CW00552923

Martyn Lloyd-Jones (1899-1981) and Twentieth-Century Evangelicalism

STUDIES IN EVANGELICAL HISTORY AND THOUGHT

A full listing of all titles in this series
appears at the close of this book.

Martyn Lloyd-Jones (1899-1981) and Twentieth-Century Evangelicalism

John Brencher

Foreword by J.C.G. Binfield

paternoster
publishing

First published 2002 by Paternoster Press

Paternoster Press is an imprint of Paternoster Publishing
P.O. Box 300, Carlisle, Cumbria, CA3 0QS, U.K.
and P.O. Box 1047, Waynesboro, GA 30830–2047, U.S.A

08 07 06 05 04 03 02   8 7 6 5 4 3 2

British Library Cataloguing in Publication Data
A catalogue record for this book is available from the British Library

ISBN 1–84227–051–6

Typeset by A.R. Cross
Printed and bound in Great Britain
for Paternoster Publishing
by Bell & Bain Ltd., Glasgow

To Elizabeth
for her patience, support
and love

Contents

FOREWORD

Martyn Lloyd-Jones was a pulpit prince at a time when the churches were still rich in such men even if some contemporaries felt that their day was already past. Nobody vanishes more rapidly than the preacher and no influence is easier even for the sympathetic historian to underestimate than the preacher's. The distinctive tone, which both informs and transforms the message, dies with the last hearer. Sometimes it lingers in the rhetoric of the printed page, but more often it is buried in anecdote and today that burial is all but complete. The sermon, and therefore the preacher, has lost its primacy even in Protestant worship. The significance in the Reformed churches of a preached theology has been downgraded. Those who devoted their lives to such preaching have suffered accordingly. They do not count.

Martyn Lloyd-Jones was pre-eminently such a preacher. He was what earlier generations would have called a divine, a professional man of parts with undisputed authority as educator, theologian and biblical expositor, minister, and preacher. Throughout the long middle of the twentieth century he attracted large congregations to what was already an old-fashioned preaching centre. But these were intelligent men and women on the young side attracted by a commanding and demanding gospel proclaimed by a powerfully credible man. 'The Doctor's' Westminster Chapel had been—indeed strictly speaking still was—a famous Congregational church, but those who filled it now were no denominationalists and Lloyd-Jones was certainly no denominationalist. Reared a Welsh Calvinistic Methodist, he could have held Welsh Presbyterianism in the palm of his hand, and he could have done the same with English Congregationalism. The conservative evangelicalism which marked him out in churches with strong, perhaps dominant, liberal wings, need not in fact have hampered his position in those churches. That, however, was not to be his path. Westminster Chapel was steadily detached from the Congregationalism to which it had given much and from which it had received much. Yet its minister's growing role among evangelicals remained as ambivalent as it was powerful. Lloyd-Jones's critics found him a profoundly negative, even destructive force, although none could gainsay his magnetism.

John Brencher sat under Lloyd-Jones in his prime. The value of this biographical study is that it conveys its subject's stature without lapsing either into hagiography or denigration. It is authoritative because it is both admiring and critical. It persuades the reader that the student of the

British twentieth-century religious scene must not ignore Martyn Lloyd-Jones.

Clyde Binfield
Sheffield,
February 2002

Preface

This book was originally a doctoral thesis written in 1997 within the History Department of the University of Sheffield to demonstrate the significance of the life and ministry of David Martyn Lloyd-Jones in post-war British evangelicalism,

In fact I was part of that evangelicalism so the subject was not entirely academic. I first attended Westminster Chapel in 1951 when Lloyd-Jones was at the height of his powers, and was one of those 'enthusiastic Friday-nighters' who made their way to Buckingham Gate in all weathers to hear his exposition of the Epistle to the Romans. And being a Londoner I had access to his pulpit contemporaries, W.E. Sangster, Leslie Weatherhead and the like, and to meetings and events that feature in this work.

Inevitably such a prominent ministry attracted a great deal of attention in its day, but in academic circles Lloyd-Jones is largely unknown, at least in current church history studies, and that invited my attention. I aimed to show that, so far as Protestant churches in England and Wales were concerned, no history of the period can afford to ignore him. It is my contention that despite differences of opinion and self-marginalization Lloyd-Jones was and has remained a major force in evangelical thinking.

In order to understand how this developed the present work has been structured along thematic lines highlighting events, persons and questions. The study begins by setting the stage with a biographical chapter and goes on to examine the kind of impact that Lloyd-Jones's preaching had on Christians of all denominations. He believed preaching to be the greatest need of the day and the position of this book is that preaching was Lloyd-Jones's greatest contribution to twentieth-century Christianity. As a preacher he attracted one of London's largest congregations and chapter three looks at the history and nature of Westminster Chapel comparing it with neighbouring ministries, and establishing the kind of people who went to hear him.

Chapters four and five ascertain the factors which shaped Lloyd-Jones's views on the church and show how his Reformed evangelicalism led in a separatist as opposed to an ecumenical direction, and finally to a position which was neither Congregational nor Presbyterian. While he favoured unity among believers his separatist ecclesiology only exacerbated the situation and left evangelicals more divided than before. Chapters six to eight evaluate Lloyd-Jones's background, the nature of his leadership and the extent of his influence—factors which either shaped or were the outcome of his ministry—and looks at the issues which these questions raise.

Finally, it was not my intention to go into print and I long resisted doing so. Yet such was the interest of influential friends that at last I succumbed and was persuaded to change my mind. So to them I am grateful, as I am to Jeremy Mudditt and Paternoster Press for seeing the project through, to Rev. Dr Ian Randall and Rev. Dr Anthony R. Cross for their help in editing and typesetting the book, and to Nottingham Alpha Graphics for their technical expertise and assistance.

John Brencher

York, August 2001

Abbreviations

AECW	Associating Evangelical Churches of Wales
BEC	British Evangelical Council
BOTT	Banner of Truth Trust
CCEW	Congregational Church in England and Wales
CERF	Congregational Evangelical Revival Fellowship
CMF	Christian Medical Fellowship
CUEW	Congregational Union of England and Wales
CYB	*Congregational Year Book*
EA	Evangelical Alliance
EMW	Evangelical Movement of Wales
FIEC	Fellowship of Independent Evangelical Churches
IFES	International Fellowship of Evangelical Students
IVF	Inter-Varsity Fellowship
IVP	Inter-Varsity Press
JETS	*Journal of the Evangelical Theological Society*
JURCHS	*Journal of the United Reformed Church Historical Society*
MLJRT	Martyn Lloyd-Jones Recordings Trust
SCM	Student Christian Movement
UCCF	Universities and Colleges Christian Fellowship
WCC	World Council of Churches
WChA	Westminster Chapel Archives
YMCA	Young Men's Christian Association

Introduction

In May 1968 David Martyn Lloyd-Jones retired from one of London's most celebrated Nonconformist churches. He had been at Westminster Chapel thirty years, twenty-nine as full-time pastor and one year as associate pastor. It was the close of the age of the great metropolitan platform orators when men such as Leslie Weatherhead at the City Temple, W.E. Sangster at Westminster Central Hall and Lloyd-Jones drew large crowds. They were a social phenomenon and although it may be hard to imagine now, they were as much a part of the cultural and intellectual life of London as its concert halls and theatres. There are, of course, active churches in London today but there is nothing with which to compare the ethos and collegiality generated by these kinds of ministries.

At the time these men were stars in the firmament of their churches and, in his day, Lloyd-Jones was probably the most influential and widely quoted evangelical in Britain. So he deserves to be recognized and understood. But they had their critics as well as their admirers and Lloyd-Jones was no exception: for some he was a prophet and a second Spurgeon, while for others he was a mere curiosity, but whatever the response his story has a place in recent church history. The path which he took is not only of interest to hermetic groups such as the Calvinistic and evangelical, but because of its ramifications has a wider application and is a contribution to our understanding of his times.

There are a number of accounts of his life which vary in size and importance. A short memoir up to 1968 appeared in C.E. Fant and W.E. Pinson (eds.), *20 Centuries of Great Preaching*, Vol. XI (1971), in which he was apparently ranked among all who had gone before him, and this carried an evaluation of his sermons and preaching by J.I. Packer. The first complete biography was a slim paperback by J. Peters, *Martyn Lloyd-Jones* (1986), but the major work was I.H. Murray's two volume biography,*The First Forty Years* (1984) and *The Fight of Faith* (1990). There were two family assessments by Christopher Catherwood, *Five Evangelical Leaders* (1984) and *Martyn Lloyd-Jones: A Family Portrait* (1995), and a third volume edited by C. Catherwood, *Chosen By God* (1986), was a selection of tributes and recollections. A. Spangler and C. Turner edited *Heroes* (1991) which has a chapter on Lloyd-Jones by J.I. Packer, and there are shorter references to his life and work in numerous books and articles. All of these have their place but I am particularly grateful for I.H. Murray's substantial and well-documented study which is, as yet, the best in the field. I have consulted Murray throughout and although we were contemporaries at Westminster Chapel, our views do not always coincide. For one thing, apart from an opening chapter for those

unfamiliar with his life, I have followed a thematic rather than chronological approach and, for another, I have found it necessary to be more
critical of the important episodes in Lloyd-Jones's career. Mine is a less
soothing view than some would like and by no means mirrors Murray's
work. It is an attempt to look at the life and work of Lloyd-Jones from a
wider point of view and to offer a more realistic assessment within the
limitations of this book.

That there is room for a more open and rigorous discussion of matters
which, at the time, were of the greatest importance is evident from the
limited amount of criticism that has yet appeared. Donald Macleod
offered some useful comments in 'The Lloyd-Jones Legacy'[1] which one
wishes had been more fully developed, and J.I. Packer,whose observations
are always astute, has been critical in a number of articles, but all too
briefly.[2] There was a twelve page critique on Lloyd-Jones and the gifts of
the Spirit by Peter Masters in 1988,[3] and a number of letters and articles
have appeared which I refer to in the text. There has also been some
criticism from fundamentalists in America,[4] but on the whole the critical
element has been restrained. And yet that someone so successful should
be minoritarian and 'against the stream' on so many issues and in such
an eclectic age is a matter ripe for investigation.

It has not been my intention either to safeguard or enhance the
reputation of Lloyd-Jones. I have looked upon him neither as icon nor
object of scorn. Some information has not been easy to come by. Such
was his stature and influence that few people even now are prepared to
express their criticisms in print and the overwhelming view among
evangelicals who knew him is still adulatory. Much of the source material
lies hidden in the minds of people who have much to say but are unwilling to do so. Others agreed to talk anonymously, and these are indicated in the text as 'Personal Information.' Thus, twenty years after his
death, there is still a strong interest in preserving a particular view of the
man and for many it is a case of 'Touch not mine anointed, and do my
prophets no harm.'[5]

There have been other restrictions. For example, Evangelical Alliance
records are in good shape from 1846 to 1946 but thereafter there has

---

1   *The Monthly Record*, Free Church of Scotland, October 1983, pp.207-209.
2   E.g. J.I. Packer, 'A Kind of Puritan', in C. Catherwood (ed.), *Chosen by God*
(Crowborough, 1986), pp.33-57.
3   P. Masters, 'Opening the Door to Charismatic Teaching', in the *Sword and
Trowel* 1, September, 1988, No.2, pp.24-35. The article argues for a cessationist view.
4   An unidentified American magazine referred to Lloyd-Jones as 'the devil's
agent, dividing evangelicals in Britain'. *Christianity Today*, 12 December, 1969, Vol.
XIV, No.6, p.35. See also R. Gromacki's review of *The Unsearchable Riches of Christ* in
JETS 1982, Vol.25, p.247.
5   1 Chronicles 16:2 and Psalm 105:15.

been little attempt to collect and preserve material. So far as the important events of 1966 went, all that exists are some brief *Council Minutes* and a statement in *Unity in Diversity* (1967). In the case of the Fellowship of Independent Evangelical Churches there are no archives and church returns are not retained beyond five years, and soon it will be one year. With regard to Westminster Chapel I am grateful for permission to consult their archives and have had many of my questions answered, but because some deacons who had served under Lloyd-Jones were still in office at the time of this research, it was felt that 'Deacons' Meeting Minutes' for the period should remain confidential, and I respect the diaconate's decision. As to the immediate family of Martyn Lloyd-Jones the feeling was that all the source material in their possession had already been made available to Iain Murray and that, apart from the Christopher Catherwood publications, there was nothing they could add. It is their intention to lodge his papers in the National Library of Wales at Aberystwyth.

But such has been the accumulation of other evidence that it has not been difficult to interpret events and make an appraisal. I have used sermons as primary sources and these include unedited tape recordings as well as others with minimal editing. Apart from published and unpublished material I have included many interviews and letters which have been refreshingly frank and fair-minded. There is of course always the danger of confusing hearsay with hard evidence but I have made every effort to avoid this. All my correspondents and interviewees had first-hand knowledge of what they refer to and in many cases they were at the heart of the Westminster ministry. None of them, whatever their criticism, failed to acknowledge the positive side of Lloyd-Jones's achievements and the substance of their comments is either corroborated by other sources or form part of a general trend. In addition, I have avoided anecdotal material, of which there is much, and kept my own reminiscences to a minimum.

With regard to the term 'evangelical', because labels have come to mean different things to different people and are often used loosely, some clarification is required. It should be said straight away that evangelical identity is not monolithic. Among the post-Keele Anglicans, for example, evangelicals have become more diverse and exploratory, and among non-Anglican evangelicals some have been content to defend the old battle-lines while others are more liberal and yielding. So there is a variety and development within evangelicalism which raises a problem of definition. However, since this study is almost exclusively confined to one form of evangelicalism the definition I have used is that of the Doctrinal Basis of the Inter-Varsity Fellowship (now the Universities and Colleges

Christian Fellowship) as expressed in *Evangelical Belief.*[6] This ten-point statement bears all the hallmarks of Lloyd-Jones's ministry and has an emphasis which is similar to other contemporary conservative evangelical groups. Its main features emphasize the core of evangelicalism: the infallibility and authority of Scripture, the universal sinfulness of man, and redemption through personal faith in Christ. 'Evangelical' is, therefore, a theological term summarizing one form of the Christian faith. We should also note that 'evangelical', at least in conservative circles, is not synonymous with 'evangelistic'. Evangelism, while closely related to its biblical roots, is the practice of spreading the Christian gospel. The evangelistic element is certainly a crucial factor in evangelicalism but it is possible to practise evangelism without being theologically conservative. The term 'Reformed' is used in its older sense and refers to Christians who follow more closely the theology worked out by John Calvin and his later exponents.

The footnotes and bibliography contain references to people who have willingly helped me. In particular I would like to thank C.D.T. James, Assistant Archivist at Westminster Chapel, for taking the trouble to answer many questions and point me in the right direction on a number of occasions. Also to W.V. Reynolds, Honorary Secretary of Westminster Chapel, and to the deacons for giving me access to most of the archives. To J. Elwyn Davies, General Secretary of the Evangelical Movement of Wales, I.D.G. Pickering Treasurer, the Presbyterian Church of Wales, London Presbytery, Tony Ruston of the Martyn Lloyd-Jones Recordings Trust, Murdo MacLeod, Business Manager of the Banner of Truth Trust, and Edwin E. King, who in spite of ill health, has shown considerable patience and given me a generous amount of his time. I am also grateful to Tv Dafydd Ifans, Assistant Keeper of Nonconformist Records, Department of Manuscripts and Records of the National Library of Wales, Aberystwyth, for various English translations from the Welsh which I have used. I should also like to thank my correspondents and friends, all of whom are named in the bibliography, who not only gave me of their time but whose writing and conversation has sharpened my ideas and given me a wider view. Lastly, my thanks to Professor J.C.G. Binfield, my supervisor at the University of Sheffield, who has provided valuable suggestions and encouraged me to complete the work. I am grateful too for his Foreword.

None of these people are to be held responsible for my arguments and conclusions, some of which they may find it impossible to agree with. But for those who feel that I have gone too far I would assure them that my intention has been to provide a critical assessment without being destructive. That he, like all men, had feet of clay does not affect my view

---

6   *Evangelical Belief* (1973), pp.9-10

that Martyn Lloyd-Jones was unrivalled as an expository preacher in the twentieth century. That I was able to sit under his ministry at Westminster Chapel from 1950 to 1959 and intermittently for the next nine years was an experience which had an extraordinary effect upon my life and ministry and, for better or worse, has not wholly ceased today.

I am indebted to the librarians and custodians of records in the following locations: the Evangelical Library, Chiltern Street; Dr.Williams's Library, Gordon Square; the United Reformed Church Library, Tavistock Place, now at Westminster College, Cambridge; the Friends House Library, Euston Road; the Evangelical Alliance, Kennington Park Road; the British Evangelical Council, St. Albans; the British Library at Bloomsbury, Stanmore and Boston Spa, and the university libraries at London, York and Sheffield. In addition I must thank the Banner of Truth Trust, Edinburgh, and Kingsway Publications, Eastbourne, for their help in supplying statistical information.

All quotations from the Bible are from the *Authorized Version* of 1611, not because this is always the best translation, but because it was the version most commonly used by Lloyd-Jones.

Finally, there are a number of unresolved points which, because of lack of space, have been omitted. His position on politics, gender, education, the Keswick movement, Billy Graham and mass evangelism, for example, might have warranted further chapters but since they are not issues which were central to his life and ministry we have only referred to them occasionally where the subject arises. It was felt that this book has a cohesion of its own without further extension and although these are undoubtedly interesting topics they are, none the less, marginal.

CHAPTER ONE

The Life:
'This gifted little Welshman'[1]

David Martyn Lloyd-Jones died of cancer on St. David's Day 1981. He had been a preacher for more than fifty years, fifty-four if we include his first sermon in Wales in Newport on 11 November 1926.

Preaching had been the preoccupation of his life and the catalyst of his ministerial career. He expressed little interest in social reform or politics but had a great deal to say about the church and preaching. His vigorous contribution to a revival of interest in evangelical churchmanship and Calvinistic theology placed him in a position of leadership so that when he died the Nonconformist evangelical world was deprived of an authoritative voice and persuasive standard-bearer. Within the more Reformed constituency, at least among Free Churchmen, there was none to take his place in the forseeable future. He had been the minister of only two churches, Sandfields, Aberavon, from 1927 to 1938, and Westminster Chapel, one of the most prestigious Free Church pulpits, as co-pastor with G. Campbell Morgan until April 1939, and then as full-time minister, remaining there until his resignation in 1968.

Lloyd-Jones was the product of a robust Welsh background, a Protestant Nonconformist who was second to none in his defence of the Reformation and eighteenth-century evangelicalism. But although he had a lifelong interest in church history he was very much a child of his times, a man of the twentieth century, responsive to the opportunities and stresses it created. His ability to express historic doctrine in contemporary terms accounted largely for his success as a preacher and was as much appreciated by fellow ministers as congregations. And, as Lloyd-Jones's medical background would lead us to expect, he was particularly responsive to people, his sermons showing an unremitting interest in the human condition in the way he exposed the symptoms, discovered the cause and suggested the cure, as he saw it, for twentieth-century man and his needs.

---

1   I have borrowed these words from an editorial in *Christianity Today*, 8 February, 1980, Vol.24, No.3, p.144.

Martyn Lloyd-Jones was born in Donald Street, Cardiff, on 20 December 1899, a little over a year before the death of Queen Victoria. He was the second of three sons born to Henry and Magdalene Lloyd-Jones.[2] Harold, the eldest and a law student at Aberystwyth, died at the age of twenty, while Vincent, the youngest, who had 'read all of Walter Scott and the works of Charles Dickens by the time he was fifteen',[3] later entered Jesus College, Oxford, becoming President of the Oxford Union in 1925. He was appointed a Judge of the High Court in 1960 and knighted for his services in that year.[4] He outlived Martyn by five years.

Henry Lloyd-Jones was originally a Congregationalist and his convictions were not evangelical. Murray suggests that his attendance at the Calvinistic Methodist Chapel in Llangeitho was because there was no real alternative.[5] He had become deeply attached to the liberal teaching of R.J. Campbell who had gone to the City Temple in 1903 as Joseph Parker's successor, and was attracted to Campbell's bestseller, *The New Theology* which appeared in 1907. This book was a blend of Christian humanitarianism and liberalism in which the focus of attention was on achieving social change through education and political action. Early twentieth-century Nonconformity had been strongly attracted to the social values of men like Keir Hardie, a deeply religious man with close affiliations to Congregationalism,[6] and Campbell had shared a platform with Hardie on several occasions. Yet much as he admired Campbell and shared his social concerns, it is unlikely that Henry Lloyd-Jones would have accepted all of his left-wing politics. According to Christopher Catherwood, Martyn Lloyd-Jones followed the fiery Welsh radical David Lloyd-George,[7] but so had his father until the rivalry of Asquith and Lloyd-George in 1916 when the latter ousted the former as Prime Minister. Henry, like many Liberals of his day, probably had misgivings about the First World War, especially the introduction of conscription, which Lloyd-George strongly endorsed and over which Asquith hesitated. For Martyn, the answer to lifeless churches lay not in an alliance between politics and religion but in a return to the old fire and convictions of the Methodist fathers who were, in his view, the epitome of

---

2   See Table 1: The Lloyd-Jones Family, p.235.

3   David Mathias Lloyd-Jones, interview with author, 19 October, 1996.

4   *The Times*, 25 September, 1986, p.20.

5   I.H. Murray, *D. Martyn Lloyd-Jones: The First Forty Years 1899-1939* (Edinburgh, 1982), p.4.

6   Hardie was a member of Old Cumnock Church and a lay preacher and evangelist in his early days.

7   C. Catherwood, *Five Evangelical Leaders* (London, 1984), p.51.

first-century Christianity.[8] Campbell's philosophical idealism was not for him.

This apart, Martyn owed much to his father. Elizabeth Catherwood speaks of her grandfather as 'not a very well educated man' but one who 'read the newspapers carefully and methodically' and was 'interested in the whole world around him'. Evidently the family members were all avid readers and Elizabeth draws attention to a strong literary tradition in the family. Martyn's older brother Harold read widely, wrote poetry, and knew Robert Graves and Siegfried Sassoon, and his younger brother when he was at Oxford knew Ronald Knox, met Evelyn Waugh and was in the same tutorial group as C.S. Lewis.[9] It would be difficult not to see all of this having some effect on Martyn, a point made by a 1935 correspondent who described his upbringing as 'a most potent formative influence'.[10] It was. His mother, Magdalene, had originally been a Tory and was attached to the Church of England, which must have made for some interesting debates. Of his parents, Martyn said that his father was 'the kindest character I've met' and of his mother, that she was the most 'generous and open-hearted' woman, 'a very quick thinker...more intelligent than my father'.[11]

At some point in the spring of 1906 the family moved from English-speaking Cardiff, 'Where Henry carried on a grocery business',[12] to take on the General Store at Llangeitho in Cardiganshire (now Dyfed), a small Welsh-speaking farming community whose religious fame lay in the 1730s when Daniel Rowland had been a curate there. Such had been Rowland's impact on the area that a number of revivals had spread throughout the Principality, but the effects of a revival that made 'the neighbouring hills and valleys ring with the joyful sound of salvation and praises to the Lamb'[13] had long since vanished. The 1904-05 revival had seemingly had little effect on Llangeitho and religion existed only as a strong tradition, something Lloyd-Jones trenchantly remarked upon later when he said that 'Llangeitho had lost the fire and the rejoicing of the Methodist Revival to the same extent as Westminster Abbey had lost the life and vitality of the Early Church'.[14]

8   D.M. Lloyd-Jones, *The Puritans: Their Origins and Successors* (Edinburgh, 1987), p.213.

9   F. and E. Catherwood, *The Man and His Books* (London, 1982), p.16.

10   *The Christian*, 28 November, 1935, p.13.

11   Murray, *The First Forty Years*, p.299. As a matter of interest, William Glyn Hughes Simon, High Churchman and distant cousin of Bethan Lloyd-Jones became Archbishop of Wales on 17 July, 1968. He remained in office until August 1971. G.H. Edwards, letter to author, 30 May, 1996.

12   *The Western Mail*, 3 February, 1927, p.11.

13   E. Evans, *Daniel Rowland* (Edinburgh, 1985), p.358.

14   Murray, *The First Forty Years*, p.3.

By 1911 Martyn had won a scholarship to the County School in the old town of Tregaron, four miles from Llangeitho, where he developed an interest in history and, according to a report in *The Welsh Gazette*, the years spent at this school 'were the most important ones of his life'. His estimate later, however, was that because of homesickness these were not altogether happy years, although he speaks highly of his masters who were 'Welshmen to the core'.[15] One of the most lasting impressions made on him at this time was the 1913 Assembly of Welsh Calvinistic Methodists which met at Llangeitho to commemorate the bicentenary of the birth of Daniel Rowland, and judging by the number of times he refers to Rowland in his lectures and sermons one can see how seminal that Summer Association was. Not that he could remember all that was said though the whole affair, he claimed in 1980, deeply affected his adolescent mind and created the beginning of 'an interest in the Calvinistic Methodist Fathers which has lasted until today'.[16]

When Lloyd-Jones was fifteen his father's business in Llangeitho became bankrupt through over-expansion and under capitalisation, and after a period of uncertainty the family moved to a dairy and milk business at 7 Regency Street, Westminster, in September 1914. As business picked up he was able to enter Marylebone Grammar School where he distinguished himself in the London University Senior School summer examinations of 1916, passing in seven subjects and gaining distinction in five. After a preliminary examination and interview he was admitted to St. Bartholomew's Hospital as a medical student in October 1916. He was sixteen years of age. Five years later he had taken his MRCS, LRCP and MBBS (Bachelor of Medicine and Bachelor of Surgery) with a distinction in medicine. By 1923 he had gained an MD for his research on subacute bacterial endocarditis, subsequently published as an appendix in C. Bruce Perry's *Bacterial Endocaritis* of 1936, and in 1925 he became MRCP, all of which, as G. Davies says, was achieved at an exceptionally early age.[17]

There is no doubt that these years in medicine from 1916 until he resigned for the ministry in 1927 (when he was chief clinical assistant to Lord Horder in the hospital medical unit) had a powerful influence on his life and determined his whole approach to homiletics and pastoralia. Although his great passion was preaching he never ceased to be a physician, at least in theory, as his long association with the Christian Medical Fellowship shows: 'though I am not in the profession now', he

---

15 *The Welsh Gazette*, 29 December, 1927, unpaginated, and Murray, *The First Forty Years*, p.25.

16 D.M. Lloyd-Jones, *The First Forty Years*, p.27.

17 *Ibid*, p.28, and Catherwood (ed.), *Chosen by God*, p.61. He was elected MRCP 'by the quarterly Comitia [full meeting of Fellows] on Thursday, 29 January 1929.' G. Davenport, Librarian, Royal College of Physicians to C.D.T. James, 4 October, 1991. Used with permission.

said in 1973, 'I am still a great admirer of what I regard as the greatest of the professions'.[18] He kept abreast of medical developments throughout his life and that was no mean achievement in a climate of rapid change. At a Quarter Centenary Dinner of the Christian Medical Fellowship at the Royal College of Physicians in 1972, he remarked, 'I have made it my custom throughout the years to read on Saturday night the *British Medical Journal* and latterly, the medical newspaper known as *Pulse*'.[19] He also read *The Practitioner* 'as a stimulus'. These habits continued for a lifetime, as did his esteem for his old medical school: 'I am proud to remember that in 1923 we were celebrating the foundation of the oldest and greatest hospital in London, the Octocentenary of St. Bartholomew's.'[20] This was when he became Lord Horder's assistant.

We are not, therefore, looking at two mutually exclusive careers—doctor then preacher—a point grasped early on by *The Christian*, which described him as 'the doctor-preacher'.[21] Rather, in most respects Lloyd-Jones combined the two. Of course his preaching was to take up the majority of his time from 1927 onwards, but the good natured debate between Gaius Davies—a 'Barts' friend of Martyn—and Omri Jenkins, a ministerial associate, as to whether he was essentially a physician or preacher was somewhat beside the point: he was both. And this is a view shared by his daughter and family who had come to the same conclusion: 'we in the family think that probably both were right'.[22]

The Spirit's Quickening

Despite his chapel-going and interest in religious questions at this time, Martyn was not, measured by his own criteria, a Christian. It is quite likely that as a young person he had thought he was and that he had got used to the idea before really knowing what it meant. He had heard many of the great preachers of his day and we may assume that events from Llangeitho onwards had played their part in conditioning him. But the assumption that he had always been a Christian or had become one by

---

18   D.M. Lloyd-Jones, *Healing and Medicine* (Eastbourne, 1988), p.116.

19   D.M. Lloyd-Jones, *On Treating the Whole Man* (London, 1972), p.6.

20   D.M. Lloyd-Jones, *Will Hospital Replace the Church?* (London, 1969), p.4. As a student, Horder had been a member of Lyndhurst Road Congregational Church, Hampstead, but later became an agnostic. See 'Membership Lists' for Lyndhurst Road now in the Dr William's Library. See also T.J. Horder, *Fifty Years in Medicine* (London, 1953), and T.M. Horder, *Baron Horder: The little genius* (London, 1966).

21   *The Christian*, 28 November, 1935, p.13.

22   F.and E. Catherwood, *The Man and His Books*, p.33. G. Davies and O. Jenkins were among the speakers at the Thanksgiving Service in Westminster Chapel on 6 April 1981, at which the author was present.

ritual or upbringing 'was not a true assessment of my condition'.[23] Some time in 1923, the exact date is not known, he reached an evangelical experience of the gospel when the 'Holy Spirit quickened me and awakened me to the realization of certain profound and vital truths taught in the Bible'. That was his carefully worded answer to the question, 'Why am I a Christian?' written in the 1960s. It was that kind of experience which was reflected in the type of preaching which, according to the novelist Rhys Davies, was to touch 'the romantic heart of Wales'.[24]

It was not the date or any element of the spectacular in conversion that impressed Lloyd-Jones, as a couple of sentences in a 1976 sermon show: 'I remember the ancient discussion that used to occupy time and attention in the Sunday School and Bible Class as to whether conversion was sudden or gradual; there were always two sides. But I would point out that the wrong question was being discussed. The question was not so much whether conversion was sudden or gradual. The vital question surely is "Have you been converted?"'[25] He did believe in conversion as a sudden event but he could also analyse the stages in conversion as he did in a 1932 sermon on 'Repentance' and in a 1933 sermon on 'Missing the Mark'.[26]

The Spirit's quickening of Lloyd-Jones in his early twenties was not the direct cause of his entry into the ministry. For one thing it was not his conviction that all Christians should automatically take up preaching. For another, as we shall see later, there was in his mind the necessity of the hidden call of God. Yet for all this the idea of the Christian ministry must have struck a responsive chord. 'As a youth', he told reporters from *The People* in 1939, 'I felt called to the ministry. In deference to my father's wishes, however, I took up medicine instead. But the first chance I had I went back to my first love.'[27] The origins of the impulse to enter the ministry are not altogether clear. There is no reference to his father's wishes in Murray's account where Lloyd-Jones refers to 1913 and says he had chosen 'to be a doctor'. The motivation, evidently, was that his great-grandfather on Magdalene's side had been a doctor and, in addition, he had been impressed with a local boy who had returned home after qualifying in medicine. This may have impressed his mother and father. Whatever the explanation it enabled him to say, 'I received every

---

23   'For many years I thought I was a Christian when in fact I was not. It was only later that I came to see that I had never been a Christian and became one.' D.M. Lloyd-Jones, *Preaching and Preachers* (London, 1971) , p.146.

24   R. Davies, *My Wales* (London, 1937), p.117. Lloyd-Jones's answer was printed in *This I Believe* (Glasgow, n.d.), p. 5, a booklet containing the testimonies of fourteen people, published for the North of England Evangelical Trust.

25   *Westminster Record*, August, 1976, Vol.51, No.8, p.96.

26   D.M. Lloyd-Jones, *Evangelistic Sermons* (Edinburgh, 1983), p.148.

27   *The People*, 30 April, 1939, p.6.

support and encouragement from my parents'.[28] Nevertheless, the earlier newspaper report might indicate that he had youthful feelings towards the ministry which he had not shared with his family. There is no reason to doubt the journalist's sentiment that 'Dr. Lloyd-Jones smiles when he thinks of the strange part a boyish ambition played in his career'.[29] It may well have been so.

As yet, however, he was not clear as to where his future lay. Murray draws attention to how successful and promising his career was at this time. Not only had he become the youngest assistant to the Royal Physician, Lord Horder, but Sir Bernard Spilsbury, Chief Pathologist at the Home Office, also wanted him for his private practice. *The Daily Telegraph* obituary says he had begun 'practising as a consultant physician' in Harley Street, and on the eve of his entry into the ministry 'he was offered the post of Assistant Professor of Medicine at St. Bartholomew's Hospital'. So, although the language was unacceptably extravagant to Lloyd-Jones, *The People*'s article entitled, 'Left Riches and Fame to Become Poor Pastor', was not far off the mark.[30] No wonder, then, that he did not leave medicine without a struggle. It would have been quite reasonable to have combined the two things by remaining a physician while preaching as well. But, as he explained in an interview of 1980, this was not convincing: 'it did not satisfy'.[31]

He had already felt the conflicting demands of God and mammon: 'they grip the personality', he said, 'they demand our entire devotion; they want us to live for them absolutely'. What he had heard at medical dinners where the top people were present had disturbed him. So any decision that he made had to be without compromise; it was either medicine or preaching. The struggle 'went on throughout my last eighteen months in medicine. I literally lost over twenty pounds in weight.'[32] But after his MRCP examination in 1925 he had made up his mind. In September 1926 he presented himself and was approved for the ministry by the London Presbytery of the Welsh Presbyterian Church (Calvinistic Methodist Church) and by November he had preached his first sermon at the Bethlehem Forward Movement (Sandfields), Aberavon. *John Bull* in its 'Outspoken Messages to Celebrities, Notorieties and, Occasionally, Nonentities' addressed Lloyd-Jones's decision in terms of unveiled amazement: 'Though still under thirty years of age, your fame as a heart specialist stands upon the rock of solid achievement.

---

28   Murray, *The First Forty Years*, p.26.

29   *The People*, 30 April, 1939, p.6.

30   *The Daily Telegraph*, 13 March, 1981, p.16; Murray, *The First Forty Years*, p.110, and *The People*, 30 April, 1939, p.6.

31   C.F.H. Henry, 'Martyn Lloyd-Jones: From Buckingham to Westminster', *Christianity Today*, February 1980, Vol.24, No.3, p.155.

32   *Ibid.*

Nevertheless you have decided to turn your back upon a promising career, holding emoluments almost without limit, to take up a pastorate at Port Talbot at a salary of £300 a year.' On 8 January 1927 he married Bethan Phillips[33] and on 1 February he arrived with his wife at Sandfields as their new minister. So began his half century in the ministry.

Aberavon

His move from Harley Street to a poor Glamorganshire district could hardly have been a greater contrast. For one thing, as a young consultant he would probably have earned a salary of £3,500 upwards. In 1927 Lloyd-Jones was offered £225 a year by the Sandfields congregation together with manse and rates and thirteen free Sundays annually. So from fashionable London he went to a tough quarter of Aberavon's dockland where working-class men struggled with unemployment and poverty. But it was among the tinplate workers, the miners and dock-labourers that he wanted to be: 'I deliberately went to South Wales, to a small mission centre of 93 members, to do pioneer work.' He vigorously denied that there was any element of sacrifice in what he did: 'I gave up nothing', he said, 'I received everything. I count it the highest honour that God can confer on any man to be a herald of the gospel.'[34] 'Nor did he look upon it as a change of career as *The People* later suggested, 'surrendering one great career the doctor found another'. He was simply following a conviction that God had called him or, to use his wife's words, 'the guidance of God' was 'as clear and inevitable as a route on the map'.[35]

He had arrived in Aberavon without any experience of running a church and without any formal theological training, but neither matters seemed to trouble him. However this was not satisfactory for some, who were quick to question the wisdom of a theologically untrained man taking on a pastorate. 'Dr. Jones claims no training in Divinity, and has fulfilled none of the requirements necessary for recognition as a minister

---

33   *John Bull,* 25 December, 1926, Vol.XL, p.16. They were married at the Welsh Presbyterian Church, Charing Cross Road. Bethan was also a qualified doctor although she did not practise. Her father, Tomos Phillips, was a native of Newcastle Emlyn, where Bethan's grandfather had been a minister of Bethel Calvinistic Methodist Chapel for more than fifty years, the same church where Martyn's funeral was conducted fifty-five years later. See Table 2: The Phillips Family, p.236

34   E.D. Radmacher, 'A Review of Romans, Vol.3', *Christianity Today*, 8 October, 1971, Vol.16, No.1, p.156, and *Monthly Record*, The Free Church of Scotland, April 1941 , p.88.

35   B. Lloyd-Jones, *Memories of Sandfields 1927-1938* (Edinburgh, 1983), p.95. These words were used of his move to Westminster Chapel from Aberavon, but they were equally applicable to his first pastorate.

of any English Christian Church', declared D. Winter Lewis in the correspondence columns of *The Western Mail*.[36] The London Presbytery of the Welsh Presbyterians had approved him as a suitable candidate for the ministry, but they had not ordained him. When Martyn went to Sandfields it was only with the status of lay-preacher and it could only have been a tactically wise move that he was sent to a Forward Movement mission station rather than a fully constituted church. Such matters were not unimportant to so precise a group as the Welsh Presbyterians and the kind of problem that had to be faced is illustrated by an anonymous writer of 'Church Notes' in *The Western Mail* in 1926. He pointed out that an applicant for ordination had been opposed by Principal Owen Prys on the grounds that he 'had read Divinity at Cambridge and not at Bala'.[37] Owen Prys was President of the Forward Movement, so not unnaturally the writer was interested to know how he would respond to the case of Lloyd-Jones, and his argument contained some valid anxieties. For example, does the fact that a candidate is willing to make sacrifices as a proof of his sincerity satisfy the criteria of ordination? Is it sufficient to say that an applicant shares common ground with the denomination's historical theological beliefs? Or is it enough to accept the fact that a person is well trained in another discipline: 'is this sufficient ground to qualify for ordination as an efficient Christian minister?'[38] How would the Association resolve the issue?

The Welsh Presbyterians of Owen Prys's day were in a dilemma over Lloyd-Jones. The fame of the Harley Street man and the success he was already having as a preacher made the ordination question an urgent one. It was debated over the winter of 1926-27. According to Lewis there were those who 'desired to hasten his ordination' in spite of Association rules, and 'Church Notes' also calls attention to 'the haste evidenced by some leaders to secure the ordination of Dr. Martyn Lloyd-Jones to the ministry of the Presbyterian Church'.[39] In the event their hand was forced. Such was the demand for the preaching of Lloyd-Jones beyond the Aberavon mission station that the authorities had little choice but to ordain him and waive some of their usual procedures. When the next Association of the Presbyterian Church of Wales met at Jewin Chapel in London, the Forward Movement recommended that he should be ordained forthwith.

But it was not automatic. He still had to subject himself to some denominational procedures. He appeared before the Board for the

---

36   *The Western Mail*, 3 February, 1927, p.7.
37   Owen Prys was Principal of the Calvinistic Methodist College at Trevecka which moved to Aberystwyth in 1906, and amalgamated with Bala College in 1922. He was Principal from 1891 to 1927.
38   *The Western Mail*, 3 February, 1927, p.7.
39   *Ibid.*

examination of ministerial students and when he was asked to 'give a word about his experience' his response was so passionate that the decorum of the occasion was shattered as 'a brother shouted out until the building reverberated, "Praise Him!" and the congregation was in tears'. The matter was concluded in October 1927, when the Association used Whitefield's Memorial Church in Tottenham Court Road for their four days of meetings. Lloyd-Jones had been asked to address the Youth Meeting on the Monday night and he did so with his customary vigour. *Y Goleuad* noted that an ordination service was held on Wednesday night, 26 October, and that Lloyd-Jones's ordination in 'Whitefield's Tabernacle—his great hero' was a happy coincidence.[40] H.P. Roberts, commenting later on this occasion and comparing him with other Welsh preachers, declared that Lloyd-Jones 'is a type on his own, he is not in the class of the preachers of the great festivals'.[41] His individuality had already made its mark.

He went through the process and was officially recognized as an ordained minister, though he could be equally enthusiastic about George Whitefield who had been ordained and about Howell Harris who had not. His interest was not in ecclesiastical protocol but in great preaching and the 'divine' ordination of a man who, in the pneumatological sense, 'comes from God'.[42]

If the proof of a man's calling to the ministry is to be found in the results of his preaching, Lloyd-Jones's years in South Wales provided the evidence. Despite economic depression, or perhaps because of it, his preaching attracted great crowds. 'The doors of the chapel where he preached were opened two hours before the service began', said Rhys Davies, no friend of evangelicalism. He continued: 'I have never seen a building so unhygienically packed.' The ground floor and extensive gallery 'steamed with bodies that were piled up to the walls in a warmth that was stifling'.[43] This is the picture we have from newspapers and records. During his first year he had fifty-four preaching engagements outside Aberavon—mostly midweek gatherings—while the church at Sandfields itself grew: 'In my eleven and a half years the church grew to

---

40   J.R. Evans, *Y Goleuad* (Weekly News of the Presbyterian Church of Wales), November, 1927, Vol. 57, No.51, p.2. George Whitefield was, in Lloyd-Jones's view, 'the greatest evangelist England has ever produced', and he described his preaching as 'apostolic and seraphic'. Lloyd-Jones, 'John Calvin and George Whitefield', in *The Puritans*, pp.126, 122. There are also numerous references to Whitefield in many of Lloyd-Jones's sermons.

41   H.P. Roberts, letter in *Y Goleuad*, February 1933, Vol.63, No.8, p.5.

42   D.M. Lloyd-Jones, *Knowing the Times* (Edinburgh, 1989), p.265.

43   Davies, *My Wales*, pp.117-118.

530 members and the attendance ran about 850.'[44] It is not surprising that there was media interest and this would almost certainly account for some of his followers. Even so, it was by any standards a significant rate of growth from the original ninety-three members. Bethan Lloyd-Jones records midweek meetings of two or three hundred, all-weather Whit Monday marches through the town and processions 'headed by the Doctor and the solid block of men who walked with him'. But it was under the influence of full-blooded evangelical preaching that the majority were converted, including his own wife Bethan: 'In those first two years God graciously used Martyn's morning sermons to open my eyes and to show me myself and my needs.'[45]

Such preaching was common knowledge in the South Wales of the early 1930s and sometimes newspapers picked it up. In rather extravagant language *The Sunday Dispatch* said that Lloyd-Jones 'and his wife set in motion a revivalist movement that is sweeping Wales', and *The People*, under the subheading 'Mystic Eyes', declared that 'to hear him preach is to know you are in the presence of no common man'.[46] Inevitably there was as Gwyn Williams said, 'a romantic element' in a young man with the prospect of a brilliant future coming from London to minister 'in the poor districts of Sandfields'. None of the articles impressed Lloyd-Jones; indeed, 'some of it annoyed me greatly'.[47] All the same, if we strip away the embellishments we are left with a description of the kind of ministry which did much to revive Calvinistic Christianity all over Wales. It was remarkable especially in the south, given the economic and social circumstances, the interest in Socialism and the apparent advance of secularization among the working-class, but it was no less startling in places like Anglesey, Wrexham and the north in general where 'Modernism had come in like a flood'.[48] Spacious Nonconformist chapels were filled and by 1932 Lloyd-Jones was making regular visits to the north at least once a month. A correspondent in *The Cymric Times* of 1932 spoke of large congregations at Water Street Chapel, Carmarthen,[49] and there were other similar reports.

In the same year Lloyd-Jones was in North America. He wrote that 'it was my pleasure to preach for nine Sundays in Canada, in Toronto, in 1932', at Sherbourne Street Presbyterian Church. The minister, Richard Roberts, was not an evangelical but he had heard of his fellow

---

44   Murray, *The First Forty Years*, p.184, and editorial, 'For Whom Proclamation was Paramount', *Christianity Today*, February 1980, p.156.

45   B. Lloyd-Jones, *Memories of Sandfields*, pp.34 and 11.

46   *Sunday Dispatch*, 1 May, 1938, p.6, and *The People*, 30 April, 1939, p.6.

47   G. Williams, 'A Physician for Aberavon', *The Evangelical Magazine of Wales*, April 1981, Vol. 20, No. 2, p.14, and *Christianity Today*, February 1980, p.155.

48   Murray, *The First Forty Years*, p.249.

49   *The Cymric Times*, 4 April, 1932, p.3.

Welshman's fame and had invited him to cover the 'dead months' of the summer period. According to Bethan, who was with her husband, congregations grew to such an extent during the nine weeks that people were sitting on the pulpit stairs and 'special police were sent to control the traffic'.[50] *The British Weekly*, which was just beginning to take notice of him, wrote of 'a very deep impression [made] upon large congregations' in America and the editor of *The Christian World*, referring to a letter of Richard Roberts, said that 'Dr. Lloyd-Jones has taken the city by storm'.[51] During these weeks in Toronto he was invited by T.T. Shields to preach at his Baptist church in Jarvis Street, an interesting invitation in some respects since Shields's practice of confounding his enemies and making 'mincemeat of the liberals' was never Lloyd-Jones's idea of preaching. Bethan described this 'Canadian Spurgeon' as a good evangelical preacher, but 'according to many, spoiling his ministry by his increasing diatribes against liberals and Roman Catholics'.[52] Lloyd-Jones was also invited to preach at the Chautauqua conference near Buffalo, his first visit to the United States. Chautauqua had been an evangelical Methodist centre but by 1932 it had become rather nondescript theologically and more of a platform for a variety of subjects and speakers. In fact in the year that Lloyd-Jones was there two of the speakers were Mrs Franklin D. Roosevelt and the agnostic Julian Huxley. Lloyd-Jones was not among the well-knowns, indeed he was unknown, but by the final evening of the conference he was preaching to nearly six thousand in a huge concert auditorium.[53]

At home he continued to become more widely known. On 3 December 1935, he was the closing speaker at a 'Great Demonstration at the Royal Albert Hall, London, under the auspices of the Bible Testimony Fellowship' in which he was introduced by George Gordon, second Marquess of Aberdeen, as 'one of Christ's physicians'.[54] Lloyd-Jones noted that it was 'the night when the old Crystal Palace burnt down', but it was neither this nor the crowd which heard him preach 'with exception-

---

50   Lloyd-Jones, *Preaching and Preachers*, p.147: *The British Weekly*, 8 September, 1932, Vol.XCII, p.437, and B. Lloyd-Jones, *Memories of Sandfields*, p.50.

51   *The British Weekly*, 8 September, 1932, p.437, and *The Christian World*, 1 September, 1932, p.3.

52   B. Lloyd-Jones, *Memories of Sandfields*, p.51. Thomas Todhunter Shields was the 'English-born son of a Methodist preacher turned Baptist, who ministered at Jarvis Street, Toronto, from 1910 to 1955. Jarvis Street was a leading Canadian Baptist Church'. Clyde Binfield, *Pastor and People* (Coventry, 1984). Further references to Shields occur in George A. Rawlyk and Mark A. Noll (eds.), *Amazing Grace* (London, 1994).

53   Murray, *The First Forty Years*, pp.274-275.

54   *Christianity Today*, February 1980, p.155: *The Christian*, 28 November, 1935, p.19, and 12 December, 1935, p.22.

al force and persuasiveness'[55] that made it a special occasion so far as Lloyd-Jones was concerned.The significance was the frightening prospect of G. Campbell Morgan being among his auditors. Morgan was so impressed that 'almost the next day I got a letter from him inviting me to preach in Westminster Chapel'. The combination of circumstances 'proved to be a turning-point in my story'.[56] He accepted the invitation, and on 29 December 1935 Lloyd-Jones occupied the Westminster pulpit. He had been introduced to Morgan earlier, but the Royal Albert Hall meeting was the first time Morgan had heard Lloyd-Jones preach, not as Jill Morgan says, in the United States, which would have been at the time of his 1937 visit to Philadelphia.[57] It was at the Philadelphia meetings that Lloyd-Jones guessed what was in Morgan's mind: 'Just as I began to preach I saw him pulling out his watch; he was going to time me. I knew intuitively that he was weighing an invitation to me to join him.'[58] He was right. Jill Morgan was not far off the truth when she said that her father-in-law was 'impressed by his method and ability' and that in his whole approach Lloyd-Jones 'was a man after his own heart'.[59]

London

It was inevitable given his growing reputation that Lloyd-Jones would sooner or later move on to a prominent city pastorate. 'Table Talk' in *The British Weekly* for 17 January 1938 sensed this: 'it is expected that he will shortly receive a call to an important London charge'.[60] He had been in South Wales for eleven and a half years. Campbell Morgan, now in his seventy-fifth year, was looking for an associate at Westminster Chapel and Lloyd-Jones was his choice. Not that others had not tried. An offer to become minister of 'the prosperous and fashionable Marylebone Presbyterian Church' earlier in 1938 had been declined: 'it was a great disappointment to us that Dr. Jones prefers to remain in Wales', J. Chalmers Lyon, Moderator of the church during the interim, told *The Sunday Dispatch* at the end of April.[61] By September of that year Lloyd-

---

55   G. Fielder, *Lord of the Years* (London, 1988), p.81. Lloyd-Jones's memory must have failed him here. The Crystal Palace burned down a year later on 1 December, 1936.

56   *Christianity Today*, February 1980, p.155, and D.M. Lloyd-Jones, *Centenary Address* (London, 1965), p.15: 'I shall never forget how he frightened me before the meeting.' Morgan had gone out on that night to hear Lloyd-Jones, and he made it clear he would have gone out for no one else.

57   Jill Morgan, *A Man of the Word* (London, 1952), p.302, and Henry, 'From Buckingham to Westminster', p.155.

58   Henry, 'From Buckingham to Westminster', p.155.

59   Morgan, *A Man of the Word*, p.302.

60   *The British Weekly*, 27 January, 1938, Vol.CIII, p.333.

61   *Sunday Dispatch*, 1 May, 1938, p.6.

Jones had accepted a six month arrangement with Campbell Morgan and by late 1938 *The Christian World* declared that he 'has now been invited to the permanent co-pastorate'.[62] In early 1939 Morgan intimated that Lloyd-Jones had decided in favour of a more lasting role at Westminster Chapel and Samuel William Hughes, General Secretary of the Free Church Federal Council for the next six years and who stood with Morgan on that occasion, spoke of a 'continuance of Dr. Campbell Morgan's ministry'.[63]

An outstanding thirty-year ministry lay ahead, but doctrinally it was far from a continuance. 'Personally', Morgan said in a letter of 1936, 'I take the second position [the Arminian] and believe that it is possible for a man to fall away from grace.'[64] To Lloyd-Jones there was nothing 'more monstrous...than the idea that you can fall away from grace',[65] and that view followed him throughout his life. In many respects it is remarkable that Campbell Morgan should turn to Lloyd-Jones as his successor. Morgan was part of a broader evangelical tradition, including men like Dwight L. Moody, Samuel Chadwick and F.B. Meyer from the preceding generation. Morgan was, in the best sense, a pulpiteer, a supporter of the Keswick movement with a declared premillennial approach to prophecy. Lloyd-Jones, on the other hand, was more in the tradition of George Whitefield, emphasizing the doctrines of the Protestant Reformation. Lloyd-Jones was an amillennialist,[66] although he rarely mentioned his prophetic views in public. He was no friend of the Keswick movement and cared little for a professional or clerical approach to the ministry. If, however, Morgan was looking for the continuation of Westminster Chapel as a preaching centre, subsequent events were to show how right he was.

It did not take long for Lloyd-Jones to make his mark at Buckingham Gate. The London correspondent of *The Western Mail* estimated crowds of 'not less than two thousand'—Westminster Chapel seats about that number when full—and reported that he was 'drawing congregations as crowded as those that wait on Campbell Morgan's ministry'. In a perceptive piece of journalism, Kenneth Woodfleet asked if 'a new prophet had arisen who would carry a commanding note to a sermon-surfeited

---

62   *Christian World*, 29 December, 1938, p.9.
63   *The British Weekly*, 27 April, 1939, Vol.CVI, p.61.
64   Jill Morgan, *This Was His Faith* (London, n.d.), p.238.
65   D.M. Lloyd-Jones, *God's Way of Reconciliation* (Edinburgh, 1972), p.154.
66   For Lloyd-Jones's millennial position see *The Final Perseverance of the Saints* (Edinburgh, 1975), pp.82-91. On pre-, post- and a-millennialism see also his *Maintaining the Evangelical Faith Today* (Lonodn, 1952), p.16; *What is an Evangelical?* (London, 1971) in *Knowing the Times*, p. 353; and *Great Doctrines Series*, Vol. 3 (London, 1998), pp.215-226.

generation?'[67] The 1930s was an auspicious time for London pulpits. There was what Douglas Thompson described as 'the near-legendary three-point ministry of Methodist star preachers in London.' Donald Soper had arrived at the Kingsway Hall on 17 September 1936 and Leslie Weatherhead had gone to the City Temple in the same year. In September 1939 W.E. Sangster succeeded Dinsdale Young at the Central Hall, Westminster, in what was to become an outstanding ministry lasting sixteen years, and A.D. Belden concluded his ministry at Whitefield's Memorial Church in the same year. All these men with widely differing views—Soper with his red tie and Christian Socialism, Weatherhead with his pastoral psychology, Sangster the saintly 'preaching engine' with his suffocating style of piety, and Belden a leading pacifist[68]—preached to large congregations. So Lloyd-Jones was not unique in this respect.

Under the heading 'A Tribute to Westminster Chapel', *The British Weekly* carried a full account of J.A. Hutton's address prepared for delivery at the induction of Lloyd-Jones to the co-pastorate on Monday, 4 September 1939. After a brief remark about his medical aptitude, he concluded by saying that Lloyd-Jones had come to London 'at a time when the world needs thinking, responsible men' who were not so much spectators but participants in the battle that was against the Anti-Christ himself.[69] It was stirring stuff but it was never preached nor was there ever an Induction Service. The meeting was cancelled when war became inevitable and this was a merciful deliverance for Lloyd-Jones who disliked such occasions. There had been a 'Welcome Meeting' for Martyn and Bethan Lloyd-Jones at Westminster Chapel on 18 May 1939 when representatives of all the church organizations spoke, including Campbell Morgan,[70] but the idea of an Induction Service was not revived. Until August 1943 Lloyd-Jones was co-pastor of Westminster Chapel, and he then became the sole pastor.

The four years 1935-39 were the chilling years of Rhineland remilitarization. When war was declared on 3 September 1939, the fear of mass bombing soon depleted congregations and after the Phoney War of September 1939 to June 1940, Hitler's Luftwaffe launched its assault on Britain. In the bombings of 1940 and 1941 *The British Weekly* reported that 'no fewer than 260 churches have been damaged more or less seriously by enemy action'.[71] During May 1941 the House of Commons was destroyed and among other well-known landmarks Westminster

67 *The Western Mail*, 5 November, 1938, p.9, and *The Christian World*, 1 September, 1932, p.10.
68 D. Thompson, *Donald Soper* (Nutfield, 1971), pp.65 and 68. 'City Temple for popsies; Kingsway for Bolshies and Central Hall for saints', p.68.
69 *The British Weekly*, 7 September, 1939, Vol.CVI, p.377.
70 *Westminster Record*, July 1939, Vol.13, No.7, pp.130-136.
71 *The British Weekly*, 15 May, 1941, Vol.CX, p.59.

Abbey, Westminster Hall and Lambeth Palace were damaged. All Souls, Langham Place also suffered: 'a bomb fell on the Queen's Hall next door and the steeple and roof of All Souls fell in. It was closed from 1940 to 1951.'[72] Westminster Chapel, although hit three times and once by an incendiary bomb which 'was promptly dealt with',[73] remained standing, as did the Methodist Central Hall half a mile down the road. Lloyd-Jones later recalled that 'in a flying bomb attack, a bomb dropped just across the road in June 1944, and blew off half the chapel roof', and for most of the summer of that year about 150 people 'met in a borrowed hall'.[74]

But although these were, in the view of Leslie Weatherhead, days of 'huge empty churches',[75] Lloyd-Jones went on with his evangelical preaching. To a crowded Free Church College, Edinburgh, in March 1941, he gave three addresses on 'The Tragedy of Modern Man' (published under the title, *The Plight of Man and the Power of God* in 1942) giving reasons for the war and its causes. Earlier, in September 1939, he had not been reluctant to make his position clear: 'War is just a part and an expression of the one great central problem of sin': 'God permits war in order that men may bear the consequences of their sins as punishment',[76] and it was this forthright kind of preaching with its full offer of a curative salvation which attracted visitors and servicemen in the 1940s. It also brought him invitations to preach widely: 'during the war I travelled extensively throughout Britain at least two days a week for combined meetings and special services'.[77] In February 1941, he was in the pulpit of John Henry Newman and the next day he lunched with Nathaniel Micklem at Mansfield College, speaking in the Sheldonian Theatre in the evening. On the Friday of that week he lunched with C.S. Lewis and dined with John Marsh, chaplain of Mansfield and later its Principal, preaching at Christ Church Cathedral in the evening.[78]

Lloyd-Jones received invitations to speak at many of the Free Churches and was generally accepted by the Free Church Federal Council largely, no doubt, because its secretary, S.W. Hughes, was his friend, although it is clear from a letter that he was not at one with all the Council members.[79]

---

72   John Stott, tape recorded conversation, 16 November, 1991.

73   Morgan, *A Man of the Word*, p.310.

74   Henry, 'From Buckingham to Westminster', p.159. This was the Livingstone Hall, headquarters of the London Missionary Society.

75   *The British Weekly*, 20 March, 1941, Vol.CIX, p.250.

76   D.M. Lloyd-Jones, *Why Does God Allow War?* (London, 1940), p.96.

77   Henry, 'From Buckingham to Westminster', p.159.

78   I.H. Murray, *D. Martyn Lloyd-Jones: The Fight of Faith 1939-1981* (Edinburgh, 1990), p.52.

79   *Ibid.* Lloyd-Jones spoke of politics, misunderstanding and disagreement. Among others in the Council Chamber—there were about forty in all—were A.E. Garvie,

He was invited to preach at the 'anniversary of the evangelical conversion of John Wesley' at the Central Hall, Westminster, on 24 May 1941. The celebration included a sermon by Leslie Weatherhead in the afternoon which was followed by an open-air service on Kennington Common, neither of which Lloyd-Jones attended. Three non-Methodist speakers shared the evening service. Ernest Brown MP was a Baptist as well as Minister of Health in Winston Churchill's coalition government: he 'made a serious claim for Calvinism' and its need to be 'blended with Arminianism'. Lloyd-Jones spoke as a Welsh Calvinistic Methodist and acknowledged the influence of John Wesley's biography as well as his 'incomparable' journals before developing his theme of conversion. 'Methodists must think more carefully over the discrimination between the "once born" and the "twice born". Decision may not mean conversion', he argued, a position which may not have appealed to everyone present although it had the 'mark of approval' of the audience.[80] Alan C. Don, later Dean of Westminster, was the other speaker.

As President of the Inter-Varsity Fellowship of Evangelical Unions in England he gave his presidential addresses at the annual Easter conference and his influence extended to other areas. In July 1941 he attended an informal two-day conference of the Biblical Research Committee at Kingham School, Oxfordshire, which was concerned with plans for a more scholarly presentation of evangelical theology. The long-term strategy was that students and others alike should benefit from evangelical scholarship.[81] In a two-pronged attack Lloyd-Jones gave a paper, 'The Causes of Recent Weakness', in which he dealt with liberalism and criticized the undue emphasis of some churches on such subjects as the Second Advent, Keswick holiness and easy believism. His general counsel and advice were well received in IVF circles.

The early 1940s also brought the emergence of the Evangelical Library in London and the founding of the Westminster Fellowship. The Beddington Free Grace Library was the brainchild of Geoffrey Williams whose large collection of rare Puritan and evangelical books—20,000 by 1928—was originally housed in 'a few "Do it yourself" sheds and later in a brick building' in Beddington, Surrey.[82] When Lloyd-Jones first saw the collection on a cold January day in 1939, he felt like 'the Queen of Sheba on the occasion of her visit to Solomon'. It was after the conver-

---

Sydney Berry, Scott Lidgett, Howard Belden, Leslie Weatherhead and W.E. Sangster and the latter, like Lloyd-Jones, 'never said one word', p.59. The occasion: was a private meeting of the Council leaders.

   80   *The British Weekly*, 29 May, 1941, Vol.CX, p.75.

   81   Murray, *The Fight of Faith*, pp.70-76. See also 'The Extent of the Influence', pp.239-240.

   82   *Ibid*, p.82, and D.M. Lloyd-Jones, 'Presidential Address', Evangelical Library, 1965, p.13.

gence of Williams and Lloyd-Jones in late 1938 that the latter became convinced that such a collection 'should be somewhere in the heart of London within easy reach and access'.[83] It was not until January 1945, however, that the Evangelical Library officially opened at 55 Gloucester Road, South Kensington, and in 1948 moved to its present site at 78A Chiltern Street in a building just off Baker Street and within half a mile of the old London Bible College buildings in Marylebone Road. Lloyd-Jones retained his interest as President of the Library until 4 December 1979, when he chaired his last meeting of the committee. By this time the Library had become a major resource of over 50,000 books with branches in five continents.

The Westminster Fellowship was originally a private forum of about a dozen ministers and Christian leaders who began to meet sometime in 1941. It arose partly through Lloyd-Jones's IVF contacts and it is possible that he also had the Saturday night Brotherhood meetings in Aberavon in mind. It was unexpectedly augmented in 1942 when an IVF study group at Oakhill Theological College, Southgate, under the guidance of the Vice-Principal, Alan Stibbs, was invited to join the Fellowship at Westminster.[84] Writing to Philip Edgcombe Hughes, then curate of St. John, Deptford, and later Visiting Professor of New Testament at Westminster Theological Seminary, Philadelphia, Lloyd-Jones said: 'A number of us, including the Rev. Alan Stibbs, have started a new fellowship of evangelical ministers and clergy.'[85] This was to remain a quarterly meeting until it was disbanded in 1966. As a forum for discussion and encouragement it was in every respect an important development. It was transdenominational: Anglicans like Stibbs were as welcome as Free Churchmen and equally made their contributions in papers and debates. So far as Lloyd-Jones was concerned, the Fellowship had the added benefit of introducing him to a broader spectrum of evangelical life. He also became known in Crusader Union, Scripture Union and Children's Special Service Mission circles, largely through his friend A.J. Vereker, who was Secretary of a Joint Committee of these organizations.[86] Under the chairmanship of Lloyd-Jones, the Westminster Fellowship was predominantly a re-assertion of evangelical Protestantism.

---

83   Lloyd-Jones to Geoffrey Williams, 4 January, 1939. Letter in the Evangelical Library and used with permission.

84   Murray, *The Fight of Faith*, p.87.

85   Letter to P.E. Hughes, 3 February, 1942, in D.M. Lloyd-Jones, *D. Martyn Lloyd-Jones Letters 1919-1981* (Edinburgh, 1994), pp.61-62.

86   Murray, *The Fight of Faith*, p.89. Vereker, Secretary of the Crusader Union, 1919-47, held leadership positions in a number of evangelical and interdenominational organizations, and was a member of the first Council of London Bible College. On the latter see I.M. Randall, *Educating Evangelicalism: The Origins, Development and Impact of London Bible College* (Carlisle, 2000), *passim*.

It compounded theology, apologetics and church history within the discipline of propositional revelation and was to be an influence on evangelically minded ministers for the next twenty-five years.

In Sole Charge

In July 1943, G. Campbell Morgan resigned his pastoral charge at Westminster Chapel. He was now in his eightieth year and had begun 'to have trouble in entering the pulpit owing to rheumatism, and various other evidences of weakness began to appear'.[87] But he had also felt the strain of the German Blitzkrieg: 'London is going through a tremendous ordeal. I have not been in bed for six weeks', he wrote in his diary for 8 October 1940. In the remaining two years of his life one of his pleasures was to hear other preachers, and of Lloyd-Jones he said, 'I cannot tell you with what pleasure I listen to him...it is mighty preaching, most appropriate for these days.'[88] The retirement of Morgan meant that Lloyd-Jones was now in sole charge. After the veteran preacher's death on 16 May 1945, Lloyd-Jones spoke of him as 'a grand orator' and something of an institution, occupying in the religious life of London 'the same place as Sir Henry Wood in the musical life of London'.[89] In time Lloyd-Jones was himself to become something of an institution. During the war years his ministry 'was a centre of inspiration to large numbers of men on leave from the various Armed Forces'[90] and by the 'war's end roughly 500 people attended quite regularly'. By 1945 a new congregation was developing and 'in 1948 attendances reached 1,300– 1,400 people and we opened the first gallery'.[91]

Lloyd-Jones also commanded wider attention throughout this period. On 10 May 1944 he addressed the Congregational Union 'on the Call to Evangelism' and the next day shared the platform with the Rt. Hon. Stafford Cripps MP in a meeting 'arranged by the Social Service, the Women's and the Temperance Departments of the Congregational Union at Westminster Chapel'.[92] No record of what Lloyd-Jones said survives but it is unlikely that he would have shared Stafford Cripps's view of social salvation 'as the means of perfecting the rule of God on earth'.[93]

---

87   Lloyd-Jones, *Centenary Address*, p.14. As a child Rowlandson recalls Morgan at this time being supported on each side by a deacon while he was preaching 'because his legs would not hold him'. Maurice Rowlandson, tape recorded conversation, 1 August, 1991.

88   Morgan, *A Man of the Word*, pp.308, 318.

89   *Westminster Record*, July, 1945, Vol.19, No.7, pp.61, 63.

90   Lloyd-Jones, *Will Hospital Replace the Church?*, p.20, editorial note.

91   Henry, 'From Buckingham to Westminster', p.159.

92   *CYB*, 1945, p.34.

93   S. Cripps, *Towards Christian Democracy* (London, 1945), p.9.

In May 1945, the Congregational Union was again holding its annual meetings at Westminster Chapel. Lloyd-Jones had earlier insisted that the end of the war should be commemorated and there is a reference to his preaching at a Victory-in-Europe day Service of Thanksgiving on 8 May. An editorial in the *Congregational Quarterly*, probably written by Albert Peel, complained that the 'Victory celebrations played havoc with the May meetings, and few of the important matters for consideration received the attention it deserved'.[94] Few, however, could have begrudged the time to savour such a historic moment. On 5 January 1948, Lloyd-Jones again shared a platform with Stafford Cripps, now Chancellor of the Exchequer, this time at a World Evangelical Alliance universal week of prayer gathering at Westminster Chapel.

In the 1950s Lloyd-Jones reached the peak of his powers. The highly successful Festival of Britain in 1951 'brought throngs to London, and for the first time since Campbell Morgan's day the Church was again completely filled as 2,500 persons at times crowded the auditorium, first gallery and balcony'.[95] The '2,500' and the 'at times' refer to occasions such as Good Friday and Easter Sunday, but numbers on more normal Sundays were certainly in excess of 1,500. This did not go unnoticed by *The Congregational Monthly*, which said that Westminster Chapel 'is now the largest Congregational Church in London'.[96] Oddly enough, the article refers to the chapel as Campbell Morgan's church, with no mention of Lloyd-Jones, the man who had, without question, made it London's largest Congregational church. Another occasion when the Chapel was almost completely full was on the morning of 10 February, 1952, the first Sunday after the death of King George VI, when Lloyd-Jones preached one of his rare sermons based upon a contemporary event, praising 'a King who was loyal to his office' and presenting 'the Christian view of the State and the Crown and the Office'.[97]

The picture, therefore, was of an influential ministry: 'when I joined in 1953',wrote Betty Micklewright, 'the Chapel habitually used the first

94   *Congregational Quarterly*, 1945, Vol.XXIII, Part 3, p.200.
95   Henry, 'From Buckingham to Westminster', p.159.
96   *Congregational Monthly*, May, 1951, p.50. With regard to seating capacity at the Chapel until 1902 the *CYB* figure was 3,000 sittings, then it was 2,500. At a recent count by the author, downstairs seating amounted to about 900, or perhaps 1,200 if wall seats and sittings around the pulpit are included, some of which have been removed, and the two galleries about 1,000 with wall seats. Obviously, views on seating capacity changed over the years as did fire regulations which may account for the disparity of numbers.
97   D.M. Lloyd-Jones, *Honour to Whom Honour* (London, 1952), p.7.

gallery as well as the ground floor'.[98] The only other London churches which could approach such numbers were the Methodist Central Hall and All Souls, Langham Place, where John Stott attracted about a thousand people. As the decade progressed, however, Lloyd-Jones' preaching received less attention from the newspapers and even references in *The British Weekly* became rare. Increasingly 'the great divide' between Lloyd-Jones and other Christians became more evident. He had grave misgivings about what he saw as doctrinal indifferentism and alternative views of Christian truth which, in his opinion, did not reflect the 'fundamentals of evangelicalism'.[99] These were the issues that opened up the gap between Christians in the 1960s and came to occupy much of his time and attention.

In March 1968 Lloyd-Jones became ill and required medical attention: 'I suddenly faced a situation in which I at any rate might no longer be here', he said at a meeting of the Evangelical Library on 8 November that year.[100] The illness was not the reason for his retirement from the pastorate at Westminster Chapel but, as he said, it was a 'precipitating factor in what was becoming an increasing conviction'. He recovered and could have continued at Westminster Chapel but he was in his sixty-ninth year and had 'completed 30 unbroken years in the ministry of Westminster'.[101] The conviction was that he should give more time to publishing his sermons, preparing 'spiritual reminiscences' and accepting 'invitations from various parts of the world'.[102] His retirement was sparingly noted in the press: 'London's longest preaching marathon'— *The Daily Telegraph*; 'the end of an era'—*The Western Mail*; and 'one of the most influential Free Church ministries of our time'—*The Methodist Recorder*.[103] His retirement lasted thirteen years during which time he preached many times to wider audiences.

---

98   B. Micklewright, letter to author, 19 October, 1991. Betty Micklewright is the daughter of M.J. Micklewright, deacon and assistant secretary at Westminster Chapel during the war.

99   Lloyd-Jones, *Knowing the Times*, p.252. On these fundamentals see his *Maintaining the Evangelical Faith Today*, pp.18-19.

100   D.M. Lloyd-Jones, *An Urgent Appeal* (London, 1968), p.6.

101   D.M. Lloyd-Jones, 'Letter of Resignation', 30 May, 1968. Copy in possession of author.

102   Henry, 'From Buckingham to Westminster', p.161, and Lloyd-Jones, 'Letter of Resignation'. He never did prepare biographical material, nor did his predecessor, Campbell Morgan.

103   *The Daily Telegraph*, 11 June, 1968, p.14; *The Western Mail*, 3 June, 1968, p.5; *Methodist Recorder*, 25 July, 1968, p.11. A.E. Gould who wrote the *Recorder* article, was Chairman of the Congregational Union of England and Wales 1965-66. He was the minister of London Road Congregational Church, Chelmsford.

On 8 April 1969 Dr and Mrs Lloyd-Jones made their last visit to America, not returning until 9 September, their longest visit abroad. He travelled extensively but the most significant event was his sixteen lectures at Westminster Theological Seminary, Philadelphia, on preaching, afterwards published as *Preaching and Preachers*. After 1969 he increasingly spent more time preparing his sermons for publication and completed six volumes in his series on *Romans* and seven on *Ephesians*. His interest in the Evangelical Library continued, as did his association with the Westminster Fellowship, the Evangelical Movement of Wales[104] and the Christian Medical Fellowship. The latter had been a distinguished relationship, as Douglas Johnson pointed out. He had chaired the London Medical Group for over fifteen years and had addressed annual breakfasts during three British Medical Association meetings.[105] His published lectures to the Christian medical world demonstrate how familiar he was with current practice and developments, but more importantly, they contained contributions to debates on healing, drug abuse and demonic possession.

On 7 November 1979, Lloyd-Jones preached for the last time from the pulpit of Westminster Chapel. In the following May he was at the Methodist Central Hall, Carlisle, St. Vincent's Free Church, Glasgow, and Baker Street Congregational Church, Aberystwyth, preaching in Welsh in the afternoon and English in the evening.[106] On 8 June 1980, he preached his last sermon at the opening of Barcombe Baptist church in Sussex and on 1 March 1981, he 'passed on to the glory of which he so often preached'.[107] Bethan Lloyd-Jones died on 5 February 1991 at the age of ninety-two, and was buried beside her husband in Gelli cemetery, Newcastle Emlyn, Dyfed.

---

104 His last Evangelical Library committee meeting was on 4 December 1979, and he spoke for the last time at the Westminster Fellowship on 3 December 1980. His final appearance at the Bala Ministers' Conference had been in June 1978. See Murray, *The Fight of Faith*, pp.718 and 702.

105 Lloyd-Jones, *Healing and Medicine*, p.9.

106 *The Banner of Truth*, July, 1980, Issue 202, p.6.

107 *The Evangelical Times*, April, 1981, Vol.XV, No.4, p.10.

CHAPTER 2

Preaching the Word:
'Pericles and Demosthenes'

When, in July 1945, Lloyd-Jones described the late G. Campbell Morgan as a man for whom 'preaching was the supreme passion of his life', he might well have been describing himself.[1] If Morgan directed all his gifts to this one end, Lloyd-Jones did the same. And as Morgan attracted members of different denominational backgrounds so too did Lloyd-Jones. Those who differed with Lloyd-Jones on other counts were generous when it came to admiration for him as a preacher. John Stott, Rector of All Souls, Langham Place, acknowledged that 'in his heyday in the 1950s, he was superb', and Sir Norman Anderson, first Chairman of the House of Laity in the General Synod of the Church of England, considered him 'the outstanding evangelical preacher of his day'.[2]

The expository approach of Lloyd-Jones was intellectually demanding and required the fullest attention of those who listened. Yet it was precisely this kind of preaching that he made a touchstone: 'Does exposition of the Truth in preaching appeal to you? Do you like it? Do you enjoy it? Would you like to know more about it? If you can say "Yes" to these questions you possess good presumptive evidence that you have new life in you.'[3] Certainly, none could fail to be impressed by the expository commitment to exposition of Lloyd-Jones. Thirteen years on the *Epistle to the Romans*, eight years on the *Epistle to the Ephesians*, six years on the early chapters of the *Gospel of John*, three years on the early chapters of the *Acts of the Apostles*, two years on the *Sermon on the Mount*, besides which there were many shorter series such as twenty-one sermons on *Spiritual Depression* in 1954, twenty-four on *Revival* in 1959 and twenty-four on *Baptism with the Spirit* in 1964. For those who had

---

1   *Westminster Record*, July, 1945, Vol.19, No.7, p.1.

2   John Stott, tape recorded conversation, 16 November, 1991, and also T. Dudley-Smith, *John Stott: The Making of a Leader* (Leicester, 1999), pp.233-234; Sir Norman Anderson, letter to author, 6 May 1991.

3   D.M. Lloyd-Jones, *The Law: Its Function and Limits* (Edinburgh, 1973), p.152.

'good presumptive evidence' of new life sermons such as these were a theological education and a comprehensive syllabus of evangelicalism.[4]

The Nature of His Preaching

What, then, was the nature of Lloyd-Jones's preaching? Could it be said that there was a formula which could be mastered and used by any intelligent, prayerful person or was it more complex with an element of mystery about it? There was a recognizable format to his preaching, it is true, but it was rooted in this transcendental element: to use his own words, it contained 'an existential meeting with God'.[5] What this amounted to was that preaching in and of itself was the primary means by which God made himself known. It was not the only means of faith but it was the major one appointed by God. So there were two strands in the preaching of Lloyd-Jones: there was the unpredictable spiritual part which arose from a God-given message and there was the personality of the preacher himself. In other words, each sermon was at the same time human and divine, which is why Lloyd-Jones expected people to be moved by the power of the truth not merely to understand it.

But an inbuilt sense of God and passion in his sermons was not his alone. Any preacher worthy of his calling had the same singularity of purpose. Campbell Morgan, for example, could not understand a 'man not being swept sometimes right out of himself by the fire and the force and the fervour of his work',[6] and the *Yorkshire Evening Post* reported of W.E. Sangster that as his sermon proceeded, 'the fire was burning in him and his voice rose with tempestuous force' until, in the end, his 'arms were flashing like rapiers, commanding attention, driving his main points home'.[7] There was a passion and an intense seriousness which the man in the pew felt as preachers like Lloyd-Jones expounded Scripture. There is a full treatment by Tony Sargent of the element of sacred anointing in the preaching of Lloyd-Jones.[8]

The preaching style of Lloyd-Jones owed a great deal to his medical training. Doctors are taught to determine the nature of a disease and make the relevant prescription for its cure, and that was the background that moulded Lloyd-Jones's preaching. As he said, medicine is 'an

---

4   Cf. I.M. Randall, *Evangelical Experiences: A Study in the Spirituality of English Evangelicalism 1918-1939* (Carlisle, 1999), p.159: 'The gradually increasing influence which Lloyd-Jones exerted on English conservative evangelicalism from the mid-1930s was to result in theological and expository preaching becoming much more evident within the worship of conservative evangelical congregations.'

5   Lloyd-Jones, *The Puritans*, pp.360, 356.

6   G.C. Morgan, *Preaching* (London, 1937), p.56.

7   *The Yorkshire Evening Post*, 16 November, 1953, p.3.

8   T. Sargent, *The Sacred Anointing* (London, 1994).

applied science', concerned with 'the treatment and cure of disease', and
so is 'the Christian faith and the Christian message' which is a 'remedy
for the cure of sin'.[9] If the wrath of God rests on all men and women
outside of Christ, and if people are to be called to give account of themselves to God on the Day of Judgement, an exact diagnosis is necessary.
It may be said, however, that there is a trace of contradiction here.
Medical diagnosis carries with it a sense of fallibility and it may be wise
on occasions to take a second opinion. Lloyd-Jones would not have been
unaware of this but when it came to an infallible Bible there was no room
for flexibility. In one respect this was arrogant since it disregarded the
feelings of Christian leaders who equally sincerely held alternative views.
On the other hand, believing as he did in one form of truth alone,
evangelicalism, he could not act otherwise. In the pulpit he was a physician of souls, a diagnostician, and the ailing condition of man dem-
anded precision. It was the Bible alone which uncovered the needs of
men and prescribed the remedy, and for that reason Lloyd-Jones was,
first and last, a minister of the Word.

Another factor was his capacity for logic and argument. He had an
almost clinical concern for clarity of thought and 'a superbly analytical
and logical mind'.[10] In effect, he never ceased to be a protege of Lord
Horder and this was noted by Gaius Davies who was a medical student at
St. Bartholomew's Hospital in 1947: his preaching was 'the Socratic
method in action', a style of teaching and reasoning he 'had learned in
his early training with Horder' and then 'applied to the Christian life'.[11]
Logic was undoubtedly one of the things which attracted him to
Calvinistic thought and it was this that impressed Lloyd-Jones about the
writings of the Princeton theologian, B.B. Warfield: 'he had a mathe-
matical mind... His precision and logical thinking appear everywhere...
No theological writings are so intellectually satisfying and so strength-
ening to faith.'[12] But he used logic and the Socratic method not only
because it attracted him but because it was a way of training people to
think and this was a more far-reaching feature of his ministry. It was his
contention that if people could be taught how to think about God and
man and the world by using biblical principles, the Holy Spirit would do
the rest by bringing people to salvation. Whether the majority of people
could follow his deductive preaching and process of logic is perhaps

9   D.M. Lloyd-Jones, *The Approach to Truth: Scientific and Religious* (London,
1963), pp.3-4.
10   F. and E. Catherwood, *Martyn Lloyd-Jones: The Man and His Books* (London,
1963), pp.3-4.
11   C. Catherwood (ed.), *Martyn Lloyd-Jones: Chosen by God* (Crowborough,
1986), p.63.
12   These words are taken from Lloyd-Jones's 'Introduction' to B.B. Warfield,
Biblical Foundations (London, 1958), pp.8-9.

doubtful. His sermons were usually fifty or more minutes long and to follow arguments and reasoning for that length of time would require a higher degree of concentration than most congregations were capable of giving. Fortunately, as Frederick Catherwood says, Lloyd-Jones 'had the power to clothe his clinical analysis with vivid and gripping language, so that it stayed in the mind'.[13] For some, however, it was 'intolerable' and monotonous.[14]

Lloyd-Jones believed that in preaching logic was not cold or dispassionate because it was always done with the salvation of sinners in mind. To use Lloyd-Jones's own definition of preaching, it was 'Logic on fire! Eloquent reason!'[15] Such a combination of cumulative argument 'superbly organized and magically clear',[16] and lively passion, was arguably the most crucial factor in Lloyd-Jones's preaching. It urged people to think and to go on thinking about the kind of questions that Lloyd-Jones deemed important. In this way he taught doctrine and theology, not as an intellectual exercise, but as a means to new life itself.

It was a fusion of logic and fire that formed the contrast between the lecture and the sermon. Lectures vary as much as the people who give them, but generally speaking they are the presentation of ideas or information which may or may not carry the approval of the lecturer and they are normally given with a view to further discussion and enquiry. By contrast: 'the true preacher does not seek for truth in the pulpit; he is there because he has found it'.[17] The apostle Paul, for example, 'was not a lecturer, he was always a preacher',[18] and that is what Lloyd-Jones found so appealing about men like George Whitefield, John Wesley, Howell Harris and Daniel Rowland. It was the distinction he made in the case of Jonathan Edwards—'the man most like the apostle Paul'[19]— whose ministry in eighteenth-century New England was so successful: 'Edwards did not lecture about Christian truths. I am told frequently these days [1976] that many preachers seem to be lecturers rather than preachers.'[20] This may have been a comment about preachers who were less eloquent or about men who were more concerned with precise doctrine than saving souls but it hardly applies to the other great London ministries of his day. Men like Sangster and Weatherhead were not

---

13   *Evangelical Times*, April, 1981, Vol.XV, No.4, p.9.

14   Maurice Rowlandson, tape recorded conversation, 1 August, 1991.

15   Lloyd-Jones, *Preaching and Preachers*, p.97.

16   C.E. Fant and W.M. Pinson (eds.), *Twenty Centuries of Great Preaching* (Texas, 1971), Vol.XI, p.268.

17   D.M. Lloyd-Jones, *The Sons of God* (Edinburgh, 1975), p.47.

18   D.M. Lloyd-Jones, *The Final Perseverance of the Saints* (Edinburgh, 1975), p.12.

19   Lloyd-Jones, *The Puritans*, p.355.

20   *Ibid*, p.359.

lecturers in the pulpit. For Lloyd-Jones the primary function of the preacher was inspirational: 'It is not merely to dole out information, or lecture on the books of the Bible, or lecture on doctrine... His supreme task is to inspire people.'[21] The two were not complementary.

The Decline of Great Preaching

These references to a formal lecture style were part of what he saw as the decline of great preaching in the twentieth century. His contention was that the church had suffered and become largely ineffective because of a deterioration in preaching and he gives as his reasons for this a general feeling that preaching was out of place in the modern world, decline in oratory in general, a weakening of belief in revealed truth and the authority of Scripture, a reaction against the great pulpiteers of the late nineteenth century, a widespread failure to understand the nature of the sermon, a change of emphasis in sermon content and, finally, the belief that preaching was open to every Christian. This array of alleged failings contains some useful insights into Lloyd-Jones's view of preaching.

When Lloyd-Jones spoke about preaching in the modern world what most concerned him was a tendency towards 'group discussions' and dialogue as a better way of evangelism than set-piece sermons.[22] What he had in mind were panels of experts and public debates on the radio or television, and sometimes in a church, where people would ask questions and put forward their ideas as in a Brains Trust or University Debating Society. In his opinion these were 'generally nothing but sheer entertainment' and in the case of the experts any discussion of Christian topics was doomed to failure since 'the man who is not a Christian is incapable of entering into a discussion about these matters'.[23] Lloyd-Jones would not join such panels although he admitted the remote possibility that God could use such occasions and that 'the illumination' of the Holy Spirit might dawn upon a listener.[24] Donald Soper had no such reservations: he had been a regular broadcaster since 1940 and by the late 1950s was often on screen as well as on the radio.[25] Lloyd-Jones valued debate and could spend time in long discussions with people at a private level, but when it came to public pronouncements on religion and Christianity he was horrified that people should take their lead from a panel of experts rather than a preacher.

As for radio and television it was not the medium so much as its limitations which Lloyd-Jones opposed. He had appeared on both, but

---

21   D.M. Lloyd-Jones, *Inaugural Address* (London, 1977), p.6.
22   Lloyd-Jones, *Preaching and Preachers*, p.45.
23   *Ibid*, p.49.
24   *Ibid*, p.50.
25   D. Thompson, *Donald Soper* (Nutfield, 1971), p.126.

these were special occasions, and for most of his life he refused to use them because they were 'inimical to true preaching'.[26] He objected to the use of television on several counts: one was the time-limit of programmes which he said tended to produce 'short snappy messages'.[27] He was unhappy with the pre-recording and preparation of religious programmes and the kind of control that was necessary to fit a service into a schedule because it militated against the freedom of the Spirit and restricted the preacher. To an outsider this element of divine right, for that is what it was, would have appeared as arrogance, but it was not so much vanity as a conviction that only God should direct the preacher: 'The pew does not dictate to the minister as to what he is to do', and although 'the minister also must not dictate, it was 'the Lord himself who determines'.[28] So it was not the listener who was in control, nor was it the radio or television authorities. He sympathized with their position but for a preacher to observe such time-limits was to be fettered and chained: 'from the standpoint of true preaching...the exigencies of arranging programmes' were irrelevant.[29] He also objected to the impersonal nature of broadcasting where a speaker was cut off from his audience, and he deplored such things as 'television technique' which, in his mind, destroyed the whole concept and idea of preaching.[30] Even watching a service of worship on television introduced an element of entertainment so far as the viewer was concerned because however good that service might be it was only ever one of many choices and was slotted in among programmes which were entirely different.

The juxtaposition of the 'freedom of the Spirit' and restrictions of time, whoever imposed them, was certainly arbitrary. What in practice he meant by such freedom was a fifty- or sixty-minute sermon as against a shorter one. He had a horror of short sermons and defended himself by telling his congregation: 'You Christian people [are] in too much of a hurry to get home to your televisions. Give your preachers time. These mighty truths cannot be declared in a few minutes.'[31] Whether God, who is sovereign in every circumstance, would disapprove of the shorter sermon as against the longer one is open to question. But Lloyd-Jones's feelings were in line with his dislike of organization and his views on the primacy of preaching. Had he wanted to, he could easily have used a fifteen- or twenty-minute 'slot' without modifying his message and could have done it as effectively as others had done. In the event a

---

26   D.M. Lloyd-Jones, *Preaching and Preachers*, p.247.

27   D.M. Lloyd-Jones, *Revival* (Basingstoke, 1986), p.7.

28   D.M. Lloyd-Jones, *Christian Unity* (Edinburgh, 1980), p.202.

29   Lloyd-Jones, *Preaching and Preachers*, p.248.

30   Lloyd-Jones, *Knowing the Times*, p.264.

31   D.M. Lloyd-Jones, tape recorded sermon on 1 Thessalonians 1:5, August 1967. MLJRT No.5725.

somewhat romantic view of preaching and an unwillingness to adapt prevented the use of what could have been an invaluable outlet, and it is unfortunate that he continued to see radio and television more as a threat than an ally.

Lloyd-Jones also spoke about the church itself being an obstacle which stood between people and the truth. What he had in mind were moves within churches to accommodate modern man and his objections to faith and religion. He was ready to admit that there was a great deal wrong with the church—'traditionalism, formality and lifelessness'—and that some churches were little better than 'a social club',[32] but if the church had, generally speaking, ceased to believe in the miraculous and the supernatural it had made a rod for its own back. That there was an absence of powerful preaching which gripped and moved the listener was not only a sign of weakness, it was evidence that God was displeased with his people. As a result, the churches were empty and people found their faith elsewhere.

His reference to the decline in oratory, which he called Baldwinism, is interesting.[33] When sixteen years of age Lloyd-Jones had sat with his brother Harold in the Strangers Gallery at the House of Commons to listen to men like H.H. Asquith and David Lloyd-George, but his comment in 1962, when Harold Macmillan was Prime Minister, reflected his feeling that there were no great speakers left: 'who would think of wasting his or her time by going to listen to a debate in the House of Commons today?'[34] He was impressed with the oratory of men like Lloyd-George and later Winston Churchill and, to his way of thinking, it was no accident that during two world wars both leaders were great orators. The point was that 'men who could speak, who could deliver a message' were the kind of men who made history and brought about results—'One thinks of Pericles and Demosthenes and others'—and this was characteristic of his heroes Whitefield and Wesley. Baldwin, on the other hand, 'conveyed the suggestion that if a man is a great speaker he is a man whom you cannot trust and is not quite honest'.[35] This distrust of the orator and preference for 'simple and plain and honest statements' had, according to Lloyd-Jones, penetrated church circles and produced 'a prejudice against preaching' and 'religious Baldwinism', as he called it, was part of a general outlook in which the spoken word and preaching in particular had declined.[36]

Lloyd-Jones's reference to Pericles and Demosthenes was taken from Plutarch and conveys exactly this link between speech and action.

---

32   Lloyd-Jones, *Preaching and Preachers*, p.10.
33   Stanley Baldwin was Conservative Prime Minister from 1923-29 and 1934-37.
34   D.M. Lloyd-Jones, *Presidential Address*, Evangelical Library, 1962, p.17.
35   Lloyd-Jones, *Preaching and Preachers*, pp.12 and 11.
36   Lloyd-Jones, *Presidential.Address*, 1962, p.17.

Demosthenes spoke as if 'possessed with some divine spirit' and his speeches roused the Athenians and Greeks to raise an army of footmen and horsemen as well as the money to sustain them against Philip of Macedonia.[37] Pericles 'thundered and lightened in his oration to the people, and...his tongue was a terrible lightning', and, if Plutarch is to be believed, it was his 'rhetoricke and eloquence' which successfully conducted the Peloponnesian War between 431-404 BC.[38] Such illustrations fitted well with Lloyd-Jones's views on preaching. But eloquence is a two-edged sword and what Lloyd-Jones did not say was that Demosthenes after rousing the people to fight 'fled like a coward, and did no valiant act', and Pericles, in Plutarch's opinion, not only achieved victory in the Peloponnesian War but was *the cause of it!*[39] So perhaps Baldwin had a point.

A further cause for decline in the view of Lloyd-Jones was the showmanship and professionalism of certain ministers. He argued that there had been a reaction against nineteenth-century pulpiteers, men like Henry Ward Beecher, who dominated their churches and 'were experts at handling congregations and playing on their emotions'.[40] His view of pulpiteerism was that it contained a strong element of showmanship and that oratory had become an end in itself and preaching a form of entertainment. Such ministries, wherever they were to be found, lacked substance and drove people away from true preaching. But it has to be admitted that great numbers of people did hear the gospel through such men. Not all princes of the pulpit were pulpiteers in the pejorative sense and in the end men like Henry Ward Beecher, C.H. Spurgeon, Campbell Morgan, W.E. Sangster and Lloyd-Jones himself were all masters of the pulpit in their own way. There was something of the thespian in all of them and without exception their purpose was to influence if not manipulate great crowds one way or another. Lloyd-Jones was right to draw attention to the dangers of showmanship in the pulpit but it is equally true to say that such elements might attract rather than repel and there were undoubtedly those who went to hear Lloyd-Jones simply because they enjoyed it.

37 *Plutarch's Lives* (Oxford, 1928), Vol.VI, pp.126, 131, 140-141.
38 *Ibid*, Vol.II, pp.12, 26.
39 *Ibid*, Vol.VI, p.142, and Vol.II, p.44.
40 Lloyd-Jones, *Preaching and Preachers*, pp.13-14. Pulpiteer is a word used to describe a kind of preaching which is unknown in Britain today. Its nearest comparison would be some of the American fundamentalist preachers—for example, M.G. 'Pat' Robinson or Jerry Falwell. Henry Ward Beecher was an American Congregational minister famous for his witty and dramatic preaching, and for his interest in political and social reform. He was a great moralist, and a liberal so far as the Bible went. He was minister of the Plymouth Church of Brooklyn, 1847-87.

Perhaps his most potent and personal reason for a decline in preaching had to do with the need for a specific sending call from God. Without the intervention of a heavenly sending, no 'man has a right just to set up and start preaching'. It was his belief that far too many men were preaching who were not called to do so.[41] His definition of a sending call contained five elements: an inner conviction which was 'a kind of pressure ...brought [by God] to bear upon one's spirit'; the recognition of a gift by other 'spiritually minded' members of the church; a concern for the 'lost estate and condition' of men; a constraint 'that you can do nothing else'; and a hesitancy derived from 'a sense of unworthiness' and weakness.[42] It was a high view of preaching based as much on his own route into the ministry as on biblical teaching, but the deduction was clear: the call of God meant the blessing of God and where there was no call preaching declined. He deplored the rise of lay-preaching and the idea 'that a preacher is a man who earns his living in a profession or business, and preaches, as it were, in his spare time'.[43] He did allow 'exceptional circumstances' where a man felt called to preach full-time but where his church was not financially strong enough to support him: 'I would not call him, strictly speaking, a lay-preacher; he is a man who, for the time being, has to earn his livelihood, partly, by doing something else in order to make his preaching possible.'[44]

Such a distinction, based as it was on a rarefied view of preaching, is hardly convincing. There is no evidence, for example, that there is any difference between one man or another so far as God's call to preach is concerned. It is true that certain men in the New Testament were solemnly set aside to be full-time evangelists and preachers but it is equally true that there was a church in Rome before the apostle Paul arrived and that the spread of Christianity throughout the Roman Empire owed a great deal to artisans and professionals who also preached. It may be that some men had not reached the heights of a Campbell Morgan or Lloyd-Jones but this could be said of almost any preacher, both lay or clerical. In the

---

41   Lloyd-Jones, *Knowing the Times*, p.260.

42   Lloyd-Jones, *Preaching and Preachers*, pp.104-107.

43   *Ibid*, p.101.

44   His predecessor, Campbell Morgan, would not have agreed with Lloyd-Jones on this subject. Morgan had a Lay-Preachers' Guild at Westminster Chapel 'to enrol Christian men who feel called to the work of lay preaching, and to send such men as supplies to the help of Mission Halls and other places'. S. Harlowes, *Notable Churches and Their Work* (Bristol, 1911), p.16. There were specific rules of membership such as attendance at quarterly classes, an examination, 'a probation of at least one year' and membership of the Chapel.

spread of the gospel and the support of the churches, lay-preachers have played a prominent part in church life.[45]

But if there was disapproval of 'uncalled' men becoming preachers, or hesitancy over lay-preachers, women in the pulpit were an even greater problem. So far as Lloyd-Jones was concerned gender was a non-regotiable fundamental. On the question of ordaining women into the Christian ministry and allowing them to preach to mixed congregations the biblical position had not changed: the New Testament instructed women to keep silent in the churches, forbade them to teach men and, on the analogy of Christ and the church, taught the wife to submit to her husband.[46] This is why, in 1977, Lloyd-Jones saw no place for female students in the new London Theological Seminary: 'This being a Theological Seminary, no women will be admitted', because to train women as preachers would be to go against the Word of God.[47]

Holding People Spellbound

But why did Lloyd-Jones's preaching attract such crowds and why was he a 'magnet', to quote the *Methodist Recorder*, 'at a time when many influential voices have been trying to tell us that the day of preaching was over, and that no preacher, however gifted, could expect the crowded congregations of earlier, more church-conscious days?'[48] To the outsider it was something of a puzzle. Sunday services at Westminster Chapel were austere and simple: there were no choirs, no soloists and no variation in the order of service from one year's end to the other. The interior of the Chapel was, and is, impressive for its spaciousness and Victorian style, but apart from some geometric stained glass there was no adornment, no banners or paintings or mosaics; just a vase of flowers on the communion table and two thousand seats facing a large circular rostrum. There was a powerful Willis organ behind the platform but this was used only as a means to assist the singing. The focus of the whole building was the

---

45   R. Tudur Jones, *Congregationalism in England 1662-1962* (London, 1962), p.409. This suspicion of lay-preaching was understandable but it showed little concern either for Free Church tradition or for churches which relied regularly on laymen for their ministry. Lloyd-Jones could have been more sympathetic since the first eight months of his Aberavon ministry was as a lay-pastor.

46   Cf. 1 Corinthians 14:34-35, and 1 Timothy 2:11-14.

47   Lloyd-Jones, *Inaugural Address*, p.10. For Lloyd-Jones's treatment of this and the whole issue of womanhood, see *Life in the Spirit* (Edinburgh, 1973) , pp.103-126; *The Law*, pp.18-23; *Spiritual Gifts* (4) Tape 3315 and (iii) Tape 3314, MLJRT. On Campbell Morgan's Sisterhood and Lloyd-Jones's view of women by comparison, see below.

48   *Methodist Recorder*, 25 July, 1968, p.11.

pulpit, a large red Bible, and the preacher himself.[49] Lloyd-Jones was an insignificant-looking figure, short in stature and pugnacious in appearance, 'with a great domed cranium, head thrust forward, a fighter's chin and a grim line to his mouth'.[50] There was a Welsh lilt to his voice but he did not have a voice like Sangster nor a gift for open-air preaching like Soper. He relied heavily on a public address system. His style of preaching was not demonstrative, he used few illustrations and no humour, and his sermon delivery was intellectual and deductive. Yet, in the experience of Viscount Tonypandy, his 'preaching penetrated one's very heart', and according to *The Christian*, he had the 'ability to hold the largest congregation spellbound'.[51] To the non church-going public the ends and the means were contradictory; as *The Observer* put it: 'He has a Bible in front of him and can locate texts like a computer. Nobody so much as coughs', but 'whether it's what he says, or how he says it, something is terribly convincing'.[52]

There were a number of convincing components. For example, although his approach to worship seemed out-of-date and old-fashioned his language was not archaic and what he said was always relevant to the occasion. He knew how to speak to the times, often without directly referring to a situation. In 1939, one month after Hitler's occupation of Prague and when London was humming with the inevitability of war with Germany, *The Evening Citizen* of Glasgow carried a report of a Lloyd-Jones sermon under the heading 'Easter in London' in which 'Churchman' wrote of a closely reasoned discourse 'without a single illustration except from the Bible' and went on to say, 'I do not think the word crisis was ever used; there was certainly no reference to the international situation, and yet everything he said was intensely applicable to the problems facing us in these days'.[53]

More significant was his note of authority and assurance. Forty years after hearing Lloyd-Jones address the Lawyers' Christian Fellowship, it was this authority which remained in the mind of Lord Denning, who remembered him as 'a speaker of the first quality' and a man who had

---

49   The Bible was a gift to Westminster Chapel from Dr. Harris Elliot Kirk, minister of Frank Street Presbyterian Church, Baltimore, in 1947. 'I am one of those who likes to have a pulpit Bible', Lloyd-Jones, *Preaching and Preachers*, p.75.

50   A. Spangler and C. Turner (eds.), *Heroes* (Leicester, 1991), p.60.

51   Viscount Tonypandy (George Thomas), letter to author, 4 November, 1989; *The Christian*, 21 October, 1966, p.1.

52   *The Observer Magazine*, 19 March, 1967, p.12.

53   *Glasgow Evening Citizen*, 15 April, 1939, Vol.LXXV, p.10. The sermon was printed in the *Westminster Record*, Vol.13, No.5, May, 1939. It was a Good Friday morning.

spoken with clarity and conviction.[54] Whatever the occasion this note was there: 'This message is from God', he would say,[55] and he was full of such phrases as 'I am absolutely certain', 'I make no apology for saying', 'this is the only answer', 'I do not hesitate to say', and 'there is no other hope in the world tonight'.[56] Even more effective was the way he scolded his listeners as if to arouse their sense of guilt and foolishness, something picked up by Mati Wyn in *The Welshman*: 'The Doctor hurled his truths at the congregation, and the congregation were highly pleased by this. He called us fools, stupid fools if we rejected God and refuted Christ. And he emphasized the word "fools" again. And from the gallery came many an "Amen' and "Praise be to God" from keen listeners.'[57] He had the ability to make people feel that to believe any other word than his was spiritual and intellectual suicide.

But this was not unique. Politicians are equally persuaded of their cause and so were the preachers and prophets in whose line Lloyd-Jones stood. Hesitancy and apology win few converts and people respond to positive leadership especially when they live in uncertain times. An authoritative message with clear-cut answers is a safer option than doubt. Lloyd-Jones would have denied that he had any authority believing it all came from God, but given the kind of words he used, his often weighty style and the forceful nature of a man who took no pleasure in losing an argument, it is difficult to avoid the conclusion that his sermons were as much the product of talent and personality as anything else. He feared nobody, high or low, and it was this unflinching, confrontational style that was his theme when preaching to a group of young people in September 1978: 'Much of the failure of the Christian Church during this present century has been due to the fear of man. The Church has been afraid of educated people' and has become 'apologetic and nervous' which is why the Church has lost its authority and boldness.[58] So the preacher, as a man called of God, should be fearless. Pastoral

---

54 Lord Denning, letter to author, 25 April, 1992. The meeting was in Westminster Chapel Institute Hall ,where about 300 lawyers and others gathered, one of whom was the Right Honourable Lord Justice Denning, who was Lord Justice of Appeal, 1943-57. Lloyd-Jones's sermon was published by the Lawyers' Christian Fellowship as *The Centenary Message*, 20 February, 1952. In his presidential introduction Lord Denning said Lloyd-Jones was 'not a lawyer himself, but the brother of a Queen's Counsel whom you all know well', *ibid*, p.3, a reference to Vincent Lloyd-Jones, appointed a High Court Judge in 1960.

55 D.M. Lloyd-Jones, *I am not Ashamed* (London, 1986), p.46.

56 All of these are quoted from one sermon on Ephesians 2:4, April, 1967, and most of the expressions were used more than once.

57 *Y Cymro* (*The Welshman*), 21 August, 1958, p.10.

58 D.M. Lloyd-Jones, tape recorded sermon on Acts 5:32, 18 September, 1978. MLJRT, tape no.5731.

dominance of this kind, seen in Lloyd-Jones's own ministry, allowed for no hesitation: to be indefinite was a sign of weakness and was distracting to an audience which had assembled primarily to hear God's Word, and it was this highly commanding note which drew the crowds to Westminster Chapel. In fact, the man and his message blended to such an extent that people felt as though they were in touch with God through the exhortations of his servant.

Given the nature of his personality, there is little doubt that whatever the numinous element the full explanation of Lloyd-Jones's preaching lies as much in the man himself as his message. Such was the presence and influence of the man that many 'would go to listen to the Doctor even if he was going to read from the telephone book'.[59] Edward Mace, in *The Observer*, thought it 'must be instinct; actors have envied it'.[60] But it was a combination of factors. He was not a typical Welsh speaker and there was no 'hwyl' about his preaching; but he had what Packer described as an 'electric quality of communication'. This something he had in common with great actors: 'Olivier had it a lot, Gielgud and Donald Wolfit had it in a coarser form', and the effect was 'a sort of human magic'.[61] People wanted to hear him and were drawn to him. There was a kind of vibrancy about his preaching, a compelling power, and a same sense of urgency. The performance of the preacher lingered in people's minds.

The People Who Listened

We should also consider the kind of people who listened to Lloyd-Jones. After all, the sermons were demanding and people had to sit patiently while he slowly built up his arguments and reached a climax fifty minutes later. Between 1948 and 1968 congregations averaged 1,500 on Sunday mornings and about 2,000 on Sunday evenings. These were people who, apart from visitors, 'regularly travelled by bus and train through all weathers into central London, sometimes from as far away as the south coast'.[62] Who were they? The overall picture reveals a surprising range of social groups. A.E. Gould wrote of 'large numbers of young men and women, medical and other students, and youngsters earning their living in

---

59   J.I. Packer, tape recorded conversation, 5 June, 1992.

60   *The Observer Magazine*, 19 March, 1967, p.12.

61   J.I. Packer, tape recorded conversation, 5 June, 1992. The 'hwyl' is 'a Welsh preaching device for exciting the congregation to religious frenzy by breaking into a wild chant': William Sargant's definition. See D.M. Lloyd-Jones, *Conversions Psychological and Spiritual* (London, 1959), p.29, and Murray, *The Fight of Faith*, p.146. *Conversions* was a critique of William Sargant's book *Battle for the Mind* (1957), in which Sargant questioned the nature of Christian conversion.

62   *Methodist Recorder*, 25 July, 1968, p.11.

London',[63] and this is confirmed from other sources. Gaius Davies wrote of 'a large group of...medical students of many denominations [who] went to Westminster for the regular, systematic teaching',[64] and Chua Wee-hian, General Secretary of the International Fellowship of Evangelical Students, who had come from Singapore to study theology in London in the 1950s, spoke of 'large crowds of students' of all nationalities who 'furiously took notes during the sermons'.[65] Although he does not say so, a large number of these would almost certainly have come from London Bible College.[66] Evangelical Anglicans also went to hear him in the 1950s and 1960s: Alec Motyer was at that time working at Clifton Theological College (now Trinity College, Bristol) and recalls that when 'any of our men were in London on Fridays or Sundays they would invariably sit at the Doctor's feet'.[67] Some went to John Stott for one service and to Lloyd-Jones for the other.

There were also politicians, men like Cledwyn Hughes and George Thomas, professionals like Margery Blackie, homoeopathic physician to the Queen, and a variety of special visitors like Professor R.V.G. Tasker who attended on Sunday evenings for a time: 'he forsook liberalism and told me that under my ministry he became convinced of original sin and the wrath of God'.[68] Uganda's William Nagenda and Festo Kivengere were at a Sunday morning service in 1959 when Lloyd-Jones was preaching on revival, and Arap Moi, later President of Kenya, attended when a student.[69] Chua Wee-hian talks of Ghanaian Christians and others who also attended. Among the most noted was Emil Brunner, Professor of Systematic and Pastoral Theology in the University of Zurich: 'I listened to Emil Brunner give a lecture at King's College on Tuesday evening on "Predestination and Human Freedom." He was very stimulating. He came to listen to me on Sunday evening and came in to see me at the close of the service!'[70] A reporter from the *Liverpool Daily*

63   *Ibid.*
64   Catherwood (ed.), *Chosen by God*, p.60.
65   *Ibid*, p.118.
66   The author can recall the concern of Ernest Frederick Kevan, the first Principal, that too many of his students attended Westminster Chapel regularly when they could have supported smaller churches in the London area. He had the highest regard for Lloyd-Jones as a preacher but probably saw the dangers of following one man too closely.
67   Alec Motyer, letter to author, 10 June, 1991.
68   Catherwood (ed.), *Chosen by God*, p.99. Tasker had been Professor of New Testament Exegesis, King's College, London.
69   *Ibid*, pp.119, 278. William Nagenda, an Anglican, was one of the leaders in the East Africa revival, which began in Rwanda and spread into Uganda in the 1930s. He died in 1956. Festo Kivengere was also one of the leaders in the revival and later became Bishop of Kigezi, Uganda.
70   Lloyd-Jones, *Letters 1919-1981*, pp.74-75, from a letter to his friend P.E. Hughes.

Post in 1954 'was impressed with the number of families present. They came in—father, mother, daughter...to their own special seats.'[71] In his annual letter for 1961, Lloyd-Jones expressed his pleasure at seeing young families 'growing up in our midst' and he was obviously pleased with the increasing number of people staying for lunch and tea on Sundays, and spending the whole day at the Chapel.[72] This is a useful comment because it shows his concern that the whole family should come under the sound of the gospel. There were some children in his Westminster congregation although not many.

Lloyd-Jones was not unconcerned about children and their duties, as his sermons on Ephesians 6 show,[73] and he did, on one occasion, preach at an Easter service at Greenford County Grammar School in April 1954: 'I was allowed 15 minutes but took 20! ...the 550 children, masters and mistresses, and the local clergy and ministers...listened very well.'[74] So far as we know, the only concession he made at Westminster Chapel was to include a children's hymn at Christmas. This may have been dictated by the nature of his ministry and the size of his congregation but his feeling was that preaching was a word for all and children were expected to learn, if only by imbibing the climate of worship. Young adults did attend his services as we have seen—'Nurses in their uniforms...young families and students of all colours and races[75]— but most of them were in higher education and the children, by and large, were members of Chapel families. So far as church services were concerned the impression was of a general absence of young people between the ages of sixteen and twenty-five years.

The constituency of the congregations, therefore, was mixed, but the majority of the crowd were ordinary middle-class people from London and the suburbs. They left no written records of what they felt and thought but they voted with their feet by coming in their hundreds. Whether they followed all his arguments is impossible to say but it is certain that they warmed to his plain-talking and intellectual style. It would be unreal to deny that there was also an element of sycophancy although it was more marked outside of his Westminster ministry. There is little question that the crowds who attended his British Evangelical Council conference addresses or his sermons to ministers at the Bala or Puritan Studies meetings contained a number of men who 'liked' listening to him and travelled long distances to do so. But if Lloyd-Jones had his followers, his coterie of admirers who hung on his every word, the

71   *Liverpool Daily Post*, 8 June, 1954, p.3.
72   D.M. Lloyd-Jones, 'Annual letter to members of Westminster Chapel', January 1961.
73   Lloyd-Jones, *Life in the Spirit.*
74   Lloyd-Jones, *Letters 1919-1981*, p.120.
75   *Y Cymro*, 21 August, 1958, p.10.

same could be said of Campbell Morgan, Sangster and Weatherhead. It was not that these men contrived such a situation, indeed they may have deplored it, but because of their impact and reputation as public figures it became inevitable.

Comparative Congregations

In the 1960s All Souls, Langham Place, and Westminster Chapel were the two outstanding expository ministries in London. John Stott became Rector of All Souls in 1950 remaining until 1975. He was twenty years younger than Lloyd-Jones but there were striking similarities in their preaching. Stott was well known for his powers of expository evangelical preaching and for his gift as a teacher. He was not a rhetorician but he had an analytical mind and this attracted a strong congregation. Stott and Lloyd-Jones were influential: Stott with his executive capacity making an impact on evangelicalism in the Church of England, and Lloyd-Jones with his gifts for leadership and preaching among Nonconformist evangelicals. They had their differences, as we shall see, but Stott was quick to acknowledge that they 'shared the same degree of conviction about the gospel',[76] and in his review of *Preaching and Preachers*, he did 'not hesitate to urge all preachers to study and digest this book. The reading of it certainly both challenged and blessed me.'[77]

Of the London ministries within a two mile radius of Leicester Square, the primary ones in the 1940s and 1950s were W.E. Sangster, Leslie Weatherhead and Martyn Lloyd-Jones. The Westminster Central Hall had the largest capacity with about 3,000 seats and if Sangster filled these seats, as the evidence suggests, then he had the largest Nonconformist congregation in London. The City Temple and Westminster Chapel had about the same seating capacity so apart from overflow facilities for special occasions the two Sunday congregations at 1,500-2,000 were about the same. As to the nature of these congregations they were as mixed in social and educational backgrounds as Westminster Chapel. At the City Temple there were people of all ranks from a Cabinet Minister to Harley Street doctors, civil servants, lawyers, students, artisans and clerks, and Methodist Central Hall audiences comprised large numbers of visitors as well as 'men and women of the lower middle class...university students, and several professional families'.[78] Bloomsbury Central Baptist Church enjoyed a wide range of listeners including local residents,[79] and

---

76   John Stott, tape recorded conversation, 16 November, 1991.

77   *Church of England Newspaper*, 3 December, 1971, p.11.

78   H. Davies, *Varieties of English Preaching 1900-1960* (London, 1963), p.194.

79   See F. Bowers, *Called to the City* (1989), *passim*, and also her *A Bold Experiment: The Story of Bloomsbury Chapel and Bloomsbury Central Baptist Church 1848-1999* (1999), *passim*.

All Souls drew doctors, nurses and other professionals as well as a good number or ordinary Londoners. Kingsway Hall in the 1940s and early 1950s was well attended and in those days 'they came in their hundreds, keen, younger generation worshippers, many beyond the reach of any conventional cleric',[80] and, again, they came from all kinds of backgrounds.

Placing these congregations side by side there is little to distinguish between them.[81] From 1930 to 1960, years of suffering, uncertainty and reconstruction in Britain, powerful preaching continued to exercise its influence. In general terms the City Temple attracted a more emotive listener who benefited from the holistic approach of Weatherhead, the kind of person who was not looking for a theological system so much as a way of life. The Central Hall was a centre for people who liked the passion and pragmatism of Sangster, Kingsway Hall catered for the ideals of Christian Socialism with a new and fairer world in mind, and West-minster Chapel was for the kind of people who enjoyed a more doctrinal and theological sermon, but beyond this it is difficult to go. There is no doubt that great preaching drew crowds and each man had his own followers, people who believed in them and what they were doing. And for reasons which are not clear, in each case there was a kind of inter-action between speaker and listener which meshed together: possibly it was uncertainty combined with a felt need for authoritative answers and leadership in an increasingly complex world which was growing more hostile to religion and the church.

But if it was credible answers that attracted people, what has to be noted is the difference of character and presentation of these ministers. Allowing that these men found their source of authority in the kind of message they gave and that each of them preached Christ according to his own understanding of the Christian faith, and given that they were university men, most of them with higher degrees,[82] temperamentally they could hardly have been more different. Sangster was passionate, imaginative, his sermons 'like Greetings telegrams, admirably embroid-ered with imagery' and carefully constructed.[83] Weatherhead, not an orator in the conventional sense, had a more conversational style with a

---

80   Thompson, *Donald Soper*, p.57.

81   See Table 3: Some comparative membership figures for the London area, p.237.

82   Sangster, Soper and Weatherhead had London PhDs, Lloyd-Jones had a London MD. Stott had a double first from Cambridge, while Soper had also achieved a first at the same university.

83   Davies, *Varieties of English Preaching*, p.206.

voice which was 'soft and liquid',[84] whereas Soper had a more masculine and commanding voice resembling a 'resonant baritone actor's voice'.[85]

Clearly, such men were easy to listen to and no matter what the content of their sermons it was the voice and a sense of the dramatic which held the crowds. This is what lay behind the *Liverpool Daily Post* assessment of Lloyd-Jones in 1954:'words flowed in a fluent stream from the preacher's clipped, almost harsh voice', and it was compelling.[86] He was preaching from Ephesians 6 on the whole armour of God, a dramatic passage of Scripture, and 'pointing with upraised hand to an invisible sword, putting on with gestures the helmet, the breastplate, the girdle, and the shield made us conscious of the immense, menacing presence of the dark, unresting forces of evil. We felt they were right there outside the sanctuary walls—in Victoria Street, in all the streets of London and of the world'.[87] In the end, we have to say that these great ministries were the result of credible and powerful personalities. Each of them was a gifted communicator so that whether it was the Calvinistic, confessional formalism of Lloyd-Jones or the more liberal message of Weatherhead, the effect was the same: thousands were pleased to hear their words and follow their message.

The Demise of Great Preaching

What is difficult to understand is the demise of this kind of preaching. Adrian Hastings suggests that the 'mid-1950s can be dated pretty precisely as the end of the age of preaching: people suddenly ceased to think it worthwhile listening to a special preacher'.[88] The view of Father Robert Brooks and General Coutts in *The Observer* article of 1967 was that the day of the long sermon was 'out for good' and Edward Mace, who wrote the article, felt that Lloyd-Jones was 'the last, in London anyway, of the great oratorical preachers'.[89] The question they had asked—'Can today's preachers find a substitute for the thunderous old-style sermon?'—was significant if only because the question had been asked at all. Certainly, since the resignation of Lloyd-Jones from Westminster Chapel in 1968 there had not been a modern equivalent to these princes of the pulpit, and the question is, Why?

---

84   J.C. Travell , 'Leslie Weatherhead', *JURCHS*, October, 1990, Vol.4, No.7, p.452.

85   *Liverpool Daily Post*, 28 May, 1954, p.6.

86   *Liverpool Daily Post*, 8 June, 1954, p.3.

87   *Ibid.*

88   A. Hastings, *A History of English Christianity 1920-1985* (London, 1986), p.465.

89   *The Observer Magazine*, 19 March, 1967, p.10.

Lloyd-Jones would have found the answer in the unfaithfulness of the church and the absence of a 'Demonstration of the Spirit' and divine power,[90] and he was probably right, but there were other factors. With the rise of the ecumenical movement, for example, there was a subtle shift away from preaching to a more liturgical emphasis and where fellowship was a priority concern. There was still preaching but it was shorter and, set within an ecumenical ethos, tended to be more conciliatory and less individualistic: it was the communion table not the pulpit which mattered most. This was found among Nonconformists as much as Anglicans. Another development was the charismatic renewal movement which arose in Britain in the early 1960s. It produced some gifted preachers, men like David Watson of St. Michael-le-Belfrey, York, and Michael Harper, originally on the staff of All Souls, but it also aroused a pronounced interest in other spiritual gifts and the miraculous, and allowed for more open worship and audience participation. Preaching was less formal although it was just as determined to influence people's minds. Outside of the church, as we have seen, political speeches tended to be more Baldwinian and less Churchillian and in that sense the day of the rhetoricians had passed. In addition to this most Protestant churches in post-war Britain had suffered a decline in membership and it became apparent that there was a loss of certainty and nerve in the face of rising liberalism and secularism.

Nonconformity not only became weaker in its churches but at university level it had lost men like A.S. Peake, H.H. Rowley, C.H. Dodd, T.W. Manson and H.Wheeler Robinson, all of whom were outstanding scholars and churchmen. Peake was the son of a Primitive Methodist minister and remained in that denomination all his life: he was the first occupant of the Rylands Chair of Biblical Exegesis at the University of Manchester, 1904-29, and as such was the first non-Anglican to hold a divinity chair in an English university.[91] Rowley had been a missionary in China with the Baptist Missionary Society before he took up his professorship at Manchester. Dodd was a Congregationalist and Norris-Hulse Professor of Divinity at Cambridge, 1935-49. Manson was a Presbyterian and Professor at Manchester, 1936-58, and Wheeler Robinson, a Baptist, was Principal of Regent's Park College, Oxford, 1920-42. They were not evangelicals as Lloyd-Jones understood the word but they were biblical scholars. Between 1904 and 1958 their part in the training of ministers and, therefore, influence upon the churches had been significant.

But there is another and much stronger factor: the emergence of television. The majority of people in Britain in the 1950s did not have a

---

90   Lloyd-Jones, *Preaching and Preachers*, pp.304-305.
91   J.T. Wilkinson (ed.), *Arthur Samuel Peake, 1865-1929* (London, 1958), p .69.

television set, yet within the next ten years it became widespread and by the late 1960s it had become a major factor in the control of the social environment. In public life men like Harold Wilson and after him other politicians used the intimate style of television as a way of communicating their ideas. Even more forceful speakers like Margaret Thatcher and Arthur Scargill made extensive use of television to present their case to the nation.[92] And so did a whole range of other interest groups including the church. It is true that important speeches continued to be made both in Parliament and elsewhere, and ministers went on preaching but, essentially, electronic communication had taken the place of set-piece speeches in front of great crowds. With a few exceptions, society no longer turned out to halls and meeting places for their instruction or entertainment. For Lloyd-Jones it was substituting men of strength with 'grinning ninnies', his term for 'television personalities',[93] but whether he liked it or not television and not the pulpit had become the more significant means of communication. As we have said, Lloyd-Jones would not have rated this kind of sociological factor very highly, but whatever the reason, the 1950s and 1960s saw the demise of a preaching tradition that had come down through Spurgeon and others. The only possible exception was the evangelist Billy Graham. Lloyd-Jones was not wholly discouraged and believed that great preaching would not finally perish though it might be in eclipse: 'in God's time it will come back'.[94]

It was not just great preaching which men like Lloyd-Jones, Sangster and Weatherhead produced, it was also a unique experience of worship to which large numbers of people responded. Great preaching makes for great congregations and there was a kind of synergism in such meetings, a climate of expectancy as people gathered under the power of the Word. Lloyd-Jones recognized this associational element: 'What a wonderful place God's house is... Many a time I have thanked God for His house. I thank God that he has ordained that His people should meet together in companies, and worship together. The house of God has delivered me from "the mumps and measles of the soul" a thousand times and more—merely to enter its doors.'[95] It was the combination of influential preaching and good listening that blended to make an 'oldfa fawr'[96] and

---

92   Harold Wilson, Prime Minister 1964-70, 1974-76, Margaret Thatcher, Prime Minister 1979-90. Arthur Scargill, President of the National Union of Mineworkers since 1981.

93   Lloyd-Jones, *Inaugural Address*, p.7.

94   *The Observer Magazine*, 19 March, 1967, p.12.

95   D.M. Lloyd-Jones, *Faith on Trial* (London, 1965), p.39.

96   D.M. Lloyd-Jones, 'Religion and Features of Nationality', Radio Wales, 1943. 'Oldfa fawr' is the Welsh phrase for a great meeting, 'something to remember and to speak about for years, and possibly for eternity', *ibid*.

it was this living contact Lloyd-Jones had in mind when he spoke of 'an interplay of personalities and minds and hearts' between people and preacher.[97] Weatherhead also felt that preaching was not only a matter of instruction but a means of worship. In the Preface of *That Immortal Sea,* the point of preaching was said to 'give men and women a glimpse of Jesus',[98] or as his son put it, 'To make God real'.[99] But the 'deep and profound silence' at the end of a service, 'a hush which no-one wanted to break',[100] was a characteristic of all good Nonconformist services and was found as much at Westminster Central Hall as Westminster Chapel. At the heart of it all was a sense of divine immanence and it was this ingredient of mystery which enhanced the atmosphere of Christian people gathering together. Campbell Morgan had also spoken about a 'spirit of expectation' in his meetings and this is what Jill Morgan meant: 'for the most part people were waiting and hungry for the Bread of Life'.[101] In other words it was a feeling that God might visit his people at any moment: 'The whole glory of the ministry is that you do not know what may happen... Suddenly, unexpectedly the touch of the power of the Spirit of God' may break in and it was this which made preaching and a service of worship unique for Lloyd-Jones.[102] This explains why he was not happy with 'once-ers':'We must convince them of the importance of being present at every service of the church. Every service!' in case 'something really remarkable' should take place and they miss it.[103]

These, then, were the kinds of factors which attracted people to the great preaching centres of post-war London. Some will regard these years as a bit of late Victorianism. Others will see great preaching as an extraordinary but repeatable occurrence. Of Lloyd-Jones himself, all the evidence points to his being one of the twentieth century's greatest preachers. That so many and so varied a crowd went to hear him is an indication in itself of the charm and inspiration that was in his voice and of the prophetic note which filled his sermons and spoke to his times. He was of the old Welsh Calvinistic Methodist school and the best illustration of his own definition that preaching is 'theology on fire'.[104]

But although as a preacher Lloyd-Jones was in touch with people in numerous countries and across the British Isles, the heart of his ministry was, for thirty years, at Westminster Chapel, and in the next chapter we

97   Lloyd-Jones, *Preaching and Preachers*, p.227.
98   L. Weatherhead, *That Immortal Sea* (London, 1953), pp.7-8.
99   K. Weatherhead, *Leslie Weatherhead: A Personal Portrait* (1975), p.11.
100 Travell, 'Leslie Weatherhead', p.453.
101 Morgan, *A Man of the Word*, pp.127-128.
102 Lloyd-Jones,*Preaching and Preachers*, pp.153-154.
103 *Ibid.*
104 *Ibid*, p.97.

turn to its history, its changing character and Lloyd-Jones's position on a number of relevant issues.

CHAPTER 3

Westminster Chapel:
'A cathedral of Nonconformity'

Until 1967, the year in which Westminster Chapel cut its links with the Congregational Church in England and Wales (CCEW), Westminster was a Congregational Church, its Trust Deeds of 25 December 1842 directing its officers and members to uphold and preach the religious doctrines held by the Congregational Union of England and Wales (CUEW). Its ministers were for the most part noted Congregationalists and to trace the history of Westminster Chapel is to trace the course of Congregationalism in Britain: its large auditorium often the venue for annual assemblies and its platform the scene of some historic decisions.

The kind of Congregationalism into which Westminster Chapel came as a new member in 1841 had only been in existence eleven years, but successive issues of the *Congregational Year Book* (*CYB*) give some idea of the growth of Congregationalism during these years. For example, the number of churches, branch churches and mission stations in Great Britain and Ireland in 1848 was 2,173, and in England and Wales in 1859, 2,236. By 1865 the number of Congregational churches in England and Wales had grown to 4,347 and in 1904, when Campbell Morgan commenced his first Westminster ministry, there were 4,615. In 1939, when Lloyd-Jones became co-pastor, there were 3,435; in 1966 when the CCEW was formed, 2,747; and in 1969, 2,386.

The first Westminster Chapel was built, according to Albert Peel, during 'six of the most important years in the history of the Union'.[1] New foundations had been laid, churches and County Associations were joining the Union and there was an increasing urgency for building more places of worship.[2] Much of this had to do with two men, Thomas and Joshua Wilson. Thomas Wilson, 'Congregationalism's "most striking layman" in the nineteenth century', had entered his father's business as

---

1   A. Peel, *These Hundred Years* (London, 1931), p.16.

2   The Congregational Union was originally an affiliation of County and District Associations of churches which joined the Union over a period of time. For example, in 1883 there were thirty-seven Associations with eight still outside, although these joined one by one over the next few years. See *ibid*, p.68.

a silk-manufacturer but retired a wealthy man in 1798 to give himself to Christian work and chapel-building. Much of his time was given to the Hoxton Academy, a Congregational theological college, of which he was Treasurer from 1794,[3] but between 1790 and 1840 he became instrumental in re-opening or founding a number of Congregational chapels in London and the provinces. Joshua Wilson also had a part in the formation of the CUEW: he was Secretary from 1832-36, Treasurer 1864-74, a Trustee of the Union and a prime mover in the later development of the Memorial Hall and Library.[4]

Joshua had his father's vision for Congregationalism. His concern for chapel-building extended from the 1840s to the early 1870s, and when asked by the 1861 Assembly how best to celebrate the bicentenary of the ejectment of 1662 he suggested fifty chapels to be opened 'before 24th August, 1862', and the foundation stones of fifty more to be laid 'on that day'.[5] Our interest in him lies in the fact that his was the first name to appear on the Westminster Chapel Trust Deed. It had been the intention of his father to found a chapel for the 'teeming population' of Westminster since 1832 and after 'several attempts to obtain suitable ground', a freehold site in Castle Lane was secured.[6] This makes the Castle Lane building one of his earliest London chapels and it also establishes that Westminster Chapel, largely through Joshua Wilson, was a Congregational church from the beginning.

Where people came from to form the original church is not clear. There was a dissenting chapel somewhere in the Westminster area which had stood on a piece of land belonging to Lord Dartmouth and had opened on 26 June 1807.[7] It is possible this work had declined, leaving a remnant of independently-minded believers without a chapel. Such a group may have continued in the area and as such would have pre-dated Westminster Chapel, but this is not certain. The most likely explanation is that the founding party was the Congregational Union itself which, looking for ways to build more churches in the London area, knew of the derelict site at the corner of James Street and Castle Lane and decided to build there. It was certainly in line with John Angell James's call to

---

3   *Ibid*, p.46, and A. Peel, *The Congregational Two Hundred* (London, 1948), p.115.

4   Peel, *These Hundred Years*, pp.411, 238, 47.

5   Peel, *These Hundred Years*, p.238.

6   P. Collins, 'Thomas Wilson 1764-1843' (15 September, 1979), p.10. Unpublished typescript. WChA.

7   *Ibid*. Lloyd-Jones said, 'I have read many times of a Nonconformist place of worship in Westminster in the eighteenth century but it is very difficult to discover where exactly it was.' D.M. Lloyd-Jones, *Centenary Address* (1965), Westminster Chapel, p.6. But even if it were discovered the link between them and the chapel would remain uncertain.

'build, build, build' and not wait 'for congregations to be gathered before we build', and it was in the mind of Shec Harlowes who wrote that although the first building 'was opened for public worship on May 6th, 1841', a church was not formed until October of that year.[8] In fact a cornerstone 'was laid on August 3, 1840 by Charles Hindley Esq., MP',[9] and on 4 October 1841 the 'Declaration of the Church meeting at Westminster Chapel' made it a 'regular' Congregational church. According to the *CYB* for 1841, membership at that date was only twenty-two but they formed a church and it took only eight months to find their first minister, Samuel Martin, who remained at Buckingham Gate for the next thirty-five years.[10]

The 'Declaration' of 1841 and the Trust Deed of 1842 both draw attention to the Congregational nature of Westminster Chapel. In the former it was described as 'a house of God for Divine Service, according to the Congregational Faith and Order', and the latter committed the chapel to upholding 'the religious doctrines held by the Congregational Union of England and Wales'. The terms of the Deed obliged a minister to give assent 'to the aforesaid Denomination of Independent Protestant Dissenters' and preach the doctrines of the CUEW, but as we shall see, this did not prevent the appointment of J.A. Hutton in 1923 and Hubert L. Simpson in 1928, both Presbyterians.

Circumstances had of course changed in 1967 when Lloyd-Jones asked P. Raynar, one of his deacons, if 'in his opinion it was competent for the Members of the Church to decide to join the FIEC', and to do so 'without the agreement of the Trustees'.[11] It was Mr Raynar's view that such deeds should 'be interpreted by reference to the situation ruling at the time when the *Trust Deed* was entered into', but in fact there was no infringement of doctrine since Westminster Chapel remained staunchly Independent and Protestant under Lloyd-Jones. The only thing that had changed was the demise of the CUEW and some of the evangelicalism of

---

8   Peel, *These Hundred Years*, p.149, quoting John Angell James in 1839. The 'English Congregational Chapel Building Society' was formed in March 1853: by May, £7,000 had been promised towards the fifty new chapels in five years, *CYB*, 1853/54. S. Harlowes, *Notable Churches and Their Work* (Bristol, 1911), p.4. Harlowes's account uses information supplied by A.E. Marsh, Church Secretary under Campbell Morgan. Marsh used brief notes collated from what was published in the newspapers at the time.

9   Charles Hindley, Liberal Member of Parliament who sat for Ashton-under-Lyne from 1835 until his death. M. Stenton, *Who's Who of British Members of Parliament*, Vol.1, 1832-1885 (Hassocks, Sussex, 1976), p.193. Hindley was a Moravian although he frequently worshipped among Congregationalists when in London.

10   For the comparative church membership figures during different pastorates, see Table 4: Westminster Chapel Statistics, p.238.

11   'Notes of a Deacons' Meeting' (n.d., but early 1967). Mr Raynar was also a solicitor. The Trustees were the CUEW.

Joshua Wilson's day. As Raynar pointed out, there had been 'no departure from the terms of the Trust' and their entry into the FIEC would make no difference to what they believed. Raynar's view was very much in line with Lloyd-Jones's opinion on the usefulness of trust deeds, covenants or other arrangements which he felt should not be allowed to restrict the people of God. Criticizing 'certain tyrannical ideas' of the Pilgrim Fathers, he disagreed with the notion 'that the conditions of church membership and church government could be so laid down that the church could continue like that in perpetuity':'we cannot legislate for posterity'.[12] On the other hand, Lloyd-Jones was ready to say that he believed 'wholeheartedly everything which is contained in the church covenant of Westminster Chapel... I would not be able to stay there as minister for a moment if this were not true', but it was probably 'the belief of the Independent Protestant Dissenters'[13] which most impressed him about the document.

The first Westminster Chapel was built 'to supply the urgent wants of a wicked city, where scenes of vice and wretchedness abound in the immediate neighbourhood of the Queen's palace, the courts of law, and the Houses of Parliament.'[14] It was built with the help of the Metropolis Chapel Building Fund Association on the site of the old Westminster Infirmary which had moved to a new site in 1831. Charles Hindley, whose name appears on the corner stone, promised £1,000 and such was the urgency of the need for a chapel in Westminster that Thomas Wilson 'advanced £2,500' towards the purchase of the site.[15]

The Present Building

An early engraving shows a Greco-Roman style of building with imposing pediments and columns, and a spacious tree-lined forecourt. It was built by John Tarring[16] to seat 1,500, but such was the success of Samuel Martin's ministry—'In 1863 the applications for sittings at Westminster Chapel had for some time exceeded by several hundred the

---

12   D.M. Lloyd-Jones, *Unity in Truth* (Darlington, 1991), p.91. He goes on to quote with approval some words of John Robinson, one of the Pilgrim Fathers: 'I charge you before God and before his blessed angels that you follow me no further than you have seen me follow the Lord Jesus Christ. If God reveal anything to you by any other instrument of his, be as ready to receive it as ever you were to receive any truth by my ministry.'

13   *Barn (Opinion)*, April 1963, p.71.

14   Collins, 'Thomas Wilson', p.10.

15   Collins, 'Thomas Wilson', pp.10-11.

16   John Tarring, architect of the Memorial Hall, Farringdon Street. He 'designed many chapels in London and in the country; styled the Gilbert Scott of the dissenters'. See F. Boase, *Modern English Biography* (London, 1965), Vol.III, p.878.

number which the building could provide'[17]—that by 1865 it had been
demolished and replaced by a larger building designed to accomodate
3,000 persons. The present building, designed by W.F. Poulton,[18] was
opened on 6 July 1865 and completely covered the original site. Its
design was a mixture of Classical and Romanesque in polychrome brick
with a tower on one side and a series of steps across the front of the
building rising from the pavement on Buckingham Gate to an entrance
behind three central arches. The cost amounted to £18,000.[19] The most
impressive aspect of the design was the span of the auditorium with its
ornate iron balustrades, columns and cantilevers supporting two galleries
and giving unrestricted views of the pulpit. In some respects it looked
more like a Victorian Music Hall than a church and according to a
newspaper cutting of the time, the span of the roof was greater than 'any
other edifice in London, except Covant Garden Theatre'.[20] It was, and
still is, impressive, but it did not please everyone.

Officially it had the best acoustical properties, but Lloyd-Jones felt the
building was so bad it 'killed Men. It would have killed me beyond any
doubt... But fortunately this thing [the microphone] has been invented,
and it enables me...to exercise my ministry.'[21] He referred to Samuel
Martin, who died when he was only sixty-one years old: 'I am persuaded
in my mind that it was this building that killed him. He had continual
trouble with his voice and throat.' And 'owing to his weakness', even
Campbell Morgan 'could not be heard, and they had to provide a loud
speaker system before I came here'.[22] Even so, Lloyd-Jones thought that

---

17   *CYB*, 1879, p.330.

18   William Ford Poulton of Poulton and Woodman, Reading. Poulton was a prolific
and successful Victorian architect. He designed a number of Congregational churches in
the 1850s and 1860s, including the French Congregational Church in St Helier, Jersey,
which in some respects was similar to Westminster Chapel with its open timber roof and
requirements of a centralized auditorium. Among his other designs was the Town Hall in
Wokingham, Surrey. R. Dixon and S. Muthesius,*Victorian Architecture* (London, 1978),
p.232.

19   *CYB*, 1866, p.326. Originally there was a steeple but this was removed when it
became dangerous in 1929. In 'The Church', see n.19 below, the Chapel was described as
being 'in James Street...near the Wellington Barracks'. Buckingham Gate was the gate
into St. James's Park beside Buckingham House, later developed into Buckingham Palace
by George IV. James Street extended from Victoria Street to the Palace and came to be
known as Buckingham Gate, possibly at the end of the nineteenth century. G.
Bebbington, *London Street Names* (London, 1972), pp.104-106.

20   'The Church' (Centenary of the Building of the Chapel), 6 July, 1965, p.2.
Unpublished typescript. WChA.

21   Lloyd-Jones, *Centenary Address*, pp.21, 8.

22   *Ibid.* The reference to Morgan was to his declining years. Otherwise he had no
difficulty being heard. J. Harries, for example, gives several instances of how easily
Morgan was heard at Westminster Chapel and concludes that, 'After forty years of

Westminster Chapel was 'a wonderful pulpit to preach from. Though the place is so big the congregation is nevertheless near the preacher. It is almost unique, in my experience, in that respect.'[23] But not all ministers liked it. Arthur Porritt remarked that Westminister was 'Variously described as a "cave of the winds" and "a Charing Cross Station of a Chapel"' which 'oppressed Jowett sorely'.[24] There is much truth in this: from the pulpit desk the auditorium is cavernous. To preach in a building which is 130 feet long, 67 feet wide and 50 feet high requires a good voice as well as a good sermon. Lloyd-Jones had the latter but when the public address system failed, as it did on occasions, it was difficult to hear what he said.

Still, it was a fine example of mid-Victorian chapel-building. Lloyd-Jones, of course, did not see it that way. To him it was the product of 'a carnal spirit', not an architectural achievement, and when he called Westminster Chapel a 'Nonconformist cathedral' it was not a compliment so much as a criticism of the Nonconformist 'desire to be respectable' and 'to look big in the sight of the world'.[25] He was probably right. Victorian Neo-Gothic and numerous other styles were used to produce some impressive public buildings. It was not only Congregationalists, for Baptists, Presbyterians and Methodists all had gothic windows, colonnades or campaniles. However large congregations require large buildings and architects had a duty to design buildings which were appropriate to the surroundings. A vast unadorned barn of a building is not necessarily spiritually preferable. Yet, for Lloyd-Jones it was a matter of principle: an impressive building had little value if it had been achieved 'at the expense of the Spirit and loyalty to the truth'.[26]

The same argument arose with respect to the church organ. The Henry Willis organ, built in 1879 'at a cost of £1,600' in memory of Samuel Martin, was considered after its restoration to be 'one of the finest in the country'.[27] Originally it stood at the porch end of the church, but in 1905 it was moved to its present position behind the pulpit. The old organ, by this time redundant and presumably inadequate, was 'sold to a chapel in Wood Green for £100'.[28] For Lloyd-Jones, by installing a larger instrument, the 1879 congregation were 'competing with the

---

incessant use' his voice was 'as smooth and pliant as it was in "the gay nineties", ere Queen Victoria came to her second Jubilee.' J. Harries, *G. Campbell Morgan* (London, 1930), p. 188.

23   Lloyd-Jones, *Centenary Address*, p.21.
24   A. Porritt, *John Henry Jowett* (London, 1924), p.198.
25   Lloyd-Jones, *Centenary Address*, p.8.
26   *Ibid*, p.20.
27   Stanley Curtis, 'The Church Organ', *Westminster Chapel News*, September/October 1981, pp.13-14.
28   *Ibid*.

Church of England' by wanting 'one of the best organs in London', though Stanley Curtis, church organist from 1951-75, saw things differently.[29] That the organ was one of the finest in the country was not, in Curtis's opinion, 'the objective, consideration being given solely to its suitability and effectiveness as a means of praise and worship'.[30] It would, perhaps, be difficult to exclude some element of pride altogether, yet for those who heard Curtis play it was not a 'carnal' experience but a spiritual one: he raised the level of worship at every service.

Lloyd-Jones cannot have been unaware of this. Even so, he felt that such an instrument was excessive and expensive and this again became apparent when an overhaul was necessary in 1965: 'We are now having it cleaned and reconditioned at a cost of over £2,000', he said, but when he was warned that a future reconstruction would be needed 'at an estimated cost of £15,000', his comment was, 'I shall probably not be here then, but let me say this for the guidance of those who will be here. If you do that...I say you are forfeiting every right to expect God to bless you. To spend £15,000 on reconstructing an organ in an age like this I regard as nothing but grievous sin.'[31] In practice, however, a congregation the size of Westminster Chapel needed a powerful instrument to lead its worship—Lloyd-Jones certainly did not have the voice to do so—and there is no doubt that the hymns and psalms he so often chose would not have sounded the same without their inspired accompaniment. The 'grievous sin', if that is what it was, was committed in 1981.[32]

Here, then, was 'a cathedral of Nonconformity' which until 1947, when Westminster Chapel's relationship to the CUEW became nominal, had held an important place in London Congregationalism. Of the nine ministers (excluding assistants) who served the Chapel up to 1968, two

29   Lloyd-Jones, *Centenary Address*, p.9. Again, it was the 'carnal spirit' of Victorian Nonconformity and evidence of an 'inferiority complex showing itself in an attempt to produce a "cathedral" that can stand comparison with Westminster Abbey', *ibid*, p.8.

30   Curtis, 'The Church Organ', p.13. Curtis was no mean organist. A bronze and silver medallist for piano and organ at Trinity College of Music, London, he made a number of broadcasts and appeared in concerts at the old Queen's Hall and around the country. He produced a Long Playing record—*Organ in Contrast* (Apollo Sound A5 1004/Stereo, 1968)—which was a demonstration of the Westminster Chapel organ. He was elected member of the Royal College of Organists on 12 June, 1926, and was a member until his death on 15 December, 1975. The Royal College of Organists, letter to author, 27 October, 1995.

31   Lloyd-Jones, *Centenary Address*, p.9.

32   In 1981 a complete reconstruction and overhaul of the organ—although it 'has never been high on our list of priorities'—cost £72,000. *Appeal For Renovation of Organ Funds*, April, 1981.

were Presbyterian, one Calvinistic Methodist and six were CUEW accredited men.[33]

Its Nine Ministers

So what kind of church was Westminster Chapel under its nine ministers, and did it change? In most respects Westminster was not unlike any other Congregational church of its day. It reflected current social needs and theologically its position was that of the CUEW. In other words, it was a combination of spirituality, intellectual development, compassion and recreation. There was another factor, however, unique to Westminster Chapel: its vast accommodation and 145 foot-high campanile stood near to some of Britain's greatest institutions and this endowed it with its own importance.[34]

Between 1842 and 1878 when Samuel Martin was minister, a whole range of activities was established. The Sunday Schools were actually founded four months before the foundation of the church in June 1841, fifteen months before Martin arrived. They had originally been connected with the West London Auxiliary of the Sunday School Union (South West District).[35] By September 1842 Martin had become its President and *Sunday School Minutes* for 1862 show that on average '20-30 attended' teachers' meetings,[36] which suggests a total Sunday School of about 200.

According to Lloyd-Jones, Martin was 'full of ideas' and made 'a great impact on the City of Westminster', a view shared by Albert Peel who wrote that Martin 'did much for the regeneration of Westminster, then one of the most degraded districts in London'.[37] He had 'meetings for people described as "down-and-outs", beggars and tramps'.[38] He 'lectured frequently and successfully at Exeter Hall for the Young Men's Christian Association', and was active on the committee of Westminster Hospital and presented a communion plate to the hospital chapel in

---

33   The two Presbyterians were John A. Hutton and Hubert L. Simpson. Lloyd-Jones was the Calvinistic Methodist.

34   Westminster Abbey, Buckingham Palace, St. James's Palace, the Houses of Parliament, Wellington Barracks, the Home Office, Victoria and Belgravia are all within twenty minutes of the Chapel.

35   *Westminster Chapel News*, May/June, 1982, p. 2.

36   *Ibid*, p.23.

37   Lloyd-Jones, *Centenary Address*, pp.6,8, and Peel, *These Hundred Years*, p.187.

38   Lloyd-Jones, *Centenary Address*, p.8. The foundation stone of the old Intermediate Hall which lay behind the Chapel and is presently underneath the refurbished lounge, shows that the Hall was once the school room and was opened in 1843, one year after Martin's arrival. It was here that work among the 'down-and-outs' was largely focused.

1862.[39] When Martin was chairman of the CUEW in 1862, Westminster Chapel entertained the Autumn Assembly: 'in addition to dinner at the Tavern each day, there was a tea at Stepney Meeting and a breakfast in a room "tastefully decorated, as well as bountifully supplied with provisions" at Westminster Chapel'.[40]

The impression, therefore, is of a flourishing, socially active church, strongly committed to neighbourhood needs but not neglecting national questions. Under Samuel Martin the combination of good preaching, extensive pastoring and a lengthy pastorate produced one of London's strongest churches and Westminster Chapel did not enjoy the same kind of success again until the arrival of Campbell Morgan in 1904.

In Henry Simon's time, 1878-87, three other Sunday Schools began joining with the Chapel on special occasions such as flower services and flower shows, and a harvest festival was introduced at this time.[41] In 1883 the Congregational Union suggested Westminster Chapel take over Buckingham Chapel in Palace Street, Pimlico, for evangelistic purposes. This was begun in March 1884, and became known as the Westminster Chapel Mission, A.W. Hewitt being given the oversight.[42] Hewitt introduced Bible classes, evangelistic services, social evenings, a temperance society, a Band of Hope and other agencies with the Chapel's approval and this continued until the lease ran out in 1892, when the work was transferred to Westminster Chapel itself.

In W.E. Hurndall's day the emphasis was similar. In a pastorate of only sixteen months he 'launched out into various and numerous activities, established a "Men's Own" at Westminster Town Hall, together with a "Woman's Own" at Westminster Chapel', and had the same interest in 'the poor and lowly and underprivileged'.[43] In his previous pastorate at Harley Street, Bow, his 'Men's Own' group grew to a membership of 'nearly one thousand' and his interest in personal evangelism brought about a church-based enterprise which was said to be 'One of the largest tract distributing societies in London'.[44] It was a combination of these kinds of interests—evangelism, lively preaching and, again, a wide-ranging pastoral ministry—that he brought to Westminster Chapel and

---

39   *CYB*, 1879, p.331, and C.D.T. James, letter to author, 1 November, 1995.

40   Peel, *These Hundred Years*, p.243.

41   This was the Bessborough, Castle Lane and Horseferry Road Sunday Schools. *Westminster Chapel News*, May/June, 1982, p.23.

42   *Westminster Chapel News*, July/August, 1979, p.19. Alfred Walter Hewitt was Westminster Chapel evangelist from 1878 to 1915. He conducted open-air services in the Chapel area and continued his work through four pastorates. Lloyd-Jones commented that 'he did great work...[and] was honoured by all who knew him', *Centenary Address*, p.11.

43   *CYB*, 1897, p.200, and Morgan, *A Man of the Word*, p.139.

44   *Ibid*.

which produced 'a swiftly-growing prosperity' and increase in Sunday congregations.[45]

During the ministry of Richard Westrope, 1896-1902, the impression is that Westminster Chapel became more of a Christian social centre. Lloyd-Jones spoke of 'advanced socialistic views' and felt that Westrope's ministry 'was very similar to that of...Lord Soper today'.[46] He probably took this from the *Westminster Record*'s description that Westrope was an 'advanced Radical holding strong Socialistic views, his great desire...to establish at Westminster a "People's Church", institutional, having clubs for men and women, a labour bureau [and] people's lawyer'.[47] Westrope's preaching was aimed 'to win the consent of the whole man' and Sunday evenings were, in his own words, to be a 'gathering point for distressed and scattered souls...a rallying place for all who are wearied of conventional religion', but Lloyd-Jones was probably right to say that 'his attempt to appeal to the man in the street...was not a success'.[48] By the time he resigned from Westminster Chapel in 1902, membership numbers were down to 245 and a source of income from property interests which was used 'to make good the difference between income and expenditure' had been 'expended early' that year.[49] In the end it is likely that Westrope's social concerns and growing disillusionment with an ordained ministry were factors in his move to the Society of Friends in 1907. After the resignation of Westrope in June of 1902, 'the fortunes of Westminster Chapel...reached their lowest ebb', and in the months that followed, 'Sunday services were conducted in one corner of the great auditorium'.[50]

The Morgan Years

Fortunes changed in 1904 when George Campbell Morgan (1863-1945) returned from North America to become minister.[51] Such was the interest

---

45   *Ibid.*

46   Lloyd-Jones, *Centenary Address*, p.11.

47   *Westminster Record*, June, 1905, Vol.1, No.6, p.141.

48   *Ibid*, pp.140-141, and Lloyd-Jones, *Centenary Address*, p.11.

49   Harries, *G. Campbell Morgan*, p.76.

50   *Ibid*. According to the *Labour Prophet*, April, 1896, Vol.V, No.52, p.58, Westrope was 'forced out' of his pastorate at Belgrave Chapel, Leeds, 'because leading lawmen thought he was too radical in politics'. He was a member of the Christian Social Brotherhood of which he was treasurer and had done 'useful work among the unemployed in the Castleford area', *The Friend*, 28 March, 1941, Vol.99, p.156. He preached his last sermons at Westminster Chapel on Sunday 8 June, 1902, and in 1907 joined the Society of Friends with another ex-Congregational friend, Percy Alden. *CYb*, 1907, p.47.

51   He had left Tollington Park in 1901 to take up conference work at East Northfield, Massachusetts, a centre under the direction of D.L. Moody, until his death in 1899.

in his return that on 2 November, at a service of recognition, William
Robertson Nicoll, editor of the *British Weekly*, spoke of Morgan's 'heroic
thing', and Charles Silvester Horne of Whitefield's Memorial Church,
spoke of a 'chivalrous and courageous enterprise'.[52] On Sunday 3 November, Morgan's first services at Westminster Chapel, the whole ground
floor was crowded and before long the first gallery was filled also.

But if under Morgan Westminster Chapel once again became a comprehensive social structure in which minister, officers and staff controlled
an extensive array of church activities, Morgan did not do it by himself.
A condition of his acceptance was that Albert Swift, his lifelong friend,
would join him and it was only when that was settled that Morgan agreed
to come.[53] Swift's organizational abilities played an important part in the
new developments, something which Arthur E. Marsh continued in 1908
when he became assistant and Church Secretary.[54] The new development
which was used to reach 'the people of the slums of Westminster and the
sleek, outwardly smiling streets of Kensington' was the Sisterhood, and
by the end of 1904 Morgan had 'ordained' four young women for the
work.[55] By 1911 the Sisterhood had grown to nine full-time workers who
wore a distinctive uniform of navy blue and scarlet.[56] They sat together
during Sunday services and among the areas of responsibility in the 1911
Sisterhood was a Woman's Employment Register, Study Circle Leadership, superintending of the Primary Department of the Sunday School
and Young People's Institute, teaching at all levels of the Sunday School,
church visitation, church membership matters, secretarial, editing the
Westminster Record, and management of the *Westminster Pulpit* and the
chapel bookstall. In addition they had the oversight of Communion
Circles Classes, took part in the Benevolent Committee and one of them,
Sister Dora, was Missionary Secretary.

Morgan was 'beyond cavil...the mainstay of the work in the years immediately following
Moody's death.' Harries, *G. Campbell Morgan*, pp.74-75. Morgan preached extensively
throughout America and remained in this work until his call to Westminster Chapel in
1904.

52   *The British Weekly*, 3 November, 1904, Vol.XXXVII, pp.115, 99.

53   *Westminster Record*, January, 1905, Vol.1, No.1, p.15. 'I knew that Dr.
Morgan would not come to Westminster unless I promised to be with him, and I felt it
would be a great responsibility for me before God if I hindered Dr. Morgan from taking up
this great work.' *The Christian Age*, 26 October, 1904, Vol.LXVI-17, p.258.

54   A.E. Marsh had been studying for the ministry at Princeton Theological
Seminary but after only a year he was invited to become Morgan's assistant and Church
Secretary. Earlier he had been Morgan's private secretary. Harlowes, *Notable Churches
and Their Work*, p.6. Marsh stayed at the Chapel for over fifty years and was Church
Secretary until 1961. He died in 1962. *Westminster Record*, December, 1962, Vol.37,
No.12, p.183.

55   Harries, *G. Campbell Morgan*, pp.87, 4.

56   Morgan, *A Man of the Word*, p.146.

These were gifted women, carefully chosen by Morgan. One had taken a course at the Westhill Training Institute at Bournville to prepare herself for Primary School leadership and one had been Honorary Residential Secretary at the Central Institute of the YWCA in Hanover Square. All were experienced in social and church work, some having secretarial and nursing skills, and one was 'an artist of exceptional ability'.[57] According to Jill Morgan, among later Sisters one was a doctor, one was a graduate of London University and one was married to the General Secretary of the London Missionary Society.[58] And when *The Christian Age* carried an interview with Albert Swift on prospects for the new ministry in 1904, Swift spoke particularly about reaching the more 'aristocratic "flats"': 'We are having a lady—a lady by birth and training, and one who desires above all to give herself up to the work of God—who we shall turn loose, as it were, upon the well-to-do people.'[59]

It was a formidable team and there is no question that these women contributed substantially to the success of Westminster Chapel as a local church. In his 'Editorial Note' for October 1908, Morgan acknowledged 'the burden of oversight and responsibility' undertaken by the Sister-hood: 'We do not hesistate to say', Morgan continued, 'that, apart from the work done at Westminster during the past four years by our Sisters, the results obtained would have been impossible'.[60] The congregation had the diaconate, A.W. Hewitt the full-time evangelist, and the Vergers, but the backbone of the Westminster Chapel social structure was the Sisterhood and Morgan had no reservations about women in positions of responsibility in church. Indeed, his desire was for more women and for this he appealed: 'Are there not many young women of leisure and of means who could devote themselves to such work... results would be

---

57   *Ibid*, p.147.

58   *Ibid*, pp.146-147. The doctor was Charlotte Murdoch of Baltimore. Sister Josephine was the BA graduate 'equipped when the need arose to teach a class in New Testament Greek', and the wife of the London Missionary Society General Secretary was Mrs A.M. Gardiner.

59   *The Christian Age*, 26 October, 1904, p.258. This may have been Lady Kinnaird wife of the eleventh Baron Kinnaird, who presided at the Recognition Service of Campbell Morgan and Albert Swift on Wednesday afternoon, 2 November, 1904, at a table 'backed by the flags of Great Britain and America'. *The British Weekly*, 3 November, 1904, p.83. Kinnaird had been in touch with Westminster Chapel for forty-five years and had 'had the privilege very early in my life of making the acquaintance of Mr Samuel Martin', *ibid*. On the other hand, Congregationalism included women from a wide social background and Swift's reference could have been to the Honourable Mrs Henley (née Maitland) who joined Westminster Chapel in 1906.

60   *Westminster Record*, 10 October, 1908, Vol.IV, No.10, p.218.

beyond computation if twelve or twenty such daughters of the King should join our ranks for training during the next year.'[61]

Integral, too, was a choir of around sixty voices, a League of Prayer, Junior Church Membership, Lay Preachers' Guild, Missionary Circle, Literary and Social Guild and Mothers' Meeting. The Men's Slate Club inculcated 'the principle of thrift and provided benefit during periods of sickness', and a Coal Club was a savings account and means of provision 'during the winter months'.[62] There was also a Cripples' Parlour, a Dorcas Guild to make clothing for the poor, a Benevolent Society—'to provide help among the sick and poor who live in the parish and immediate neighbourhood'[63]—a Visitation Committee, the Brotherhood, and Bible Teachers' Association. There were two publications: the *Westminster Pulpit* which started in 1905 and continued until 1909, and the *Westminster Bible Record*, the organ of the Bible Teachers' Association which started in 1910 and ceased in 1916. The *Westminster Pulpit* was published again in May 1927 as the *Westminster Record* and has continued to the present time.

It is little wonder that Lloyd-Jones described Westminster Chapel under Campbell Morgan as a 'highly organized institutional Church'.[64] Through the burgeoning of evangelistic and youth activities under Swift, the extensive social concern of the Sisterhood and the popular preaching of Morgan, Westminster Chapel became one of the largest Congregational churches in central London.

There were three other pre-war pastorates: J.H. Jowett, J.A. Hutton and H.L. Simpson and while each had their own styles Westminster Chapel remained much as Morgan and his associates had made it. Jowett, 1918-22, a distinguished Congregationalist, had succeeded R.W. Dale at Carr's Lane, Birmingham, in 1895. He went to New York in 1911. When he returned to England in 1918 it was with 'a new emphasis on social and

---

61   *Ibid.* Morgan's diaconate was all male but though it was always men who supplied the Westminster pulpit, he had nothing in principle against women preachers. The difference between Morgan and Lloyd-Jones on this issue was their background. Morgan had been closely associated with the Salvation Army and Wesleyan Methodism in his early days and to the end of his life he had a high regard for Salvationists and their mixed-gender ministry. Lloyd-Jones came from a male-dominated Welsh Presbyterianism where women played a supportive rather than leadership role.

62   *Ibid*, p.17.

63   This was a nineteenth-century equivalent of family income support and social services. Applicants were given immediate relief through local tradesmen and suppliers and some were provided with food and shelter through the Salvation Army. Money for the Society came from voluntary gifts and a Christmas morning collection.

64   Lloyd-Jones, *Centenary Address*, p.12.

international implications of the Gospel'.[65] Hutton, 1923-25, resigned to become editor of *The British Weekly*. When he concluded his two-year ministry, a resolution of Westminster Chapel stated 'a deep appreciation of the interest shown [in] the welfare of the schools and Young People's Institute' and for Mrs Hutton's work in 'the Women's League and the Dorcas Guild'.[66] Hubert L. Simpson, 1928-33, continued in the same tradition.

So there was very little change in the kind of church Westminster Chapel was between 1841 and 1939. The number of church activities and level of organization were greater in Morgan's day but there had always been a variety of mid-week meetings, societies and youth work. As a local church the strength of Westminster had been in its structure of departments and activities, while as a centre of preaching it had continued to be popular among all classes of people. Apart from the vacancy years of 1902-04 and 1925-28 when the Chapel was at its lowest ebb, the tendency was towards high attendances, the strongest years being those of Samuel Martin and Campbell Morgan. It is also apparent that a church which is socially as well as spiritually orientated can be a success.There does not have to be a dichotomy between the two, as Lloyd-Jones suggested, and John Huxtable's dictum that the church 'must have a sociological as well as a spiritual manifestation' was not so far from the truth.[67] But what kind of church was Westminster under Martyn Lloyd-Jones?

The Chapel under Lloyd-Jones

When Campbell Morgan resigned from Westminster in June 1943 after sixty-seven years of preaching,[68] the character of Westminster Chapel had already begun to change. Numerous air raids, evacuation and transport problems had reduced church attendances, so that by 1940 Morgan's collegiality and elaborate structure of activities had largely disappeared, and Lloyd-Jones did nothing to revive them. A Sunday Prayer Meeting was started by Lloyd-Jones in 1942 and the Sunday School reopened in 1943. The Friday evening Bible School became a meeting for fellowship and discussion in the Institute Hall, but by 24 October 1952 Friday night

---

65   *CYB*, 1925, p.153. The 'new emphasis' was mainly as 'a champion of unity of the Churches.'

66   *The British Weekly*, 8 October, 1925, Vol.LXXIX, p.39. The report also spoke of 'the influence of his strong and virile ministry during the two years in which he has been in office in the Westminster Church.'

67   J. Huxtable, 'God's Sovereignty over the Church', in F.R. Tomes (ed.), *Christian Confidence* (London, 1970), p.124.

68   Morgan, *A Man of the Word*, p.316. He became Minister Emeritus and reached eighty years of age on 9 December 1943. He died on 16 May 1945.

meetings had moved back into the church and become more like the original Bible School. By 1957 church activities on Sundays included pre-service Prayer Meetings, an afternoon Sunday School, Young People's Class, Women's Bible Class and Bible Study with Discussion. Week-nights included a Monday Prayer Meeting, Tuesday afternoon Women's Meeting, a monthly Dorcas Guild on Wednesdays, a Thursday Bible Study Class with Discussion, and Friday evenings. A creche was 'provided during the Morning Service...for the convenience of parents with babies and small children', and in October 1954 the 'serving of coffee, tea and biscuits after the Friday and Sunday evening services was started...by our deacon Mr. G. Hasler'.[69]

All this was a far cry from the 'Shoeblack Brigade' of Martin's day or the 'Orchestral Band' of Morgan's early years.[70] The idea of Westminster Chapel as a centre of social life was, for Lloyd-Jones, the product of a nineteenth-century mentality which had failed to meet spiritual needs. That there had been vigorous preaching no one could deny, but in spite of conversions and professions of faith the material welfare or social side of the gospel had been 'inherited from Victorianism' and left the church in post-war Britain weak and powerless: 'The sooner we forget the nineteenth century and go back to the eighteenth...the better.'[71] What he especially had in mind was 'organist tyranny', 'choir tyranny' and what in Wales became known as '"the demon of the singing"' which had caused more quarrelling and divisions in churches than practically anything else.[72] True, 'many a preacher has had great trouble in his ministry with a difficult organist', but it may also be said that good organists and choirs have had their troubles with difficult ministers and poor standards of music.[73] Lloyd-Jones was not averse to singing or to the organ, indeed his argument against Christians who sing nothing but psalms without accompaniment was that the church should be free to sing the whole range of psalms, hymns and spiritual songs 'as an expression of...joy and happiness to-

---

69   *Westminster Record*, 'Church Notes', all issues from the mid-1950s, and Dorothy M. Thompson, 'Gleanings from the Archives' (n.d.). WChA.

70   *Ibid*, January, 1905, Vol.1, No.1, p.19, and February, 1906, Vol.2, No.2, p.48.

71   Lloyd-Jones, *Preaching and Preachers*, pp.265-266.

72   *Ibid*, pp.266-267.

73   Speaking at the Memorial Service of E. Emlyn Davies, FRCO, in 1951, Lloyd-Jones admitted: 'I am afraid he must have suffered much at my hands, because I am conservative in these matters, and I often probably imposed considerable restrictions upon him. I tend to have my favourite hymns...and I am afraid he may have groaned inwardly many a time, but he never revealed it to me.' *Westminster Record*, July, 1951, Vol.25, No.7, pp.85-86. Davies was organist at Westminster Chapel 1916-51.

gether', and occasionally he chose a hymn with a chorus.[74] His criticism had mainly to do with conditioning and formality, and he was sensitive about this wherever it arose. Some people 'seem to think that the right thing to do in the house of God is just to go on singing choruses and a certain type of hymn until you are almost in a state of intoxication', he said, but 'that may be of the very devil'.[75] His criticism was also aimed at those who, in his view, were more interested in music than the truth. He disliked what he called a 'formal service...such as you have in a cathedral',[76] although it has to be said that there is a degree of formality in any church service, even at Westminster Chapel. But it was all part of an attack on those who look upon church as an aesthetic experience, 'a beautiful service in a beautiful setting' with 'very short sermons'.[77]

His point with respect to music in public worship was that, given how powerful music can be, it should be controlled. Nothing should be allowed to detract from the pulpit. The greatest work was preaching, not singing, and all the emphasis was to be on that. If there had to be organists and choirs in churches—and he would 'abolish choirs alto-gether' in favour of congregational singing—ministers should ensure that the organist and 'every member of the choir' were Christians and that 'the preacher should choose the tunes as well as the hymns, because sometimes there can be a contradiction between the two'.[78] So far as the abilities of the organist went these were not to be inflicted on churches and it was this element of unobtrusiveness and lack of showmanship which impressed him about the playing of E. Emlyn Davies at Westminster Chapel: 'His idea was not to show what he could do, not to impose his gifts and powers upon us...everything in the service must be subservient to the one great end of bringing glory to God.'[79] Lloyd-Jones's whole conception of church music and the dignity of services was

---

74   *Westminster Record*, September, 1968, Vol.43, No.9, p.132, and July, 1951, Vol.25, No.7, pp.84-85. Earlier, in Aberavon, he had been 'the "star turn"' when he sang 'one of the old favourite hymns in a quartet. He could read the part—bass for him—easily and well, given the sol-fa, and not the old notation!' Bethan Lloyd-Jones, *Memories of Sandfields 1927-1938* (Edinburgh, 1983), p.41. Mrs Lloyd-Jones was describing a Whit Monday march which turned out to be wet and stormy: 'we were all herded into the chapel' filling it 'from door to pulpit and from floor to ceiling', *ibid*. Such references to his singing in such a way are rare indeed.

75   Lloyd-Jones, *Faith on Trial*, p.44: 'a certain type of hymn' was almost certainly a reference to songs with a high level of repetition, little theological content and with a distinct emphasis on personal experience.

76   *Westminster Record*, September, 1968, pp.139-140.

77   Lloyd-Jones, *Faith on Trial*, p.43. See also Lloyd-Jones, *Will Hospital Replace the Church?*, p.6, where 'beautiful singing' was described as 'a pleasant form of "escapism"'.

78   Lloyd-Jones, *Preaching and Preachers*, pp.266-267.

79   *Westminster Record*, July, 1951, p.135.

the old dissenting view of public worship where people sang together
under the minister's direction and where the only eccentricities were
those of the sermon.

At Easter 1939, the choir of Westminster Chapel consisted of only five
ladies (some may have been on holiday). By 1945 it had gone altogether,
as had the Sisterhood, the Young People's Institute, the Saturday Evening
Praise, Prayer, and Missionary Rally, Junior Church Membership,
Communion Circles, the Lay Preachers' Guild and youth movements, the
Brotherhood, the Visitation Committee and the Bible Teachers'
Association. What remained of the Morgan era was the afternoon Sunday
School, the Women's Meeting and the Dorcas Guild. In some respects
these changes were to be expected, as Lloyd-Jones said:'the Hospital
...has taken over the healing of the sick' and the 'State has...taken over
the administration of social relief, education and much else'.[80] There was
now no need of the Men's Slate Club or a Cripples' Parlour. But the
absence of such activities at Westminster Chapel was less an indication of
changing times than a view of the local church.

Healing the sick or bringing aid to those in need is important, as the
New Testament shows, but Lloyd-Jones's point was that healing was not
Christ's primary purpose: the priority of Christ's ministry was to deal
with the problem of sin and restore people to a right relationship with
God. The ministry of healing was a 'by-product' or 'incidental function' to the main purpose of making sinners right in the sight of God,
and this was Lloyd-Jones's reason for leaving medicine in the first
place.[81] The real business of a church is prayer, preaching and Bible
study and this is what he meant by a 'God-centred' church. Churches
which 'became the centre of social life' with 'all sorts of cultural clubs'
or 'organized games', as many had been in 'the pre-1914 period', were
man-centred. Where this led to socio-political preaching it was 'largely
responsible for emptying the churches'.[82] Whether this was so or not, and
it was not in Morgan's case, Westminster Chapel prospered under the
influence of Martyn Lloyd-Jones.

The Chapel under Lloyd-Jones then was very different. From the
beginning he had been critical of what he had inherited and by 1945 had
gradually dismantled most of it or at least done nothing to preserve or
revive it. But the new régime was achieved at a cost and it generated such
feelings that for the first few years of his ministry at Westminster, Lloyd-
Jones experienced opposition. Murray draws attention to 'influential

80   Lloyd-Jones, *Will Hospital Replace the Church?*, p.19.
81   *Ibid*, p.11. 'I saw men on their sick beds, I spoke to them of their eternal souls,
they promised grand things. Then they got better and back they went to their old sin! I
saw I was helping these men to sin and I decided that I would do no more of it. I want to
heal souls.' Sermon, 28 April, 1929, quoted in Murray, *The First Forty Years*, p . 80.
82   Lloyd-Jones, *Preaching and Preachers*, p.34.

members of the congregation from pre-war years, including men in the leadership of the diaconate'[83] who opposed him, although he does not identify them. When Margery Blackie, converted under Campbell Morgan, first heard Lloyd-Jones's sermons she 'did not take kindly to him' and was 'even somewhat prejudiced against him', such was the difference between the two men.[84] In a letter to A.G. Secrett in 1943, Lloyd-Jones confessed to being 'terribly lonely at Westminster for the whole of the first year. Indeed I could scarcely believe that it was actually possible for a church to be so spiritually cold'.[85] And there was a touch of homesickness as he missed the fellowhip and friends in Port Talbot.[86]

At the same time it was no easy matter to labour under the shadow of a famous person, and this was also the problem faced by Glyn Owen in 1969.[87] When Lloyd-Jones went to Westminster Chapel in 1939 such was the esteem which surrounded Morgan that Lloyd-Jones and his approach to church affairs were not well received: in 'my first two years I went through hell'.[88] Morgan's daughter 'accused him of trying to ruin her father's work' and Blackie 'felt he had not co-operated with Dr. Morgan as he should have'.[89] According to one estimate, although 'the blitz'

---

83   Murray, *The Fight of Faith*, pp.100-101.

84   Constance Babington Smith, *Champion of Homoeopathy* (London, 1986), p.76. In due course, Blackie 'was able to find in him a wise counsellor and understanding friend'. Later, when writing *The Patient, Not the Cure* (London, 1976), she thanked Lloyd-Jones for reading the proofs and for continued advice as she 'turned to him again and again', and to 'his wife Bethan', who 'also made valuable comments', *ibid*, p.157. For Blackie's high regard and close relationship with Campbell Morgan and his wife, see pp.59, 74-76, 97.

85   Lloyd-Jones, *Letters 1919-1981*, p.86. A.G. Secrett was one of his deacons.

86   At the Memorial Service for E. Emlyn Davies, Lloyd-Jones said: 'I always used to like the way, when he came back from holiday, he used to tell me how he felt home sick. I knew exactly what he felt, and he was one of the few people who could sympathize with me when I felt the same!' *Westminster Record*, July, 1951, p.86.

87   *Life of Faith*, 18 October, 1969, p.3. Glyn Owen was appointed to Westminster Chapel in September 1969 and commenced his ministry in October. Although he stayed until 1974 such were the memories of Lloyd-Jones that 'his years at Westminster were difficult years'. George Hemming, interview, 6 February, 1995. As R.T. Kendall said, 'My advantage was that the church was already empty when I got there.' Tape recorded conversation, 8 October, 1991. Kendall arrived in 1977. So far as the Chapel went in 1968, Kendall did not believe 'there was a preacher in the whole world who could have kept it going'. In that sense, it was fortunate for Campbell Morgan that there was a Lloyd-Jones to follow him, but there was no such person in 1968.

88   'Personal Information 1'.

89   *Ibid*. Morgan had two daughters, Ruth and Kathleen Annie, both of whom were devoted to their father's ministry. Kathleen became Morgan's secretary and travelled with him in Britain and in America. Our source does not say which daughter it was, but given their loyalty and devotion, it could have been either. See Harries, *G. Campbell Morgan*,

dispersed many of the people to other parts of the country, 'perhaps 20-25% of Campbell Morgan's congregation'— some still office bearers— 'remained at Westminster in the 1940s'.[90] Still, most of the old guard had either died or moved away by the 1950s and others, according to Mrs Lloyd-Jones, 'became his firmest friends'.[91]

A Local Church?

The changes in Westminster Chapel between 1939 and 1966 were a matter of principle. The principle was that benevolent societies, concerts, clubs and suchlike activities were extraneous to spiritual life and were the sign of a dead church rather than a living one. Lloyd-Jones was convinced that if 'the Protestant Fathers and the Puritans could return and look at the modern Church' they would not recognize it: 'they did not have brotherhoods and sisterhoods, and divisions according to ages, and organizations and clubs and leagues and badges'.[92] The local church was a separated society, a gathering of the new-born who focused on doctrine, the breaking of bread and prayer, on the glory of God and the salvation of mankind. Yet in spite of all the effort Lloyd-Jones made in his preaching to discover the real nature of the church it is curious that in the case of Westminster Chapel he offered little guidance. On the wider issues he was unequivocal—the fellowship of believers, spiritual gifts and styles of worship, the history and purpose of the church, and relationships with other churches. But when we turn to the pragmatics of church polity and government he was uncertain if not random. Given that the marks of a Congregational church are the worship of God, preaching of the Word, administration of baptism and the Lord's Supper, pastoral care, discipleship and evangelism, there were discrepancies. Worship, preaching and the sacraments were in place but the function of elders and deacons was not clarified, there was no acknowledgement of baptism in public worship, no collective action of the church to visit and evangelize the locality, no programme of pastoral care or preparation for church membership and no parity between minister and assistant. In his early years at Westminster he had, according to one source, tried to lay down a basis of faith but it foundered on the question of priorities: 'He wanted to insist that the sacraments were placed within secondary truth' and not among

---

pp.222-223, for Kathleen's assessment of her father. On Margery Blackie see *Champion of Homoeopathy*, p.76.
90   Betty Micklewright, letter to author, 19 October, 1991.
91   Murray, *The Fight of Faith*, p.101.
92   Lloyd-Jones, *Christian Unity*, p.274.

the primary functions of the faith,[93] and this is a view confirmed by his lectures and sermons.

In the matter of ruling or teaching elders and the question of deacons Lloyd-Jones was adamant that the subject was never meant to be central. Iain Murray has it that he 'opposed any consideration of the introduction of elders at Westminster Chapel' and this is almost certainly true.[94] Lloyd-Jones hardly ever mentions the subject but he admits in a lecture on 'The First Congregational Church' in 1966, that Henry Jacob had elders and deacons.[95] It is interesting that he concluded his paper with a warning against rigidity and the need to keep an open mind. In practice he retained a diaconate of twelve, and by doing so continued the pastor-deacon arrangement of his predecessors which was the traditional CUEW position. He would have agreed with the Congregational Moderators that the 'office of the elder has been fused with that of the deacon'.[96]

Increasingly the Westminster Chapel deacons were happy to let Lloyd-Jones have his own way. In the early days some had taken longer to persuade than others and there were times when 'he let meetings go on until midnight or after until he got his own way', but even then he did not convince all of them.[97] When Lloyd-Jones wanted to take Westminster Chapel out of the CUEW in 1947, the minutes of the church meeting record that in the diaconate 'it had the support of all, save one Deacon'.[98] But not all of the older deacons had difficulty with the change of ministry. A.E. Marsh, who had served under Morgan since 1907, had no trouble adapting to Lloyd-Jones. He carried on as Church Secretary with Lloyd-Jones's approval without a break until 1961, and in his retirement address on 16 March 1961, spoke of Lloyd-Jones's 'magnificent expository ministry' and in particular, of his 'Studies in the Sermon on the Mount', 1950-52: 'I shall use a good deal of my spare time' to see that this 'shall be known all over the world'.[99]

---

93   Edwin King, tape recorded conversation, 31 March, 1995. This may also have contributed to his earlier difficulties. See also Lloyd-Jones, *Great Doctrines*, Vol.3, pp.32-34, 36.

94   Murray, *The Fight of Faith*, p.790 n.2. For Murray's view see 'Ruling Elders—A Sketch of a Controversy', *Banner of Truth*, April, 1983, pp.1-9.

95   Lloyd-Jones, *The Puritans*, pp.156, 164.

96   The Moderators, *The Deacon* (London, 1957), pp.30, 47. For a short history of deacons from the Congregational point of view this is a useful book. When the United Reformed Church was founded in 1972 it was agreed that deacons in Congregational churches 'should continue so for such remaining years of their elected life, provided that on re-election they should be ordained as elders.' J. Huxtable, *As it seemed to me* (London, 1990), p.57.

97   George Hemming, 6 February, 1995.

98   'Minutes of the Church Meeting', 16 October, 1947. WChA.

99   A.E. Marsh, 'Retirement Address', 16 March, 1961. Unpublished typescript. WChA. 'In 1924 I wrote a littlebook on the Diaconate, entitled, *The Responsibilities of*

As time went on newer deacons became more deferential towards their minister.[100] Whether the deacons understood the issues involved in his preaching or were sympathetic to his views is another matter. One of them in the 1950s, according to one observer, 'who was always on the door was a liberal...and only H.C. Todd was clear about the ecumenical movement'.[101] If this is true, it is rather striking. The rest of them were 'more interested in general biblical truths and not so concerned with all Lloyd-Jones's talk about secession and the church', as was evident in the Billy Graham Greater London Crusade when one of his deacons became a chief steward at Harringay.[102]

Baptism

On the matter of baptism and its mode Lloyd-Jones was for a long time undecided. At Port Talbot he sprinkled believing adults, but up to the 1950s he had not baptized anyone at Westminster Chapel and was 'confused' over the subject.[103] By the 1960s, however, he was happy to sprinkle adults again,[104] and these were recorded under the heading of 'Membership Matters' in the *Westminster Record* supplement which appeared three or four times a year, as was the dedication of infants. Of the latter it was his practice to dedicate infants at the close of the Sunday morning service when requested, but at no time did he baptize the children of unbelieving parents or immerse, although there was a baptismal pool under the floor of the Institute Hall which Morgan had installed and used during his first pastorate.[105] When people asked for

---

the *Deacons to the Minister of the Church.*' This book, no doubt privately produced, has not been found.

100 R.T. Kendall's comment was: 'In those days when he called his deacons together they simply rubber stamped his decisions'. Tape recorded conversation, 8 October, 1991. Herbert Carson's view was that 'he got away with so much because he had so many yes-men around him'. Tape recorded conversation, 15 April, 1995.

101 'Personal Information 1'. H.C. Todd, Church Secretary 1961-71, had been connected with Spurgeon's Tabernacle through his family and had a strong evangelical background. *Westminster Chapel News*, May/June, 1982, p.24. He had also been treasurer and helper at the Evangelical Library for twenty-one years. I.H. Murray, *Not a Museum But a Living Force* (London, 1995), p.12.

102 'Personal Information 1'.

103 See also Lloyd-Jones, *Great Doctrines Series*, Vol.3, pp.35-46. Lloyd-Jones 'would say about baptism, "Don't ask me; I am as confused as you are!"'

104 'I myself only baptize adult believers...by sprinkling.' Lloyd-Jones, *Letters 1919-1981*, p.170.

105 The baptistry was built in 1904. Morgan originally baptized by immersion as appears in Morgan, *This Was His Faith*, pp.232-233, but when he returned from America for his second Westminster pastorate in 1936 he used sprinkling, possibly because the baptistry had deteriorated. The baptistry was re-opened for the first time since 1917 on

immersion in George Hemming's day they were referred to Paul Tucker, minister of East London Tabernacle, and when Herbert Carson was assistant he baptized 'two at Welwyn Evangelical Church, one in Highgate Chapel and one in a chapel...in Surrey where the family had personal links'.[106]

This was understandable since Lloyd-Jones was not an immersionist by conviction. Our point here is that the significance of baptism and its overt implications were lost, at least so far as the Sunday congregations were concerned, and there was no public recognition of the great spiritual realities for which the sacrament stands. This reluctance to come to terms with the practice of baptism occasionally appeared in his sermons,[107] but it is clear from what he said that baptism was of secondary importance whatever its mode, and its practice was confined to a personal duty and given no place in Sunday worship. When he did baptize it was in the Institute Hall at a church meeting so the public element was removed and baptism became more a sign to the person themself rather than a witness to the whole congregation or to the wider public.[108] The irony is that given the importance of baptism in the New Testament and in the life of the Christian church, so far as the Sunday congregations at Westminster Chapel were concerned the sacrament hardly existed. For Baptists and those who held more decided views on the subject it was not easy to accept that baptism was unimportant in the overall scheme of things, and Lloyd-Jones almost certainly did not realize how unacceptable baptism as a secondary truth was to immersionists, and many who 'welcomed him as a special speaker...would not have done so as pastor'.[109]

The position of Westminster Chapel on the mode and practice of baptism was not rigid. The 'Declaration' of 1841 has only a general

---

Sunday 8 April 1979 when R.T. Kendall baptized twenty-two people by immersion. *Westminster Chapel News*, May/June 1979, pp.10-11. A new baptistry was built in 1990 as part of the refurbishment of the rear halls and the new one 'is approximately in the same place as the old one... It is in what we now call the Main Hall, but years ago was called the Intermediate Hall.' Bill Reynolds, Honorary Secretary of Westminster Chapel, letter to author, 15 January, 1996.

106 Herbert Carson, tape recorded conversation, 15 April, 1995. This was over a period of two years, 1965-67. Carson, who had been an Anglican and a paedobaptist, left the Church of England in 1965 and became a convinced Baptist.

107 See, for example, *The New Man* (Edinburgh, 1992), pp.34-37, 'John Bunyan: Church Union', in *The Puritans*, pp.390-411, and Lloyd-Jones, *Great Doctrines Series*, Vol.3, p.35.

108 The New Testament suggests that baptism was a public event, not a hidden act. See, for example, the baptizing of Christ in Luke 3:21-22, the public nature of the Great Commission in Matthew 28:19, and the instance in Acts 8:36-39. Generally speaking, the history of the church bears this out by giving prominence to the sacrament of baptism, whatever its mode or practice.

109 George Hemming, 6 February, 1995.

reference to 'obedience to all the doctrines, ordinances and laws of Christ', and the Trust Deed of 1842 states that ministers should belong to the denomination of Independent Protestant Dissenters and 'preach the religious doctrines held by the Congregational Union of England and Wales'. The 'Constitution and Law' of the CUEW defines member churches as those 'in which the privileges of Membership and eligibility to office are not dependent on the opinions held regarding the subjects or mode of Baptism'[110] and this view was carried forward in later constitutions.

By 1925 the general practice of Congregational churches was of infant baptism, not as indicating baptismal regeneration but as an act of dedication, and the recommendation was that 'Every church should possess a font' and that baptism by sprinkling should be 'made part of the ordinary [Sunday] morning worship', usually following the last hymn, and this wider view and practice became accepted in the majority of cases.[111] The question of the mode of baptism at Westminster Chapel was not a matter of controversy. That it changed from time to time was no infringement either of the documents we have cited or the spirit of Congregationalism. In any case, as we have seen, Lloyd-Jones had an almost cavalier indifference to trust deeds and the like, 'believing it was not possible to keep people true to the faith in the future' by such provisions.[112] The only church that mattered was the present one and so far as baptism was concerned the right approach was to treat it as a secondary matter: 'I care not whether a man is a Presbyterian or a Baptist or an Independent or Episcopalian or a Methodist, as long as he is agreed about the essentials of "the faith"', and baptism was not among 'the essentials'.[113]

Pastoral Care

Pastoral care at Westminster Chapel under Lloyd-Jones was also a marginal affair and almost exclusively confined to those who came to his vestry each Sunday. This is not to imply that he never visited the sick or that his vestry ministry was ineffective: on the contrary, there was real compassion and where there were deeper problems people returned for help over a number of Sundays. Nor are we unaware of the help he gave to people wherever he preached or to fellow ministers over the telephone

---

110 *CYB*, 1871, p.xii.
111 T.T. James, *The Work and Administration of a Congregational Church* (London, 1925), p.59.
112 George Hemming, 6 February, 1995.
113 *Westminster Record*, July, 1963, Vol.38, No.7, p.111. He did of course care about these affiliations and the question as to what were essentials and what were not was far from clear.

or at conferences, but in the case of Westminster Chapel there was no organized pastoral care and Murray's biography does not mention this issue.

The explanation, at least for Lloyd-Jones, rested in the special nature of his ministry. He made this clear in 1959: 'Though we do not meet personally as frequently as I should like, owing to the exceptional circumstances in which we are placed, I am nevertheless conscious of being in a special relationship to you as your Pastor.'[114] But it is difficult to know what that 'special relationship' was since he never knew the majority of his congregation and had no contact with them beyond the Sunday services. If 'exceptional circumstances' was a reference to West-minster Chapel as a preaching centre and to out-of-town engagements during the week, the same could be said of Campbell Morgan. The difference was that Morgan established a team of workers to carry out the church's obligations to its own members and the neighbourhood. In Lloyd-Jones's day hospital visitation was left to the assistants and any others who may have had a particular interest. In some cases this may have been effective but at its best it was a rather hit-or-miss affair.

Equally haphazard was entry into church membership. There were no 'Rules of the Church' or 'Duties of Church Members' as there were in Samuel Martin's time, no member of staff to oversee membership matters like the Sisters in Morgan's day and no preparation of candidates. Some went to see Lloyd-Jones and some did not: it was wholly at his discretion and the transfer of members 'did not exist'.[115] Names were mentioned at a deacons' meeting and the Church Secretary 'made sure this was then voted on [at] the next Church Meeting': none questioned Lloyd-Jones's wisdom—it was entirely in his hands.[116] New members received a booklet of numbered, monthly communion cards, presumably to follow up those who did not attend the Lord's Table regularly, and the 'right hand of fellowship' was given to new members as it had been in Morgan's day, at the close of a morning communion service.[117] The only other hint of

114 D.M. Lloyd-Jones, 'Annual Letter to Members of Westminster Chapel', January, 1959.

115 Church membership in Lloyd-Jones's day was by special recommendation: 'He interviewed the person and if he was satisfied, recommended membership.' The same procedure applies today. Bill Reynolds, 15 January, 1996.

116 *Ibid.* 'No doubt the church did not overturn the recommendation.'

117 In fact this had become standard practice among Congregationalists: See D.H. Stockwell, *What About Church Membership?* (London, 1956), pp.79-80. Although in the author's experience there was no letter or indication of welcome other than the communion cards, 'the right hand of fellowship', given by Lloyd-Jones, was generally considered to be enough. To belong to Westminster Chapel in the 1950s and 1960s was more of a privilege than a relationship. The author's communion cards for 1966 show his absence from the Lord's Table on several occasions, but no enquiries were ever made.

organization was a 'Roll of the Friends of Westminster Chapel' which included the names of the members who had moved away from London but wished to keep in touch: the origin of this is uncertain.

Assistants

We have also said that there was no parity between the minister and his assistant at Westminster. Assistants were appointed by Lloyd-Jones alone. They were not church members so they did not attend church business meetings or, for that matter, deacons's meetings. They had to be ready to step in at any moment should Lloyd-Jones be sick and they were dismissed without the need of consultation with others. Because they were 'assistants to the minister' and not 'assistant ministers' they were a personal choice, although their appointment was confirmed by the deacons. With the first assistant, Iain Murray, 1956-59, 'The Doctor proposed that he should invite Mr Murray' and that 'a Bursary of £450' be provided, and these proposals were 'agreed'.[118] There were two reasons for the first appointment—'the need of some assistance in order to provide sufficient week evening meetings, in addition to the Friday Evening Lecture', so releasing Lloyd-Jones for preaching engagements 'in all parts of the country' and to provide time for Murray to continue his research.[119] The meetings Murray took included the Monday Prayer Meeting which was attended by twenty-five to thirty people, and Wednesday Bible Study, but he was not invited to preach either on Sundays or Fridays.[120]

The position of assistant varied with circumstances. For Murray it was a means of enabling him to settle his future. With the second assistant, George Hemming, 1959-65, it was a 'tent-making situation' and a break after a seven-year pastorate at Union Congregational Church, Leigh-on-Sea. For Herbert Carson, 1965-67, it was a breathing space on leaving Anglicanism, and with Edwin King, 1967-69, it was a matter of keeping various meetings going at Westminster Chapel while continuing with his own pastorate at New Town Baptist Church, Chesham. All of them were expected to lead a Sunday afternoon Bible Class, the Monday Prayer Meeting and Wednesday Bible Study, and in most cases, to undertake pastoral visitation where necessary. Hemming, who 'came almost entirely for pastoral help', undertook hospital visitation, taught mathematics part-

---

Cards were issued each January or late December, but apart from a Bible text for each month, the only other information it carried was the name of the minister, address of the church, candidate's number—641 in this case—and a list of the twelve deacons inside the back cover.

118 'Minutes of the Deacons' Meeting', 17 July, 1956. WChA.

119 *Ibid.*

120 The first time he preached on a Sunday at the Chapel was during the vacancy, 2 March 1969. *Westminster Record*, Vol.44, No.3, p.48.

time at a Technical College in Slough and preached 'somewhere in Greater London' every Sunday.[121] Like Murray he was not invited to preach either on a Sunday or Friday at Westminster. Carson, a University of Dublin graduate, also preached widely through the London area, and to supplement his stipend he lectured part-time at All Nations Bible College (now All Nations Christian College) in Ware, Hertfordshire. Carson, of course, was not a young minister serving an apprenticeship: 'I had been an Anglican parson for nearly twenty years and being in a university city at St. Paul's I was quite prominent.'[122] Carson brought with him much skill as an expositor and preacher,[123] and Lloyd-Jones acknowledged this when Carson resigned and went to Hamilton Road Baptist Church, Bangor in Northern Ireland: 'We shall ever be grateful for the fellowship and co-operation of such a faithful and courageous contender for The Faith.'[124] He also differed in that he was the first assistant of Lloyd-Jones to preach at the Chapel: 'I preached the first Sunday after Christmas, the first Sunday after Easter and on four Sundays in the summer',[125] but there was no formal agreement or contract either with Carson or any of the others.

The heaviest load fell on his final assistant, Edwin King. Like the others he had visited the sick and taken weddings and funerals,[126] but when Lloyd-Jones fell ill in March 1968, he became immediately responsible for the services. He was invited by the deacons to take one Sunday a month during the vacancy 'for which I would receive £21; I would take

---

121 George Hemming, 6 February, 1995.

122 Herbert Carson, letter to author, 20 January, 1995.The church was St. Paul's, Hills Road, Cambridge, where he had a large congregation and a considerable following of undergraduates.

123 Carson was a gifted author. He contributed an exposition on *The Epistle of Paul to the Colossians and Philemon* in the Tyndale New Testament Commentary series in 1960, was the author of four other books, and contributed an article to the *New International Dictionary of the Christian Church* (1974).

124 Lloyd-Jones, *Letters 1919-1981*, p.178. By 'courageous' Lloyd-Jones was referring to Carson's secession from the Church of England in 1965, an account of which was given in his *Farewell to Anglicanism* (Worthing, 1969).

125 Herbert Carson, tape recorded conversation, 15 April, 1995. In fact in the summer pulpit arrangements for 1965, he preached for the whole of August—five Sundays—Prof. G.N.M. Collins, Ieuan Phillips, W.J. Grier and Leith Samuel preached one Sunday each. Carson also preached four Sundays during August and September 1966, four Sundays during the same months in 1967, and on 26 May 1968.

126 Until 1961, A.E. Marsh took many of the weddings and funerals for Lloyd-Jones and latterly H.Carson and E. King played their part. Lloyd-Jones took such services when he was available but he rarely preached at them. Before Carson went to Westminster in 1965, 'when I was still a vicar at St. Paul's, Cambridge, I was asked to preach at a wedding at the Chapel. Lloyd-Jones did not usually speak at weddings. He took the service and I preached.' Tape recorded conversation, 15 April, 1995.

the Friday Evening Bible Study regularly and could drop the Wednesday meeting'. This continued until Glyn Owen was appointed in 1969.[127]

The position of assistant under Lloyd-Jones, then, was very different from that of Campbell Morgan and Albert Swift who were co-pastors. Of Swift Campbell Morgan said: 'He is not my assistant. We are colleagues in this work. The duties he is going to undertake are quite as important as anything I can do.'[128] But Lloyd-Jones was more solitary and never enouraged a 'curate' type of situation, let alone a colleague of equal standing. Possibly he was not the kind of man who could have had a powerful assistant, or maybe he did not want the challenge or difficulties that an assistant of this kind might bring. It could also be said, however, that his style of leadership was a phenomenon of the time when preachers like Dinsdale Young, W.E. Sangster or Leslie Weatherhead overshadowed their officers and assistants. Whatever the explanation, there is little doubt that Westminster Chapel and the assistants themselves would have benefited from a properly organized assistantship with well-defined areas of work. Had they been there at the invitation of the church things might have been very different after his resignation.

Thus although Lloyd-Jones became convinced that Independency was the most Scriptural form of church government, in practice he never ceased to be a Welsh Presbyterian minister[129] and heir to a tradition that went back to the Victorian period. He was a product of his own past and he was also the product of his training and experience as a medical consultant, which explains why, for Margery Blackie, 'Lloyd-Jones ...appeared much more like a doctor in his consulting room than a minister in his chapel'.[130] As one of his deacons said, his vestry ministry was reminiscent of 'a Harley Street consultant seeing his patients, the church parlour being the waiting room and the deacon on duty being the receptionist'. Murray agrees: 'to an extent', Lloyd-Jones 'ran his vestry

---

127   Edwin King, 31 March, 1995. King preached on Friday evenings, 8 March to 18 June, 1969, without a break.

128   *The British Weekly*, 10 November, 1904, Vol.XXXVII, p.115. 'The vast opportunities on the other side of the Atlantic appealed to me with almost irresistible force, but the conviction that there was a strategic point in danger of slipping out of the hands of the Church was too strong, as I came to be convinced that I, with the help of one other man, could hold it...when Albert Swift...said he was willing to stand with me, the matter was settled. So I came.' G. Campbell Morgan, 'How I came to Westminster Chapel', in *Westminster Record*, January, 1905, Vol. I, No.1, pp.14-15.

129   He refers to the Presbyterian Church of Wales as the 'denomination to which I belong', *Centenary Address*, p.16, and he remained on their ministerial list until his death.

130   Smith, *Champion of Homoeopathy*, p.76.

interviews as a specialist runs his consulting room'.[131] None of these observations goes far enough. Lloyd-Jones ran the whole of Westminster Chapel as a consultant's practice, although with one difference: he had no registrar. This may have been acceptable medical practice but it was not what is generally understood as Congregational church practice. So once again we are left with a contradiction. On the one hand he recognized differing gifts and functions in the local church, but on the other, he offered no guidance as to how these gifts and functions might operate. This 'Chief' had no 'firm'.[132]

In all these matters—the relative unimportance of the diaconate, reluctance over the sacrament of baptism, the absence of any programme of church-based local evangelism and the lack of organized pastoral care—Westminster Chapel could not in the usual sense of the word be described as a local church. By definition a local church is a witness to the gospel in its own neighbourhood and parish. There were, as we shall see, those who showed initiative and this included the assistants themselves, but this said, in all other respects Westminster Chapel was held together by one man.

A Preaching Centre

Lloyd-Jones was not altogether unhappy with the idea of Westminster as a preaching centre —it had been such since Morgan's day—and he had successfully used the Chapel as a base for reviving evangelicalism in England: even so while this was an outstanding achievement and although it had the effect of enhancing Westminster Chapel as a centre of Christian teaching, it did so at a cost. Lloyd-Jones evidently saw this and apparently warned new members on several occasions that there was 'no such thing as pastoral care' at Westminster,[133] and he was right.

---

131 *Evangelical Magazine of Wales*, December/January, 1986/87, Vol.25, No.6, p.12, and Murray, *The Fight of Faith*, p.405.

132 The 'Chief' was a word used to describe medical consultants and the 'firm' was his team of registrar, housemen, junior doctors and their staff. In the 1920s Lloyd-Jones had been chief assistant to his 'Chief', Lord Horder. Murray, *The First Forty Years*, p.55. As a minister Lloyd-Jones was an independent consultant who rarely delegated his responsibilities. His assistants and diaconate hardly amounted to a 'firm'!

133 Edwin King, 31 March, 1995. This was not unique. The first pastor, Samuel Martin, responded to requests for pastoral visits but went on to say: 'It may readily be inferred that the Pastor of a large Church can have no time for calls and visits of a merely friendly nature, and this notice is appended to the Church Rules to prevent disappointment.' Declaration of the Church of Christ, Meeting in Westminster Chapel, October, 1841. WChA.

If in any sense Westminster Chapel could be said to be a local church it was, to quote Lloyd-Jones, 'just barely' so.[134] There was certainly an inner circle of friends, what Frederick Catherwood calls 'a core of the church', 'a strong church "family" who stayed for most of the day on Sunday'.[135] Another member of the Catherwood family thinks that 'in terms of "body life" nothing could have been stronger than the Chapel!'[136] But it is difficult to see how these sentiments can be viewed as anything other than wishful thinking. If this 'inner circle of friends' was a family which lunched together, talked, shared thoughts and discussed problems, why could no such provision be made through house groups, for example, for people who lived at a distance but who regularly attended the Chapel? After all, if it could be said that those who were free to spend all day Sunday at the Chapel 'were the Church family, the nucleus who under God supported the whole work',[137] the same might also be said of people who met for prayer and fellowship in the Greater London area or beyond. Yet no effort was made to reach the wider fellowship or consolidate the membership of the six to eight hundred members. The majority remained outside the inner circle. In any case, zeal for the strength and harmony of a 'core' church cannot excuse the fact that, in practice, Westminster Chapel was not a local church as we would understand it.

Lloyd-Jones's idea of a gathered church, so fundamental to historic Independency, was real enough, but his continual emphasis on preaching, doctrine, prayers and the encouragement of a godly fellowship separate from the world tended to overshadow all other issues. The priesthood of believers needs to be earthed in Christian responsibilty and it is here that some organization is useful as a counterbalance.[138] In the end it must be said that so far as Westminster Chapel went Lloyd-Jones did not have a doctrine of the church. It was an autocracy, or at its best a 'benign dictatorship'.[139] In theory Westminster Chapel was Congregational. In reality, however, it was more a Presbyterian than Congregational or Independent church.

Lloyd-Jones allowed the CUEW to hold its assemblies at Westminster Chapel. He was not the first to do so: when Samuel Martin was chairman of the CUEW in 1886 the Autumn Assembly was held at the Chapel and

---

134 R.T. Kendall, 8 October, 1991. 'I asked him twice over on one occasion if Westminster Chapel was a church and he answered, "just barely": those were his actual words.'

135 F. Catherwood, *At the Cutting Edge* (London, 1995), pp.148, 64.

136 C. Catherwood, *A Family Portrait* (Eastbourne, 1995), p.74.

137 Catherwood, *A Family Portrait*, p.74.

138 For one of the best discussions of these issues see P.T. Forsyth, *Faith, Freedom and the Future* (London, 1955), pp.290, 336, 447.

139 R.T. Kendall, 8 October, 1991.

over the following years there were many other occasions. But it became incongruous in the 1950s when the Congregationalist debate was moving towards ecumenical union and a more corporate church, and in 1966 when Congregationalists adopted a wider definition of 'church' following their declaration of the covenant when the CUEW became the Congregational Church in England and Wales (CCEW).[140] It would be interesting to know what delegates themselves thought as they crowded the pavement outside of the Chapel and saw Lloyd-Jones's name on the noticeboards: some might have regretted his self-imposed isolation. Others would not have heard Lloyd-Jones since he was never present at Congregational assemblies, but for those who did know him John Marsh was probably right to say that he was 'tolerated' as 'an extreme' and no more.[141] But others used the Chapel during these years. The London Bible College held its annual meetings there until 1954 when it switched to the Metropolitan Tabernacle; so too did the Trinitarian Bible Society, the Strict Baptist Mission and the FIEC, and in 1966, Michael Harper, curate to John Stott at All Souls, was allowed to hold charismatic meetings in the Institute Hall.[142] So Westminster Chapel was a useful venue for many.

Some of these meetings raise interesting questions. Why, given the strength of his views, did Lloyd-Jones allow[143] denominational Congregationalism to expound its ecumenical intentions and proposals for union from the very pulpit where he had so strongly denied it? Or, knowing his antipathy to women ministers, what of the induction of Elsie Chamberlain as Chairman of the CUEW in May 1956 at the same desk from which he preached week by week?[144] Evidently Lloyd-Jones

---

140 *Congregational Monthly*, August, 1966, Vol.XLIII, pp.16-17. The BBC film of the event shows the formation of the new Congregational Church at Westminster Chapel. On the platform were John Huxtable, Maxwell Janes, Ernest Gould, Norman Goodall, H. Cunliffe-Jones, Elsie Chamberlain, John Marsh, Sir Harold Banwell and Kenneth Thorndyke—the leaders of English Congregationalism in the 1960s.

141 John Marsh, letter to author, 8 April, 1991. As a measure of Congregational feeling over ecumenical issues, E.S. Guest of Sawbridgeworth Congregational Church, Hertfordshire, from 1956, recalls that he 'was greeted with catcalls and boos from the 2,500 members' of the 1966 CUEW May Assembly, when he made 'a call for Scriptural principles to be maintained'. E.S. Guest, tape recorded conversation, 11 February, 1992. This was, of course, how Guest remembers it but whether all did 'boo' him is another matter. Many may have voiced their dissent on Scriptural grounds.

142 Edwin King, 31 March, 1995.

143 The practice, inherited from Campbell Morgan's day, was that when a request for a letting was received by the Church Secretary, it was approved by Lloyd-Jones who, on the whole, chose to continue the tradition and not be restrictive.

144 *The Sphere*, 26 May, 1956, p.268, carried a photograph of the event with the comment: 'The Rev. Elsie Chamberlain is inducted in London. She is seen at the Westminster Chapel in Buckingham Gate during the ceremony when she was made chairman of

dissociated himself from much of what was said and done at these meetings, but the fact remains that the majority of his evangelical sympathizers would have considered it compromising to rent their church premises to those who held opposing views.

None could have known in 1939 how much the nature of Westminster Chapel as a social institution would change under Lloyd-Jones and how little of Campbell Morgan's church would remain after 1945. Some activities, reflecting a changing society, died out anyway but others ceased as a matter of principle and some for lack of resolution. In one respect Westminster was an outstanding success. For almost thirty years and at a time when in general the number of church members was declining and congregations falling, Lloyd-Jones regularly attracted large congregations in central London by preaching alone. The reason Westminster Chapel attendances increased from less than 500 in the early 1940s to around 1,500 and more by the 1950s, and maintained their momentum until 1968, was that he preached the Chapel full. People went because they wanted to hear Lloyd-Jones and the absence of a choir or any other aid beyond the simplicity of four hymns, two prayers and a Bible reading made no difference. A plain poster announcing, for example, 'Studies in Paul's Epistle to the Romans' was all that was needed to draw five or six hundred people each Friday evening for thirteen years.

Nonetheless, all great ministries come to an end. When they do, it is hardly surprising if there is a vacuum. Inevitably people will change their habits. Those who had travelled into London over long distances to hear Lloyd-Jones no longer had the same incentive and by the time Glyn Owen arrived in October 1969, most of these had gone. So too had a variety of other visitors. Students at colleges in London and the South East, ministers with a free Sunday, people on holiday or travelling through London would no longer come for the stimulus of a Lloyd-Jones sermon. For some it demonstrated the fallacy of placing too much importance on any 'human personality',[145] but that was always the danger with a powerful speaker. As Maurice Rowlandson said, great preaching centres were 'a bit like a petrol station' where people went 'to be filled up on Sundays'.[146] That of course is also true of ministers'

---

the Congregational Union of England and Wales.' The first woman minister in the CUEW, Constance Coltman, was from King's Weigh House Congregational Church: she was ordained 17 September, 1917, at the age of twenty-eight. See Elaine Kaye, 'Constance Coltman—A Forgotten Pioneer', in *JURCHS*, May, 1988, Vol.4, No.2, pp.134-146.

145 Gilbert Kirby, tape recorded conversation, 6 August, 1991.

146 Maurice Rowlandson, tape recorded conversation, 1 August, 1991.

conferences, conventions and the like, and Lloyd-Jones was not unaware of this.[147]

It was also the case that people had looked on Westminster Chapel as their theological alma mater, becoming familiar with a speaker of national and international significance, and some would find it difficult to settle under another minstry. Many did, like Geoffrey Thomas, join another local church,[148] but others may not have found it so easy to sit under new ministries and forms of worship. Christopher Catherwood's rosy picture of Westminster Chapel people, fortified by 'the benefit of years of the Doctor's teaching', going into local congregations and making 'an enormous difference' to their lives,[149] is highly optimistic.

After Lloyd-Jones announced his resignation to his deacons on 29 May 1968, he suggested they set up a Pastorate Committee composed of the diaconate and six members of the church under the chairmanship of T. Omri Jenkins, a fellow Welshman and General Secretary of the European Missionary Fellowship.[150] Jenkins, styled 'Moderator' in the *Westminster Record* from September 1968 to September 1969, recommended Glyn Owen[151]—minister of Berry Street Presbyterian Church, Belfast, since 1959—to the Committee and his name was put to a church meeting in September 1969 and duly accepted.[152] Whether it was wise to appoint another Welshman so soon after the departure of Lloyd-

---

147 'The problem of Westminster as a church, is that people simply do not know one another and it is difficult to see how they can. It is the old question of a church or a preaching centre.' D.M. Lloyd-Jones in a letter to his daughter Elizabeth, cited in Murray, *The Fight of Faith*, p.178. His answer was a week night prayer meeting though this did not solve the problem either.

148 *Evangelical Magazine of Wales*, April/May 1987, Vol.2, No.2, p.15. 'I was received into the Buckhurst Hill Baptist Church in April 1970'.

149 Catherwood, *A Family Portrait*, p.74. While admitting that many did blend into other fellowships, in the author's experience, a number of local churches 'suffered' rather than prospered at their hands.

150 'Mr Owen is Welsh, like his predecessor.' *Westminster Record*, September, 1969, Vol.44, No.9, p.143. *Evangelical Magazine of Wales*, April/ May 1987. Geoffrey Thomas was one of the deacons. He remained on the Committee until Glyn Owen was appointed, then resigned because of 'the demands' of his solicitor's practice in Woodford. His place was taken by Frederick Catherwood.

151 Owen had heard Lloyd-Jones on his visits to Wales and had received the *Westminster Record*. He had been associated with the Evangelical Movement of Wales, and was joint editor of the *Evangelical Magazine of Wales* from its inception until he left Wrexham in 1959. *Life of Faith*, 18 October, 1969, p.4.

152 Edwin King, 31 March, 1995. Owen was away on holiday at the time. Owen preached for the first time at Westminster Chapel on 3 November 1968, then again on 9 February 1969. There was a Welcome Service on Friday, 17 October 1969. *Westminster Record*, Vol.43, No.11, p.176; Vol.44, No.2, p.32; and Vol.44, No.10, p.159.

Jones and on such a low turnout of church members[153] is not our concern here. It is simply a fact, however, that church attendance figures for that autumn were under 500 on Sundays and less that 100 on Friday evenings.[154] How much the Committee of deacons and six church members played in the choice of a successor is not clear, but in the opinion of one general church member, it 'was nearly a year before the church was called to prayer over the issue' and the 'general feeling at Westminster Chapel during the vacancy was one of confusion'.[155]

While the ministry of Martyn Lloyd-Jones was a great achievement therein also lay a problem. In a sense no one could succeed him. Such was his impact on the Westminster Chapel congregation that whoever followed him was certain to have a hard time. The trouble was that the building became interlocked with the man and, for a while at least, it was difficult to imagine the Chapel going on without him. Had there been a more viable assistantship or the appointment of a co-pastor and possible successor, things might have been very different.

---

153 According to Edwin King, about 160 were present at the church meeting, and Owen received just over sixty per cent of the vote. Edwin King, 31 March, 1995. Hemming says a 70% vote was needed and about 70% voted in favour. George Hemming, 6 February, 1995. For one person present when the vote was taken, the estimate of numbers present was higher—possibly up to 200, but the vote in favour was lower. 'Personal Information 4'. Whatever the figure, 'many of us were amazed that Glyn Owen accepted with such a low percentage in favour', so 'Personal Information 4'. Exact figures are not available, but membership at the time was around 700.

154 Edwin King, 31 March, 1995.

155 'Personal Information 4'. If this is a reference to Omri Jenkins's 'Annual Letter to Members of Westminster Chapel', January, 1969, it was eight months, although in his letter Jenkins refers to 'considerable numbers' who 'have recently come together to call upon the Lord'. For Edwin King, Westminster Chapel in 1968 'was like an ocean-going liner in the midst of the Atlantic with nobody on the bridge.' Edwin King, 31 March, 1995.

CHAPTER 4

Incipient Romanizing:
'What reasons have we for not coming together?'

If ecumenism had drawn together most of the talents and leaders of the twentieth-century church it certainly held no attraction for Lloyd-Jones. On the contrary, by the mid-1960s he felt so strongly that the World Council of Churches was 'a menace to the true meaning of the Gospel'[1] that he publicly called upon evangelicals of all denominations to separate and form a new and doctrinally faithful fellowship. Before coming to these events, however, it would be helpful to identify some general areas of apprehension which became crucial to his thinking on the church.

One of his anxieties in 1951 was of 'a new denominationalism' with increased 'self-consciousness' among religious groups 'to emphasize their own particular identity and outlook'.[2] He did not say who these groups were, but went on to speak of men 'animated by a mere party spirit' and of 'friends and allies' who appear to be fighting 'for their own particular theological party' more than for the truth itself.[3] Among the 'friends and allies' of those days John Stott had begun to attract evangelicals and was soon to be at the centre of an 'impending Evangelical renaissance'[4] among Anglicans. We will refer to James Packer later, but as a Puritan Conference man and a continuing Anglican he was especially suspect, as we shall see. Both Stott and Packer did much to show that biblical awareness and membership of the Church of England were not necessarily inimical. There was a growing interest in the Fellowship of Independent Evangelical Churches (FIEC) which was enlarging its register of ministers and churches, and these all believed denominationalism to be 'contrary to New Testament teaching'.[5] The

---

1   'Threat to Religious Liberty', British Evangelical Council News Release, 1 March, 1966. A report of an address by Lloyd-Jones on Plumstead Common on 1 March.

2   Lloyd-Jones, *Maintaining the Evangelical Faith Today*, p.5.

3   *Ibid*, p.6.

4   K. Hylson-Smith, *Evangelicals in the Church of England 1734-1984* (Edinburgh, 1989), p.288.

5   *Unity in the Evangelical Faith*, an introductory leaflet, The Fellowship of Independent Evangelical Churches (London, n.d.), p.2.

FIEC, with its brand of alternative unity, had long dissented from the ecumenical movement and by the end of Lloyd-Jones's life had strengthened its separatist and theological position. In *Maintaining the Evangelical Faith Today*, Lloyd-Jones spoke of 'false prophets' and 'unreliable guides' who lead the church astray.[6] Nathaniel Micklem, in 'some plain speaking', interpreted the contents of this 'little pamphlet' as a recrudescence of 'Romanism with its typical anathema on all who do not conform',[7] but Lloyd-Jones's attack was against principles, not persons, and in spite of the severity of his pronouncements on ecumenism and theological reductionism he did not fail to acknowledge the presence of evangelical sympathizers 'in all denominations'.[8] If a person had faith in Christ, however fragile that faith, Lloyd-Jones would recognize it, but when it came to an ecclesiological view the only answer to error was separation.

The crux of his objection to denominationalism was that it imposed human authority on Christian people and overshadowed the lordship of Christ and promptings of the Spirit in the government of the church. There were those who were 'regulated by tradition' and who placed 'reason, human understanding and philosophy' above the Bible itself, and he especially equated 'the tyranny of denominationalism' with 'the tyranny of Roman Catholicism': it was a fear of growing 'central powers and committees' and 'of a world-wide Church with yet more centralized authority'.[9] It was not that denominations in themselves were wrong. What troubled him was their often liberal theology and ecumenical tendencies.[10] By 1977 he was even more convinced of the matter and suggested that even to speak about 'mainline' denominations was a mistake: 'they are not on the main line.They have gone astray...they are mixed denominations'.[11] This was essentially the reason why his association with the London Bible College ceased in the 1950s.[12] Although Lloyd-Jones had almost everything in common theologically with Ernest F. Kevan, LBC's first Principal, what disturbed him was Kevan's opening up of ministerial and academic opportunities for his students by way of London University degrees so that they could find recognition within the

6   Lloyd-Jones, *Maintaining the Evangelical Faith Today*, pp.8-9.

7   *The British Weekly*, 19 March, 1953, Vol.CXXXIII, p.6.

8   *Y Cylchgrawn Efengylaidd* (*The Evangelical Magazine*), November-December 1948, Vol.1, No.1, p.2.

9   *Ibid*, p.5.

10   *Ibid*, p.6. Where a denomination held to evangelical principles he was happy to go along with it. At Slough Tabernacle on 1 November 1974, he told Pentecostals, 'Don't stand in denominationalism. Belong to a denomination but don't stand fast in it'. Tape recorded sermon preached at the Memorial Service of W.T.H. Richards.

11   D.M. Lloyd-Jones, *Unity in the Truth* (Darlington, 1991), p.168.

12   See Randall, *Educating Evangelicalism*, p.104.

Baptist Union and other denominations.[13] The same view, although brist-
ling with dislike of the Church of England, is reflected in his *Inaugural
Address* at the opening of the London Theological Seminary in October
1977, when he referred to 'certain Free Church evangelical students' who
had entered 'Anglican Colleges for their training' which 'as a Nonconformist and Free Churchman...rouses my ire'.[14] As a generalization,
Christopher Catherwood's suggestion that Lloyd-Jones believed 'denominationalism stunted true growth' was true insofar as 'paper declarations'
and 'dead orthodoxy' took the place of life in Christ,[15] but most mainstream leaders would have said much the same thing. Still, denominational and institutional Christianity for Lloyd-Jones was subversive of
autonomy in the local church.

Traditionalism

If the tyranny of denominationalism was intolerable so too was the
spectre of traditionalism. At the end of his lecture on 'that notable event
which took place in 1662', Lloyd-Jones reminded his listeners of the
need for vigilance 'to observe all authoritarian tendencies and all
tendencies to ecclesiasticism and the hierarchical principle in the life and
activities of churches, or groups or councils of churches', issues which
were especially urgent 'as churches look more and more to and frat-
ernize increasingly with Rome'.[16] This last comment, made as it was
against a background of international ecumenical activity, was not without some foundation. In 1958 a new and conciliatory Pope had arrived in
Rome with a passion for church history and *aggiornamento*,[17] and he
established the Secretariat for Promoting Christian Unity—an event which
for the first time allowed for a deeper and broader ecumenical debate

---

13   On Kevan, see G.W. Kirby, *Ernest Kevan: Pastor and Principal* (London, 1968).
There was also the feeling that London Biblie College had abandoned its original
position and David Mingard reported that early in 1977 Lloyd-Jones had been told that
LBC 'was no longer able to give a good theological training', and this he accepted. D.
Mingard, tape recorded conversation, 28 April, 1995. By June of that year a decision had
been taken to establish the London Theological Seminary.
14   D.M. Lloyd-Jones, *Inaugural Address* (London, 1977), p.3. This was mainly a
reference to David Jackman who had gone to assist Leith Samuel at Above Bar,
Southampton, in 1976. He had trained for the ministry at Trinity College, Bristol. See
also Randall, *Educating Evangelicalism*, pp. 205-206.
15   C. Catherwood, *Five Evangelical Leaders* (London, 1984), p.104, and D.M.
Lloyd-Jones, *What is the Church?* (London, 1969), pp.11, 16-17.
16   D.M. Lloyd-Jones, *1662-1962* (London, 1962), pp.5, 47.
17   John XXIII had been a young professor of church history at Bergamo. 'In the
mouth of John XXIII [aggiornamento meant] not only adaptation to the age but also an
inner renewal.' H. Jedin, K. Repgen and J. Dolan (eds.), *History of the Church* (London,
1981), p.99.

within the Roman Catholic Church. Later that year (2 December)
Geoffrey Fisher became the first Archbishop of Canterbury to visit Rome
since Archbishop Arundel in 1397, and in 1961 the Church of England
appointed a representative in Rome 'to act as a two-way link between the
Archbishops and the Pope'.[18] In the same year evangelism and
ecumenism had been interconnected in the World Council of Churches at
the third plenary assembly in New Delhi and in October 1962, the
Second Vatican Council was opened with the charge to 'move nearer to
the unity willed by Christ in the truth'.[19] Hylson-Smith recognizes that
these developments were 'highly dangerous and even heretical' to non-
Anglican evangelicals like Lloyd-Jones.[20] Lloyd-Jones's views were not
formed in a vacuum: 'There are movements afoot and meetings taking
place', he said in 1962, which 'makes it imperative that we should
understand something about what is happening'.[21] In this sense he was as
much a part of the ecumenical scene as anyone else except that his view
of events called for separation and not inclusion.

To return to the spectre of traditionalism, Lloyd-Jones was 'suspicious
of increasing liturgical tendencies in worship...as expressed in the
wearing of gowns and robes and in processions—in Free Churches as well
as in the Anglican Church', and the increase of bureaucracy in church
life in general.[22] Of course the wearing of a gown or surplice does not
ineluctably preclude true religion, although for Lloyd-Jones an escalating
ecclesiasticism was a threat to New Testament simplicity which exalted the
'service' at the expense of the sermon. But even evangelical principles
can deteriorate and he was as ready to warn his fellow evangelicals against
fossilized Christianity as he was to alert others: 'We must not preserve our
evangelical principles simply because they have a venerable pedigree',
but concentrate on a 'living and dynamic' experience which was self-
authenticating.[23] What he feared was an incipient romanizing of Protestant church life and to this he could not be indifferent or neutral: 'The
Roman Catholic Church and all the churches which follow her speak
much about tradition but for the most part it is of human, not divine
origin.'[24] The old sixteenth-century tension between Scripture and tradition was no dead issue. Paul VI, probably smarting over the struggle
between the intransigent and progressive forces among the Second

18   E. Carpenter, *Cantuar* (London, 1988), p.502, and Hylson-Smith, *Evangelicals in the Church of England*, p.343.
19   Jedin, Repgen and Dolan (eds.), *History of the Church*, p.107.
20   Hylson-Smith, *Evangelicals in the Church of England*, p.344.
21   D.M. Lloyd-Jones, *Roman Catholicism Today* (London, n.d.), p.1.
22   Lloyd-Jones, *1662-1962*, p.47. He always wore a black Geneva gown in the Westminster Chapel pulpit, but rarely in other churches.
23   Lloyd-Jones, *Maintaining the Evangelical Faith Today*, p.6.
24   D.M. Lloyd-Jones, *The Christian Soldier* (Edinburgh, 1977), p.207.

Vatican Council fathers, wrote to Cardinal Ottaviani: 'The Church does not derive assurance of salvation from Scripture alone, tradition is the living teaching office of the Church, which authoritatively interprets and complements Scripture.'[25] In other words, although Bible reading was more freely encouraged, fidelity to ecclesiastical tradition was also required.

In a sermon on 29 January 1961, later published under the title *Roman Catholicism*, Lloyd-Jones vigorously condemned the Roman system as 'a counterfeit' and, using apocalyptic language, declared that 'she is, as Scripture puts it, "the whore"'.[26] The conviction that the Pope is Antichrist and his church a false church has a long history and in this Lloyd-Jones adopted a fairly standard seventeenth-century view. We may see how strong this view was by his comment that Rome 'binds the soul of her people absolutely, as much as Communism does, as much as Hitler did under his horrible system'.[27] In the shadow of the World Council of Churches meeting in New Delhi, he spoke about resisting 'Romeward tendencies, yes, even unto blood, because if the drift towards Rome prevails...everything is lost'.[28] In 1962 he warned of assimilation and later in 1969 he spoke of the menace of absorption by 'minor changes'.[29] At the same time, however, he was not unwilling to acknowledge the presence of a biblical doctrine even within the Roman system. The problem was Catholic 'insistence on obedience and conformity to things not taught in the Scriptures' which amounted to 'Christ plus something' else,[30] and this undermined the evangelical concept of free grace and reversed the doctrine of justification by faith alone. Stripped of its accretions, Lloyd-Jones recognized that even Rome had elements of 'the truth' in it and in a surprisingly candid remark of 1954 he admitted that 'from the sheer standpoint of orthodoxy and doctrinal beliefs I find myself nearer to many a Roman Catholic than to many within the ranks of Protestantism'.[31] What he had in mind was the

---

25   Jedin, Repgen and Dolan (eds.), *History of the Church*, p.40. A letter to Cardinal Ottaviani, 18 October 1965.

26   Lloyd-Jones, *Roman Catholicism Today*, pp.2, 4. The quotation is from Revelation 17:1, 4, 6: 'the great whore', 'the woman arrayed in purple and scarlet', 'the woman drunken with the blood of the saints, and with the blood of the martyrs of Jesus'.

27   *Ibid*, p.7.

28   D.M. Lloyd-Jones, *Presidential Address* (London, 1961), p.20.

29   D.M. Lloyd-Jones, *The Basis of Christian Unity* (London, 1962), p.5, and *Presidential Address*, p.23.

30   D.M. Lloyd-Jones, *Spiritual Depression* (London, 1965), p.181.

31   *Ibid*, p.187.

doctrinal ambiguity and drift of much Protestant Christianity in Britain into 'theological insouciance'.[32]

The Ecumenical Movement

So far as ecumenical politics were concerned it appeared, in the 1960s, that the inevitable outcome would be a World Church presided over by the Pope. There was no secret about the desire of church leaders for cross-denominational fellowship and co-operation, but Lloyd-Jones's fears were presumptuous. It was by no means clear that churches wanted to relinquish their traditions and distinctive beliefs: according to the Congregationalist John Huxtable, church unity did not mean '"giving in" to everybody but finding some way of expressing the riches we all have'.[33] The idea of a World Church was undoubtedly in mind when the Anglican-Roman Catholic International Commission of 1976 spoke of 'a special position of the Bishop of Rome in a reunited Church',[34] but over thirty years on from Lloyd-Jones's Luther address of 1967, the dreaded monolith has still not materialized and seems less likely to do so. The only unions across denominational frontiers have been the coming together in 1972, after earlier abortive efforts, of the Presbyterian Church of England and the Congregational Church in England and Wales as the United Reformed Church, with the Churches of Christ joining it in 1981. In 1955 the Church of England and the Methodist Church began conversations which went on to a final report in 1973, but although the Methodists were largely in favour of union the scheme foundered predictably on the issues of episcopacy and the ministry. Talks between Anglicans and Presbyterians came to nothing and a multilateral approach through the Churches Unity Commission in 1976 also failed. In Wales there had been some rapprochement between Nonconformists and Anglicans which concluded in a 'Covenant for Unity' but this was tied into the disestablishment question and was described as a 'near disaster...from which they emerged bruised and lacerated'.[35] So this also came to nothing. Thus, overall, apart from the United Reformed Church,

---

32   Catherwood (ed.) *Chosen by God*, p.173. This was also noted by K.S. Latourette, *The Prospect for Christianity* (London, 1949), p.140: 'The doctrinal content of Protestantism appears to be weakening as that of the Roman Catholic Church is not. Large elements of Protestantism seem to be departing from the historic faith.'

33   *Congregational Monthly*, January, 1967, Vol.XLIV, p.1.

34   Jedin, Repgen and Dolan (eds.), *History of the Church*, p.473.

35   D. Walker, *A History of the Church in Wales* (Penarth, 1976), p.172. The Presbyterian Church of Wales was not involved in conversations with the Church of England, the Presbyterian Church of England or the Congregational Union of England and Wales, although they believed in church union and did not stand outside the modern ecumenical movement.

organic church union in Britain had not been realized and all the dialogue and good intentions had, by 1981, achieved little. The World Church paradigm had not yet unfolded although there had been a measure of co-operation and intercommunion. Even so, these were busy decades in ecumenical activity and it was against this background that we must see Lloyd-Jones's fears and misgivings.

It would certainly be unjust to assume that all ecumenically-minded Christians had little interest in biblical truth, but viewed from the standpoint of Lloyd-Jones the modern ecumenical movement demonstrated 'man's attempt to revive the church by his own methods', and in a reference to the prophet Ezekiel, he likened the World Council of Churches to the coming together of a 'number of dead bodies' desperately in need of life.[36] This was colourful rhetoric, but underlying it was an unremitting fear of doctrinal reductionism because the ecumenical movement as he saw it was a move to homogenize and dilute the faith and therefore something to be resisted at all costs. In 1965, John A.T. Robinson had called for a 'cessation of hostilities' between Roman Catholics and Protestants and an end to the 'civil war in Western Christendom': the Reformation was over and, according to the Second Vatican Council, so too was the Counter-Reformation, but it was not over for Lloyd-Jones.[37] The doctrine of the Reformers was nothing less than a renaissance of New Testament Christianity and although the historic event had past, each new generation of Protestants should reaffirm the same core of belief. It was a simple choice between daylight and darkness.[38]

Obviously such a view excluded exploratory discussion and this is evident in much of what Lloyd-Jones said. In a sermon in 1931 he warned of 'beautiful generalities' and the kind of syncretism which made the followers of Buddha, Mohammed and Confucius 'brethren with Christians' and going towards the same goal.[39] In his 1952 apologia he counselled the Inter-Varsity Fellowship to stand 'more vigorously than ever' and 'refuse to surrender any single part of what is vital to the full evangelical faith as recorded in the Holy Scriptures'.[40] He was totally convinced that there could be no fellowship unless there was commitment to identity of doctrine and, dictatorial or not, he felt obliged to stand against men who felt that 'the old certitudes' were no longer attainable.[41]

36   Catherwood (ed.), *Chosen by God*, p.262.

37   J.A.T. Robinson, *The New Reformation?* (London, 1965), pp.9-10, and Jedin, Repgen and Dolan (eds.), *History of the Church*, p.147: 'Its ecumenical stance has reduced denominational strife and brought about the end of the Counter-Reformation.'

38   Any deviation was 'a denial of the Evangelical, the only true faith', D.M. Lloyd-Jones, *Luther and his Message for Today* (London, 1967), p.27.

39   D.M. Lloyd-Jones, *Evangelistic Sermons* (Edinburgh, 1983), pp.79-80.

40   Lloyd-Jones, *Maintaining the Evangelical Faith Today*, p.4.

41   K. Slack, *The British Churches Today* (London, 1970), p.142.

His response to this kind of rethinking was more precisely to define the doctrine of the church, but by doing so he began to subordinate the principle of fellowship and maximize doctrine—'Practice and behaviour are the result of the application of doctrine which has already been laid down'.[42] His argument turns upon the premise that the church cannot have unity without agreement in the truth and this he showed from the Acts of the Apostles, 'where fellowship follows doctrine'.[43] He came to the same conclusion when addressing his IVF audience in 1952: 'There must be real agreement concerning the doctrines... If there is uncertainty in such matters there cannot be real fellowship',[44] and 'real fellowship' included such matters as the plenary inspiration of Scripture and a particular view of the church. It is little wonder that in the broader arena of differing church traditions, theological conservatism of this kind was regarded as divisive.

His arguments against the ecumenical movement clustered around the nature of the church and its pneumatic foundation. Much of his concern was with the local assembly and the most he would concede to a global view was that the church is a 'unity of essence of being', that is to say, a spiritual family born out of 'the mystical union which subsists between the three Persons of the blessed Holy Trinity'.[45] In other words, the church is a community of the new-born 'not merely an association of friends'; it consists of those who have experienced 'the operation of the Holy Spirit in the act of regeneration'.[46] Anything less 'is not the unity of which our Lord speaks in John 17'.[47] So while he could speak of pragmatic details so far as a gathered church goes, anything beyond that has little support in his definition of the church. And because the 'one body' is essentially pneumatic and God-given it can never be the outcome of human effort nor can it be arrived at by discussion or dialogue: 'You are already enjoying it', he said: 'all you have to do is preserve it'.[48] Such a proposition excludes any territorialization and prohibits any view of a state or national church—'the whole notion of a State Church is a complete contradiction of the basic statement of the New Testament about the nature of the Church'.[49] The church is a fellowship of saints not a collection of religious people and it is within these parameters that he spoke about getting 'the saints together' and evangelical unity.[50] The

---

42   Lloyd-Jones, *The Basis of Christian Unity*, p.18.
43   *Ibid*, p.59, and Acts 2:42.
44   Lloyd-Jones, *Maintaining the Evangelical Faith Today*, p.13.
45   Lloyd-Jones, *The Basis of Christian Unity*, p.13.
46   *Ibid*, p.14.
47   *Ibid*.
48   *Ibid*, p.26.
49   Lloyd-Jones, *What is the Church?*, p.12.
50   *Evangelical Magazine of Wales*, April 1975, Vol.14, No.2, p.l.

church, therefore, is not a voluntary society but an involuntary body of people who share the same elemental experience of evangelical truth. Its membership can only be consistent where each local assembly is comprised of people who have been converted and 'born of the Spirit'.[51]

So the uniqueness of the church as a unity of essence and custodian of truth was a concept which he believed needed definition and defence, though equally important was the remnant principle. The remnant was a kind of church within a church and consisted of those who 'persisted in loyally seeking to do God's will when all else had defaulted'.[52] It was an extension of his quest for 'doctrinal and ethical purity',[53] and he used the idea to refute the argument that cross-denominational union would make for spiritual strength, impress unbelievers with an undivided church and facilitate the preaching of the gospel. To establish his point he used the story of Gideon in which an army of three hundred instead of thirty-two thousand was used to defeat the Midianites. It was this teaching—that the Lord can save 'by many or by few'—that he brought to bear on the contemporary situation.[54] This was underpinned with reference to the broad and narrow way of the Gospels and warnings of 'false prophets' and 'grievous wolves'.[55]

As a consequence any margin of tolerance for alternative views was inconceivable because it had become a matter of principle not to yield: 'We must not be afraid of the charge that "You think that you alone are right"! Yes, we do think that we are right; but we are not alone.'[56] However, for non-evangelicals it was an intolerable position and a *British Weekly* editorial of March 1953 spoke of an arbitrary selection of texts. A disturbed Alan Braybrooks, writing from Mansfield College, Oxford, criticized the IVF for adopting such a 'divisive and schismatic' attitude.[57] Braybrooks called for a public statement from the IVF committing itself to a policy of evangelism which encouraged Christians to work 'within the historic denominations',[58] but there was no response. Ten years later, in *The Basis of Christian Unity*, Lloyd-Jones referred to Martin Luther, who had stood alone against opposing forces, 'defying some twelve centuries of tradition'.[59] But most contentious of all was his 1966 address

---

51   Lloyd-Jones, *What is the Church?*, p.16.

52   Lloyd-Jones, *Maintaining the Evangelical Faith Today*, p.12. See also Lloyd-Jones, *The Puritans*, p.147.

53   Lloyd-Jones, *Maintaining the Evangelical Faith Today*, p.12.

54   Judges 7:2-8. The quotation is from 1 Samuel 14:6.

55   Lloyd-Jones, *Maintaining the Evangelical Faith Today*, p.10.

56   *Ibid.*

57   *The British Weekly*, 19 March, 1953, Vol.CXXXIII, p.6, and 9 April, 1953, Vol.CXXXIII, p.9.

58   *The British Weekly*, 9 April, 1953, Vol.CXXXIII, p.9.

59   Lloyd-Jones, *The Basis of Christian Unity*, p.63.

at the Second National Assembly of the Evangelical Alliance when he harnessed the remnant principle to an appeal for evangelicals to come together. We will come to this episode shortly, but we may note here that Lloyd-Jones's views of a faithful few seceding from doctrinally mixed denominations was not acceptable to John Stott, the chairman, who insisted that the doctrine of the remnant was a description of the covenant people of God not of a church within a church: 'In the Old Testament Isaiah had a kind of school of discipleship but they did not secede from the people of God',[60] and in the New Testament neither Jesus nor the apostles used it in such a way. But Lloyd-Jones's idea of the remnant was intrinsic to his theory of separation.

There was much less interest in the church at a more practical level. When he spoke about 'the purity of the church, both in doctrine and in life',[61] he did not hesitate to 'suggest that such steps as should be taken to ensure the purity of the Church' should follow.[62] But although he publicly spoke of the exercise of discipline, in practice he took little action. He did not expel the unworthy from church membership or inflict any other disciplinary measure. Privately he advised, in debate he corrected what he believed to be wrong, but it went no further. Church archives up until the 1950s reveal notes of discussions on the Congregational Union and church affiliation, missionary and financial affairs and other similar items, but there is no mention of discipline in any form. He did not 'fence' the Lord's Table with warnings against the unsaved or unworthy believer, but opened the communion service on the Pauline premise that a man should 'examine himself, and so let him eat of that bread, and drink of that cup'.[63] Each person was responsible to God for his own actions, but if matters became difficult, there was always the vestry at the end of the service.

October 1966

The direction of this chapter so far has been a general one—to identify some of the apprehensions which Lloyd-Jones had about the ecumenical movement—and it must be clear already that he was not by nature a crossbench man. He could not be evangelical and ecumenical. It is time, however, to be more specific and to show how these and other developments provoked him into action. It is also to answer the question why he made his appeal for evangelicals to come together in 1966.

In the middle of his twenty-ninth year as Pastor of Westminster Chapel Lloyd-Jones wrote in his January 'Letter to Members' that 1966 had

---

60   John Stott, tape recorded conversation, 11 November, 1991.
61   Lloyd-Jones, *The Basis of Christian Unity*, p.64.
62   Lloyd-Jones, *Maintaining the Evangelical Faith Today*, p.14.
63   1 Corinthians 11:28.

been 'an astonishing year which has witnessed momentous events'.[64] On his mind was the covenanting together of the Congregational Churches of England and Wales, a Roman Catholic priest preaching at Westminster Abbey 'for the first time since the Protestant Reformation', the official visit of Archbishop Michael Ramsey to Rome, a 'united procession of all the churches of Westminster (apart from ourselves and the Baptist Church in Horseferry Road)' from Trafalgar Square to an ecumenical service in Westminster Cathedral at which Cardinal Heenan preached, and 'on top of all this', a meeting in June in St. Martin-in-the-Fields 'at which representatives of all the world religions took part'.[65] As he said, 'in the light of all this...I made an appeal at a meeting held in Westminster Central Hall in October'.[66] So far as evangelicalism in Britain in the 1960s goes and so far as the subsequent influence of Lloyd-Jones was concerned, the effect of 18 October 1966 was considerable. It was here that he took the opportunity to express his more narrowly defined view of the church in a public manner.[67]

Gilbert Kirby, on behalf of the Evangelical Alliance Commission on Church Unity, had invited Lloyd-Jones to speak on Christian unity at the opening meeting of the Alliance's Second National Assembly of Evangelicals which was held at the Methodist Central Hall, Westminster. The First National Assembly had met in September 1965 and had called for a Commission to study 'various attitudes of Evangelicals to the Ecumenical Movement, denominationalism and a possible future United Church'.[68] The concern of the EA was a part of the growing interest in unity during the 1960s and was partly a reaction to the 1964 British Faith and Order Conference at Nottingham, which envisaged a reunion of the historic churches in the '1980 Resolution' of the British Council of Churches.[69] There was a climate of inclusivism which, if it did nothing else, highlighted the disunity of Protestantism. The Commission consisted of seven members of the Executive Council under the joint chairmanship of R. Peter Johnston, Anglican, and John Caiger, Baptist. To form their *Report* they interviewed representatives from ten church groupings and two London churches, Grove Chapel, Camberwell, and Westminster Chapel, and in addition received a number of written submissions from

---

64   D.M. Lloyd-Jones, 'Annual Letter to Members of Westminster Chapel', January, 1967.
65   *Ibid.* John Carmel Heenan, Archbishop of Westminster 1963-75 and Cardinal, 1965-75.
66   *Ibid.*
67   For another account see A.E. McGrath, *To Know and Serve God: A Biography of James I. Packer* (London, 1997), pp.116-128.
68   *Report of the Commission on Church Unity* (London, 1966), p.3.
69   *Ibid*, p.10.

smaller denominational groups.[70] The findings of the *Report* were published a year later and made available at the Second Assembly. Its conclusions recognized and encouraged stronger links 'between evangelical churches of various traditions', but denied that there was any 'widespread demand at the present time for the setting up of a united evangelical Church on denominational lines'.[71] Some kind of 'fellowship or federation of evangelical churches at both local and national level' might be useful but what they had in mind was not an alternative grouping but a stronger Alliance.[72] Put more simply, the findings indicated that the majority of evangelicals at that time were happy to stay where they were.

The scandal in the evangelical sector was not so much the disunity of churches but that Christians with the same core beliefs were disinclined towards each other. It was not that historic distinctives as such were obsolete: it was a matter of people standing apart even though they were agreed in the essentials of the gospel. Until now the majority of evangelicals had been happy with a personal ecumenism based on piety and faith, but ecumenical developments had alerted the leaders of evangelicalism and many came to see that something more positive was needed. For Lloyd-Jones the hope of keeping the 'lines of communication open'[73] was not enough because many of the churches in membership with the EA were also members of ecumenically favourable denominations. The only answer so far as he could see was for the 'custodians of the faith of the Bible' to come together outside of the ecumenical movement,[74] but this disenfranchised other Christian groups and declared Independency to be the best understanding of the Scripture. It was a narrow trajectory which allowed for no debate and was largely a pessimistic reaction to the religious climate of the day.

Given all this, it is surprising that with his known separatist views Lloyd-Jones should have been asked 'to say in public what he had said in private' at the opening meeting of the Assembly.[75] A. Morgan Derham

70   These were the Church of England Evangelical Council, the Methodist, Baptist and Congregational Revival Fellowships, the British Pentecostal Fellowship, Christian Brethren, Free Church of England, Church of Scotland, Free Church of Scotland and the Presbyterian Church of England. The minister of Grove Chapel at the time was Iain Murray. Among the smaller groups that appeared in the *Report* were the Salvation Army, the Strict Baptists, Independent Methodists, Churches of Christ [Disciples], Wesleyan Reform Union, Moravian Church, Countess of Huntingdon's Connexion and there are brief references to evangelicals in Wales, Scotland and Northern Ireland.
71   *Report of the Commission on Church Unity*, p.11.
72   *Ibid*, p.4.
73   *Ibid*, p.12.
74   Lloyd-Jones, *Knowing the Times*, pp.255-256.
75   D.M. Lloyd-Jones, *Unity in Diversity* (London, 1966), p.7.

defended the choice of speaker by suggesting, a little naively perhaps, that there was 'a very real difference between his giving evidence to a group like the Commission which is made up of his theological peers and delivering a statement to a general public assembly'.[76] What emerged in the sermon was fairly straightforward. Initially he argued, as the ecumenists were arguing, that in the face of a lost world where the church was largely ridiculed, the unity of Christians 'must also be visible'.[77] But matters had been complicated by the rise of the World Council of Churches and an entirely new situation existed. Not only was there talk about churches coming together, but the attitude of Protestants towards Rome was changing. Evangelicals, Lloyd-Jones alleged, had no answer to the charge that they had little interest in church unity, but now a unique and perhaps unrepeatable opportunity had opened up for evangelicals to be more positive. 'Are we content', he said, to be 'nothing but an evangelical wing of a church?', a paper church that will eventually include Roman Catholicism?[78] Turning ecumenical events to his advantage, he suggested that if others were 'prepared to put everything in the melting pot' evangelicals should also start afresh by taking a new look at the New Testament. He briefly tackled 'the sin of schism' and concluded that 'to leave a church that has become apostate is not schism' but 'one's Christian duty': schism he defined as 'a division among members of the true visible Church' over secondary and less important matters.[79] Schism, therefore, could only be committed by true believers since they alone were the 'body of Christ' bound by doctrine and experience. To break with unbelievers or heretics was not schism but a Christian necessity.

A New Grouping?

Thus far it had been a familiar Lloyd-Jones argument and added nothing new to his earlier position, or, indeed, to his statement to the Commission on Church Unity in 1965. What was new was the hortatory application: 'Let me therefore make an appeal to you evangelical people here present this evening. What reasons have we for not coming together?'; and again, 'Do we not feel the call to come together, not occasionally, but always?'[80] The successors of the Reformation should unite in the truth because upon this contingent action the Holy Spirit would bless his Word and his people. It was an unmistakeably secessionist peroration and concluded with the hope that the modern ecumenical debate might have

76   A. Morgan Derham, letter to K.I. Paterson, 26 October, 1966. Used with permission.
77   Lloyd-Jones, *Knowing the Times*, p.247.
78   *Ibid*, p.251.
79   *Ibid*, p.253.
80   *Ibid*, p.254.

spurred evangelicals on to face their problems and bring them 'together as a fellowship, or an association, of evangelical churches'.[81]

The sermon was printed in a summarized form in *Unity in Diversity* by the EA in 1967. The introduction to the résumé made it clear that a full transcript of the address was available but Lloyd-Jones himself did not want it to be printed. In his opinion not enough time had been allocated for him to develop his theme into a more formal paper and what he said was, in his view, appropriate only to that 'living occasion': it was 'not the form in which he would couch his statement' if he had prepared a sermon for the printed page.[82] But what did he mean? The majority of his printed works were of 'living occasions', corrected a little, certainly, but never so as to lose their original sermonic form. In fact there is little difference between his papers and his sermons—they were all equally well reasoned and passionate. If the appeal of that night were a valid one and if it were as unique and important an occasion as he claimed, why should it not be publicized for others to consider as was his equally powerful call to evangelicals at the British Evangelical Council conference later in 1967? It would certainly have put the record straight since his sermon was, whether he liked it or not, widely reported in the Christian press. The most likely reason for his reluctance to go into print may well have been a political one in that he wished to distance himself from the broader forum of the EA which had neither endorsed his call nor shown any interest in secession. Hardly any had responded to his appeal and there had been little real debate on the issues he raised. Certainly by December 1966, when he was writing his January 'Letter to Members' of Westminster Chapel, he spoke of the need for 'close fellowship with all similar and like-minded churches',[83] which hinted at his dissatisfaction with the Alliance's mixed constituency and suggested that he might be looking elsewhere for a basis of unity. It was no secret how he felt about Anglicanism and while evangelical Anglicans remained members of the Alliance there could be little hope of the kind of unity that he envisaged. In addition, he might also have wanted to ease the tension that had arisen from that meeting. Whatever the reason it was not until 1989, eight years after his death, that a full transcription of the address was printed.[84]

Powerful as his sermon was (and he was at his best that night, 'giving his opportunist instincts full rein, he pulled out all the stops'[85]) evangelicals did not come closer together. The chairman, John Stott, rose

---

81   *Ibid*, p.257.
82   Lloyd-Jones, *Unity in Diversity*, p.7.
83   D.M. Lloyd-Jones, 'Annual Letter to Members of Westminster Chapel', January, 1967.
84   Lloyd-Jones, *Knowing the Times*, pp.246-257.
85   Catherwood (ed.), *Chosen by God*, p.45.

at the conclusion of the address to dissociate himself from the appeal and the gap widened.[86] For Kenneth Paterson, minister of Trinity Road Chapel, Tooting, it was 'the moment of a lifetime',[87] but for Alec Motyer, also a friend of Lloyd-Jones, 'the call did nothing for the church at large' and 'left a lasting legacy of division and suspicion'.[88] A. Morgan Derham, the newly appointed General Secretary of the Evangelical Alliance, wrote later saying that 'in the perspective of twenty-four years' his call 'must be judged an irrelevancy from which the evangelical world is still re-covering'.[89] David Winter, also on the platform that night, felt that Lloyd-Jones totally misjudged the feelings and loyalty of Church of England evangelicals,[90] and Kenneth Slack, formerly minister of the City Temple, regarded his effort to separate 'the conservative Evangelicals in mixed Churches' as a 'notable failure'.[91] *The English Churchman* valued the issues raised by Lloyd-Jones as an 'opportunity of taking positive action in the ecumenical sphere', but questioned secession and cited the Anglican-Methodist talks on unity as a scheme 'for union between Evangelicals'—not exactly what Lloyd-Jones had in mind.[92]

The argument came to centre on what Lloyd-Jones really did ask for: whether it was for a loose fellowship, which already existed partly in such groups as the FIEC, or whether he had a new denomination in view. His closest allies were as ready to defend him as others were to attack. Leith Samuel, then minister of Above Bar, Southampton, while acknowledging 'the Doctor's general feelings about Anglicans', said that at 'no time did he ever advocate a new denomination only a loose fellowship or association of churches'.[93] Iain Murray offers the explanation that he was pleading 'for bigger and bolder thinking and especially for thinking which would keep obedience to the gospel as the decisive issue': keeping the gospel as his first commitment, Lloyd-Jones's hope was for 'a basis of association in which churches could work and operate together with a minimum of control'.[94] A few pages later, Murray quotes with approval the *English Churchman*'s report which, he says, gets 'the emphasis of what Lloyd-Jones said right'—by which he may have meant that there was less talk of secession and more of moderation.[95] Even so the article

---

86   The most recent account is to be found in volume two of T. Dudley-Smith's biography of Stott, *John Stott: A Global Ministry* (Leicester, 2001), pp.65-70.

87   *In Step*, Broadsheet of the British Evangelical Council, Autumn, 1990.

88   Alec Motyer, letter to author, 10 June, 1991.

89   *Third Way*, December, 1990, Vol.13, No.12, p.35.

90   David Winter, letter to author, 3 October, 1991.

91   *Church Times*, 30 May, 1986, p.6.

92   *The English Churchman*, 28 October, 1966, p.6.

93   *Monthly Record*, Free Church of Scotland, April, 1984, p.90.

94   Murray, *The Fight of Faith*, p.511.

95   *Ibid*, p.527.

does not hide the hope that the Anglican authorities would devise 'a formula which will enable those evangelicals who so desire to remain in the Church of England without straining their consciences unduly'.[96] Lloyd-Jones had, in the context of a 1959 sermon on revival, repudiated 'the formation of a new evangelical denomination as the right response to ecumenism'.[97] But by 1966 and certainly by 1967 the nature of the church had become more central to his thinking.

As to the shape of the new grouping there is some reason to think that he placed more weight on some kind of united evangelical church than some have allowed. Gilbert Kirby thought that 'his dream was that people would leave and regroup' although, as it turned out, it was only 'a pipe-dream'.[98] R.T. Kendall, the present minister of Westminster Chapel and someone who knew Lloyd-Jones well during the last four years of his life, thinks that the appeal was a political mistake but that what he said was a 'deliberate and intentional' move towards a new evangelical alignment.[99] There was nothing incidental or casual about what he said and there was no doubt that he 'thought something would happen',[100] and such an intention was undeniably present in his pastoral letter where he referred to his appeal for 'all truly Evangelical people in all the denominations to come together and to form local Evangelical churches which should be in a loose fellowship together'.[101] But there were other reactions. For Motyer it was a case of disbelief: 'I cannot make up my mind to this day whether the Doctor really meant what he said... In subsequent conversation I came to wonder whether he had really expected to be taken seriously.'[102] To men like Motyer and Stott it seemed suprisingly naive of Lloyd-Jones to expect that men reared and trained in the Church of England and committed to its theological foundations would want to come out and leave it all. James Packer, an ardent admirer of Lloyd-Jones's preaching, concluded that it 'failed to convince',[103] and John Huxtable, who in 1972 became the first Moderator of the United Reformed Church, was relieved that the call to 'a sort of true Protestant

96   *The English Churchman*, 28 October, 1966, p.6.
97   D.M. Lloyd-Jones, *Revival* (Basingstoke, 1986), p.167.
98   Gilbert Kirby, tape recorded conversation, 6 August, 1991. Kirby was EA General Secretary 1956-66. His tenure of office terminated three months before the Central Hall meeting.
99   R.T. Kendall, tape recorded conversation, 8 October, 1991. 'I sat at his feet for four years, visiting him every Thursday from 11 to 1 p.m., and I was in and out of his house on Fridays and Sundays.'
100 *Ibid.*
101 D.M. Lloyd-Jones, 'Annual Letter to Members of Westminster Chapel', 1967.
102 Alec Motyer, letter to author, 10 June, 1991.
103 Catherwood (ed.), *Chosen by God*, p.45.

Church' failed 'largely because wiser counsels prevailed'.[104] For Kirby the whole idea was not earthed or grounded: 'he was not a man to set up an organization', and therefore it 'largely evaporated the next day'.[105]

What, then, was the outcome of this appeal? *The Baptist Times* in its leader of 27 October, suggested that instead of increased fellowship, once again 'Evangelicals are divided about unity'.[106] For Kirby the whole affair was an embarrassment, both 'the shock' of the appeal and 'John Stott's understandable reaction. The whole thing I regarded with a great deal of sorrow and wished I had not arranged it in the first place.'[107] For Maurice Rowlandson, one of the eager young men in the auditorium sitting on the edge of their seats, it was a 'great excitement' especially after the chairman's altercation: 'it was like a breath of fresh air to have debate like this'.[108] In an oblique comment Walter Bottoms of *The Baptist Times* took up the united evangelical church theme in his report: 'what kind of Church would it be?', and asked, whether it would be 'Independent or connexional; ritualistic or pentecostal?'[109] True, this was probably a tongue in cheek remark, but it was a pertinent issue in that these were the very kinds of thing which roused the passions of Christians. Furthermore it is too easy to say that Lloyd-Jones was not interested in organization or that this kind of alternative ecumenism rose above ecclesiastical preferences because he clearly sat uneasily with some evangelical forms of worship, for example, those of the Free Church of Scotland. The EA, not a little embarrassed by the whole affair, played the matter down and 'pleaded for a spirit of patience and mutual respect between brethren who differ from one another on matters of interpretation'.[110] In effect, the EA maintained its status quo of a broader basis for 'free mutual association', as Derham wrote on the eve of the Assembly, or as the editor of *Crusade* put it, 'without a massive secession of Evangelicals from the historic Churches'.[111] Whatever might be said of Lloyd-Jones's sermon, there was undoubtedly a 'never again' feeling in a meeting of the Executive Council of the Alliance which recorded in its 'Minutes' of 20 October, 'that in future only one public rally should be held during the Assembly, which should be informative and inspir-

---

104 J. Huxtable, *As it seemed to me* (London, 1990), p.43.

105 Gilbert Kirby, 6 August, 1991.

106 *The Baptist Times*, 27 October, 1966, p.1.

107 Gilbert Kirby, 6 August, 1991.

108 Maurice Rowlandson, tape recorded conversation, 1 August, 1991.

109 *The Baptist Times*, 27 October, 1966, p.2.

110 *Ibid.*

111 *Crusade*, October, 1966, Vol.12, No.10, p.13, and November, 1966, Vol.12, No.11, p.13.

ational'.[112] For Walter Bottoms, the whole affair had 'an air of unreality about it' in view of a lack of any widespread demand for such a grouping, but for R.S. Luland, 'the report did not reflect the true position', and he believed 'that many Baptists were moving towards secession'.[113]

It is unfortunate that no record was kept by the EA to show how many withdrew from their denominations as a result of Lloyd-Jones's call, but the truth of the matter is that although there was a flurry of debate and excitement very few actually seceded, so statistically there was little to record. According to Gilbert Kirby, 'We lost two Council Members around that time' and they withdrew 'without any acrimony'.[114] When the two men (John Caiger and T.H. Bendor-Samuel) resigned from the Council, 'there was no other reason than its attitude to ecumenicity'.[115] In fact the EA suffered very little. Kirby had himself already resigned as General Secretary earlier that year to become Principal of London Bible College though he remained a firm supporter of the Alliance. Leith Samuel agreed that 'very few came out of the "mainline" denominations' and on the FIEC list of accredited ministers, 'less than two dozen men' had come from other denominations, men who 'like myself [Leith Samuel] had seceded for conscience sake long before the Doctor's' call.[116] Motyer, Packer and R.T. France—all Anglicans—felt that the appeal had very little impact in the short term and put the withdrawal numbers at two, which seems to be the general opinion. E.S. Guest, Secretary of the Evangelical Fellowship of Congregational Churches, agrees that few seceded 'because of the appeal. In the long term people began to come out but in our denomination we had a background of evangelical fellowship already going on.'[117] It could be said that A. Morgan Derham, though not a seceder, was the most unfortunate casualty of the event as he fell between two camps, the EA and the BEC, and he continued to look upon the 1966 event as a grievous dividing of the

---

112 'Minutes of the Executive Council of the Evangelical Alliance', 20 October, 1966.

113 *The Baptist Times*, 27 October, 1966, p.16.

114 Gilbert Kirby, 6 August, 1991.

115 T.H. Bendor-Samuel, letter to author, 5 November, 1991.

116 *Monthly Record*, April, 1984, p.90.

117 E.S. Guest, tape recorded conversation, 11 February, 1992. Alan Gibson, General Secretary of the BEC, in a response to Derham's 'irrelevancy' felt that 'the last 24 years have seen even greater readiness among many evangelicals to co-operate in ecumenism with those who deny the gospel than with those who are committed to gospel absolutes. If there were need for such warning in 1966 then how much more relevant is that call in the year when the Roman Catholic Church has taken up full membership of the re-vamped ecumenical bodies in the United Kingdom.' A.F. Gibson, letter to the editor of *Third Way*, 14 December, 1990, Vol.14, No.1, p.35.

evangelical community in the United Kingdom.[118] The Executive Council of which he was a member passed a resolution on 15 December 1966, saying that 'it would be most desirable for the EA and BEC to be seen to be working closely together', although this was not to be the case for some years.[119]

In reality it was mainly the evangelical Anglicans who were most estranged, not from the gospel but from Lloyd-Jones, who, according to Motyer, had exercised a 'profound influence among evangelical Anglicans' at one time.[120] But even if Lloyd-Jones had announced a concrete plan for a new church it is highly improbable that it would have made any difference to them. There had been some unofficial discussion about secession, as Stott candidly admits: 'One of the topics discussed in the Eclectic Society in the 1950s was whether we should stay in the Church of England and on what grounds.'[121] But by the spring of 1967 at Keele, 'we had made a strong decision to remain in the Church of England as witnesses'.[122]

Stott's Postscript

It might of course be argued that John Stott's postscript to Lloyd-Jones's sermon went some way to make the appeal a 'cause célèbre'. At the time Stott, with his expository preaching, was at the height of his powers. In 1966 congregations at All Souls 'varied between 600 and 800', and forty-five members were serving as missionaries overseas.[123] Stott had been at the centre of a revival of Anglican evangelicalism since the 1950s and his refounding of the Eclectic Society in 1955 had provided a seminal forum for evangelicals under the age of forty.

So here were two men, Lloyd-Jones and Stott, in many respects completely different and yet at one in their preaching and equally hardhitting in their claims for Christ, who were without doubt the most prominent evangelical leaders in Britain at the time and who equally demonstrated the possibility of holding evangelical convictions while retaining intellectual integrity. All of this made the public clash of 1966 memorable and significant.

Rightly or wrongly, Stott's remarks turned a sermon into a debate and underlined the disparity among evangelicals on the extent of non-

---

118 *Third Way*, 14 December, 1990, p.35.

119 'Minutes of the Executive Council of the Evangelical Alliance', 5 December, 1966.

120 Alec Motyer, letter to author, 10 June, 1991.

121 John Stott, 11 November, 1991.

122 *Ibid*. R.T. France has said that by 'then [1966] evangelical Anglicans were well on the road to Keele'. Letter to author, 7 November, 1991.

123 Francis Whitehead, letter to author, 7 November, 1991.

negotiable truths. For some, the ecumenical movement had become a fundamental consideration affecting the very gospel itself and although this was a familiar stance for Lloyd-Jones and his followers, many in the Central Hall that night were hearing it for the first time. It brought such issues out into the open and into the public domain. But the postscript was not Stott's only contribution to the meeting. Under the heading of 'Chairman's Remarks' he was given ten minutes in which 'to speak on why in good conscience I could remain a member of the Church of England' and this was before Lloyd-Jones's address.[124] He did not exclude 'the possibility of secession altogether but he felt sure that that time had not yet come'.[125] Stott's argument was that the Church of England should be judged by its official formularies such as the *Thirty-Nine Articles* and *Prayer Book*, not by some theological deviation, and Lloyd-Jones had responded to this 'by saying that the Church I belonged to was a paper church, and this was the heart of the debate'.[126] Lloyd-Jones's point was relevant to all confessional groups, but it would be difficult not to see his allusion to a 'paper church' as a direct reference to the evangelical Anglicans.

Even so, despite such disapproval, it was not to this that Stott objected so much as to the pre-emption of debate and possibility of hasty action. 'We are here to debate', he said, 'appeal should have come at the end. I believe history is against what Dr. Lloyd-Jones has said. Scripture is against him... I hope no one will act precipitately. We are all concerned with the same ultimate issues and with the glory of God.'[127] The reason Stott intervened before the final hymn was twofold: it was thought to be improper to issue an appeal on the eve of an Assembly that was called to debate this very issue,[128] and such was the strength of Lloyd-Jones's preaching that he 'could forsee many young men going home and writing their resignations that night. I wanted to damp down their enthusiasm and ask them to think about it and wait until the Assembly had discussed the matter.'[129]

Whether Stott's concluding remarks are seen as an intrusion or a necessity will depend on one's point of view. According to David Winter, Editorial Secretary of the EA at the time, the Council had agreed that Stott could respond as chairman if he felt it right to do so. This is confirmed by John Caiger who was also with the platform party and was present when Morgan Derham advised Stott that if Lloyd-Jones's statement gave serious embarrassment he must feel free to speak afterwards as

124 John Stott, 11 November, 1991.
125 Lloyd-Jones, *Unity in Diversity*, p.8.
126 John Stott, 11 November, 1991.
127 Murray, *The Fight of Faith*, p.525.
128 John Stott, 11 November, 1991.
129 *Ibid.*

chairman.[130] Stott does not remember anticipating a problem:'we knew the topic on which he would speak [but] we had no idea that he would actually issue an appeal to people to leave their churches'.[131] Eric Fife had apparently foreseen the outcome when he met Gilbert Kirby at Wheaton, Illinois, in April 1966. According to an article he prepared for *Eternity* magazine in 1981, Fife had 'warned him that the Doctor could be expected to give a call for ministers to leave their predominantly liberal denominations'.[132] For T.H. Bendor-Samuel, a member of the original Commission who interviewed Lloyd-Jones, Stott 'over-reacted', and for Derek Prime, the mistake, if there was one, was in having the same man 'as both speaker and chairman of such an important meeting'.[133] Caiger saw Stott's remarks as a 'very justifiable qualifying note', but considered that 'strictly speaking it was ultra vires because as chairman he should have been objective, but he felt so involved with evangelicals in the Anglican Church, especially as their leader, that he felt compelled to speak'.[134] Stott later apologized to Lloyd-Jones 'for misusing the Chair' but not for what he said. In his view 'the number of people who protested at my words was about evenly matched by the number who thanked me for speaking out (they were not by any means all Anglicans), because they believed it was a responsible attempt to de-fuse a very emotional situation'.[135]

The intention then was to study the subject of Christian unity the next day. Nonetheless the night before could not be ignored and any real discussion would need to take into account the points raised both by

---

130 David Winter, 3 October, 1991, and John Caiger, tape recorded conversation, 11 February, 1992.

131 John Stott, letter to Eric Fife, 9 September, 1981. Used with permission.

132 A. Morgan Derham, 26 October, 1966, and E.S. Fife, 'The Doctor Under Attack', a brief article prepared for *Eternity* magazine, 1981, but not printed so far as is known. The occasion of the meeting was the Congress on the Church's Worldwide Mission. According to Fife, Kirby's response to his warning was that Lloyd-Jones 'had made it clear that he would do exactly as I predicted but that the Council of the Evangelical Alliance had assured the Doctor that he had the freedom to do that. Gilbert Kirby explained that it was intended to demonstrate how tolerant the Alliance was.' Fife, 'The Doctor Under Attack'. There appears to be some misunderstanding here. There is no evidence that the Council knew Lloyd-Jones was going to issue an appeal for secession and Kirby has no knowledge of it. In view of the purpose of the Assembly which was to debate the whole issue of evangelical unity, it is highly unlikely that such a call would have been approved, at least not on the first night.

133 T.H. Bendor-Samuel, 5 November, 1991, and Derek Prime, letter to author, 27 November, 1991.

134 John Caiger, 11 February, 1992.

135 John Stott to Eric Fife, 9 September, 1981. 'I felt it right to make this apology because I was 20 years younger than he, and some people had been offended. I still stand by it because what I did was a technical breach of the rules of chairmanship.'

Lloyd-Jones and Stott. The question of what happened is important for several reasons. From the Alliance's point of view it could be said that the Second Assembly largely failed in what it set out to do. True, the *Report* of the Commission on Church Unity was passed but it did not satisfy Lloyd-Jones and his followers who, within twelve months, were to form the groundswell of a revived BEC. Nor could it provide much of an alternative to the growing awareness among evangelical Anglicans of their own identity in the Church of England, as the Keele Congress was to show. So far from keeping evangelicals together there was a noticeable change of direction among the Anglicans towards openness and experiment, and among some of the Free Churchmen there was an opposite shift towards reactionary conservatism. From the point of view of Lloyd-Jones the following day's debate was particularly important: would the Assembly heed the issues he raised, and would there be a serious discussion of them? Whatever the outcome, the rally of the night before was a watershed in that Lloyd-Jones was not invited to address the Alliance again and thereafter Lloyd-Jones dissociated himself from the broader and more centrist platform of the Alliance, although not from his friends in it.

Evidence relating to the next morning's debate is sparse, but an address was first given by Julian Charley, an Anglican, which counterbalanced Lloyd-Jones's statement and put the case for 'a united territorial Church' with a warning against a 'perfectionist/individualistic outlook' which could 'never make any headway in the matter of unity'.[136] For the second part of the morning, discussion was related to the need for evangelicals of whatever denomination to stay together in the unity of the Spirit, and the conclusions of the *Report* of the Commission were passed, as were the fourteen resolutions of that day. These stated that the current 'accelerated movement towards the Roman Catholic Church' was 'a movement away from Biblical Christianity', that Christians of all denominations should not be excluded from 'the historic right of access to the Lord's table in the Church of England', and that loyalty to the Person of Christ and belief in the Old and New Testaments as the inspired Word of God should encourage evangelicals to remain united and be patient with each other although they may 'differ in matters of interpretation'.[137] The remaining resolutions related to sexual morality, Christians in society, community service, Sunday observance, missionary strategy, evangelism and the encouragement of young people. The Assembly also endorsed the Commission's conclusion that there was 'no widespread demand...for the setting up of a united evangelical Church', and confirmed the Alliance's opinion that it 'was uniquely fitted to

---

136 Lloyd-Jones, *Unity in Diversity*, p.24, where the paper is printed in full.
137 *Crusade*, December, 1966, Vol.12, No.12, p.33.

provide a framework for effective co-operation on the part of evangelical churches in general, whatever their denominational affiliation'.[138] Most of this was passed nem con.

But did this peaceful conclusion bear any relation to the arguments raised the night before or had Lloyd-Jones been tactfully ignored? One member of the Assembly, Kenneth Paterson, 'was so aroused' by the opening rally that he 'typed out a resolution' the same night 'to the effect that this assembly deplores the action of the chairman and supports the call made by Dr. Lloyd-Jones', and asked for serious discussion of the issues raised.[139] It was seconded by Alan Gibson, then minister of Stanmore Evangelical Free Church, Winchester, who welcomed the motion as a means 'to carry forward the discussion' but regretted that 'it was never put to the meeting because, in the Council's view, the substance of the motion was contained in another motion which was to be put to the meeting'.[140] The official explanation was provided by Derham in response to a letter from Paterson later that month: 'We discussed it very carefully—that is, the Chairman and the Secretariat—before the meeting, but we felt that it would so deflect the Conference from its main purpose and it would introduce such a personal element into the discussion at the very start that it really would not be a right and proper thing to do, bearing in mind the overall purpose for which we were met.'[141] There was a standard procedure to allow emergency resolutions but the Paterson resolution did not fall into this category.

Under the heading 'Immediate Reactions' the 'Executive Council Minutes' of 20 October, Item III, states that Resolutions 'should definitely come from the churches represented at the Assembly', and Item IV says that 'Careful consideration should be given to the acceptance or otherwise of last-minute amendments.' Item III outflanks any embarrassing moves by personal members and Item IV enables the Council to eliminate redundant resolutions. The conclusion of Derham was that the discussion and subsequent vote showed that the Alliance majority opinion was against separation from denominations, but had Paterson's resolution gone forward, it might have been a different story. Lloyd-Jones's two fundamental questions (whether evangelicals were content to go on being a peripheral influence in their denominations, and what the real nature of the New Testament church was) remained unanswered and, so far as Alan Gibson is concerned, it was a matter of sorrow that people 'were unwilling to face the challenge so clearly

---

138 *Report of the Commission on Church Unity*, p.11.

139 *In Step*, p.1.

140 Alan Gibson, tape recorded conversation, 14 November, 1991.

141 A. Morgan Derham to Kenneth Paterson, 26 October, 1966. Letter used with permission.

presented to the National Assembly of Evangelicals in 1966'.[142] Others
would argue that the challenge lay inside the denominations not outside
them, and that Lloyd-Jones's view of the church did not correspond to
what Scripture teaches. Whichever was right, the clash between Stott and
Lloyd-Jones went some way to accelerate polarization within British
evangelicalism.

Westminster Fellowship

Six weeks later, on 29 November, in the vestry of Westminster Chapel, 'a
rather dispirited' Lloyd-Jones announced to Caiger, Secretary of the
Westminster Fellowship, 'I am closing the Fellowship today. The Anglicans are not with us.'[143] It was the first casualty of his failure to bring
about a new evangelical grouping. The closure of the Fellowship was a
unilateral act and depended on no committee or joint decision, not even
Caiger 'knew what he was going to do until that day', and it aroused
astonishment and sorrow among the members.[144]

From its inception in 1941 the Westminster Fellowship had been a
success. From very small beginnings eventually two hundred men in
pastoral charge met monthly on Monday mornings in the parlour of
Westminster Chapel to hear papers read and to share their problems and
difficulties. It was a forum of wide interest and discussion included
medical, historical and pastoral issues as well as straight theological
debate. The only other meeting in London for evangelical ministers at
the time was the Eclectic Society which John Stott had re-founded. It was
not a conscious parallel to the Westminster Fellowship but there were
similarities as well as differences. Stott had been influenced by an upswell
of evangelical interest among some of the younger ministers in the
Church of England and what he visualized was a gathering of young men
of his own generation for informal fellowship, discussion and prayer. Its
growth was largely spontaneous and there had been no attempt at
promotion, though it is noticeable that Stott, unlike Lloyd-Jones with the
Westminster Fellowship, was ready to develop an infrastructure for the
society which he outlined for prospective members. It was a touch of
wisdom that ensured its future growth. By 1966, when many of these
young clergymen heard Lloyd-Jones give his Westminster Central Hall
sermon, the Eclectic Society had seventeen affiliated groups in different
parts of England as well as one in Northern Ireland. These kept in touch
'through Residential Conferences...the exchange of membership lists and
other literature', and in addition provision was made in the four Greater

---

142 Alan Gibson to the editor of *Third Way*, 14 December, 1990. Letter used with
permission.
143 John Caiger, 11 February, 1992.
144 *Ibid.*

London Groups for a Senior Group for members who had reached the over-forties.[145] Lloyd-Jones, on the other hand, was not inclined to organize anything beyond the immediate agenda of a meeting and was suspicious of 'men [who] set themselves up to form their own organization'.[146] In fact it was not until the closure of the Westminster Fellowship in 1966 that he conceded the need for a written statement of belief with requirements for membership, and even then it was minimal. Had he been a less autocratic figure (in practice the Fellowship was very much a one-man band) and had he been willing to extend the Westminster Fellowship idea—with its blend of mutual encouragement and instruction—through a network of ministers' fraternals nationwide he might have gone some way towards realizing his hope of evangelical unity.

Among the similarities, membership of the two groups was by nomination and election and in both cases members were expected to hold a full commitment to the Scriptures as the Word of God. As a reliable primary source the Bible was always the central axis of debate and none held to it more ardently than Lloyd-Jones and John Stott. So that however wide the range of discussion—'and we could be as radical as we liked in the application of Scripture'[147]—it was always contained within this view of Scripture. As to membership, the original Eclectic Society, founded in 1783, admitted some non-Anglicans but the revived movement provided for Church of England clergy alone. The great difference between the two groups was, in the end, the difference between two personalities. Lloyd-Jones dominated the Westminster Fellowship and was patriarchal, indeed, men went to hear his latest words. The value of his utterances, and in particular the value of his private sessions as a pastor of pastors,[148] meant that members travelled from the north of England as well as from the south and west to be there. Stott was quite different: 'we had nothing like that'.[149] Each of the affiliated groups in the Society made its own arrangements regarding the composition of its

145 J. Stott, *The Eclectic Society* (London, 1967), p.2. See also Dudley-Smith, *John Stott*, pp.304-308. The original Eclectic Society was founded by John Newton, Rector of St Mary Woolnoth, Lombard Street, in 1783. Other members included Richard Cecil of St John's Chapel, Bedford Row, who was one of the leaders of the Evangelical Revival, and Thomas Scott, the Bible commentator. Among others who became members were Charles Simeon of Holy Trinity, Cambridge, and John Venn, Rector of Clapham. *Ibid*, p.1.
146 Lloyd-Jones, *What is the Church?*, p.5.
147 Stott, *The Eclectic Society*, p.2. The Anglicans might have been more radical than the Dissenters.
148 Catherwood (ed.), *Chosen by God*, p.200. 'The Westminster Fellowship was nicknamed the Westminster Confession because so many ministers unburdened their hearts to the Doctor about the problems they faced in their churches.'
149 Stott, *The Eclectic Society*, p.2.

committee and officers, and although there were guidelines leaders were strictly 'primus inter pares'. Whether Lloyd-Jones's brand of leadership was a strength or weakness will depend on how one sees the Westminster Fellowship, but if the real focus of attention was the counsel and wisdom of its chairman, any other arrangement would have been an anticlimax.

Until 1966 the Fellowship was open to all who took a conservative evangelical position, so that within its own criteria of theological certainties it had been a tenable form of cross-denominational unity. But the developing ecumenical movement was forcing churchmen to reconsider the issues. A difference of opinion had opened up and this was too serious a matter to be ignored, especially in a fraternity of ministers where Lloyd-Jones was the chairman. So strong were his feelings that he was ready to close the Fellowship although not, in the event, irrevocably. According to Iain Murray's notes, Lloyd-Jones was unwilling to see the Fellowship 'degenerating into strife and wrangling', but for John Caiger, Secretary of the Fellowship from 1955 until the death of Lloyd-Jones in 1981, it was a strong reaction to what happened at the Central Hall: 'the Doctor was outraged and hurt [by Stott's response] and I think on reflection that the presence of the evangelical Anglicans who were quite happy to stay in their denomination had, by doing so, become a reflection on what he was trying to say'.[150] If it was a rebound from the Central Hall meeting it was not only Anglicans who provoked his frustration: others 'also felt unable to take so definite a stand', and Leith Samuel spoke of 'a number of sincere and godly...Baptists who ceased to meet at Westminster following the 1966 watershed'.[151] But while some aspects of the Central Hall meeting had exacerbated matters, for Lloyd-Jones the closing of the Westminster Fellowship was not an entirely spontaneous reaction if, as alleged, he had already expressed some concern for the future of the group a year earlier.[152] Caiger's point, that keeping company with men who disagreed with his separatist stance would be a reflection on what he was trying to say, was a valid one. Lloyd-Jones had said as much in 1963: 'What is the value of expressing criticism if in practice and in action you are saying, We are one of them after all?'[153] Given the intransigence of Lloyd-Jones's separatist ecclesiology on the one hand and the more open nature of denominational evangelicalism on the other, the closing of the Westminster Fellowship was not surprising.

Between the two sessions on that November day when he closed the Fellowship there had been some discussion about the possibility of saving

150 Murray, *The Fight of Faith*, p.529, and John Caiger, 11 February, 1992.

151 T.H. Bendor-Samuel, 5 November, 1991, and Catherwood (ed.), *Chosen by God*, p.201.

152 Murray, *The Fight of Faith*, p.506. Murray's notes of an unpublished address to the Westminster Fellowship at Welwyn, 16 June, 1965.

153 Lloyd-Jones, *Knowing the Times*, p.191.

the meeting and, although Caiger had not been included in this discussion, a suggestion had been put to Lloyd-Jones which attracted his
approval. This is clear from the afternoon session when an announcement
was made, probably by Bendor-Samuel, 'that the Doctor had expressed
his willingness to continue as chairman if the Fellowship desired it, but
the Fellowship must be on a more specific basis than it had been'
hitherto.[154] It was unfortunate that the decision to close the Fellowship
had not been taken in collaboration with its Secretary, but this was part of
the problem of the Reformed wing of conservative evangelicalism at that
time, so much of which had come to centre on Lloyd-Jones. But it was
not his wish that the meeting should die altogether. What he wanted was a
positive response from the members, a declaration of intent which
reflected his own theological preferences, and this is precisely what happened. The lunch-time discussion had rescued the Fellowship but Lloyd-
Jones had imposed his own terms. When it re-emerged the following year
with a narrower basis of fellowship up to a third of the members had
gone and, in terms of quality, 'it was a serious loss'.[155] In the meetings of
the following January and March Lloyd-Jones spoke 'about the previous
events but explained that he wanted to discuss other questions than just
the ecumenical one', and since those who had differed with him were no
longer present, 'the meeting should move on to other matters', and
'there was no opposition expressed'.[156]

Now that he had cleared the air something could be set out in print
which asked for consent to evangelical doctrine and required 'opposition' to the ecumenical movement.[157] Until then men had been
proposed for membership and their names brought before the meeting
for a vote of approval. In the reconstructed Fraternal there was a 'Statement of Principles' governing membership to which all members had to
adhere, and five of the six principles affirmed dissatisfaction with the
nature of ecumenism. James Packer believes that Lloyd-Jones set 'the
trajectory of required agreement for evangelical unity unbiblically high',
but the 'Statement' amounted to more than this because in Principle Five
pressure was placed on men who remained in doctrinally mixed denominations to 'seek to know the mind of God concerning the steps which
they should take'.[158] Evidently 'the mind of God' was on the side of the
separatists, and although the 'Statement' concedes that not all evangelicals 'see eye to eye with us' the implication was that non-separating
brethren were compromisers. Caiger comments that 'it even went as far as

---

154 John Caiger, 11 February, 1992.
155 *Ibid.*
156 T.H. Bendor-Samuel, 5 November, 1991.
157 Westminster Fraternal, *Statement of Principles* (1967).
158 J.I. Packer, letter to author, 7 June, 1991, and *Statement of Principles.*

that'.[159] It was not surprising that Alec Motyer spoke of a 'two-tier membership' where 'pride of place was given to those committed to a secessionist position'.[160] What Principle Five did was to place a matter of opinion within the definition of 'an uncompromising Gospel basis' and that was a serious if not sectarian development.

Those who approved of the new Fraternal naturally saw things in a different light. Their view was that there was little profit in continuing debate at cross purposes where people were 'talking on different presuppositions', and this was something the Eclectic Society recognized for their membership.[161] If the aim was for ministers to move towards an evangelical fellowship of churches, and it was so expressed in Principle Six, to hold an opposing view would be contentious since the matter was no longer open for debate. In the event the inclination towards a regrouping of churches was not a practical option. It may have been exhilarating to share ideals and discuss pastoral problems with a select company of like-minded men, but in reality men could only move when churches were ready to move with them and 'for various reasons not enough of the men could persuade their churches to move. The best that could happen was for a closer fellowship between the churches of the Fraternal ministers.'[162] If Lloyd-Jones saw the Westminster Fellowship or Fraternal as a prototype of church unity, and it is likely that he did, then his hopes of a new grouping of evangelicals failed again to get off the ground, this time among his closest friends. But there was another and parallel casualty of the advancing separatist movement and that was the suspension of the Puritan and Reformed Studies Conference which met each December.

The Puritan Conference

The Puritan Conference was formed in 1950 and started as a study group under the aegis of the Tyndale Fellowship.[163] The first Conference was

159 John Caiger, 11 February, 1992.

160 Alec Motyer, 10 June, 1991.

161 Alan Gibson, 14 December, 1990, and Stott, *The Eclectic Society*, p.2: 'It is limited to "conservative" evangelicals simply because, knowing a priori that we share the same basic convictions and pre-suppositions, we can discuss with real freedom and without having to waste time on preliminaries.'

162 Alan Gibson, 14 December, 1990.

163 In 1938 the Inter-Varsity Fellowship had formed a Biblical Research Committee which was concerned to bring a more intellectual approach to evangelicalism. In 1942 the Tyndale Lectures commenced at the annual conference for theological students and in 1945 Tyndale House in Cambridge was opened for biblical research, and at the same time the Tyndale Fellowship for Biblical Research emerged. F.F. Bruce, *Evangelical Quarterly*,

announced in *The Christian Graduate* when Lloyd-Jones was to speak on 'The Distinctive Theological Contribution of the English Puritans'.[164] It was the brainchild of two Oxford students, Raymond Johnston and James Packer, who went to Lloyd-Jones's vestry to float their vision of such a forum, asking for 'his help in making it a reality'.[165] At the beginning the conference met in the parlour of Westminster Chapel but this was soon too small and they moved upstairs into the Institute Hall. By 1955 about sixty attended and this rose to around 300 by the 1969 Conference. In some respects Packer became almost equal to Lloyd-Jones in the Conference, while for some he 'was looked upon as the Doctor's number two'.[166] Like Lloyd-Jones, Packer was strongly influenced by Protestant doctrine and Puritanism and did much to establish an intellectually defensible gospel in the face of an intimidating liberalism and a largely pietistic evangelicalism. Packer's scholarship, coupled with Lloyd-Jones's preaching, did much to redeem evangelicalism from a theological backwater and gave new meaning to biblical Calvinism.

What was it, then, that brought this formidable partnership to a close? What 'led to individual estrangements, from which the present writer [Packer's own words] was not exempt?' And why in some evangelical circles did Packer 'cease to be, in England, the oracle he once was?'[167] So far as Lloyd-Jones was concerned the reasons were to be found in Packer's ecclesiology. In 1968 Lloyd-Jones offered his own annotation on the cleavage in stark chiaroscuro: 'It is, alas, a time of conflict and trial, indeed a time of tragedy when old comrades in arms are now in different camps. It is not that one in any way questions the honesty or the sincerity of such friends. There is only one explanation and that is, "an enemy hath done this." Never has that enemy been more active or more subtle.'[168] Both men had carried a torch for Puritan godliness, but the difference was that Packer was an Anglican whereas Lloyd-Jones was by now a convinced Independent. It was never Packer's intention to secede,

---

1947,Vol.19, No.1, p.52. Bruce had become a leading member of the Tyndale Fellowship.

164 Lloyd-Jones, *The Puritans*, p.iii.

165 Catherwood (ed.), *Chosen by God*, p.66. See also McGrath, *To Know and Serve God*, pp.37, 38, 49-54.

166 Alec Motyer, 10 June, 1991, and Catherwood (ed.), *Chosen by God*, p.37. Packer graduated from Corpus Christi, Oxford, in 1948 and went on to complete a DPhil on Richard Baxter in 1954. He had been a Curate at Harborne, Birmingham, 1952-54, a lecturer at Tyndale Hall, Bristol, 1955-61, Warden of Latimer House, Oxford, 1962-69, Vice-Principal of Tyndale Hall, 1970-72, and Associate Principal of Trinity College, Bristol, 1972-78, with Alec Motyer.

167 Catherwood (ed.), *Chosen by God*, p.46, and Alec Motyer, 10 June, 1991.

168 D.M. Lloyd-Jones, 'Annual Letter to Members of Westminster Chapel', 1968.

although Lloyd-Jones hoped he would,[169] but rather to use his energies in the battle against liberalism and against attacks on the Protestant basis of the Church of England, its worship and *Thirty-Nine Articles*. Packer was prepared to test the waters and to explore the possibility of common ground between Christians and herein was the problem since for Lloyd-Jones dialogue between diversified church groups could only amount to compromise. Packer had been a member of the Anglican-Presbyterian Conversation from 1962 to 1965 and of the Anglican-Methodist Unity Commission from 1965 to 1968. When the Anglican-Methodist negotiations faltered in July 1969,[170] mainly because of Anglo-Catholic and evangelical opposition, he was appointed by the Unity Commission of which he was already a member to carry out further study.[171] The Commission's findings were published in 1970 under the title *Growing Into Union*. The document declared that reunion was desirable so long as beliefs and practices were 'controlled by theological norms, with explicit reference to the Bible', and so long as it was a unity in diversity and 'a unity-by-acclamation', by which local church discussion and opinion was encouraged.[172] Packer commented that 'It was a final tactic to cut the official, as it seemed to me, juggernaut rolling for a proposed union scheme between the Anglican and Methodist Churches.'[173] It was not 'an "Open Sesame solution",[174] nor necessarily a fully viable scheme, but it did at least carry the argument for union forward within the traditional concept of the church as "semper reformanda."'

For Lloyd-Jones this was folly which sooner or later would result in doctrinal horse-trading, but it is difficult to avoid the conclusion that Lloyd-Jones did not want to understand what Packer was trying to do. The fact that Packer had joined with two Anglo-Catholics in discussions on church unity had the effect of closing Lloyd-Jones's mind to any further co-operation, but the truth is that Packer had never moved away

169 J.I. Packer, tape recorded conversation, 5 June, 1992.

170 On 8 July 1969, the Methodist Conference met in Birmingham and approved the Anglican-Methodist Unity Scheme by a majority vote of 76%. The Convocation of the Church of England, meeting on the same day and in joint session at Westminster, failed to achieve the required majority of 75%, the main opposition coming from the laity. P.A. Welsby, *A History of the Church of England 1945-1980* (Oxford, 1984), p.170.

171 Members of the group were, E.L. Mascall, Professor of Historical Theology, London University, 1962-73, G. Leonard, the Bishop of Willesden and later Bishop of London for the Anglo-Catholics, and C. Buchanan, tutor at St. John's College, Nottingham, from 1964 and later Bishop of Aston, and J.I. Packer for the evangelicals.

172 *Growing into Union* (London, 1970), pp.172, 174.

173 J.I. Packer, 5 June, 1992.

174 *Growing into Union*, p.175.

from his evangelical moorings as his publications clearly show.[175] As to the discussions outlined in the 'Proposals' of 1970, the conferees did not trade their doctrinal convictions: they had no sympathy with 'organizational and administrative reshuffles', they did not 'cry up unity as the palliative for all the Church's ills', and their interests did not lie in a syncretist super-church.[176]

But there is little doubt that Packer had become an embarrassment to Lloyd-Jones. To have remained in fellowship would have been seen as a compromise by the followers of Lloyd-Jones and might have brought the charge that he was lax in acting on his own principles. Since their views on ecumenism and the church were incompatible, to have continued in fellowship would, from Lloyd-Jones's point of view, divide his platform. Packer's bilateralism was a bridge too far for Lloyd-Jones. He may have thought that Packer had been weakly led by politically ambitious friends or he may simply have miscalculated the strength of Packer's commitment to Anglicanism. It is true that he had known about Packer's denominational affiliation from the start, but this had probably been tolerated because of their mutual interest in the Puritans although, at a private level, Lloyd-Jones took every opportunity to press for secession: 'he felt it was part of his task to get me out of the Church of England'.[177] By the 1960s their views on ecumenism and the church had become a rift and there can be little doubt that the publication of *Growing Into Union* had been the last straw which ended their association and precipitated the closure of the Puritan Conference.

According to the Publisher's Introduction to *The Puritans*—a collection of Lloyd-Jones's addresses to the Puritan and Westminster Conferences from 1959 to 1978—'the three non-Anglican members of the Puritan Conference Committee (John Caiger, David Fountain and Dr. Lloyd-Jones) decided that it was impossible for the conference to continue without the introduction of serious controversy'.[178] In other words, Packer had been dismissed for keeping improper company and for

---

175 In 1961 he published *Evangelicalism and the Sovereignty of God*, in 1963 *Keep Yourselves from Idols*, an answer to J.A.T. Robinson's *Honest to God*, in 1964 an Introduction for *The Works of Thomas Cranmer*, in 1965 *God has Spoken: Revelation and the Bible*, in 1966 *The Plan of God*, in 1972 *The Spirit Within You* in conjunction with A.M. Stibbs, and in 1973 his most popular work, *Knowing God*, which 'was to sell 500,000 copies in its first decade', Catherwood, *Five Evangelical Leaders*, p.193. He had written earlier books like *Fundamentalism and the Word of God* in 1958, and an introductory essay on John Owen's *Death of Death in the Death of Christ* in 1959. For a more exhaustive list see McGrath's 'Recordings of Lectures' and 'A Select Bibliography', *To Know and Serve God*, pp.291-308.

176 *Growing into Union*, pp.10-11.

177 J.I. Packer, 5 June, 1992.

178 Lloyd-Jones, *The Puritans*, p.xii.

making concessions to the Catholics, and once again, a unilateral decision
was made. Packer had been shut out.[179] In a political move, Lloyd-Jones
withdrew as chairman of the Puritan Conference at the December meeting
in 1969, and there was no further meeting until 1971 when it was
reconstituted as the Westminster Conference under the continuing chairmanship of Martyn Lloyd-Jones.

As we have shown in the case of the Westminster Fellowship the closing
of these meetings leaves room for comment. It is more than likely that in
the back of Lloyd-Jones's mind was a desire to be free to create a more
homogeneous group. He knew of the affection of his followers and in
fact it was not long before they rallied to his position. That he continued
to guide the newly formed group as vigorously as before—'it was to all
intents and purposes the old conference resumed'[180]—until within a few
years of his death at least shows how reluctant he had been to see its
demise. But if that was in the back of his mind, at the forefront was
Growing Into Union, the final evidence of Packer's compromise: 'I was
dismissed', Packer said later, 'although I did not press for a debate at that
time'.[181] There was no need for a debate since most members of the
conference knew where he stood. Commenting twenty-six years later, he
said: 'my mind has not changed since the 1950s with respect to church
unity'.[182] Packer's views were well documented in his contributions to
the ecumenical debate,[183] but none of this minimizes the peremptory
nature of his dismissal nor, indeed, of his related dismissal in 1970 as a
consulting editor of the *Evangelical Magazine*.[184]

If the showdown between Lloyd-Jones and John Stott was damaging to
evangelical unity so too was the break with Packer. It was less public,
certainly, but it is not hard to imagine how much might have been
achieved for British evangelicalism had they stayed together. The new
Westminster Conference did not actually exclude Anglicans but few

---

179   Catherwood (ed.), *Chosen by God*, p.46: 'During the '60s he occasionally put
the boot into me'. See also McGrath, *To Know and Serve God*, pp.154-161, on the break
between Packer and Lloyd-Jones.

180   Lloyd-Jones, *The Puritans*, p.xiii.

181   J.I. Packer, 5 June, 1992.

182   *Ibid.*

183   *The Church of England and the Methodist Church* (1963), *All in Each Place,
Towards Reunion in England* (1965) (edited by Packer), and *Fellowship in the Gospel*
(1968), evangelical comment on Anglican-Methodist unity and intercommunion with C.
Buchanan and G.E. Duffield.

184   Elizabeth Braund, a member of Westminster Chapel, was the managing editor,
Paul Tucker and James Packer were consulting editors. *The Evangelical Magazine* folded
soon after Packer had no further association with it. Packer says that his dismissal was
'related to the fact that I had been dropped from the Puritan Conference.' J.I. Packer, 5
June, 1992. No explanation was offered: he was merely sent his expenses.

could expect them to be comfortable under the new separatist regime. Packer, their greatest loss, now had less influence among Free Church evangelicals and turned his mind to 'greater responsibilities in the Anglican context'.[185]

---

185 By 1978 Packer had become Professor of Systematic and Historical Theology at Regent College, an interdenominational institution in Vancouver, founded in 1968.

CHAPTER 5

A Grievous Dividing:
'Unity in the truth'

Our discussion of the ecumenical question so far has not taken into account the position of Westminster Chapel and Congregationalism, nor have we shown the extent of Lloyd-Jones's separatism in relation to the British Evangelical Council. More positively, we also need to establish what he believed to be true biblical ecumenicity. These matters will be our concern in this chapter.

From a chronological point of view the withdrawal of Westminster Chapel from Congregationalism antedated October 1966 and was one of several developments which reached their climax in 1967. At a members' meeting on 20 January 1966, a motion was 'proposed, seconded and carried nem con that Westminster Chapel should not enter into the new covenant relationship of the Congregational Church in England and Wales'.[1] On 17 May, at the 154th Annual Assembly of the Congregational Union held in Westminster Chapel, BBC television cameras were present to record the Act of Covenant Service at which John Huxtable, Minister Secretary of the newly constituted Congregational Church, presented the Covenant Book to the first president, Maxwell Janes.[2] Eleven months later, Westminster Chapel affiliated to the Fellowship of Independent Evangelical Churches and through them to the BEC.[3] But for Lloyd-Jones the events which transpired between January 1966 and April 1967 were part of a longer history of disenchantment with Congregationalism.

Congregationalists had taken a sympathetic interest in the ecumenical movement since the World Missionary Conference in Edinburgh in 1910. In 1939 the General Purposes Committee had recommended that the Congregational Union join both the World Council of Churches and the British Council of Churches and men like Nathaniel Micklem, Principal of Mansfield College, Oxford, and J.S. Whale, President of Cheshunt

---

1   'Minutes of the Church Meeting' 20 January, 1966. All 'Minutes of the Church' and 'Deacon's Meetings' in this chapter are held in the Westminster Chapel Archives.

2   *Congregational Monthly*, August, 1966, Vol.XLIII, p.16.

3   The FIEC is a constituent member of the BEC.

College, Cambridge, played a vigorous part, as did A.E. Garvie, who became president of the National Free Church Council in 1924.[4] By the time Lloyd-Jones became co-pastor of Westminster Chapel in 1939, leading Congregationalists were firmly ensconced in the ecumenical movement. The post-war situation had brought a fresh impetus to establish what had been a temporary arrangement and in 1946 a provisional committee met in Geneva where it was decided that the first assembly of the WCC should be held in Amsterdam in August 1948. G. Campbell Morgan, by now retired from the Westminster pastorate, had not been impressed with this movement for unity and on occasions was 'glad to escape the political [sic] clamour that so often intruded' into Free Church Council Meetings.[5] He was not slow to express pleasure 'in the spiritual unity of the catholic Church', but 'for corporeal unity' he cared 'very little'.[6] Neither Morgan nor Lloyd-Jones became involved in denominational affairs, but in Morgan's case his reluctance to take part or 'to be nominated for the Chairmanship of the Congregational Union' arose not out of separatist convictions—he was always a loyal Congregationalist —but from a wish to direct his energies into 'the preaching and teaching of the Bible'.[7] Westminster Chapel was happy to maintain its reputation as a preaching centre and follow its minister. But Lloyd-Jones was becoming increasingly suspicious of the idea of mutual recognition between different churches and in October 1944 he warned against the 'vague generalities' of church leaders who for the sake of unity diluted the Christian message to such an extent that 'the uniqueness of the Gospel has vanished'.[8]

In Congregational circles, a new series of talks with the Presbyterian Church of England had commenced in 1945 'with the object of achieving, if possible, a scheme of union satisfactory to both denominations', but these talks had not been wholly successful and some had expressed their doubts.[9] The following year a surprising suggestion had

---

4   *CYB*, 1940, p.101. The WCC had been established at the Utrecht Conference in 1938. See also *CYB*, 1938, p.207, and 1936, p.14.

5   Morgan, *A Man of the Word*, p.177. By 'political' Morgan may have been referring to a partisan spirit or, possibly, to ecumenical discussion. In neither case would Morgan have taken much interest since he felt his only calling was to preach. He was not a committee man or ecumenical statesman.

6   Murray, *The Fight of Faith*, pp.152-153.

7   *Ibid.*

8   *Westminster Record*, March, 1945, Vol.19, No.3, p.20.

9   The first series started in 1932: *CYB*, 1934, p.65, and 1935, pp.95-98. By 1935 it was agreed that full union was not possible but joint efforts in publishing and church services were encouraged. *CYB*, 1936, pp.130-131, and 1937, pp.163-165. Further talks were suspended because of the war. On the post-war talks see *CYB*, 1946, p.31, and 1947, pp.298-306.

come from Geoffrey Fisher, Archbishop of Canterbury, that the Free Churches should take episcopacy into their systems as a preparation for a commonly accepted ministry.[10] It was not so much a plea for organic union as an effort to maintain essential Anglicanism while inviting the other churches to join it: for Fisher it was not 'desirable that any Church should merge its identity in a newly constituted union' and, so far as he was concerned, it was important to preserve the episcopal system.[11] The General Purposes Committee of the Free Church Federal Council responded to Fisher's idea by saying that 'individual Free Churches should be invited to hold conversations with the Church of England along the lines of the Archbishop's suggestion',[12] but Nonconformists were not episcopalians and Congregationalists were not uncritical of Fisher's idea for union. John Huxtable, putting the Congregational point of view, spoke of Fisher's idea 'as a sort of ecclesiastical experiment in cross-fertilization' and wondered how the office of bishop 'could be fitted into a non-episcopal system?': would 'the Moderators of the Congregational Union be consecrated?' Would future 'generations of Congregational ministers have to be ordained by Moderators: and would their orders be otherwise invalid?'[13] Moreover, what was a bishop and what was his office in the church, and how would the Anglican pattern fit in with the Free Church idea that each pastor supported by his elders or deacons was bishop in his own church?

Such questions were for discussion, not for preventing ecumenical dialogue. Indeed, for Congregationalists, a little was better than nothing: 'If we cannot have the larger unions we desire, it seems politic to seek such as are possible', and for the Presbyterian Church of England, which had welcomed Fisher's suggestions with reservations, the feeling was the same.[14] The Free Church leaders met Fisher at a Joint Conference of Anglicans and Free Churchmen on 16 January 1947 at Lambeth Palace, but in the *Report* which appeared in 1950[15] only the Methodists were ready to enter into a serious correspondence with the Church of England. But if union with the Church of England was remote, talks with the Presbyterian Church had moved foward and new possibilities had opened up by the May Assembly of 1947. *The British Weekly* picked this up and

10   Geoffrey Fisher, Archbishop of Canterbury, 1945-61. The sermon was preached at Great St. Mary's Church, Cambridge, on 3 November, 1946. The matter is well covered in E. Carpenter (ed.), *The Archbishop Speaks* (London, 1956), pp.68-71, and in W. Purcell, *Fisher of Lambeth* (London, 1969).

11   Purcell, *Fisher of Lambeth*, pp.154-158.

12   Carpenter, *Cantuar*, p.503.

13   *The British Weekly*, 19 December, 1946, Vol.CXXI, p.167.

14   *Congregational Quarterly*, October, 1947, Vol.XXV, No.4, p.299. See also the *Presbyterian Messenger*, February, 1947, p.6.

15   *Church Relations in England* (London, 1950), Report of the Joint Conference.

carried the news that after debate and 'sustained applause' in favour of union the Assembly received the *Report* of the Joint Conference of Presbyterians and Congregationalists which, as the *Congregational Year Book* recognized, amounted to a 'covenanting together to take counsel with one another in all matters of common concern', while falling short of complete union.[16]

Breaking with Congregationalism

This, then, was the background and these were the issues which caused Lloyd-Jones to think about breaking with the Congregational Union in 1947. The question had originated with a Resolution at the Church Meeting of 22 May, 'To consider whether Westminster Chapel should withdraw from affiliation with the Congregational Union of England and Wales and The London Congregational Union, or otherwise'. But since his return from America Lloyd-Jones had modified his views.[17] He had received a letter from a Congregational minister which had expressed the hope 'that the Chapel would remain in the Union and thus support the number of Evangelical ministers in the Union', and Lloyd-Jones had referred to 'The Congregational Evangelical Ministerial Fellowship, a body of 60 or 70 Evangelical Ministers, who had made a similar appeal'.[18] He had also agreed with another correspondent that, although modernism was 'rampant in many churches', there was a continuing number of ministers who remained 'steadfast in the matter of Evangelical Principles' and he did not wish to 'increase their difficulties' by withdrawing from the Union.[19] So he accepted their appeal and agreed that Westminster Chapel should remain in the Congregational Union, but it was on his terms. An amended resolution was put together at the Deacons' Meeting of 2 October 1947 and it was decided to continue the affiliation fee and remain in the Union, but 'in order to preserve the Independent nature of the Chapel' they would continue to exercise 'complete freedom of action in the allocation of monies' to churches and evangelical causes of their choice, and that 'no official delegates

---

16   *The British Weekly*, 22 May, 1947, Vol.CXXII, p.102. Also *CYB*, 1948, p. 87, and 1950, p.96.

17   'Minutes of the Church Meeting', 22 May, 1947. He had sailed from Liverpool on 16 July and boarded the Mauritania for England on 12 September. The main reason for his visit was to attend a conference at Harvard University, 18-23 August, where the International Fellowship of Evangelical Students was established. Lloyd-Jones was elected chairman and gave the conference evening address. D. Johnson, *A Brief History of the International Fellowship of Evangelical Students* (Lausanne, 1964), pp.75-76.

18   'Minutes of the Deacons' Meeting', 2 October, 1947, and 'Minutes of the Church Meeting', 16 October, 1947.

19   'Minutes of the Church Meeting', 16 October, 1947.

should be sent to any society under the auspices of the Congregational Union'.[20]

Such was the amendment placed before the special meeting of the Chapel on 16 October. It was a well-attended meeting and the reasons why Lloyd-Jones had reversed his original intention were in recorded in the minutes: 'that in the light of these appeals, together with further reflections, he felt led to modify his views and support the Amendment'. We are not told what the 'further reflections' were but the mixed ecclesiastical affiliations of the Harvard Conference which had included representatives from the Lutheran, Anglican, Baptist, Presbyterian and other churches from as far away as Europe and Australia might have made him more sympathetic to the position of other evangelicals.[21] In the event Lloyd-Jones gave his word that 'any worthy Congregational cause' would be supported 'so far as may be within our power', and the 'Minutes' show that the amendment was carried with ten dissentient votes 'and some who refrained from voting'. Among the dissentients were those who could not support 'the non-sending of Delegates to Societies' and there may be some truth in Iain Murray's suggestion that these were largely a pre-war remnant unwilling to relinquish their loyalty to Congregationalism.[22] Whether this was so or not, and it is not possible to be certain at this distance, it was no more than a temporary compromise for Lloyd-Jones.

The break, therefore, between Westminster Chapel and the Congregational Church in 1966 did not represent a shift in policy for Lloyd-Jones since his earlier views had been much the same. What was new, as we have already seen, was the zeal with which he came to insist on separation from the ecumenical movement. After more than twenty years of disillusionment with denominational Congregationalism the proposal of August 1965 by the Congregational Union to form the Congregational Church in England and Wales provided a convenient breaking point, and the relationship of Westminster Chapel with Congregationalism ceased entirely at 'a well-attended Church meeting' on 20 January 1966.[23]

The main reasons for the decision were printed under 'Special Announcement' in the *Westminster Record* the following month, and reflected the 'Minutes of the Deacons' Meeting', that is, the involvement of Congregationalism with the WCC 'which we regard as inimical to evangelical principles', and disagreement with the new proposal of the Union to form a Congregational Church, 'a definite infringement of the

---

20   'Minutes of the Deacons' Meeting', 2 October, 1947.
21   Johnson, *A Brief History*, p.139.
22   Murray, *The Fight of Faith*, p.164.
23   *Westminster Record*, February, 1966, Vol.41, No.2, p.31.

Congregational principles to which we adhere'.[24] It was to this point of principle that Lloyd-Jones referred in his December Puritan Conference paper on 'Henry Jacob and the First Congregational Church'. Indeed, his justification for considering Jacob was not only to celebrate an anniversary but to highlight what he saw as the difference between seventeenth-century Independency and modern Congregationalism with its new formation as a 'Church'.[25] He was dismissive of 'the authorities of the Congregational Union' who, he felt, 'were probably completely ignorant' of the Henry Jacob anniversary which fell around the time of the 1966 Assembly: 'though it means nothing to them it means a great deal to me'.[26]

The truth was that men like Geoffrey Nuttall and John Huxtable were not unmindful of their history but, as Huxtable said, they were unwilling to ignore 'the ecumenical spirit of the times'.[27] Jacob had founded an Independent church in Southwark in 1616, and had defined a church as 'a number of faithfull people joyned by their willing consent in a spirituall outward society or body politike, coming together in one place, instituted by Christ in his New Testament, and having the power to exercise Ecclesiasticall government and all God's other spirituall ordinances (the meanes of salvation) in and for it selfe immediately from Christ'.[28] Lloyd-Jones subscribed to this definition although not to the semi-separatism of Jacob[29] and it was this kind of statement describing the nature of an Independent church which, in Lloyd-Jones's view, had come to an end with the formation of the new CCEW.

The heart of the matter was centralization. Since the October 1904 Assembly a Council had been elected and some of its members co-opted to direct the affairs of the Congregational denomination, and in 1919 Moderators were appointed for the first time.[30] It could of course be argued that centralization was inevitable given the need for a more

24 *Ibid.*

25 Lloyd-Jones, *The Puritans*, p.149.

26 *Ibid*, p.50.

27 Huxtable, *As it seemed to me*, pp.37, 39.

28 W. Walker, *Creeds and Platforms of Congregationalism* (Philadelphia, 1960), p.78. Jacob's church became known as the Church of the Pilgrim Fathers because the London contingent who sailed in the Mayflower in 1620 were members of it. It was finally 'destroyed by enemy action' in 1941. *The British Weekly*, 27 March, 1941, Vol.CIX, p.261.

29 Jacob refused to separate 'absolutely' from other 'true visible churches and ministers' although he disagreed with Anglicanism as such. He was, therefore, an Independent, not a Separatist. Lloyd-Jones, *The Puritans*, p.157.

30 A scheme for Provinces and Moderators was approved at the London Congregational Association in May, 1919. *CYB*, 1920, p.8. See also Alan Argent, 'The Pilot on the Bridge: John Daniel Jones (1865-1942)', *JURCHS*, 1997, Vol.5, No.10, pp.592-622.

careful deployment of limited resources and it does not follow that, because final decisions on important matters rest with an Assembly or its representatives, there is no continuing congregational element. Members of an Assembly are, after all, members of the churches they represent and in this way they have the same interests at heart. Neither, so far as we know, did the Congregational Union or the new covenant relationship aspire to be surrogate churches, but for Lloyd-Jones centralization was incompatible with 'essential Congregationalism' because it violated the autonomy of a congregation's subjection to Christ and the Scriptures alone.

Lloyd-Jones was right insofar as the idea of covenanting, as used in the Act of Covenant Service in the 1966 Assembly, was a move away from original Congregationalism. Covenants and confessions by ministers, members and congregations had been an important part of Independency since the sixteenth century and had safeguarded doctrine and the gathered church principle: towards the middle of the nineteenth century there was a decline in local church covenants as new Congregational churches appeared. A.P.F. Sell has noted the influx of 'Enlightenment individualism' which arose at the same time and which encouraged a shift away from saints covenanting 'in Christ' to an emphasis on the unanimity of saints: that is, the democratic principle of 'one man—one vote',[31] and Westminster Chapel had not avoided this either. There were exceptions but 'by the 1950s' the idea of a more national covenant incorporating the denomination as a whole had evolved, and it was this broader use of 'church' which Lloyd-Jones found disturbing. The new Act used 'covenant' more widely to describe the whole CCEW, and the intention of such a 'global form of confessing'[32] was to recognize the wider communion of believers, a point which Huxtable made clear in his sermon at the formation of the new Church: 'as so often happens people who see one thing very clearly are apt to miss other things', and it took Independents 'almost 300 years to see' it.[33] The nature of modern Congregationalism did not consciously deny its roots but it had moved on to see the life of the church 'as a whole' and to recognize 'Christians of other traditions'.[34]

---

31   A.P.F. Sell, 'Confessing the Faith in Congregationalism', *JURCHS*, October, 1988, Vol.4, No.3, pp.170-215. So the old doctrinal emphasis took second place as did Statements of Faith, 'the last being dropped from the [Congregational] *Year Book* in 1928 on grounds of economy'. S. Morris Watts, 'Presbyterian-Congregational Union?', *Congregational Quarterly*, October, 1947, Vol.XXV, No.4, p.300.

32   Sell, 'Confessing the Faith', p.170.

33   *Congregational Monthly*, August, 1966, Vol.XLIII, p.16.

34   *Ibid*, p.17. Sell says that in the Act of Covenant Service of May 1951, Congregationalism chose to follow 'the risky road of combining corporate confessing with liberty under the Gospel'. 'Confessing the Faith', p.211.

The position of Westminster Chapel vis-à-vis the Congregational Union had never been strong. It had paid its annual subscription until 1947 but apart from the Chapel being a convenient amphitheatre big enough to accommodate large meetings in central London there had been remarkably few contacts. Nor had the Chapel affiliated to the London Congregational Union, although 'for many years [it] had sent a voluntary lump-sum contribution...in order to help Churches in the Eastern part of the City'.[35] Lloyd-Jones was never on the denomination's ministerial list and the letter 'A' against his name in the *Congregational Year Book* list of churches noted that he was not yet in the Union.[36] Strictly speaking, the decision of January 1966 was not secessionist since the old Union had been dissolved and the new Church was a voluntary association. It simply stood outside the proposed covenant and did not join. So the non-covenanting decision was something of a non-event so far as the Chapel was concerned, although it served to sharpen the issues and redirect the Chapel's focus. Numerically Westminster Chapel was strong enough to pursue its own course. By 1964 orders for the *Westminster Record*, which carried little more than a sermon by Lloyd-Jones, were 6,000 copies monthly, which included 1,200 sent to overseas subscribers and 2,300 sent to addresses in the United Kingdom.[37] Despite its unusual strength, however, the Chapel was not isolationist nor was it Lloyd-Jones's intention to be so. He had said as much in his annual 'Letter' of January 1967, when he wrote about 'the danger of living only to ourselves', and when giving notice of the March business meeting that year one of the questions to be considered was that 'of our formal relationship to other like-minded churches'.[38]

Turning to this meeting and the Chapel's relationship with like-minded churches, there is some evidence that Lloyd-Jones did not have things all his own way. 'Minutes' of the meeting on 16 March record a 'unanimous recommendation by Dr. Lloyd-Jones and the Deacons to the church to apply for membership to the FIEC', but no definite decision was taken: 'on a show of hands, 42 people voted in favour of postponing our decision and it was agreed that another meeting should be called as soon as possible to consider the matter further'. There is no indication as to what percentage of the meeting this number was nor do the 'Minutes' record the number present, but the issue was clearly unresolved. There

---

35 'Minutes of the Church Meeting', 16 October, 1947. This also ceased in 1947 when the Church Meeting decided to make its 'own choice of Churches to be helped' and 'to support such Churches as are governed by Evangelical Principles'. *Ibid.*

36 He remained on the Ministerial List of the Welsh Presbyterian Church from 1927 until his death, and was on the FIEC list of Accredited Ministers from 1967-1981.

37 'The Church', 6 July, 1965. Unpublished typescript, WChA.

38 D.M. Lloyd-Jones, 'Annual Letter to Members of Westminster Chapel', January, 1967.

are several possible reasons for this. Church meetings in Independent
churches are an open forum for members and in practice this extends
discussion. No doubt there was an element of this and it would appear
that there were some who had given little thought before the meeting as
to what the new alignment would mean. Others may have been loath to
sever a lengthy affiliation to Congregationalism. Murray includes this
meeting under a chapter on 'Controversy' and suggests that the matter of
affiliation to the FIEC was a difficult move for some, with 'a measure of
controversy' and tension which arose, mainly from a small group of
younger men who felt that the FIEC was not sufficiently Calvinistic.[39]
This may have accounted for a few, and no doubt for Murray himself,
but a vote of '42 people' in favour of postponement points to a more
general feeling of uncertainty rather than any arguments against the
FIEC. It was true that the FIEC did not require acceptance of the five
points of Calvinism[40] for membership but neither did it stipulate the
mode of baptism or form of local church government. Its vision of
evangelical unity was more broadly based in that it included both
Calvinists and Arminians who were united in the more primary doctrines
of evangelicalism and who stood against the ecumenical movement. It
was this broader evangelical fellowship that Lloyd-Jones and his deacons
had recommended, but members wanted more time to think. The matter
was finally resolved on 13 April when 'attendance at the church meeting
was very large'. By a show of hands the motion was 'carried by an
overwhelming majority' with 'five dissenting votes',[41] and Westminster
Chapel applied for membership to the FIEC. Once again, the number of
votes were not recorded but the wording of the 'Minutes' points to a
larger gathering than 16 March, and this being so, the five dissenting
votes suggests a nearly unanimous decision.

The British Evangelical Council

The conservative *Evangelical Times* saw the new affiliation as a 'by-
product' of Lloyd-Jones's call for a new grouping of evangelical

39   Murray, *The Fight of Faith*, p.542.

40   The five points of Calvinism summarize the central doctrines of the Synod of
Dort, 1618-19, and are popularized in the acrostic 'TULIP': total depravity of human
nature, unconditional election (or absolute predestination), limited (or particular)
atonement, irresistible grace, and the perseverance of the saints (including perfect
assurance of eternal salvation). See W.J. Seaton, *The Five Points of Calvinism* (1970).

41   'Minutes of the Church Meeting', 13 April, 1967. By 1969, there were 315
affiliated churches and missions, 266 accredited ministers, 95 accredited missionaries and
over 2,000 personal members. See *Unity in the Evangelical Faith* (n.d.), an introductory
leaflet, and *Handbook* (1969). On the FIEC, see E.J. Poole-Connor, *Evangelical Unity*
(1942), pp.174-188.

churches and an argument against those who interpreted it as a call for a new denomination,[42] but others might have seen it as his only refuge and an inevitable move if he was to avoid isolation. Lloyd-Jones had burned his boats so far as Congregationalism went, but his future did not lie with the FIEC so much as with the BEC. Here he became passionately outspoken, and was their leading speaker over the next twelve years. Although the BEC had been founded in 1952,[43] until November 1967 (when Lloyd-Jones preached on the 450th anniversary of Martin Luther's ninety-five theses) the BEC was almost unknown to the Christian public. Its interest for us here is that the Luther address in 1969 contained a further appeal for evangelical unity which was more rigorous than the Evangelical Alliance appeal of 1966, and, apart from the Mayflower sermon of 1970,[44] it was the last time Lloyd-Jones called for radical Independency in so public a manner.

The substance of his appeal this time was that the real enemy involved fellow believers, those who, although equally sincere and honest, had a faulty conception of the nature of the church and of the gospel itself. Lloyd-Jones knew that his views were causing others to become impatient with him: 'Some of us Evangelicals are constantly being charged with being spiritual detectives, and we are said to condemn a man for a dot or a comma...we are over-critical.'[45] But for Lloyd-Jones the boundaries between truth and falsehood were clearly drawn and believers must defend themselves against wrong associations. Such was his view that a destructive force was at work within the churches and that ecumenism was the ruin of biblical Christianity, that it comes as no surprise to hear him speak with increasing vigour of uncompromising separation.

In Lloyd-Jones's 1967 Luther-sermon, he made it clear that 'Neutrality at a time like this was cowardice, it is temporising where it is

---

42   *Evangelical Times*, July, 1967, Vol.1, No.7, pp.1-2: 'the Chapel's latest step will be that all such misunderstanding will be dispelled'.

43   It was founded in St. Columba's Free Church, Edinburgh, by G.N.M. Collins and Murdoch Macrae of the Free Church of Scotland, and T.H. Bendor-Samuel and E.J. Poole-Connor of the FIEC. Hywel R. Jones in D.M. Lloyd-Jones, *Unity in Truth* (Darlington, 1991), p.8. Church groups that came to be linked with the BEC are the FIEC, Evangelical Presbyterian Church of Northern Ireland, Strict Baptist Churches, Free Church of Scotland, Evangelical Movement of Wales, Evangelical Fellowship of Congregational Churches, Union of Evangelical Churches, and the Apostolic Church. In addition there are a number of local churches not identifying with any group.

44   See Lloyd-Jones, *Unity in Truth*, pp.84-101. The meeting was at Westminster Chapel and commemorated the 450th anniversary of the sailing of the Pilgrim Fathers to the New World. He shared the platform with Charles Woodbridge, Professor of Church History, Fuller Seminary, California. See also *Evangelical Times*, Double Commemoration Issue, November, 1970, Vol.IV, No.11, pp.1-4.

45   D.M. Lloyd-Jones, *President's Address*, The Evangelical Library, 1962, p.22.

not sheer ignorance of the facts'.[46] It was time for believers to withdraw from unholy alliances and enter into a fellowship of like-minded people 'such as this BEC' which, he believed, 'stood for the truth and against compromise, hesitation, neutrality and everything that ministers to the success of the plans of Rome'.[47] For those who chose to remain in the established churches and denominations while maintaining their own evangelical convictions, he was most scathing. He spoke of the 'mental reservations' and 'private interpretations' of such men who, because they remained in doctrinally mixed churches, were in fact denying the 'Articles' or 'Confessions of Faith' which they had claimed to believe. He repeated this in 1971, accusing such men of 'dishonesty, and of lying'.[48] He may have had in mind the kind of remarks made by Michael Ramsey, incoming Archbishop of Canterbury, who in 1961 had said that it was 'quite in order for a person to stand up in church and recite the *Creed* even if he has scruples about the virgin birth, provided he believes in the pattern of faith as a whole'.[49] Whatever the meaning of the latter part of Ramsey's statement, for Lloyd-Jones the 'pattern of faith' had to be matched by accurate doctrine and credal honesty. Later, in his 1971 'State of the Nation' sermon, he spoke of the 'spectacle of a bishop' and 'leaders of the Church'. The 'spectacle' was John Robinson, suffragan Bishop of Woolwich, who had stood as a witness at the trial of D.H. Lawrence's book, *Lady Chatterley's Lover*, and was in favour of publishing the unexpurgated edition, saying that Lawrence's portrayal of the sexual relationship was something sacred, like 'an act of communion'.[50] The 'leaders of the Church' were those who supported 'the Wolfenden Report recommendations with regard to homosexual practices'.[51] These were extreme cases but they served to highlight the mixed nature of the church, especially the Church of England, and made Lloyd-Jones's call for separation increasingly urgent.

Lloyd-Jones's closing address at the BEC conference of 1 November 1967 was preached to a capacity congregation in Westminster Chapel and contained an assessment of Martin Luther and a commemoration of the

46   Lloyd-Jones, *Luther and his Message for Today*, p.29.

47   *Ibid.*

48   Lloyd-Jones, *1662-1962*, p.46, and D.M. Lloyd-Jones, *The State of the Nation*, British Evangelical Council, 1971, p.8.

49   Michael Ramsey, Archbishop of Canterbury, 1961-74, interviewed by Rhona Churchill, *Daily Mail*, 2 October, 1961, p.9. O. Chadwick, *Michael Ramsey* (Oxford, 1990), pp.5 and 342.

50   *Lady Chatterley's Lover* (1928) by D.H. Lawrence was adjudged not to be obscene by a jury at the Central Criminal Court on 2 November 1960.

51   Lloyd-Jones, *The State of the Nation*, p.8. Sir John Wolfenden, an Anglican layman, presided over the Committee on Homosexual Offences and Prostitution in Great Britain between 1954 and 1957.

ninety-five theses. Principally it was a critique of the modern church and a call for evangelicals to secede. The *Evangelical Times* had no doubt about the burden of this latter-day Luther: 'Here I Stand' was the headline,[52] and few could have missed the implication of one man and his cohorts standing for the truth in a sea of unfaithfulness. *The Christian*, less separatist and anti-ecumenical, had the headline, 'Attack on Ecumenism',[53] but both were right. In most respects it was a typical Lloyd-Jones sermon containing the same kind of emphasis and illustrations that are common to a great many of his sermons, but this time there was a new element, a sting in the tail. Not only did he see doctrinal compromise in those who remained in their denominations, he went further: 'It also raises the question of guilt by association'. 'If you are content to function in the same church with such people', he said, 'you are virtually saying that though you think you are right, they also may be right... That, I assert, is a denial of the Evangelical, the only true faith.'[54]

'Guilt by Association'

By definition, therefore, 'guilt by association' was a charge that was laid at the door of fellow Christians who chose not to secede. It was not merely a protest against the contemporary zeitgeist, it was a challenge to fellow evangelicals on the subject of church affiliation and it carried all the marks of second-degree separation. Using Luther's life and message, he warned against unevangelical tendencies and clinched his argument from Revelation 18:4:'Come out of her, my people, that ye be not partakers of her sins, and that ye receive not of her plagues.'[55] The idea that evangelicals could stay within a doctrinally mixed denomination in order 'to reform it' or 'turn in into an Evangelical body' was, to Lloyd-Jones, 'mid-summer madness',[56] and that was a word not only to the Anglicans but to Baptists, Congregationalists, Methodists and all who had an official interest in ecumenism and the WCC. But it should not be forgotten that Lloyd-Jones was profoundly convinced that the ecumenical movement was an enemy of the gospel and it was against this background that he used 'guilt by association'. Indeed, such was the number of occasions on which he expressed anti-ecumenical feelings that it is not hard to see how they came to be a primary factor in his understanding of Christian truth:'if your doctrine of the church is wrong, eventually you will be wrong everywhere. If you believe in a mixed

52 *Evangelical Times*, November, 1967, Vol.1, No.11, p.1.
53 *The Christian*, 10 November, 1967, p.1.
54 Lloyd-Jones, *Luther and his Message for Today*, p.26.
55 *Ibid*, p.29.
56 *Ibid*.

denomination...of necessity you have to compromise.'[57] The nature of
the compromise was not that one agreed with the sentiments of a certain
bishop or church leader but that one associated with his views by
remaining in the same denomination. It was not Anglo-Catholics,
moderates or liberals he had in mind so much as the culpability of
evangelicals who held the same gospel in all its essential points.

To speak of 'guilt by association' implied the committing of an
offence or at least a failure of duty and since words like 'guilt', 'compromise' and 'separation' indicate disapproval, it implied a judgement of
those concerned also. It was a serious charge and one that raises certain
questions. The issue of church affiliation is clear enough, but does 'guilt
by association' mean that all serious conversation with Christians who
hold differing views is out of the question? Is it wrong to talk face-to-face
with other believers on matters of mutual interest? But if there is an
embargo on communication how will people learn from each other and
how will they live together in a yet imperfect world? Or does the offence
relate to the purity of the pulpit and the kind of men who are invited to
preach in the churches? And, perhaps most radical of all, should
evangelicals feel guilty if they do not join the BEC, since this was the best
provision for unity? But to say as much is bordering on sectarianism and,
in any case, encourages yet another ecclesiastical organization.

The problem was that although the trend of thought was clear, Lloyd-
Jones did not define what he meant by 'guilt by association'. It may
amount to any one of the above explanations or to all of them. What is
beyond doubt, however, is that it immediately polarized believers by
making separation the touchstone of orthodoxy, and at a stroke it removed a whole group of Christians from the mainstream of debate and
action. For R.W. Davey it was quite illogical: 'to talk about withdrawing
from denominations and churches...is like saying, if you are a human
being you had better not be a member of the human race because that is
the reductio ad absurdum of that kind of argument'.[58] But it could also
be argued that 'guilt by association' is unchristian because it is not
consistent with the life and ministry of Christ. He was separate, certainly,
but by virtue of who and what he was, not in the sense of encouraging his
disciples to dissociate from each other. None would doubt the severity of
Christ's words against sin and unbelief or his warnings on a variety of
subjects but when it came to judging a brother in the faith he cautioned
care.[59] Of course Lloyd-Jones knew this and John Caiger is quite right to

---

57   Lloyd-Jones, *Unity in Truth*, p.176.
58   R.W. Davey, tape recorded conversation, 12 February, 1992. Davey studied
theology at King's College, London, and later at the Evangelical Theological College of
Wales at Bridgend before he became a physician. He attended the Westminster Fellowship
and knew Lloyd-Jones well.
59   Matthew 7:1-5.

say that 'the closer you were to Lloyd-Jones the more inconsequential was this position. The further away from him people were the more they felt the impact of his statement.'[60] Nevertheless, it was said. The tape recording of the sermon conveys all the passion of his preaching and the statement is undoubtedly an indictment—'It is guilt by association'. The printed version is toned down to 'This raises the question of guilt by association',[61] but this is not a critical point. A man has the right to edit his spoken word for publication and most preachers do: nor does it change what he is saying, a view which he was to hold for the rest of his life. 'I was criticized some 8 or 9 years ago', he said in 1974, 'for using a phrase, "guilt by association". I was told you musn't say that. But now there is no difficulty because the position has changed. What I saw then to be implicit has now become explicit', and he went on to explain what he meant by citing cases of ecumenical evangelism.[62]

Reaction to the charge of 'guilt by association' reflected the division that had opened up among evangelicals. Those close to Lloyd-Jones chose either to defend him or to say little so as not to exacerbate the situation. Murray makes no mention of 'guilt by association' in his reference to the Luther address, though he does talk around the subject of separation and alignment in the following chapter, 'Controversy: An Assessment'. He does, however, allow the phrase in a quotation from James Packer and adds that this did 'not fairly reflect his [Lloyd-Jones's] position'.[63] Murray's view of Packer is somewhat partial. He seems to be saying that Packer is a man who has lost his way and gone with the tide, especially in the implication that he had changed his mind about the nature of the church itself. But, as we have noted earlier, Packer was still a convinced evangelical.

The view of Hywel Rees Jones was more direct: 'The Doctor was not advocating second degree separation' at all. 'What he was doing was questioning those who, in the previous twelve highly charged months, had repeatedly rejected a call to gospel unity in favour of denominational loyalty which countenanced serious error.'[64] But to say that 'he was not in fact charging anyone with guilt' is either to question the meaning of words or miss the point altogether. As we have said, it was a charge laid at the feet of fellow believers and this was not missed by his contemporaries.

---

60 John Caiger, tape recorded conversation, 11 February, 1992.

61 The original tape recording is available from the BEC. Being present on the night, I have to say that the phrase was less startling set within the context of what he was saying. It is undoubtedly true that although we may disagree with Lloyd-Jones's position, the sloganizing of the phrase afterwards only made matters worse.

62 D.M. Lloyd-Jones, '1 Corinthians 16:13-14'. Tape recorded sermon, 1 November, 1974. Private copy.

63 Murray, *The Fight of Faith*, pp.548-549 and 793.

64 Lloyd-Jones, *Unity in Truth*, p.20.

For Gilbert Kirby, then Principal of London Bible College and a friend of Lloyd-Jones, 'guilt by association did tremendous damage', and for Maurice Rowlandson, Administrative Assistant to the Evangelical Alliance, 'it turned brother against brother'.[65] David Winter, Editorial Secretary of the Alliance, thought that few took 'much notice', but R.W. Davey, who attended the Westminster Fellowship, found it more menacing: 'there was a sense in which you were forced to conform, rather like receiving a government Whip. You gave nominal assent...but privately there was lots of dissent'.[66] Davey highlights the dilemma of men who had grown up under the preaching of Lloyd-Jones and who had benefited from his counsel but who now felt uncertain about what he was saying on secession. To such men, an unquantifiable number, loyalty had to be balanced with conscience.

There were others—men like A. Morgan Derham—who spoke about the separatist emphasis in 1966 and 1967 as 'an error of judgement which...grievously divided the evangelical community in the UK', and this was noted by J.D. Douglas in an American publication, *Christianity Today*: 'it is irrefutable that the veteran Welsh preacher's views on separation have split evangelical ranks'.[67] The grievous dividing in Derham's case was a distinct coolness between the more inclusive EA and more exclusive BEC, and it is not hard to see the predicament of Derham who had sympathies with both sides but who felt personally betrayed. His hopes had been for a strengthened Alliance in which all evangelicals stood together, but the events of 1966 and 1967 had proved otherwise. He was not happy with these new tensions between brethren and in spite of looking on Lloyd-Jones as 'my theological guru, my pastoral exemplar, my friend and encourager', regretted that he pressed separation so far that it made his mission as the General Secretary of the EA 'impossible and I quit'.[68] The tension felt by Derham was clearly expressed in a letter to the author: 'I resigned in 1968 precisely because the promotion of the BEC made my vision for the EA impossible, and because I did not wish to be involved in controversy with my former friends and colleagues of the Westminster Fellowship of which I had been a member since the late forties'.[69] Alec Motyer, who had known Derham 'tolerably well' and who attended the Westminster Fellowship, felt that 'the whole aura of guilt by association...made real fellowship between

65   Gilbert Kirby, tape recorded conversation, 6 August, 1991, and Maurice Rowlandson, tape recorded conversation, 1 August, 1991.

66   David Winter, letter to author, 3 October, 1991, and R.W. Davey, 12 February, 1992.

67   *Third Way*, December, 1990, Vol.13, No.12, p.35, and *Christianity Today*, 19 December, 1969, Vol.XIV, No.6, p.35.

68   *Third Way*, December, 1990, p.35.

69   A. Morgan Derham, letter to author, 3 November, 1991.

true evangelicals more difficult and less warm...and there was a real fear of entering into even simple cross-barrier contacts':[70] fear, that is, of deserting Lloyd-Jones and his cause. This was the kind of observation made by Maurice Rowlandson: it was a feeling of anxiety which 'made you look over your shoulder and made people very careful of what they said; they didn't want to condemn themselves in the eyes of others'.[71] Packer's response was that although it had been made in good faith, 'guilt by associstion was viciously flawed' and entailed 'censure of [the Apostle] Paul because, having detected and corrected major errors, he failed to tell the churches that he personally was breaking off fellowship with them until he was satisfied that they had all renounced those errors'.[72]

It cannot, of course, be said that Lloyd-Jones wanted to provoke ill-feeling, but either he had not thought his position through sufficiently or he was naive in his expectations. For some, moved by the power of his preaching, it may have seemed like the beginning of a new era and a new reformation. For others it was an absurdity and could hardly gain a foothold in the mainstream denominations since all of its members would be 'guilty by association'. In practical terms all it did was to marginalize Lloyd-Jones further. The result was that instead of evangelicals coming together in the 1960s and thereafter, they split three ways: the separatists to the BEC, the Anglicans to a reinvigorated evangelical Anglicanism, and the rest to the EA. It could hardly have been further from what Lloyd-Jones had intended. For many evangelicals denominational loyalties still had their place although not to the exclusion of other Christians and, as R.T. France says, 'if anything, Lloyd-Jones's appeal...made us more clearly aware that our denominational context was more than just a flag of convenience. We became more conscious of being evangelical Anglicans, not Anglican evangelicals'.[73]

The Appeals Fail

The two calls for a new grouping of evangelicals, 1966 at the Central Hall and 1967 at Westminster Chapel, were sincerely made but they largely fell to the ground through lack of support. It is difficult not to see the Central Hall appeal as a political mistake. Until that meeting Lloyd-Jones had almost universal approval among all evangelicals, but after 1966 his influence declined amid some bitterness and polarization. Whether he would have formed a new denomination given the chance is a moot point. Publicly he denied any such intention though some who were close

---

70   Alec Motyer, letter to author, 10 June, 1991.
71   Maurice Rowlandson, 1 August, 1991.
72   J.I. Packer, letter to author, 7 June, 1991.
73   R.T. France, letter to author, 7 November, 1991.

to him are not so sure. R.T. Kendall, for example, feels that when nothing happened 'he was very disappointed. He could have done it. I think the only reason he did not have the courage to do it was that he thought it might fail. I think he hoped for vast numbers of people beating on his door to do it.'[74] But Lloyd-Jones made no plans for a new structure: this he left to others. In fact he looked upon plans and schemes with disdain and had no ambitions to be a denominational leader. His great interest was preaching, but herein lay the dilemma. Such was the effect of his preaching that he inspired many by what he said and his relentless use of logical arguments and historical illustrations made people think that what was being said was of great significance. And yet if the calls of 1966 and 1967 were so important why did he make them if he was unwilling to follow them through? Was it right to say such things then leave people dangling in mid-air, hoping that something would happen? His purpose may have been simply to alert people to what he saw as the great need of the day, but if he had no intention of following up what he said it might more accurately be described as misleading rhetoric. Or perhaps it was politics. If so, to make rejection of the ecumenical movement a core belief of Christianity was too narrow: in fact it was sectarian, no matter how concerned he was for the truth.

The allegation of 'guilt by association', coming as it did a year later in 1967, may have been a final blow aimed at less radical brethren who were not prepared to conform to Lloyd-Jones's concept of unity. But beyond the impact of the occasion it had little practical effect. Few were willing to say that Christians who spoke out against error while remaining in their churches were guilty simply by virtue of the membership they held. If that had been so, for one thing it would prejudge the integrity and motives of those who differed, and for another such wholesale secession would mean that the evangelical point of view would cease to be heard in the church at large. But the most chilling aspect of this kind of conservatism is its alienation from the fellowship of other believers and its failure to understand their struggle with current issues in an equally honest way. The closest Lloyd-Jones came to realizing his call for a new grouping of churches was to revive an existing one, that is, to associate with the BEC. There were other associations—the FIEC, for example, or the Evangelical Fellowship of Congregational Churches—but the BEC was a larger forum and could speak, so he hoped, with a corporate evangelical voice. From here he would hold the fort and make his pronouncements: 'Why do I belong to the British Evangelical Council?' he asked at Westminster Chapel in 1969: 'It is because I cannot say "yes" and "no" at the same time... I take my stand with the apostle

---

74   R.T. Kendall, tape recorded conversation, 8 October, 1991.

Paul'.[75] The implication was that to remain outside of the BEC was to
weaken the church's coherence and testimony to biblical truth and the
unmistakeable impression was that evangelicalism and the BEC were one
and the same thing.

So the BEC became a kind of flagship for 'shadow ecumenism', but in
spite of the thousands who gathered to hear Lloyd-Jones at their annual
meetings it amounted to very little, and the impact on British Christianity
today of those who take Lloyd-Jones's line is negligible. There are clear
indications that the majority of Lloyd-Jones's supporters held Independent convictions well before 1966. T.H. Bendor-Samuel, for example,
spoke about the 'vital importance of building a truly united evangelical
church' in 1964, and proceeded to say, 'we should hope and pray that
out of the present confusion one evangelical church may arise and we
should be prepared to take our place in it'.[76] And, troubled with the
issues of mixed doctrine and ecumenical tendencies, the Evangelical
Movement of Wales had formed in 1955 to encourage evangelicals in the
Principality and in 1967 churches were beginning to affiliate to it.[77] His
supporters' position was, therefore, confirmed rather than precipitated by
the appeals of 1966 and 1967. So far as evangelical Anglicans were
concerned, they too were already on the move in the 1960s. Latimer
House had been founded in Oxford in 1959 to promote theological
research and scholarly writing on current Christian questions from an
evangelical point of view, and by 1964 there had been two Northern
Evangelical Conferences in York and a layman's conference in Leeds,
while plans for the Keele Congress of 1967 were already being discussed
in 1964 by men like John Stott: 'All that was going on without any
reference to Dr. Lloyd-Jones and when he began increasingly to make
separatist noises the effect was that Anglicans progressively lost interest.'[78] So a divergence of opinion between Anglicans and Independents was already opening up in the early 1960s.

The trouble was that for Lloyd-Jones secession was not up for
discussion: all who took the opposite view were guilty of ecclesiastical
indifferentism. But for men like Stott and Packer the evangelical influence in the Church of England was growing. For them, secession would
be disobedience and would be damaging to the people of God. But more
than this, Lloyd-Jones's idea of unity at this point is open to question and

75   Lloyd-Jones, *Unity in Truth*, p.81. The meeting was the final rally held on 29
October. Having recently recovered from his illness, among his opening words were,
p.66: 'I speak as "Paul the aged", but I am very glad that the message is still the same.'

76   T.H. Bendor-Samuel, *One Body in the Lord* (London, 1965), pp.11, 13.

77   J.E. Davies, *Striving Together* (Bridgend, 1984). Lloyd-Jones had encouraged
this formation.

78   M. Saward, *Evangelicals on the Move* (London, 1987), pp.36-37, and J.I.
Packer, 5 June, 1992.

we are entitled to ask if he was right to make evangelicalism the focus of allegiance? To hold this kind of unilateral allegiance was to encourage the very party spirit that he deplored while at the same time it made the ecumenical movement the axis around which his ecclesiology was formed. For the majority of Christians, however, these were not primary issues, nor did they find any difficulty in being faithful to the gospel and remaining in their churches. Lloyd-Jones's black-and-white distinction between denominational evangelicals and independent congregations did not reflect the true state of affairs for the generality of church-goers. But it was not they who concerned him so much as the smaller number of the faithful who stood outside of the WCC and found refuge in the BEC: God's alternative provision in an age of theological syncretism: 'I believe the call to the BEC, which it has heard and already responded to, is to do in our age and generation precisely what Elijah did on Mount Carmel'.[79] Once more, it was 'the big battalions on the one side and on the other side the Luther-like figure of Elijah standing in the name of God and the truth.[80] Or as he put it on a number of occasions, it was 'Athanasius contra mundum'.[81]

The consequence of all this was that it placed those who disagreed with Lloyd-Jones among the false prophets. There was only one way to worship God—'in spirit and in truth'—and as the prophets of Baal were destroyed for opposing the true God, the church also must withstand heresy: 'You must destroy them and their teaching. And if you cannot excommunicate them because of your numerical weakness, you have got to remove yourself from their midst.'[82] That some appeared to be removing themselves gave him much satisfaction: 'I am immensely encouraged at the sight of this congregation', he said at the beginning of his Luther address in 1967: 'I am glad to find that if not exactly 7,000 there are at any rate some 2,500 and more who have not bowed the knee to Baal'.[83] Such was his conviction: 'Why this BEC? Why not join the other evangelicals?' His answer was unequivocal: 'they are mixed up with infidels and sceptics and denials of the truth'.[84]

But although there had been anti-ecumenical feelings in certain areas in the 1960s, Lloyd-Jones was alone among the other prominent London

---

79   Lloyd-Jones, *Unity in Truth*, p.156.

80   *Ibid*, p.157. The story of Elijah and the prophets of Baal is found in 1 Kings 18. It was an ideal illustration to demonstrate his distinction between true and false religion and between the confusion of other opinions and the clarity of gospel truth.

81   *Barn (Opinion)*, June, 1963, p.171.

82   Lloyd-Jones, *Unity in Truth*, p.164.

83   Lloyd-Jones, *Luther and his Message for Today*, p.3. The 7,000 is a reference to 1 Kings 19:18. The number in Westminster Chapel that night may have been nearer 3,000.

84   Lloyd-Jones, *Unity in Truth*, p.157.

ministries of the time. W.E. Sangster, his famous Methodist neighbour, 'tried hard to see fine points about all the Churches, and went to a variety of services when he could, including Roman Catholic ones': he 'was active all the later years of his life in ecumenical meetings of every description, including the British Council of Churches, the United Free Church Council, the Ecumenical Institute, the Conversations between the Church of England and the Methodist Church',[85] and that was while he remained an outstanding evangelical preacher. John Stott at All Souls was a convinced denominational evangelical and was already playing a vital part in the development of evangelical Anglicanism.

In the end, it can be argued that Lloyd-Jones's separatism was a retreat, not from biblical doctrine or from a broader ecclesiastical view alone, but from a wider field of influence in which he once was generally welcome. In the eyes of the church at large it was a retreat into self-imposed marginalization. It was also a shift in priorities. The heart of the matter for Lloyd-Jones was that differing views of the Christian church and of its core beliefs had become 'the major cause of division amongst evangelical people' and formed 'the greatest hindrance to revival' and evangelism.[86] Thus ecclesiological issues had taken on an overriding importance and this, even in the eyes of his sympathetic grandson, 'was a mistake'.[87]

Alternative Ecumenism

Our study so far has shown more of the negative side of Lloyd-Jones's ecumenical position and there has been enough evidence to suggest the nature of its problems. But the difficulties were not all on one side. It is true that there was doctrinal woolliness in contemporary ecumenism and Lloyd-Jones had little in common with most of its leaders. Moreover, given his belief that the church was to be pure and separated and not a net with all kinds of fish in it, his fears were justified since the majority of Christians did not separate but remained in their churches and therefore within the ambit of the ecumenical movement. There was, however, a more positive view of Christian unity and any attempt to assess his ecumenical position would be incomplete without the knowledge of what he did believe.

In a letter to the editor of the Welsh monthly *Barn* in 1963, Lloyd-Jones wrote: 'I believe from the bottom of my heart in church unity and

---

85   P. Sangster, *Doctor Sangster* (London, 1962), pp.301-302. W.E. Sangster was at the Central Hall, 1939-55, and was President of the Methodist Conference in 1950.

86   Lloyd-Jones, *What is the Church?*, p.4.

87   Catherwood, *Five Evangelical Leaders*, p.91.

I look on schism as sin.'[88] In his opening address at the Second National Assembly of Evangelicals in 1966 he told his congregation, 'I am a believer in ecumenicity, evangelical ecumenicity. To me the tragedy is that we are divided'.[89] What then was the positive side of his teaching on Christian unity and how could he be so passionately for and against it at the same time? We have already seen that there was a clash in his thinking between biblical unity and what was going on in the mainstream churches; we now need to show the underlying reasons and theological bases for what he did believe.

The case for an alternative ecumenism came from the premise of evangelicalism itself, and this he made clear as early as 1946: 'The question is, what is this great ecumenical church to stand for? What is she to believe? What is her foundation?' These were the issues in mind, not numbers, 'for however great a body the ecumenical church may be, she will have no influence upon the world unless she has a truth to present'. To be faithful to its roots the church must prioritize the apostolic message because what 'the Bible is concerned about is truth, and in a very extraordinary manner it ridicules our pathetic faith in big battalions and in great numbers'.[90] Lloyd-Jones's view of biblical ecumenism was a logical process within which three main areas of thinking can be identified. The first step was to ask three fundamental questions: 'What is a Christian?', 'How does one become a Christian?', and 'What is the Church?' Arising from his answers to these questions came the second part of the process, the nature of the unity itself. Lastly, and equally integral, was the centrality of doctrine.

In response to the first question the Christian is described as someone who is 'born of the Spirit', which not only means that his 'sins are forgiven' but that by virtue of the converting act he 'is a partaker of the divine nature...one in whom are essentially, the traits and characteristics of God himself'.[91] So if, by definition, the Christian is the result of an act of God in conversion and that alone, the new birth cannot be conferred through such practices as infant baptism, church membership, or the living of an irreproachable life. And this is exactly what he said in an undated and rare testimony under the title 'Why I am a Christian': 'I am

---

88   *Barn*, June, 1963, p.236. *Barn* strongly supported the Welsh language movement and bilingualism in the 1960s and 1970s. Lloyd-Jones's letter to the editor was in response to the comments of Aneirin Talfan Davies in his column 'Av Ymyl y Ddalen' ('In the Margin'), under the heading 'Yv Hyn a Gredaf' ('That which I Believe'), who was arguing against Lloyd-Jones's position on ecumenism in his *The Basis of Christian Unity*.

89   Lloyd-Jones, *Knowing the Times*, p.255.

90   D.M. Lloyd-Jones, *Expository Sermons on 2 Peter* (Edinburgh, 1983), p.5.

91   Lloyd-Jones, *The Basis of Christian Unity*, p.13. His whole thesis on Christian unity is found in this booklet, although it is generously expanded elsewhere, as I show.

a Christian solely and entirely because of the grace of God and not because of anything I have thought or said or done.'[92] It was the classic Calvinist answer: 'We are Christian not because we are good people', he said elsewhere, 'we are Christian because, though we were bad people, God had mercy on us and sent His Son to die for us. We are saved entirely by the grace of God; there is no human contribution whatsoever.'[93]

This led exactly to the more contentious second question of how a person becomes a Christian: 'Is it through the Church and its sacraments and through works alone; or is it justification by faith alone?' It was 'the old 16th century question...how is a man saved?'[94] and was firmly set within his view of history and Scripture. 'How does one get forgiveness of sins?', he asked in his Luther address: is it through indulgences or works or is it wholly fideist? 'How does one become a Christian and get this assurance of being reconciled to God? That is the question that led to the Protestant Reformation.'[95] As Luther had come to a personal experience of salvation by studying the Scripture, especially the book of Romans and its doctrine of justification by faith, so not only did he become a different man but, more importantly, his experience opened up the difference between a church-based system of salvation and one in which divine grace came directly from God without a priest.[96] Becoming a Christian was a gratuitous and sovereign act which depended on God's work rather than man's. After conversion the believer was expected to be 'throughly furnished unto all good works', but the initial conversion experience was 'not by works, lest any man should boast'.[97]

The answer to the question 'What is the Church?' is strictly tied into the other two questions and has a strong spiritual emphasis: it is a communion of saints, not an institution. It is an association of people who have been 'born again' and who because of this are members of the body of Christ. Such people are 'a spiritual society with the Holy Spirit as their companion, as the one who leads them, and the one who inspires them.'[98] In other words the church is an aggregate of all who share the same conversion experience.

---

92   D.M. Lloyd-Jones, *This I Believe* (Glasgow, n.d.), p.5.
93   D.M. Lloyd-Jones, *Faith on Trial* (London, 1965), p.89.
94   *Barn*, April, 1963, p.173.
95   Lloyd-Jones, *Luther and his Message for Today*, p.25.
96   For a popular discussion and study of Luther see R.H. Bainton, *Here I Stand* (New York, 1970). The phrase, 'the just shall live by faith' is found in Habakkuk 2:4, Romans 1:17, Galatians 3:11 and Hebrews 10:38. As Bainton rightly says, p.65, 'Luther's own experience was made normative' and 'justification by faith' became central to the evangelical understanding of salvation thereafter.
97   2 Timothy 3:17 and Ephesians 2:9.
98   Lloyd-Jones, *Knowing the Times*, p.179.

Together these questions and answers provided a structure for the kind of unity which Lloyd-Jones envisaged. It was to be Trinitarian and familial, and these concepts were at the heart of his exposition of Christ's high priestly prayer in John 17: 'the essential character of the unity about which our Lord is speaking is that it is comparable to the unity that exists between the Father and the Son Themselves. It is also comparable to the unity between the Son and the people for whom he is praying.'[99] This was the Trinitarian aspect, something he put even more clearly in a sermon on Romans 8:28-30: 'The unity of which our Lord speaks is not a mere coming together of all who call themselves Christians; it is a unity of the same character as the unity between Father and Son.'[100] So there is a clear-cut division between those who are in the world, the non-believers, and those who are separated or gathered to Christ. It is the latter 'and they alone [who] are the subjects of this unity'.[101]

The argument is circular: true believers are one because their salvation is Trinitarian and Christocentric. This is a familial relationship and a unity of essence since they all belong to the same Father. As 'a matter of blood and of essence' each family member has his or her origin in the same evangelical experience, and for this reason the unity of the church is not voluntary but inevitable. Such inevitability is a vital part of his argument: unity being involuntary, there is no need 'to create' or search for it because it is a matter of preserving what is already there. The people of God 'stand for the same things...possess the same emphasis [and] speak the same language'.[102] It is not surprising, therefore, to hear him say that 'the invisible Church is more important than the visible church', and to take this a step further, for evangelicals 'loyalty to the former may involve either expulsion or separation from the latter, and the formation of a new visible church'.[103] Separation was obviously in his mind when he said this in 1962, but to what extent is not clear. A.T. Davies certainly thought this statement was mischievous, but in his defence Lloyd-Jones argued that it was not his purpose to deny the reality of a visible church, simply to show the difference between the visible and invisible aspects, which is common knowledge to 'every Protestant Church'.[104] He made little comment on 'new', which Davies takes as 'the heart of the argument' but which Lloyd-Jones saw as the

---

99   Lloyd-Jones, *The Basis of Christian Unity*, p.12.

100   D.M. Lloyd-Jones, *The Final Perseverance of the Saints* (Edinburgh, 1975), p.348.

101   Lloyd-Jones, *The Basis of Christian Unity*, pp.9-10.

102   *Ibid*, p.24, and *Y Cylchgrawn Efengylaidd* (*The Evangelical Magazine*), November/December, 1948, Vol.1, No.1, p.13.

103   Lloyd-Jones, *The Basis of Christian Unity*, p.60.

104   *Barn*, April, 1963, p.172.

myopic reaction of someone unable to think of any church 'other than the episcopal church!'[105]

The third part of the process was the centrality of doctrine. What he believed about biblical ecumenism rested firmly on an agreed body of truth: Christian unity is 'unity in the truth'; it is the 'getting together of like-minded people'.[106] Conversely, people 'are not "one", nor in a state of unity, who disagree about fundamental questions', and in practice there needs to be 'agreement on basic points before true co-operation is possible'.[107] Any kind of unity which is less than this 'is dishonest and sinful' because it misleads the world at large: it is to 'be guilty of a lie'.[108] His point was that all unanimity in apostolic doctrine would help a fallen world in need of gospel light—'Nothing so surely drives the world away from the truth as uncertainty or confusion in the Church with respect to the content of her message'. He illustrated this from geometry: 'Without the acceptance of certain axioms and propositions in geometry ...it is idle to attempt to solve any problem; if certain people refuse to accept the axioms, clearly there is no point of contact between them and those who do accept them. It is precisely the same in the realm of the Church.'[109]

But not all truth can be defined as axiomatic and Lloyd-Jones makes a distinction between essentials and non-essentials in *The Basis of Christian Unity* and in *What is an Evangelical?*, although it is a distinction which recurs in other sermons too. The essentials, the irreducible minimum, are the full inspiration and authority of Scripture as the revelation of God, and its trustworthiness in all matters of faith, knowledge and practice, including creation, the Fall of man, the divine plan of redemption which included a propitiatory and substitutionary atonement, the need for the new birth, and the resurrection and final glorification of believers. It also included the trinitarian nature of God and the full divinity of Christ in his birth, life, death, physical resurrection, ascension and second advent, and the person and work of the Holy Spirit. These were the constituents of truth and the elements of 'essential evangelical preaching' and unity.[110] It was a body of doctrine which had been received from the past and was to be preserved in the present, and Lloyd-Jones believed that evangelicals above all others were the 'guardians and custodians' of this 'New Testament heritage'.[111] Secondary or non-essential truths were those 'matters upon which the Scriptures are not clear', and among these were

---

105 *Ibid.*
106 Lloyd-Jones, *The Basis of Christian Unity*, p.12, and *Revival*, p.167.
107 Lloyd-Jones, *The Basis of Christian Unity*, p.61, and *Barn*, April, 1963, p.171.
108 Lloyd-Jones, *The Basis of Christian Unity*, p.61.
109 *Ibid.*
110 Lloyd-Jones, *Unity in Truth*, pp.112-113.
111 Lloyd-Jones, *Knowing the Times*, p.255.

the mode of baptism, church polity, interpretations of prophecy, theories or modes of sanctification, and spiritual gifts. To divide on these kinds of issues where opinions differ even among evangelicals, was to 'become guilty of schism and...to rend the body of Christ'.[112] His definition of schism, therefore, was wholly restricted to believers: 'It is only evangelicals who can be guilty of schism. Schism means that men and women who are agreed about the fundamentals of the faith divide on matters that are not fundamental, and are of second-rate importance.'[113]

This, then, was the rationale of his position. There was no unity outside of 'the cardinal truths', and to pray, evangelize or worship with people who differed on the essentials was meaningless.[114] It was of the greatest importance, therefore, not to compromise and he constantly warned against the replacing of defined truth with 'a flabby, sentimental notion of unity' which was, in his view, characteristic of the ecumenical movement. It was a theological outlook which depended entirely on the 'absolute supremacy' of the Bible and on an Independent view of the church.[115] If church order was a matter of relative indifference, the nature of the church itself was not, and this is why it was so difficult for Anglican evangelicals to co-operate with Independents. True, the Anglicans had as much to offer as anyone else but when it came to establishment questions and inter-church relations, 'they would never be accepted as "true blue" Evangelicals'.[116]

Given the theology of Lloyd-Jones, the idea of biblical unity which he advocated was a perfectly valid one and his disagreement with those who held a more syncretistic view of the church was not unexpected. Some in the ecumenical movement might, indeed, have agreed with much of what he said,[117] but none of them could be so exclusive of other Christian views. As John Huxtable said: 'Variety must have its place within the framework of a well defined unity',[118] but that, of course, meant freedom to differ on doctrine and practice. Lloyd-Jones's doctrine and practice were so closely defined, at least in the essentials, that it left him no room

---

112 *Ibid*, p.354.

113 1 Corinthians 16:13-14. The sermon was preached at Slough Tabernacle. 'The first Epistle to the Corinthians is the locus classicus' on the matter of schism. Lloyd-Jones, *Knowing the Times*, p.186.

114 Lloyd-Jones, *The Basis of Christian Unity*, p.55.

115 Lloyd-Jones, *Unity in Truth*, p.172.

116 David Winter, letter to author, 3 October, 1991.

117 'There may be no compromise in respect of the Gospel; we all agree about that. But we should hesitate to claim that Dr. Lloyd-Jones or any other man has done more than glimpse the mystery of the grace of God, since it is only "with all saints" that we may hope to grasp the length and breadth and height of grace.' *The British Weekly*, 19 March, 1953, Vol.CXXXIII, p.6.

118 Huxtable, *Christian Unity*, p.25.

for manoeuvre. If the church is a remnant people and its ideal state Independency, as Lloyd-Jones believed, separation was inevitable. It was but a short step to 'guilt by association'.

CHAPTER 6

Wales and the English:
'A Welshman through and through'

We turn in this chapter to the question of nationality and the part it played in the life and ministry of Lloyd-Jones. Such was the nature of his nationalism that it affected the way he saw things and the way he accomplished his goals. Therefore, because Welshness so strongly coloured Lloyd-Jones's evangelicalism, it is important to include some assessment of the matter.[1]

In the first of three talks on Radio Wales in 1943, Lloyd-Jones described himself 'as a sort of Welsh exile'. When he made this comment he had been 'in London and in England'[2] for only four and a half years, yet after forty-two years of living in England he felt the same. He took his holidays in Wales, missed no opportunity to preach in Wales, and at the end of his life it was the Bible and a Welsh hymnbook 'that were his only reading'. By a piece of good fortune for a Welshman, he died on St. David's day and when he was buried five days later, it had to be in Wales: 'He couldn't have been buried anywhere else'.[3]

As we have seen the Lloyd-Jones family moved to London when Henry was looking for work in 1914.[4] The family became members of the Welsh Presbyterian Church in Charing Cross Road (formerly the Welsh Calvinistic Methodist Church in Nassau Street, Soho), and their names first appear in the 'Annual Report' to members of 1915.[5] There was no change in the 'Report' until 1918 when it was reported that Harold, Martyn's older brother, had been 'killed in action' and then

---

1   See J.F. Brencher, '"A Welshman Through and Through": David Martyn Lloyd-Jones (1899-1981)', *JURCHS*, December, 1998, Vol.6, No.3, pp.204-225.

2   D.M. Lloyd-Jones, 'Religion and Features of Nationality', Part 1, p.1 of a type-script translation by Dafydd Ifans. A series of three talks given on Welsh Radio in 1943.

3   F. and E. Catherwood, *The Man and His Books*, p.36.

4   Murray, *The First Forty Years*, pp.32-33.

5   'Mr Mrs H. Lloyd-Jones, Harold, Martyn and H. Vincent of 7 Regency Street, S.W.' 'Charing Cross Annual Report', 1915.

again in 1921 when Martyn first appeared as 'Dr. Martyn Lloyd-Jones'.[6] The 1925 'Report' records the death of Henry Lloyd-Jones[7] and by 1926 the family had moved to 12 Vincent Square, Westminster. According to the 'Chapel Report' of 1927, Martyn had withdrawn his membership paper after his marriage to Bethan Phillips at the Chapel on 8 January, after which they arrived in Aberavon in February to take up his first pastorate. When he joined Campbell Morgan at Westminster Chapel, Magdalene, his mother, withdrew her membership paper from Charing Cross and was welcomed into membership at Westminster Chapel by Certificate of Transfer at the communion service in January 1940.[8] In the same year Vincent Lloyd-Jones, who at Oxford had developed a strong interest in Catholicism,[9] moved to 24 Vincent Square.

From the end of 1914 to the end of 1926 when Martyn was a member, Charing Cross Chapel was a liberal church and something of 'a transit camp for Welsh who came to London to work or study'. It was 'a cultured church'[10] and Lloyd-Jones referred to the 'high intellectual level' of papers 'read at the Literary Society meetings on Friday evenings and the discussion that followed'.[11] But although he was appointed Sunday School Superintendent for a year these were spiritually barren years for an unconverted man:'What I needed was preaching that would

---

6   'Annual Reports', 1918, 1921. According to F. and E. Catherwood, *The Man and His Books,* Harold 'died in the flu epidemic of 1918', p.16, and David Mathias Lloyd-Jones confirms with this. Interview, 19 October, 1996.

7   See Ieuan Phillips, 'In Memoriam: A Tribute to Henry Lloyd-Jones', *Y Gorlan* (*The Fold*), Charing Cross Chapel, October, 1925. Also printed in Murray, *The First Forty Years,* pp.379-381.

8   *Westminster Record,* January 1940, Vol.14, No.2, p.36. Martyn stayed at the family home, 12 Vincent Square, with his mother and brother from September 1939, but in December he moved to The Haven, a rented house in Chatsworth Avenue, Haslemere, Surrey, travelling up to London, usually on Saturday evening. In November 1943 he moved to 2 Colebrooke Avenue, Ealing, and in July 1945 when this property was sold they lived in rented accommodation at 39 Mount Park Crescent—'a few minutes from Ealing Broadway station'. In the summer of 1965 he moved to 49 Creffield Road, Ealing, where Ann and Keith Desmond moved into the top floor, the Lloyd-Joneses occupying the ground floor. Murray, *The Fight of Faith,* pp.134, 495.

9   David Mathias Lloyd-Jones, interview, 19 October, 1996. Vincent did not become a member of the Roman Catholic Church. At Oxford he came under the influence of G.K. Chesterton, Hilaire Belloc, Evelyn Waugh and the writings of Ronald Knox. He became a member of the Thomas More Society in London and read the *Tablet* every week throughout his life. His interest in Catholicism was more 'a matter of intellectual interest than religious commitment'. Apparently there was no friction between Vincent and Martyn, who 'perfectly understood'. *Ibid.*

10   I.D. Pickering, interview with author, 10 August, 1995.

11   *Y Ganrif Gyntaf* (*The First Century*), Charing Cross Road Chapel, 1949, p.17.

convict me of sin and make me see my need... But I never heard that.'[12] The gospel that was preached by Peter Hughes Griffiths, minister at Charing Cross Chapel for almost forty years, did not have the conservative emphasis that Lloyd-Jones adopted[13] and the assumption, if that is what it was, 'that we would not have been there in the congregation unless we were Christians' was for Lloyd-Jones 'one of the cardinal errors of the Church' in general this century.[14] Even so, he remained in membership until January 1927, while occasionally visiting Westminster Chapel during the ministry of J.A. Hutton.[15] Lloyd-Jones preached 'about twice in Charing Cross after he retired', but because of his conservatism he 'was not a...popular preacher...with the members'.[16] His invitation to preach at the centenary services in 1949 was partly because he and his family had been prominent members and also because he was a distinguished figure in London church life and a convinced Welshman as well.[17]

Llangeitho

Before moving to London, however, he had grown up in a Welsh-speaking rural community and in one of the centres of Calvinistic Methodism. Under the preaching of Daniel Rowland of Llangeitho and Howell Harris of Talgarth, Cardiganshire and Breconshire had been at the heart of the 'great awakening in Wales',[18] and for Lloyd-Jones these men were among the heroes of the faith. As a child he attended the Calvinistic Methodist Chapel in Llangeitho where Rowland had been minister for fifty years and at the age of thirteen he had attended the Summer Association meetings where four or five thousand gathered to celebrate the

12   Lloyd-Jones, *Preaching and Preachers*, p.146. Lloyd-Jones placed no date on his conversion but it appears to have been around 1924-25. See Murray, *The First Forty Years*, pp.64-78.

13   'Whether we always enjoyed the gospel as we listened to him it is not for me to say.' *Y Ganrif Gyntaf*, p.19. Evidently he did not.

14   Lloyd-Jones, *Preaching and Preachers*, p.146. According to Lloyd-Jones, Griffiths dominated the church 'by the sheer force of his personality'. *Y Ganrif Gyntaf*, p.17.

15   'I belonged to a Welsh Presbyterian Church in London. But I was greatly attracted by Dr. J.A. Hutton...then minister of Westminster Chapel which I attended occasionally.' *Christianity Today*, 8 February, 1980, Vol.24, No.3, pp.155-156.

16   I.D. Pickering, letter to author, 9 September, 1995.

17   There may also have been some ill feeling over Lloyd-Jones leaving the Presbyterian Church of Wales for a Congregational pastorate. I.D. Pickering, 9 September, 1995.

18   Lloyd-Jones, *The Puritans*, p.287. On the history of Calvinistic Methodism see R. Buick, *Wales and 'Y Goleuad' 1869-1879* (Caernarvon, 1969); C.M. Book Agency, and William Williams, *Welsh Calvinistic Methodism* (London, 1872).

bicentenary of the birth of Rowland. These meetings made 'a deep impact' on Lloyd-Jones[19] and it would have been surprising, given his increasing interest, if some of the enthusiasm of those days had not rubbed off on him and if the life of Rowland had not caught his youthful imagination. Rowland, 'the greatest preacher of them all', had preached in Wales to crowds of up to 3,000 and people travelled on sacrament Sundays 'from almost every county in Wales'.[20] Above all, it was 'a Welsh movement, led by a Welshman preaching in the Welsh language'[21] and this was undoubtedly the kind of revival Lloyd-Jones would like to have seen in twentieth-century Wales. Indeed, it is not difficult to find similarities between the two men: conviction in preaching, extended exposition of the same text, a vibrant doctrine of Scripture, and belief in evangelical Calvinism.

Lloyd-Jones did, of course, meet with people who had experienced the 1904-05 revival in Wales—the South Wales minister in *Preaching and Preachers* who lacked careful sermon preparation for example—and considered himself to 'belong to that generation'.[22] But although 'the Calvinistic Methodists received an added 24,000 into membership'[23] and the revival spread to the whole Principality, north and south, there were 'many problems'.[24] He would not deny that God was present in the revival but there were 'certain tendencies to extreme mysticism in Mr. Evan Roberts' and the 'general difference in character' between this and earlier Welsh revivals was 'the lamentable failure of the preachers to con-

---

19   Lloyd-Jones, *The Final Perseverance of the Saints*, p.293; and Murray, *The First Forty Years*, p.26. The meetings were in 1913. He was 'deeply moved...and possibly the most important thing it did was create in me an interest in the Calvinistic Methodist fathers which has lasted until today', Murray, *The First Forty Years*, p.27. The occasion was also the start of a lifelong passion for revival: *Evangelical Magazine of Wales*, 19 April, 1975, Vol. 14, No.2, p.21.

20   Lloyd-Jones, *The Final Perseverance of the Saints*, p.293, and E. Evans, *Daniel Rowland* (Edinburgh, 1985), pp.214, 353.

21   C.R. Williams, 'The Welsh Religious Revival, 1904-5', *The British Journal of Sociology*, 1952, Vol.3, pp.242-259.

22   For example, see Lloyd-Jones, *Preachers and Preaching*, pp.225, 152. 'It was the second generation after the revival of 1859, and I discovered later that I had never really heard a truly convincing evangelistic sermon. I was received into the Church because I could give the right answers to various set questions.'

23   E. Evans, *The Welsh Revival of 1904* (London, 1969), p.146. To the Wesleyans were added 'over 4,000, the Congregationalists, 26,500' and the 'Anglicans and Baptists brought the total figure to...100,000'. *Ibid*. G.I.T. Machin, *Politics and the Churches of Great Britain 1869 to 1921* (Oxford, 1987), p.269, has Nonconformists increasing 'by some 82,000'.

24   D.M. Lloyd-Jones, Foreword, Evans, *The Welsh Revival of 1904*, p.6.

tinue preaching and teaching during the revival'.[25] He also referred to the absence of sermon preparation during the revival and the problems it caused afterwards: 'I knew several such men and had to try to help them a little out of the spiritual depression which in some cases...crossed the line from the spiritual to the psychological.' So things were not as he would have liked, and recalling a conversation of 'many years ago' he spoke of 'the sad decline in spiritual tone and spirituality of the Church in Wales' since the revival.[26]

Yet while the revival had proved to be disappointingly transient and had not touched Llangeitho—'By the time I came to live there' the church where Daniel Rowland had been the minister was 'of all churches that I have known, the most lifeless'[27]—there were still a lot of very devout people around. True, 'Welsh preaching [had] lost the old-time power' and the original enthusiasm had gone, but some churches had retained good congregations, probably through a strong sense of tradition. Others were not so fortunate. When Rhys Davies visited Wales in the mid-1930s he found the majority of chapels empty, and in one place '20 people sat huddled in the centre pews', the vast number of seats both downstairs and in the galleries empty.[28] A decade later Wales had failed to revive its Nonconformist traditions and the general attitude to religion was one of apathy. Writing in 1946, the view of Thomas Jones was that religion in Wales 'is not attacked, nor is it fiercely discussed...it is subjected to something worse—it is ignored as something irrelevant'.[29] Lloyd-Jones's assessment in 1963 was that 'Wales is quickly turning into paganism and is becoming popish'.[30] The same, of course, was true of England, but so far as Wales was concerned, while people turned out for cultural occasions such as the Llangollen International Eisteddfod, local eisteddfodau, or the excitement of an election, when it came to chapel life, 'Only a celebrity like Lloyd-Jones could draw a crowd'.[31]

---

25   *Ibid.* 'The mystical element was probably the most impressive thing about the revival.' Evan Roberts, an ex-collier and layman, was the outstanding preacher of the revival. See *ibid*, pp.151-152, and Williams, 'The Welsh Religious Revival, 1904-5', pp.251-252.

26   Lloyd-Jones, *Preaching and Preachers*, pp.225-226, 151. Of the 'poor fellow' who continued to neglect his studies, expecting God to 'fill his mouth', 'he emptied his church, and was more or less useless as a preacher for some fifty years afterwards'.

27   Lloyd-Jones, *The Final Perseverance of the Saints*, p.293.

28   Rhys Davies, *My Wales* (London, 1937), p.126.

29   T. Jones, *The Native Never Returns* (London, 1946), pp.13-17. This was quoted by Jones from a broadcast by Principal Gwilym Edwards in 1945. Thomas Jones was at one time a Deputy Secretary to the Cabinet and Secretary to the Economic Advisory Council.

30   *Barn*, June, 1963, p.237.

31   Davies, *My Wales*, p.126.

Nationalism and Temperament

Although his commitment to revival was strong, because he was 'a Welshman through and through' there was also a robust, lifelong nationalistic element in him, and like his father he 'carried Wales in his heart'.[32] The subject arose a number of times in his lectures and sermons, but the best source is found in 'Nationalism, Tradition and Language', a printed version of an interview with Gaius Davies in 1964. Here Lloyd-Jones distinguishes between nationalism 'according to the flesh', that is, idolizing it above others 'because you belong to it',[33] and nationalism as the inheritance of a language and tradition which are integral to upbringing and citizenship. For this he cites the apostle Paul who was 'of the tribe of Benjamin, a Hebrew of the Hebrews; as touching the law, a Pharisee', but who looked upon such things as 'dung, that I may win Christ, and be found in him'.[34] That a man is a Christian 'does not mean that he ceases to be a citizen of his own country', but it was not the United Kingdom he had in mind so much as the 'Welsh "anian"'. This 'ethos or temperament', largely preserved by language and accent,[35] was to be preserved on the grounds that real Christian faith does not violate or change a person's individuality. National characteristics remain, as do pre-conversion faculties and talents, but the problem was that indigenous Welsh culture was under attack and anglicization, as we shall see, was thought to be the main offender. To lose culture and language because of external influences, to lose the 'anian' and conform to another cultural pattern, was unthinkable for Lloyd-Jones because it 'not only betrays' a man's 'country, but also betrays human nature'. In other words, the 'man who is ashamed of his Welshness, or who tries to crucify his Welshness' by suppressing his accent, for example, 'is...doing something that I would argue the New Testament itself condemns'.[36]

---

32   Ieuan Phillips, 'In Memoriam', 1925: 'you entered Wales as soon as you crossed the threshold of his home. The Welsh tongue, the Welsh spirit and Welsh hospitality greeted you like a breeze from the hills.'

33   *Evangelical Magazine of Wales*, August/September, 1969, Vol.8, No. 4, pp.5-11. The discussion was carried in consecutive issues of the magazine, of which Gaius Davies was one of the editors. According to Graham Harrison, this interview was not well received in 'some parts of darkest England' but 'was most warmly received in black Africa'. 'Apparently they felt that it showed great understanding of colonial-type attitudes and situations, and that it brought clear biblical principles to bear on them.' *Evangelical Magazine of Wales*, April, 1981, Vol.20, No.2, p.46. The interview was reprinted in *Span*, the magazine of the Pan-African Fellowship of Evangelical Students.

34   Philippians 3:5, 8-9.

35   *Evangelical Magazine of Wales*, 1969, pp.5-6. For a striking sermon on the subject see Lloyd-Jones's *Honour to Whom Honour* (1952).

36   *Evangelical Magazine of Wales*, 1969, p.6. The reference to suppressing the Welsh accent is a reminder that Welsh was thought to be socially an inferior form of

Few today would wish to question the place of ethnic cultures or the value of regional and minority languages in society, but so determined was Lloyd-Jones to retain Welsh Christian tradition, that is the tradition of the Welsh Calvinistic Methodists, that when he moved to London he would not conform to the English pattern of doing things, either at Westminster Chapel or in Inter-Varsity Fellowship circles. Because, in his view, the Welshman has a 'higher rate of intelligence' and is 'more theologically inclined than the Englishman', his purpose in coming to England was to teach the English 'this element of depth' which they lacked. With unabashed confidence he told 'the English many times' that he had 'come amongst them as a missioner... Though I put it in a jocular form, I really mean it.' Indeed, to reverse the argument, any idea that the Welsh needed the help of the English was as 'utterly superficial' as the idea 'that Britain needs the help of America... It is we who have got the real contribution to make because of this element of depth.'[37]

Three main points arise from all this: Lloyd-Jones's understanding of the temperament, the importance for him of the Welsh language, and his belief in the superiority of the Welshman to the Englishman.

As might be expected, his view of the Welsh was favourable. His theory was that psychologically there were 'a number of different levels' in the Welsh personality each one independent of the other. Among these levels, feelings were the most superficial, but then came emotion, imagination, a sense of the melancholic and tragic, reason, clarity of argument, systematic thinking, a feeling for the truth and finally the will, which 'is not easy to reach'. It 'is possible for one level to be awake while another sleeps', which explains why the Welshman can be moved by his feelings alone, or by his interest in argument or public speaking without any further commitment—the danger of being 'religious without being Christian'. Thus the Welshman's feelings are 'merely a thin layer on the surface...underneath is the thick, strong layer...namely the mind'. The Englishman has one unified and 'totally simple character', whereas the Welshman is more complex, 'with many facets' to his personality.[38]

The result, according to Lloyd-Jones, was Welsh stability, conservatism, preference for authority and exactness of thought, and it was for these kinds of reasons that the '"Via Media" of the Church of England or Arminianism [was] too indistinct and not systematic enough for the

---

speech in some quarters: as Alan Butt says, 'many Welsh people find it convenient to lose even their accent as they rise in the world'. A.B. Philip, *The Welsh Question* (Cardiff, 1975), p.47.

37 *Evangelical Magazine of Wales*, 1969, p.9. 'He loved the other nations' but it was 'sometimes with a sardonic smile'. F. and E. Catherwood, *The Man and His Books*, p.33.

38 Lloyd-Jones, 'Religion and Features', pp.2-6.

Welshman'.[39] It was either Calvinism or Catholicism, with their more precise positions, which appealed most to the Welsh. Whether this psychology of the Welsh temperament is scientifically tenable or merely an example of unrestrained partiality we leave for others to judge, but it seems perfectly feasible that such levels of personality are present in most people. Nonetheless, the same ideas resurfaced again in 'Nationalism, Tradition and Language'. The Welshman was a mystic, 'a bit of a dreamer', emotional but not sentimental like the English. He was essentially a humble man, helpful and tending towards self-denial, but above all his thoughts were of a greater depth than his English neighbours. He instinctively took to the cut and thrust of 'discussion, questions and answers', and 'the essence of the Welsh genius' was the ability to deal with 'profound questions' and 'give expression to the truth', particularly through 'incomparable' preaching.[40] And because of 'uncommon mental abilities' the Welshman refuses 'to conform with the majority'[41] and is inclined towards preciseness and definitions: 'He prefers authority and systems which set out truth clearly in every point and which reconciles everything together.'[42] If there is a downside to being Welsh, it is that 'We are also natural actors and imitators', 'lazy by nature' and, disliking change, 'very conservative'.[43]

Such were some of the elements, as Lloyd-Jones understood it, in the nature of a Welshman. He was a dissident at heart, a protestor, an individualist and Nonconformist with a good deal of the 'serf complex' ('Cymlethdod y taeog') bred into him by 'the past history of our nation'.[44] The problem was that he belonged to a smaller and more dependent country in which 'the overwhelming direction of...social and economic life' was 'towards greater integration with the English way of life', and this was unfortunate for Wales.[45]

The dominance of a larger nation over a smaller one was nothing new, but in the case of Lloyd-Jones, we see a concern for national survival allied to a strong sense of ethnic superiority. Edwin King, for example, recalled an occasion when 'he gave an address to the Church of England Jews' Society in which he said that as a Welshman, he had a kind of

---

39   *Ibid*, p.5.

40   *Evangelical Magazine of Wales*, 1969, pp.6, 9-10.

41   *Barn*, April, 1963, p.173.

42   Lloyd-Jones, 'Religion and Features', Part 3, p.5.

43   *Evangelical Magazine of Wales*, 1969, p.6, and 'Religion and Features', Part 3, p.5. For this reason it is 'extremely difficult to reach the will of the Welshman' and to move it. 'Religion and Features', Part 3, p.6.

44   *Evangelical Magazine of Wales*, 1969, p.6. This reference is to years of poverty and tenant farming.

45   Philip, *The Welsh Question*, p.71.

affinity with the Jews'.[46] In the Old Testament the Jewish nation was also small by comparison to many other nations, yet in spite of this and of 'all its failings, and sin and weaknesses' Israel had been chosen by God to bring his revelation of the truth into the world. For much of her history Israel had been overshadowed by her neighbours and in New Testament times she was a vassal state of Rome. But Israel was a nation raised up by God 'for his own purpose'[47] and it was this Messianic element that set them apart from the other nations. While the situation with regard to ancient Israel was historically unique, the sense of isolation and special-ness was not that far from the 'inestimable value' of Welsh Christian trad-ition. It was also to the Jews he referred when answering the question as to whether Wales had 'made any particular contribution to the Church's understanding of the truth?': the 'genius of the Jew lies in his talent for expression. I believe up to a point that the same thing is true of us. This is our particular gift.'[48]

The same interest in ethnic minorities arose in a sermon on the 'Woman of Samaria' in 1964: 'I was amazed...it lent itself to the occas-ion as the condition of the Samaritans was so similar to that of modern Wales—Nationalism, interest in religion and theology, preaching etc.'[49] But it found its widest expression within the International Fellowship of Evangelical Students. There he warned 'of the dangers of Western dom-ination' and did much to encourage the indigeneity of developing count-ries such as those in Africa and Asia. Chua Wee-hian's observation was that Martyn Lloyd-Jones's Welshness 'helped considerably', and in the 1947 conference at Harvard he amused some of the delegates with a defiant comment 'when he insisted that he would not allow the English or the Church of England to formulate his Christian perception of the truth!'.[50] Whether he was as intent on keeping the English out as bringing the others in is more than likely, but to be fair much of the groundwork in overseas Christian development had been done either by English graduates or with their support.[51] Moreover, had there been Anglican colonialism or 'Western domination' the IFES would soon have folded, but the reverse was true. The implications of one group eclipsed by

46   Edwin King, tape recorded conversation, 31 March, 1995. No date was given but it was probably the late 1950s or early 1960s.

47   Lloyd-Jones, 'Religion and Features', Part 2, p.2.

48   *Evangelical Magazine of Wales*, 1969, pp.8-10.

49   Lloyd-Jones, *Letters 1919-1981*, p.117. He had preached in Birmingham on John 4.

50   Catherwood (ed.), *Chosen by God*, pp.124, 113.

51   D. Johnson, *Contending for the Faith* (Leicester, 1979), pp.273-274. National Christian Unions that had imitated a western model were 'very few', and in most countries languages and circumstances guided the Unions and the gospel was 'clearly geared to local needs'. *Ibid*.

another may also have had its ramifications in the remnant principle and
the 'Gideon scenario' of David against Goliath and Gideon against the
Midianites[52] where right triumphed over might. When Lloyd-Jones used
the quotation, 'the greatest things in this world [have] been done by small
men and small nations!', it was no tongue-in-cheek comment. That he
meant what he said appears, for example, in his lecture, 'John Knox—
The Founder of Puritanism', in which he describes the Reformer as 'of
short stature' and adds, autobiographically, 'a fact not without
significance!' That Knox was apparently 'not a handsome man' or
'distinguished in appearance as judged by modern standards'[53] was
important since it shifted the glory away from man to God. The same
thought arises in *The Weapons of our Warfare* where, quoting 1
Corinthians 10:1 and 10, he suggests that Paul 'was not of striking
appearance' but 'probably, according to all accounts, a short man with a
bald head and also suffering inflammation of the eyes'.[54] Lloyd-Jones
was of course a short man. Whether he was influenced at times by taller
people is possible, certainly Edwin King thought so,[55] and it would not be
surprising given that many of his friends were taller than he was. But that
aside, Lloyd-Jones may have been less secure than his public persona
suggested and it is possible that he shared what A.B. Philip identified as a
Welsh characteristic, 'an inferiority complex towards England and its
people'.[56] If this was so it would help explain why on the one hand he
was a Welshman and 'proud of it' and on the other how he harboured 'a
real contempt for the English'.[57]

Temperamentally the Welshman was a Celt and Lloyd-Jones believed
that Celts have 'a high regard for the importance of doctrine and a
national aptitude for theology'.[58] He argued for national differences in
emotional and intellectual outlook, and when distinguishing between
different parts of Britain he made it clear that Celtic Scotland 'had retained more of the older art of biblical exposition and theological interest
than the South', and this was true of 'Wales and Northern Ireland' too.

---

52   1 Samuel 14:6 and Judges 7.
53   Lloyd-Jones, *The Puritans*, p.262.
54   D.M. Lloyd-Jones, *The Weapons of our Warfare* (1964), p.10. The biblical
references include Paul's assessment of himself: 'who in presence am base among you',
and the remarks of his critics that 'his bodily presence is weak, and his speech contemptible', 1 Corinthians 10:10.
55   Edwin King, 31 March, 1995. 'Doctor was very susceptible to tall people, this
was one of his weaknesses.' Packer writes of 'this slight Welshman with the large domed
head', in C.E. Fant and W.M. Pinson (eds.), *Twenty Centuries of Great Preaching* (Waco,
TX, 1971), XI, p.268.
56   Philip, *The Welsh Question*, p.322.
57   John Caiger, tape recorded conversation, 11 February, 1992.
58   J. Elwyn Davies, letter to author, 3 February, 1995.

But this begs the question as to whether, if a church-by-church survey were made, it would show a lower percentage of expository preaching in England, 1900 to 1950, compared to Scotland, Wales and Northern Ireland. Much depends on what we mean by expository preaching. To find contemporary preaching weak by comparison with our 'evangelical fore-fathers'[59] was not so much a comment on the general 'religious scene' as Murray suggests, as an anti-English way of looking at things. This is clear from his further remarks in which, 'Greatly daring', he criticized 'certain aspects of English Evangelicalism' and Englishmen in particular. But if preaching had declined in England it had also declined in the rest of Britain, and if English evangelicals paid lip-service to the past it was also true that Welsh believers indulged in the same kind of backward-looking-Christianity, to 1904 and 1859, to Daniel Rowland and Howell Harris. As for 'the older art of biblical exposition' and 'preaching (in its truest meaning)'[60] perhaps there was more of it than he knew.

It is doubtful also if he was justified in distinguishing between the four ethnic groups in Great Britain on the grounds of intellectual capacity and faithfulness to God's Word. There is, it is true, a distinct Welsh culture as, indeed, there are English, Scottish and Irish cultures which are 'quite different',[61] and we can agree with Rhys Davies that there is such a thing as a Celtic sense of the visionary and poetic.[62] Genetic and environmental factors are important and Lloyd-Jones agreed: our 'views are determined by a number of accidents... Celts and Saxons start with a different bias and prejudice'.[63] But such has been the intermixing of accents and traditions in modern Britain, 'the closer integration of culture in Wales and of the Welsh economy with their English counterparts, as well as the decline of the Welsh language' itself, as A.B. Philip put it,[64] that entities such as Celtic individualism or Saxon inflexibility are found in most corners of the British Isles.

---

59   Murray, *The Fight of Faith*, p.72. This was cause six of the eight 'General Causes' of weakness in British evangelicalism outlined by Lloyd-Jones at the Kingham Hill Conference in 1941, pp.70-74.

60   *Ibid*, pp.74, 72. 'This address, delivered as it must be remembered in private, provides one of the clearest indications of ML-J's approach to the contemporary religious scene'. *Ibid*. The whole Kingham Hill address was aimed more at the English situation than any other, but number six of the eight 'General Causes' is more specific.

61   P.E. Mayo, *The Roots of Identity* (London, 1974), p.86.

62   Rhys Davies, *My Wales*, pp.14-15.

63   D.M. Lloyd-Jones, *Evangelistic Sermons* (Edinburgh, 1983), p.59. Sermon dated 1931.

64   Philip, *The Welsh Question*, p.323.

The Welsh Language

The Welsh language, however, was a matter 'of very great value' to Lloyd-Jones. He was a Welsh-speaking Welshman and his preaching among Welsh-speaking people in Wales 'added to the effect and influence of his sermons'.[65] He believed that the preservation and continued use of Welsh strengthened the 'Welsh "anian"' and to the extent 'that you lose the language you will also tend to lose this "ethos"'. So Welsh was more than a means of communication, it was 'a way of thinking and feeling, even a way of life',[66] and it was a safeguard against uniformity. What Lloyd-Jones had in mind was the violation of personality and the making of a 'standard type' of believer such as produced by cults. But the 'standard type' was also a reference to 'the establishment', that is to the English universities and the English Church.[67]

Once again Lloyd-Jones used his biblical knowledge to demonstrate his point. The purpose of a regional language like Welsh, set as it was among so many other languages and against a majority language like English, was analogous to 'the whole question of the inspiration of Scripture'.[68] Scripture was not mechanically transmitted and there was a variation of style between the writers. They were 'all controlled by the same Spirit' and directed as to what they should write, but they expressed 'their personality' in the way they wrote. Thus, if you can 'recognize Paul's style as distinct from that of John or Peter', the same is true of nationality and language. The 'peculiar quality' of Welsh was that it had the capacity to 'convey aspects of the glory of the gospel in a way which ...a Welshman alone can do',[69] and this was especially evident in the case of Welsh hymns with their 'emphasis on the heart and the affections' as well as the mind.[70] 'I am sorry for the people who do not understand Welsh!', he said, when preaching on the theme of praise and worship in 1959:[71] there was simply 'no comparison' between English and Welsh hymns.[72] Welsh was a better means of thinking and feeling about the faith, a better expression of praise. Gwynfor Evans and Ioan Rhys defined this 'peculiar quality' as something inherited from the old Welsh and the Methodist revival which 'produced, not hymns as the English

---

65   *Evangelical Magazine of Wales*, 1969, p.6, and Lord Cledwyn, letter to author, 8 November, 1989.

66   *Ibid*, and G. Evans and I. Rhys in O.D. Edwards (ed.), *Celtic Nationalism* (London, 1968), p. 221.

67   *Ibid*, p.6.

68   *Ibid*, p.10.

69   *Evangelical Magazine of Wales*, 1969, p.6.

70   *Banner of Truth*, June, 1975, No.141, p.20.

71   *Westminster Record*, November, 1968, Vol.43, No.11, p. 174.

72   *Evangelical Magazine of Wales*, 1969, p.6.

know them, but lyric poetry as great as any in the Welsh language', and Lloyd-Jones would have agreed with this. But it was not only 'the joie de vivre'[73] of the old Welsh, it was the deeper doctrinal content as well as the 'grandeur and dignity' of the language which, he was convinced, exceeded English hymns. Welsh was thought to be an ideal vehicle for the expression of theological truth and liberty of the Spirit, and it was this almost mystical element that Lloyd-Jones was unable to utilize at Westminster Chapel.[74] In effect, 'God had so gifted' Welsh Christians with this unique means of declaring the gospel that a moral and spiritual obligation rested on them to learn and use the language: indeed, it was their 'bounden duty to do so'.[75]

Yet in spite of all this, Welsh had hardly changed in five hundred years and words had to be invented and added to the language to incorporate modern forms of knowledge and expression. In that sense Welsh could not match the variety and breadth of the English language and not even Lloyd-Jones had the same facility of words in Welsh as he had in English. Since the use of Welsh was outlawed in official business in the Act of Union of 1536—'the most important manifestation of the anglicizing tradition in Wales'[76]—English had become embedded in Welsh culture as the language of commerce and industry. Of course Welsh writers and poets became a vehicle for the arts and humanities and later for the sciences as well, but whether Welsh provided a better way of thinking about the Christian faith depends upon one's point of view. Many would feel that there is little to match the 1611 King James Bible or much of the English literature that it generated.

Although Lloyd-Jones believed Christians in Wales had a duty to learn the language he was not saying that Welsh alone should be spoken. After all, Wales had been in some measure bilingual since the conquest of Wales by Edward I in the thirteenth century and Lloyd-Jones himself regularly preached in both languages. His point was that to preserve national identity, Welsh should be used and in this he was adamant: people who go to live in Wales should learn Welsh and non-Welsh-speaking Welshmen should learn their own language. 'It is laziness' not to do so.[77]

---

73   Edwards, *Celtic Nationalism*, p.234.

74   As, for example, when preaching on Christian worship from Ephesians 5:19— 'There is a Welsh hymn that puts what I am anxious to say at the moment perfectly.' *Westminster Record*, November, 1968, p.174. The use of Welsh before an English congregation would have been pretentious and out of place, and, to my knowledge, Lloyd-Jones never did so.

75   *Evangelical Magazine of Wales*, 1969, p.11.

76   Philip, *The Welsh Question*, p.42.

77   *Evangelical Magazine of Wales*, 1969, p.11.

The logic of Welshmen speaking their own language might seem plain enough, but not all Welshmen wanted to learn Welsh. Census returns for the years 1901 to 1981 show a constant decline in the number of people in Wales who could speak Welsh, and notwithstanding the efforts of the Welsh Nationalist Party, Plaid Cymru, the Welsh Language Society, a Welsh language fourth television channel, the teaching of Welsh in schools and Papurau Bro (community papers), by 1981 the figure had dropped from the 50% of 1901 to 19%. There were, certainly, spatial differences between strong heartland areas like Bala where the figure in 1971 was 80% and in Llangeitho where it was 79%, but apart from Welsh-speaking Wales which was mainly in the west of the Principality, the rate of decline over the years 1901 to 1981 was constant. Welsh church attendance had also declined. Chapel had been a major centre for integrating Welsh language and culture.[78] So despite optimistic claims from Welsh interest groups and Lloyd-Jones's conviction about the learning of Welsh, the reality was rather different. To be fair, while Welsh was a matter of 'very great importance' to Lloyd-Jones he did not share the extreme view that to lose the language was to lose everything: that was to be 'guilty of going too far'. What troubled him, as we have seen, was loss of identity, 'the slavish way that so many Welshmen' appeared to lose their individuality through anglicization, something neither the Scots nor Irish had managed to do 'in spite of having, to a large extent, lost their language'.[79]

The English

Coming to his alleged 'contempt for the English'[80] and belief in the superiority of the Welsh, on the surface it may seem innocuous enough, but underneath there were some strong anti-imperialist feelings and harmful generalizations. For example, his view was that the English were pragmatists with 'a genius for compromise'. Pragmatism and the 'via media appeals to the Englishman' because 'he likes the idea of compromise' and dislikes 'over-precise definitions'. Indeed, there is 'a hatred of definitions and precise statements'.[81] Because he is a

---

78 Chapel and language are closely related in C. Baker, *Aspects of Bilingualism in Wales* (Clevedon, 1985). As attendances at Welsh chapels declined, so did attitudes to the Welsh language change; chapel was 'no longer the main transmitter of Welsh culture', *ibid*, p.148. In the case of children between ten and thirteen years of age, 'having and preserving a favourable attitude to Welsh and relatively favourable attainments in Welsh were most strikingly linked to Welsh religious services', *ibid*, p.179.

79 *Evangelical Magazine of Wales*, 1969, p.10.

80 He was charged with despising the English by A.T. Davies, although he denied it. *Barn*, June, 1963, p.236.

81 Lloyd-Jones, *The Puritans*, pp.277, 221.

compromiser, the Englishman is an Arminian rather than a Calvinist. The
'English way of thinking' is not only superficial—'There is no depth or
depths in his character'[82]—it is 'dangerous to Protestantism',[83] which
relies on exact statements and doctrinal precision.

Put another way, the typical Englishman is 'an out-and-out empiricist
who moves carefully without knowing in what direction', rather like 'the
glory of the British Empire' which did not have 'a written Constitution. It
just happened, and with the principle of empiricism enthroned...she
"muddled through"'.[84] So, in effect, the English do not think; they have
an innate dislike of precision and rather than follow a principle, they
settle for moderation. In terms of the Christian faith this amounted to 'a
little superficial religion' with 'no great doctrinal content', and to a
nebulous 'brotherliness' which merely 'strives to create a good mankind' and no more. 'In a word', it was 'to agree with Thomas Arnold
who defined religion as "morality touched by emotion"'.[85]

The tragedy, as Lloyd-Jones saw it, was that the English way of thinking and doing things had done great harm among Welsh students who
had been heavily influenced by the Student Christian Movement which,
as we shall see in our next chapter, was more liberal and open-minded
than the Inter-Varsity Fellowship. Above all he was disturbed by the way
in which they became 'adorers of William Temple, the most typical
Englishman you could ever find', and 'one of the worst influences, not
only upon the Christian life of Wales, but upon the Welsh life of Wales'.[86]
By 1908, when Temple was only a deacon in holy orders, he had become
a popular speaker in the Workers' Educational Association, the Young
Men's Christian Association, the Student Christian Movement and other
societies, and from Iremonger's biography it is clear that Temple was
consulted by these groups as much as Lloyd-Jones was in IVF circles. In
addition, Temple was at the heart of ecumenical affairs in the early days
and presided over the founding of the British Council of Churches in
1942.[87] After 'influencing the IVF for thirty years', Lloyd-Jones
admitted in 1969 to a sense of failure that Welsh students had 'been too
ready to conform': they 'have not let me down exactly—but have been
sort of battling against me'. The trend was 'to go under the umbrella' of
the larger group and to follow William Temple and the SCM, the 'big
organization', and that was the cause of the 'present deplorable condition

82   Lloyd-Jones, 'Religion and Features', Part 15, p.15.
83   *Barn*, June, 1963, p.236.
84   Lloyd-Jones, *The Puritans*, p.221.
85   Lloyd-Jones, 'Religion and Features', Part 3, p.4.
86   *Evangelical Magazine of Wales*, 1969, p.9. William Temple, Archbishop of
York 1929-42 and of Canterbury 1942-44.
87   F.A. Iremonger, *William Temple: His Life and Letters* (London, 1948), p.413.

in Wales'.[88] That large numbers of Welsh students chose not to follow Lloyd-Jones and his Welsh way of doing things probably reflected a wider field of interest as much as anything else, but if the SCM group did 'adore' Temple it is equally true that the IVF group and similarly minded people idolized Lloyd-Jones as their leader.

Ultimately, Lloyd-Jones's feelings about 'the average Englishman' and the English way of life centred upon social status and class: 'I hope that I do not despise any person', he said in 1963,'but I admit to despising social or intellectual snobbery, and especially so in the religious realm'.[89] He also had the impression that religion and the Bible were sometimes 'valued solely in terms of England's greatness' and this had given rise to 'the charge of national hypocrisy'. Britain had been 'blessed in the past' because it had been religious, and God honours those who honour him, but when we 'advocate religion in order that we may be blessed we are insulting God' because the grounds of true worship are that he is Almighty and Holy; we worship him because of who he is. The idea that the 'more religious the nation, the more moral and the more dependable and solid is the nation' may be true, but it was a tempting proposition for 'statesmen and leaders to pay lip service to religion and to believe in its maintenance'[90] as a quid pro quo, for political purposes.

The idea of the English as the ruling class was never far away from the thinking of Lloyd-Jones. When referring to 1660 and the restoration of the monarchy in England his comment was: 'This is one of the few countries left in the world that has a monarch. This is not an accident, it is typically English. A fondness for kings and queens, a liking for titles and names, is a part of the whole outlook'. The Welsh, on the other hand, were 'a peasant people' and 'Never had the veneration for titles that is found so commonly in England'.[91] In his sermon 'What is the Church?' he makes the same distinction. He commends the subordination of nationalist feelings to the greater duty of placing 'a Christian brother before a Welshman' but in the following paragraph, speaking on separation from 'the orders of society', he refers to 'The squire! The Lord! the great men of the district; and the various gradations down until you come to the underling.' His point was fair enough: there is no room for a 'monarchical' or 'aristocratic principle' in Christianity: believers are equal although differently gifted. But his illustrations were distinctly

---

88   *Evangelical Magazine of Wales*, 1969, p.9.
89   Lloyd-Jones, *The Puritans*, p.221, and *Barn*, June, 1963, p.236.
90   D.M. Lloyd-Jones, *The Evangelical Quarterly*, January, 1942, Vol.XIV, No.1, p.14.
91   Lloyd-Jones, *The Puritans*, p.225.

anti-English, and the rich man of James 2:1-9 became '"the Lord of the Manor"'.[92]

In a letter to his friend Douglas Johnson, Lloyd-Jones said that if he were ever to write 'a best seller' (it was a tongue-in-cheek remark) his thesis would be 'that the main cause of our present ills [1940] is due to the tragic break-down and failure of the middle-class in this country [England] due especially to their aping of the aristocracy in sending their children to public schools'.[93] This was one of the reasons why he reacted so strongly to William Temple. He had been to Rugby School before going up to Oxford, and the significance of Rugby was the influence of Thomas Arnold, Headmaster from 1827 to 1842. Lloyd-Jones referred to this in a sermon dealing with 'righteousness without holiness' in 1956: 'I am afraid that in many respects Thomas Arnold of Rugby was mainly responsible for...the so-called Public School religion, which is concerned about producing a gentleman, not a saint'. The inference was that by teaching religion and morality Arnold believed people would behave 'in a nice, decent, respectable' manner and produce a 'law-abiding society', but the 'appalling thought' for Lloyd-Jones was that people could be moral and decent, and even 'enjoy public worship without knowing God!'[94]

There can be no doubt that it was Lloyd-Jones's Welshness rather than any theological position which accounted for the majority of these feelings. Lloyd-Jones had grown up in an atmosphere of antagonism between church and chapel and one of the great questions of his youth was the disestablishment of the Church of Wales. It had been a long and divisive struggle, but when it finally came and the pre-1662 endowments were 'secularised and transferred to the University of Wales and county

---

92   Lloyd-Jones, *What is the Church?*, p.12: 'and that is not an easy thing for me to say'.

93   Lloyd-Jones, *Letters 1919-1981*, pp.56-57. Such a book 'would evacuate Westminster Chapel of all who claim any relationship to the aristocracy!'

94   D.M. Lloyd-Jones, *The Gospel of God* (Edinburgh, 1985), pp.360-361, 261. See also *The New Man* (Edinburgh, 1992), p.193. Lloyd-Jones's analysis of Arnold agrees with Michael McCrum, *Thomas Arnold Head Master* (Oxford, 1989). Arnold's achievements have been both disparaged and exaggerated, but McCrum shows, p.5, that 'Goodness was more important than truth' at Rugby, and that the Bible for Arnold was 'a source of moral guidance' rather than doctrine. He believed that 'the State's chief function is education, administered by the Church', p.7, and that 'social action' rather than dogma was the only way to 'save the Church', p.7. Arnold had a very erastian view of Church and State and by 'Church' he meant only the Church of England. The qualities he required in a lower form master was that he should be 'a Christian and a gentleman, an active man, and one who has common sense', p.31. It was a Victorian and Anglican view but there is no real reason why these qualities should not co-exist or why they should appear to be contradictory. Certainly, Arnold saw them as two sides of the same coin. See also D.M. Lloyd-Jones, *Darkness and Light* (Edinburgh, 1982), pp.82, 204.

councils', it was considered by the majority of Welshmen to have been a victory for the Nonconformists.[95] What made matters worse was the sharpness of feelings that lay behind the division between church and chapel. Welsh Anglicanism was seen by many as 'an ecclesiastical version of English colonialism'[96] and since most of the landed middle and upper classes in Wales were Anglicans, it is not surprising that there was tension, especially in the Welsh-speaking heartlands where Lloyd-Jones had grown up. But just as important and as fiercely debated was the question of education in Wales. Nonconformists were in favour of a national education system under effective public control and with religious equality, which was not found in church schools. Anglicans and Catholics argued for the retention of denominational schools and they also wanted public funds to maintain them and this, for many Nonconformists, was incipient priestcraft..

Thus while he spoke against nationalism, he came very close to it himself. Indeed, if Welsh Nationalism is a protest against anglicization, Lloyd-Jones was 'on the side of the Welsh Nationalists'.[97] In that sense he did not cease to be nation-conscious. In the early days he refused 'automatically every invitation that came from England. I did not even consider them. I was called to Wales.' Eventually he accepted an invitation to speak at a Bible Witness Rally at the Royal Albert Hall in 1935[98] and thereafter his visits to England increased, but on matters Welsh there was no compromise or middle ground. In fact so determined was he at one time that when asked by Bethan Phillips, his future wife, 'whether she or Wales came first [he] had to say that Wales came first'.[99] When speaking at the centenary of Westminster Chapel in 1965 because the second pastor, Henry Simon, came from Pembrokeshire he 'did not acknowledge him as a Welshman' at all.[100]

---

95   Machin, *Politics and the Churches*, p.306. The Disestablishment Act received the Royal Assent in September 1914, but was not implemented until March 1920 when the four Welsh dioceses separated from the Province of Canterbury and became an autonomous Anglican province. See also P.M.H. Bell, *Disestablishment in Ireland and Wales* (London, 1969), and Walker, *A History of the Church in Wales*.

96   Evans, *The Welsh Revival of 1904*, p.186.

97   *Evangelical Magazine of Wales*, 1969, p.7.

98   Lloyd-Jones, *Centenary Address*, p.22. See also Murray, *The First Forty Years*, p.301.

99   Lloyd-Jones, *Letters 1919-1981*, p.6. 'That was certainly the most awful question I have yet been asked during my life. She was great enough to say that she thought still more of me for saying so.' On the other hand, perhaps she had little choice.

100 Lloyd-Jones, *Centenary Address*, p.8. There might have been an element of jocularity here but if there was, under the surface he was quite serious. 'He came from Pembrokeshire which is sometimes called "Little England beyond Wales"'. According to Evans and Rhys in Edwards (ed.), *Celtic Nationalism*, p.220, 'English had been the indigenous language of one or two areas like South Pembrokeshire for centuries'.

Yet none of this precluded criticism of the Welsh. Far from it. On preaching, for example, 'there were men who turned' it into 'entertainment [by] the over-use of illustration and stories... We had a glut of this especially in my own country of Wales.'[101] He severely criticized the Presbyterian Church of Wales and 'was very critical of his Welsh brethren over charismatic matters'.[102] His most devastating critque came in a lecture, 'The Tragedy of Modern Wales', to the Literary and Debating Society of Charing Cross Chapel in 1925 which was reported at length in the *South Wales News*. He rebuked Welshmen who 'worship degrees', and who formed 'spurious' aristocracies based on wealth, especially among the London Welsh: he attacked gambling, the membership of London Clubs where 'men ate and drank like beasts', wire-pulling in public and church life, excessive singing and the 'great abomination' of preacher politicians. Wales, once a Christian nation, had 'lost its soul' and was 'on her death-bed'. Not surprisingly, the lecture evoked a great deal of comment and produced a number of articles and letters. Editorials pronounced it a 'wild and indiscriminate abuse of his fellow country-men...an outbreak of hysteria', and in response to a letter defending him it was said, 'If Dr. Martyn Lloyd-Jones talks like this at twenty-five, we tremble to think what he will say about us when he is fifty'. Among those who spoke in his favour were Peter Hughes Griffiths, chairman of the meeting and minister of the Charing Cross Chapel, who referred to Lloyd-Jones's 'brilliant introduction' although he did not agree with all that he said, and Tomos Phillips 'the well-known eye specialist' and father of Bethan Phillips, who agreed with 'every word of it'.[103] Of course, the lecture was the product of a fiery young Welshman, but although time may have tempered some of his words he remained just as uncompromising and the lecture of 1925 could easily have been given in 1965.[104]

So far in this chapter we have not questioned the value of ethnic cultures or denied the role of nationhood in the Christian's experience. As Lloyd-Jones said, 'salvation...does not erase...national characteristics.

101 Lloyd-Jones, *Knowing the Times*, p.265.

102 Edwin King, 31 March, 1995.

103 *South Wales News*, 1925. February 7 p.7, February 9 p.6, February 14 p.4 , and February 11 p.4. There was 'loud and prolonged applause from his Welsh audience. Although seven speakers followed him, only one attempted to criticize what had been said', February 11 p.4. Lloyd-Jones apparently had no idea the lecture was to be reported but when interviewed afterwards said, 'he was not criticizing the Welsh nation as a nation but...its modern representatives'. *South Wales News*, 1925, February 11, p. 4. It was a good example of public condemnation but a softer approach in private. Perhaps Lloyd-Jones was closer to the Welsh preaching tradition than he realized.

104 For example, 'Nationalism, Tradition and Language', *Evangelical Magazine of Wales*, August/September, 1969, Vol .8, No.4, which carries the same characteristics.

It is the man or the soul which is re-born and not his...abilities nor his temperament... The personality, as such, remains the same'[105] and we agree with this. The problem is that while there is much that is commendable in what he says, he tends to generalize and much of what he said is coloured by anti-English feelings. We would not deny that the Welsh have their own brand of thinking, as do the Scots and the Irish, and it could only be blinkered reasoning which refused to admit that there were a lot of very good thinkers in England too. But much of the content of the first and third of his 1943 radio broadcasts was a parody of the English. In fact the whole series was more like an autobiographical tirade against his pet dislikes rather than a constructive discussion on an important subject. There were elements of truth in what was said, but his bold generalizing on matters of faith and practice were unconvincing. For example, he contended that Welsh services and public meetings lay great stress on preaching, whereas the English emphasis was 'on other things'. What he meant by 'other things' in this context was an 'eminent man', a 'Mayor or Lord Mayor' who was invited to take the chair, and as the guest speaker, 'to give his address—not sermon—after the choir has sung'. He was 'expected to speak on a topic of current affairs—political problems, moral problems—without raising a text from the Bible', and then the 'listeners—not the congregation—show their appreciation...by clapping their hands'. But of which church was he speaking? Occasionally it might have been true, in England or Wales, but on the whole it was inaccurate and misleading. The majority of churches were not like that. Again, he argued that English preachers 'usually' read from manuscripts 'fairly closely', producing 'an essay rather than a sermon'. But in the author's experience this was the exception: the use of notes in preaching was normal practice, but reading a sermon was rare. Similarly, 'the Englishman likes movements'—the Council of Free Churches, Student Christian Movement, Christian Endeavour, Keswick, Missionary Societies, Holiness and Prophetic movements, the Children's Special Service Mission and Young Life Campaign—whereas 'We as Welshmen, do not like a lot of small societies'; they are 'not congenial with our spirit as religious people'.[106] But why then did he associate with the Evangelical Movement of Wales, the Inter-Varsity Fellowship, the Banner of Truth Trust and the British Evangelical Council? Were not these movements and societies?

When it comes to his analysis of the English and Welsh character the same kinds of problem arise. Is it true that an Englishman's character is 'close to the surface' with 'no depth or depths', or that below the surface of a Welshman lies a 'thick, strong layer...namely the mind' with 'its love

---

105 Lloyd-Jones, 'Religion and Features', Part 2, p.5.
106 *Ibid*, Part 1, pp.3-5.

of reason and of definitions'? And is there any substance in the view that while Englishmen 'claim' to be controlled by reason 'he hates definitions and clear and plain bounderies' of thought?[107] Is it only Welshmen who think for themselves and 'believe in principles',[108] or is all this nothing more than special pleading? The latter seems more likely.

Lloyd-Jones and the Welsh

The irony of the situation is that while Lloyd-Jones had genuine feelings for Wales, his uncompromising identification with conservative evangelicalism earned him the reputation of being a fundamentalist, and 'as such he was largely ignored' by his own people. Those who held him in the highest regard were men like J. Elwyn Davies and others who had, as Davies himself said, 'come to faith in North and South Wales in the late forties and fifties' during the ministry of Martyn Lloyd-Jones, but it was significant that when he died in 1981, 'very little appeared in the Welsh press' about it.[109] The 'common people were prepared to hear him gladly', perhaps out of curiosity as much as anything else, but the majority of leaders in the Presbyterian Church of Wales 'had been considerably irked' by his outspoken convictions as had many others.[110]

As for the preservation of Welsh culture and nationality apart from preaching, Lloyd-Jones did nothing to promote it and played little or no part in London Welsh life. This was one of the points made in the editorial response to his lecture, 'The Tragedy of Modern Wales': 'where and when has Dr. Martin (sic) Lloyd-Jones done anything towards delivering Wales from its besetting sins and shortcomings?... A critic who claims the right to indict a nation should at least be able to show that he has laboured long to save it from itself.'[111] In his defence, Lloyd-Jones carried a heavy load of engagements and was frequently out of town, and when he was in Wales he probably felt that preaching in Welsh was contribution enough. On the question of nationality there was no quest for nationalism in the political sense but there was an ideal, and this was the Welsh Christian tradition based upon the Methodist Revival of the eighteenth century. But if a revived Methodism had awakened Wales to a new Nonconformity and consciousness of religion, it was hardly likely

107 *Ibid*, Part 3, pp.5, 3.

108 *Barn*, April, 1963, p.173.

109 J. Elwyn Davies, 3 February, 1995.

110 *Evangelical Magazine of Wales*, April, 1981, Vol.20, No.2, p.24. This was an embarrassment to them. Murray, *The First Forty Years*, pp.288-289. In the event, no invitation to Bala came and after he had kept Westminster Chapel waiting six months, he finally became co-pastor with Campbell Morgan in 1939. Murray, *The First Forty Years*, pp.346-351.

111 *South Wales News*, 9 February, 1925, p.6.

that Calvinistic Methodism was going to have the same effect in the twentieth century. Certainly the 1904-05 revival did nothing to restore the old position, and in 1969 his comment was that 'conditions, religiously speaking, are worse today in Wales than in England'.[112]

One should also take into account a strong element of tribalism and brotherliness in Welsh culture, especially in Welsh-speaking Wales, and a general feeling for the old values and beliefs. We are not saying that Lloyd-Jones wished to 're-establish communion with a fading Welsh way of life',[113] but there was more than a hint of the romantic in his references to the Welsh language and to the traditions of the Methodist fathers. Yet in spite of the clannishness of the Welsh, Lloyd-Jones was not a social being and, unlike other ministers, he did not have to keep his congregations together, they willingly came to him. In this sense he was on the periphery of things and although individually he helped many, it was characteristic of the man that his individualism made it hard for a large number of ministers to work alongside him.[114] Lloyd-Jones had been an individualist from the beginning.

Notwithstanding all of this, the preaching of Martyn Lloyd-Jones had a remarkable impact on his fellow Welshmen. Chapels 'all over the country invited him to prove his oratorical gifts in their pulpits'[115] and such were the numbers that attended his meetings in the 1920s and 1930s that Iain Murray used 'revival' to describe what was happening. To give two examples: an estimated 7,000 heard him at the 1935 Sasiwyn (Presbyterian quarterly meeting) at Llangeitho, and 2,000 at a meeting in Felinfoel in 1936.[116] Contemporary newspapers carried many such reports.[117] Even so, it is not our concern here to deal with the nature of his preaching so much as with its effect. Why, when Welshmen were struggling with unemployment, poverty and in some cases were growing 'impatient with the chapel' and the church, did so many people flock to hear him? It was not that he was demonstrative or had 'the old furious way' of the early revivalists.[118] In fact Lloyd-Jones had said, 'I am not and never have been a typical Welsh preacher', and when Rhys Davies went to hear him he was disappointed because instead of fire, he found 'a

---

112 *Evangelical Magazine of Wales*, 1969, p.8.

113 Philip, *The Welsh Question*, p.205.

114 D. Ben Rees, tape recorded conversation, 20 May, 1992.

115 Rhys Davies, *My Wales*, p.117.

116 Murray, *The First Forty Years*, pp.202-227, 299, 307-324. Sasiwn (the older spelling is Sassiwn) is a Welsh corruption of the English 'association'.

117 *The Western Mail, Herald of Wales* and other local and national newspapers, including *The British Weekly*, carried regular reports, as did the *Christian Herald*.

118 Rhys Davies, *My Wales*, pp.104, 118.

cold ruthlessness' in his preaching.[119] But such sermons as 'Christianity—Impossible with Men' (1928), 'Why Men Disbelieve' (1930) and 'Repentance: The Gate to the Kingdom' (1932) attracted great crowds and were relevant because they emphasized the cause of the troubles— 'the desecration of everything that is sacred and of God', and offered the answer—'to discover the mind of God' and return to him.[120]

If we accept that 'the hand of God was upon him'[121] what was happening was not unlike revival. But there were other, more 'worldly' reasons, chief of which was the celebrity factor. Lloyd-Jones did nothing to encourage media interest in his life and deliberately played down the idea of his sacrificing a medical career[122] for a less prosperous one in a poorer area of Wales. Nor, in his mind, was there anything noble about it since it had never occurred to him to go anywhere else: 'I was certain I was called to minister in Wales' where the need was greatest.[123] He had also inherited 'his father's radical views and concern for the poor and the under-privileged had had a profound effect upon him',[124] and this was probably a major factor in his going to Aberavon in 1928. But this was not how the newspapers and people of Wales saw it. The impact of his leaving Harley Street and a promising career as a consultant physician for a Mission in a depressed area of South Wales 'was, in those days, like Albert Schweitzer going out to Africa'.[125] It was a talking point, a sensation, and such were the columns of print which newspapers devoted to religious affairs in the first part of the twentieth century that it would have been unusual if Lloyd-Jones had not become well known. In that sense he had a lot going for him although he did not have the same media coverage after the late 1940s.[126] Still, it was the celebrity factor that initially caught the imagination of the Welsh: as D. Ben Lewis said: 'Listening as a child, it was this aspect of what he had given up which was

---

119 Murray, *The First Forty Years*, pp.146-147, and Rhys Davies, *My Wales*, p.119.

120 Lloyd-Jones, *Evangelistic Sermons*, pp.43, 25. This is a collection of twenty-one sermons preached between 1928 and 1937.

121 Catherwood (ed.), *Chosen by God*, p.179.

122 *Monthly Record*, Free Church of Scotland, April, 1941, p.81. 'I gave up nothing, I received everything.'

123 Lloyd-Jones, *Centenary Address*, p.22.

124 *Evangelical Magazine of Wales*, April, 1981, p.213.

125 D. Ben Rees, 20 May, 1992.

126 There are hardly any references, for example, in *The British Weekly* after 1949 in stark contrast to the 1920s and 1930s. One of the reasons for the decline of newspaper interest may have been the kind of message that he preached. Had there been an ecumenical interest it might have been different. On the other hand national newspapers were becoming less interested in religious affairs, and by the 1950s, the day of the printed sermon in a daily newspaper was long past.

present in all the conversations about him.'[127] But it was a combination not only of celebrity but of oratory and authority which brought all kinds of people to hear him, and what they heard was a voice of assurance in difficult times. Such was the interest that some 'of the poor of the valleys' saved their '"dole" money for weeks in order that they might travel to listen to him.[128]

Another reason for his success was the Welsh sense of occasion. As people went to hear David Lloyd-George and later Aneurin Bevan,[129] so they flocked to hear Martyn Lloyd-Jones, and in this sense at least, he certainly was in the great Welsh tradition of oratory and among the last to draw large congregations in Wales. These occasions were social events and people travelled in from the surrounding countryside, giving the whole day up to two or three meetings. In the early days he preached in churches where ministers were sympathetic, and many of these became annual visits, but later, when ministers moved on and in some cases were replaced with liberal-minded men, such was the strength of local feeling towards these visits that the tradition was allowed to continue: to have stopped them 'would have caused quite a stir'.[130] What was unique about this sense of occasion was that it was almost entirely Welsh. In England people went to hear W.E. Sangster, Leslie Weatherhead and Lloyd-Jones in large numbers, but there was not the same gala atmosphere. When people filled halls and churches in England to hear Lloyd-Jones the majority were evangelicals, whereas in Wales even those who disagreed or were indifferent went along—it was part of the tradition. Such was the case with Rhys Davies who was not a believer and had no wish to be 'induced...to be "saved"', and for a collier who responded to his preaching by saying that, 'as a Welshman it held and roused me, but as another man it left me cold'.[131]

The Church of England

Lloyd-Jones's parody of the English was largely driven by a lifelong distaste for Anglicanism which had its roots in his upbringing and background. In many respects it was a confrontational background in which Wales was set against England, Nonconformity against the Established

127 D. Ben Rees, 20 May, 1992.

128 *Y Goleuad* (Weekly News of the Presbyterian Church of Wales), February 1, 1933, Vol.63, No.8, quoted by Murray, *The First Forty Years*, p.308.

129 David Lloyd-George, Liberal Prime Minister 1916-1922. Aneurin Bevan, Minister of Health in Clement Atlee's Labour government of 1945 and architect of the National Health Service in 1948, and who was considered to be one of the finest orators of his day.

130 D. Ben Rees, 20 May, 1992.

131 Rhys Davies, *My Wales*, pp.119-120.

Church, and public school against state school. These were all part of the
chemistry of the situation. He could, it is true, lay aside his feelings and
talk with Anglican friends but such was his 'almost pathological loathing
of the Church of England'[132] and unwillingness to recognize that any
good thing could come out of the Church of England, even at the Reformation, that we need to consider the matter further.

In 1963, comparing cathedrals and parish churches to 'some of the
churches in the New Testament', he wrote of 'self-conceited
dignity...formal deathliness and...respectability' which was more reminiscent of 'pagan false religions...than the simplicity of the Early Church',
and of 'the spiritual famine of the ecclesia anglicana'. Quoting D.
Gwenallt Jones, who had crossed from Nonconformity via the social
gospel to Anglicanism before finally returning to Calvinistic Methodism,
he referred to the Anglican church as 'the old mother' and '"the old
traitoress"'.[133] Seven years later, at a meeting commemorating the sailing
of the Pilgrim Fathers, he cited 'John Foxe, the great martyrologist' who
believed 'there were still remnants of popery left in the Church of
England which he wished God would remove, for God knew that they
were the cause of much blindness and strife'.[134] In other words, the
Reformation had not gone far enough in the Church of England,[135] and
this was his point in 1962 when he distinguished between Puritanism and
mainstream Anglicanism. What he believed about the Puritans, who were
mostly Anglicans up to 1662, was that they were a movement 'for a pure
church, pure in practice as well as doctrine, pure in life as well as belief'.
'Essential Puritanism' was a desire that 'the Reformation of the Church
of England should be completed' and since 'the gathered church' was
'at the heart of the Puritan idea'[136] and of Scripture itself, the Church of
England could not be truly reformed until it had become congregational.
It was semi-reformed and still contained Catholic customs and traditions.
The only exception in the history of Anglicanism was the Puritan
movement, and that was 'a glorious exception', and this is how he saw his
erstwhile friend James Packer. He had regarded him 'as a latter-day

---

132 Alec Motyer, letter to author, 19 December, 1991.

133 *Barn*, April, 1963, pp.172-173. D. Gwenallt Jones was a Christian poet who
died in 1969. The quotation came at the end of a letter from Lloyd-Jones in his
controversy with A.T. Davies on Christianity. Davies, who had also moved from
Calvinistic Methodism to the Church of Wales, accused Lloyd-Jones of 'being infallible
and self-righteous as the Pharisees of old'. *Ibid*, p.171.

134 Lloyd-Jones, *Unity in Truth*, p.88. John Foxe (1516-87).

135 For example, 'confirmation' was something which the Anglicans inherited and
'just continued' from the Roman Catholic Church: 'it is simply a part of the
incompleteness of the Reformation of the sixteenth century'. D.M. Lloyd-Jones, *Joy
Unspeakable* (Eastbourne, 1995), p.47.

136 Lloyd-Jones, *The Puritans*, p.257.

Puritan' and would not acknowledge that he was 'a real Anglican' at all, predicting that his fellow-Anglicans would not accept him.[137]

Whether such a view of Puritanism is acceptable or not, and many would argue against his premise that 'a truly Reformed Church' is a gathered church, what is clear is his hostility to what he saw as 'the mechanics of worship' and a religion of externalities and doctrinal deadness.[138] Unlike the Puritans, the Church of England had no interest in going back to the New Testament and was only concerned to maintain its 'continuity and tradition' as a kind of bridge between Rome and Geneva. For Lloyd-Jones the claim 'to be Catholic as well as Reformed' was an expression of compromise and expediency, and this is what he meant by 'Anglican thinking among members of the Baptist Union, the so-called Congregational Church of England', Methodists, and other churches. By remaining in their denominations, reason rather than revelation became the controlling factor for evangelicals.[139] There were exceptions, but generally speaking, the Church of England was a lost cause and 'the greatest obstacle to revival' outside of Rome itself.[140]

He was especially critical of the first National Evangelical Anglican Congress held at the University of Keele, 4-7 April 1967, because it condemned the 'narrow partisanship and obstructionism' of earlier evangelicalism in the Church of England and pledged a new willingness 'to welcome truth from any quarter' and fellowship with other Christians whatever their differences. This was primarily an ecumenical issue but for Lloyd-Jones it was also an example of the nature of Anglicanism which, as he believed, was flawed through compromise and accommodation. He was right to say that Keele marked a change in the position of Anglican evangelicalism: it was a landmark. Delegates not only made an ecumenical commitment but were encouraged to place loyalty to the Church of England above that of loyalty to evangelicals in general, and this was clearly stated in the printed report.[141] Lloyd-Jones would not accept that men like John Stott and James Packer could be true evangelicals while at the same time nurturing a wider fellowship of Christians and, although there were exceptions—his brother Vincent, for example—he would not allow that Anglo-Catholics and Roman Catholics were Christians or that

---

137 Catherwood (ed.), *Chosen by God*, p.40.

138 Lloyd-Jones, *The Puritans*, p.257: 'God deliver us from stereotyped formal prayers!'—'they are not true to the New Testament teaching'. D.M. Lloyd-Jones, *The Sons of God* (Edinburgh, 1975), pp.165, 242.

139 Lloyd-Jones, *The Puritans*, pp.257-258.

140 John Caiger, tape recorded conversation, 11 February, 1992. Lloyd-Jones's own words. And yet almost all the leaders of the evangelical revival in the eighteenth century came from the Church of England.

141 P. Crowe (ed.), *Keele '67 Report* (1967), pp.15, 8. Also Lloyd-Jones, *Knowing the Times*, p.314. See further J.C. King, *The Evangelicals* (London, 1969), pp.120-121.

Rome would ever reform.[142] When Archbishop Ramsey, a man known for his openness towards Anglo-Catholics and liberals, was invited to speak at the Keele Congress Lloyd-Jones was 'amazed' that such a man should be 'called onto an evangelical platform... I still personally have to be satisfied that the man is really a Christian in the New Testament sense of the term at all.'[143] He was also doubtful about C.S. Lewis, and although he had written a favourable but short review of *The Screwtape Letters* in 1942, in 1963 he doubted that Lewis was a Christian.[144] Lewis was a moderate Anglican layman, neither Roman nor Genevan, but such was his popularity among conservative Christians that Lloyd-Jones thought he had 'almost become the patron saint of evangelicals', though he 'was never an evangelical and said so quite plainly himself'.[145] Obviously

---

142 On John Stott's suggestion that Rome might reform itself, Lloyd-Jones replied: 'That's impossible. I think the Roman Catholic Church will disintegrate; ...liberals like Hans Küng (who is not a Christian) will join the Church of England—he'd be happy there—while the conservatives will remain unreformed.' John Stott, 'A Visit to Dr. Lloyd-Jones', personal notes, 19 December, 1978. Used with permission.

143 D.M. Lloyd-Jones, tape recorded sermon, 1 November, 1974. Michael Ramsey had aroused a great deal of interest in his year of enthronement (1961) when he said that he expected 'to see some present-day atheists' in heaven. *Daily Mail*, 2 October, 1961. Lloyd-Jones's comment was, 'if this is true, if we are to expect to meet atheists in heaven, if a man can go to heaven who does not even believe in God, why should we ask him to believe in the Book? Why should we have a Christian Church at all?' *Free Grace Record*, Summer, 1969, Vol.2, No.11, pp.324-325. But according to John Huxtable who met him frequently, Ramsey was a man of 'honesty of thought' and 'deep spirituality', 'one of the very great Archbishops'. Huxtable, *As it seemed to me*, p.45. See J.I. Packer (ed.), *Guide-lines: Anglican Evangelicals Face the Future* (London, 1967), and *Keele '67: The National Evangelical Anglican Congress Statement, with Study Material* (London, 1967). One thousand people attended—519 clergy and 481 laymen.

144 *Inter-Varsity Magazine*, Summer term, 1942, Vol.XIV, No.5, p. 23. *The Screwtape Letters* (1941) was the first of C.S. Lewis's many books on Christian apologetics. Lloyd-Jones told *Christianity Today* (20, December, 1963, Vol.VILI, No.6) that 'because Lewis was essentially a philosopher, his view-of salvation was defective in two key respects: (1) Lewis taught and believed one could reason oneself into Christianity; and (2) Lewis was an opponent of the substitutionary and penal theory of the Atonement'. (Scrapbook cutting, page not known.) There is no doubt that Lewis had a philosophical turn of mind. He believed that reason was important in ascertaining the truth and gave much attention to imagination as a means of understanding, but his journey from atheism to rational theism did end in a full acceptance of Christian truth, and contra Lloyd-Jones we would not wish to question the validity of his conversion or faith.

145 Lloyd-Jones, *Knowing the Times*, p.21. This was the view of A.N. Wilson in his biography of Lewis: 'to the amazement of those who knew him in his lifetime, [he] has become in the quarter-century since he died something very like a saint in the minds of conservative-minded believers'. A.N. Wilson, *C.S.Lewis* (London, 1990), p.x. Lloyd-

Lewis did not meet the criteria of Lloyd-Jones's definition of a Christian. Packer's assessment that 'this kind of notional correctness was not achieved by anybody after the Apostle Paul' has some force.[146]

Intriguing, too, was Lloyd-Jones's sympathy for J.H. Newman and his search for truth. Newman had come from an evangelical family and he had immense influence on the Anglo-Catholic tradition in the Church of England. Lloyd-Jones had urged Iain Murray 'to get hold of Wilfred Ward's two-volume *Life of Cardinal Newman* which he had recently finished' and, during the 1941 IVF mission to Oxford, he was evidently pleased to have preached 'in the famous pulpit of John Henry Newman—in St. Mary's Church, where he preached while he was still in the Church of England'.[147] Lloyd-Jones was a prolific reader of all kinds of books but while the whole story of Newman 'fascinated him: where Newman had gone wrong, and how it had happened, what a great mind he had' and so on.[148] What especially caught his attention was how Newman came to see the Church of England as a compromise between Romanism and Protestantism, and how he moved to Rome. The same kind of response arose in the case of his old friend A.T. Davies who had moved to the Church of Wales: 'if he had, like Mr. Saunders Lewis turned Catholic I would understand and would see a kind of consistency although I would disagree completely'. In Lloyd-Jones's view Roman Catholics and evangelicals in Wales were 'the only two groups who know where they stand and what they believe': Anglicanism counted for nothing. The trouble with A.T. Davies and his High Church tendencies was that he had moved from a distinctive position in Calvinistic Methodism to an 'anti-theological', empiricist position and Lloyd-Jones could not understand such a defection. All he could hope was that 'some day we shall see ATD "coming to his senses"' by returning to the faith.[149] There is, of course, no question as to the antipathy of Lloyd-

---

Jones listened to a lecture by Lewis in 1941 and had lunch with him afterwards: they met again on a boat to Ireland in 1953. Murray, *The Fight of Faith*, p.52.

146 J.I. Packer, tape recorded conversation, 5 June, 1992. 'He was relating the sine qua non of true faith with being intellectually correct in terms of intellectual formulae achieved between the sixteenth and nineteenth centuries in certain streams of Protestantism.'

147 He referred to Newman as 'the main activator of the Oxford Movement and of Anglo-Catholicism' in *Barn*, June, 1963, p.237; to Newman on tradition and Scripture in *Knowing the Times*, p.341; and on the trend towards Rome and the beginning of the Evangelical Alliance in 1846, *ibid*, p.247. On the reference to Wilfred Philip Ward, *John Henry Newman* (London, 1912), see Murray, *The Fight of Faith*, p.710, and the further reference is on p.76. Newman resigned from St. Mary's in 1843 after a fifteen year incumbency. In 1845 he was received into the Roman Catholic Church.

148 F. and E. Catherwood, *The Man and His Books*, p.26.

149 *Barn*, June, 1963, p.173. John Saunders Lewis, a leading Welsh dramatist, literary historian and critic, and one of the founders of the Welsh National Party. He had

Jones to Rome and all it stood for, but it is striking how he was often more sympathetic to people in the Catholic Church than to people in the Church of England: before he died, 'a group of Jesuit priests in America' discovered his writings, and he was 'most happy' about it.[150]

It is evident from what we have seen in this and preceding chapters that Lloyd-Jones did not give sufficient credit for the doctrinal stand and intentions of Anglican evangelicals. That their doctrine of the church differed from his is clear enough both before and after Keele, but people like John Stott and James Packer, two of the leading Anglican evangelicals, also believed in the purity of the church, and Stott had said so: 'We do not believe in a doctrinally mixed church and in such comprehensiveness.'[151] Indeed, Stott's resolve to remain 'first and foremost an evangelical' was the 'probable reason' why he had not been appointed a bishop: 'I could not understand people who changed their theology on being made bishops. I'm committed to the purity of the church.' In spite of the imperfections of the Church of England, Stott could not 'disown the great majority of Anglicans as if they were not Christians': they were like 'Apollos, needing to be taught the way of the Lord'.[152] Lloyd-Jones agreed with this, at least the latter point, but remained adamant that neither Stott nor Packer, nor anyone else, would ever change the Church of England. Packer, a continuing evangelical although ecumenically involved, 'never had any qualms of conscience about the integrity' of his position, and men like Alec Motyer and Kenneth F.W. Prior, while under no illusions as to the faults of the Church of England and acknowledging Lloyd-Jones's 'deep distrust and dislike' of Anglicanism, nevertheless remained Anglican.[153]

---

grown up in a strong Calvinistic Methodist family but became a Roman Catholic in 1932. See M. Stephens (ed.), *The Oxford Companion to the Literature of Wales* (Oxford, 1986), pp.345-346.

150 See Lloyd-Jones, *Roman Catholicism*, and numerous other references in sermons and lectures. R.T. Kendall, tape recorded conversation, 16 November, 1991.

151 John Stott, tape recorded conversation, 16 November, 1991. These were his words to Lloyd-Jones.

152 John Stott, 'A visit to Dr. Lloyd-Jones', 19 December, 1978. 'I didn't add that both [Howard W.K.] Mowll and [Marcus L.] Loane had asked me to be a Sydney Coadjutor, that the Crown and Archbishop's secretary had been to see me, or that I'd declined to be nominated by friends for sees like Sheffield and Rochester.' Stott was invited to be a Sydney Coadjutor shortly before Mowll died, and Loane repeated the invitation a few years after he succeeded Mowll. The visit of the Crown and Archbishop's secretary was after Stott became Rector of All Souls in 1950, probably about 1955. The approach of 'friends' with regard to Sheffield and Rochester was sometime in 'the mid-1950s'. John Stott, letter to author, 28 July, 1997.

153 Motyer was vicar of St. Luke's, West Hampstead, 1965-70, and Principal of Trinity College, Bristol, from 1971. Prior was vicar of St. Paul's, Onslow Square, 1965-70, then Rector at Sevenoaks, Kent. When Motyer moved to London in 1965, Leith

The insistence that unless Christian truths were expressed in a certain way they were not genuine truths, effectively cut off the majority of Anglicans, although he remained friendly with some of them. Those who did go to hear him after 1966 were more cautious and 'would sift what they heard'.[154] Nor were they tempted to secede. He did not preach at All Souls although Stott had invited him, 'especially at our annual Doctors' service', although he addressed meetings of the Eclectic Society in its London groups on such topics as prayer and revival, and he did so 'after 1966'.[155] As we have said, he preached at St. Mary's in Oxford but he also attended a service at St. John's in Parkstone, Poole, when Motyer was preaching in 1960.[156] He had heard Stott preaching and there were other occasions when he was to be found in an Anglican church, but they were very few.

In fact his influence on the religious scene so far as the Anglicans were concerned was minimal. In the mid-1950s and 1960s such was the attraction of the Westminster Chapel pulpit that Anglicans and Nonconformists alike were impressed, but as he became more outspoken on ecumenical issues and, particularly after 1966, his influence declined. Nor could we say that the 'call' of 1966 inadvertently triggered a response among Anglican evangelicals as to their own position. There had been plenty of talking going on well before 1966 and 1967.[157] As Packer said, the Church of England had been 'in process of getting a total spring clean' since the 1950s.[158] *Prayer Book* and canon law revision was under way, the question of patronage had been raised, as had the value of the *Thirty-Nine Articles* and whether they should remain. Latimer House had been founded in 1959 and this in itself brought about 'a lot of ad hoc discussion' and the involvement of a number of 'top people at that time who met and formed a kind of strategy for Anglican evangelicals'.[159] So the planning for Keele went back three years to 1964 and its roots at least ten years,[160] and was going on while men like Motyer, Prior and others were visiting Westminster Chapel.

Samuel offered to propose him for membership of the Westminster Fellowship, but when he learned 'that the Fellowship was in effect erected on a secessionist basis [he] pursued the matter no further'. A. Motyer, 19 December, 1991.

154 Gilbert Kirby, tape recorded conversation, 6 August, 1991.

155 John Stott, letter to author, 31 December, 1991.

156 Alec Motyer, 19 December, 1991.

157 For Lloyd-Jones's views on the Keele Congress see *Unity in Truth*, pp.172-173, and tape recorded sermon on 1 Corinthians 16:13-14, 1 November, 1974. Private copy.

158 J.I. Packer, tape recording, 5 June, 1992.

159 *Ibid.*

160 Crowe (ed.), *Keele '67 Report*, pp.36-37.

Despite this blind spot for Anglicanism, at a personal level Lloyd-Jones had friends among Anglicans and was 'always ready to have commerce with them'. He believed that they erred by remaining in the Church of England and said so 'strongly, not to scorn them, but to try to lead them to the truth',[161] but there were some long-standing friendships. Stott 'had a very friendly relationship at a personal level right to the end' in spite of their differences, and the Central Hall disagreement of 1966 did not sour it.[162] Sir Norman Anderson was thankful for 'the warmth of his friendship and his dealing with individuals', and welcomed him as 'a man with whom I enormously enjoyed discussion'.[163] Philip E. Hughes spoke of 'the constancy of his friendship during more than thirty-five years', and Alec Motyer saw him as 'a great man and a good friend'.[164] D.R. Davies, a Welshman from Pontycymmer in Glamorgan, who moved from Unitarianism and Marxist Socialism to faith in Christ and was eventually ordained by Archbishop William Temple into the Church of England's ministry, spoke of Lloyd-Jones's preaching as an influence which 'defies analysis' and reached the depths.[165] Although Davies went through Nonconformity and settled for Anglicanism, Lloyd-Jones willingly put him in touch with Hodder & Stoughton who published his book, *On to Orthodoxy*, an account of his disillusionment with rationalism.[166]

All the same, Lloyd-Jones could never understand the appeal of Anglicanism. In the end, his anti-Anglicanism, as we suggested earlier, was essentially a Welsh view of the English. Being Welsh did not wholly account for his theology, although his upbringing and association with Calvinistic Methodism was a significant factor, but it gave emphasis to his attitude and was as much a 'national outlook' as any for which he condemned the English. Some of his criticisms of the Church of England were probably justified, this we would not dispute, but that does not allow for his lack of respect for Englishness or horror of Anglicanism. Christopher Catherwood, seeking, no doubt, to mitigate the circumstances, suggests that 'the Doctor did not ever become "anti-Anglican" per se. It was simply that in England, the Church of England was by far the biggest of the "mixed" denominations'.[167] But this does not match the

161 *Barn*, June, 1963, p.236.
162 John Stott, tape recording, 16 November, 1991.
163 Sir Norman Anderson, letter to author, 6 May, 1991. Further references to Lloyd-Jones by Norman Anderson are made in his book, *An Adopted Son* (Leicester, 1985).
164 Alec Motyer, 19 December, 1991.
165 D.R. Davies, *In Search of Myself* (London, 1961), p.194.
166 *Barn*, April, 1963, pp.173, 198. D.R. Davies, *On to Orthodoxy* (London, 1939).
167 Catherwood, *A Family Portrait*, p.128.

evidence: as one of his admirers said, 'he was never "fair" to the Church of England! It was his bête noire.'[168] Nor does it account for his singularity in the matter. He did not, for example, object to the Church of Scotland or to the Lutheran Church in Scandinavia or Germany in the same way. All of these maintained the establishment principle and the element of national recognition but they did not generate the same kind of emotion and annoyance that the Church of England did: not even his antipathy to Roman Catholicism equalled it.

As we have said, he related to certain individual Anglicans, and during his lifetime did nothing to discourage his daughters and grandson from going to Oxford or becoming term-time Anglicans,[169] but he remained 'extremely vocal' in his criticism of the Church of England[170] and of what he perceived Englishness to be. It was part of his national outlook. As he said, 'national characteristics influence the lives of religious men' and their 'understanding of the truth'.[171]

In view of all this, and it has its own significance, we need to ask how much of a leader Lloyd-Jones was? The next two chapters seek to answer this question.

---

168 Alec Motyer, 19 December, 1991. This was also Stott's view in his notes of 19 December, 1978.

169 Catherwood, *A Family Portrait*, p.173. This was Elizabeth and Ann. His grandson Christopher went to Oxford in 1973 and attended St. Ebbe's with his grandfather's 'full knowledge and permission'. Evidently St. Ebbe's had the most 'active spiritual life' in the city at the time. *Ibid.*

170 John Stott, letter to Eric Fife, 9 September, 1981. Used with permission.

171 Lloyd-Jones, 'Religion and Features', Part 2, p.6, and Part 3, p.1.

CHAPTER 7

The Nature of his Leadership:
'Standing alone against the whole world'

In the autumn of 1950 Lloyd-Jones told his Westminster Chapel congregation that there was 'nothing so unchristian in the Church today as this foolish talk about "personality"'. What he had in mind was the kind of self-confidence which attracted people to the speakers themselves rather than to God. Such 'purely fleshly and carnal' behaviour had no part to play in the work of the ministry.[1] And yet those who were listening to that Sunday morning sermon were confronted with one of the most outstanding personalities in post-war British Nonconformity.

There were other personalities who not only inspired their followers but knew how to fill pews as well. There was nothing new about this. The evangelical world has always had a tendency to produce larger-than-life figures—C.H. Spurgeon in London, R.W. Dale in Birmingham, Alexander Maclaren in Manchester. Great crowds followed great preachers. This larger-than-life element was not unique to great men alone. It was just as true of smaller churches where ministers were respected as the Lord's servant dispensing the Lord's word. Indeed, the centrality of the pastor who was at the same time teacher, counsellor, guide and example to his flock laid itself wide open to the cult of personality. Where the pulpit was pre-eminent and where the minister although fallible was seen, to use Nancy Ammerman's words, as 'a little above the messiness of the everyday world', the position of the minister 'was one of enormous power'.[2]

So although pulpit giants have largely disappeared, at least in Britain, the larger-than-life tendency in evangelicalism lives on. True, post-war society was becoming less deferential towards its leading citizens, but while some church members were more ready to question their minister, people had been doing this for years and especially if pews were not filled. If the outcome of the 1966 call for a new church grouping showed anything, it was that large numbers outside his congregation did not follow Lloyd-Jones: 'few were ready to stand with him' and for the

---

1   D.M. Lloyd-Jones, *Sermon on the Mount*, Vol. 1 (London, 1959), p.46.
2   Nancy Ammerman, *Bible Believers* (New Brunswick, 1987), pp.122, 121.

majority, his influence 'was virtually zero'.[3] Still, Lloyd-Jones was a forceful personality and it was inevitable that what he said would receive attention.

Personality

What, then, was his definition of personality and how did he distinguish between what was acceptable and unacceptable in this matter?

For this we will turn to his sermons of October 1950, where he outlined poverty of spirit, meekness and mercy. Under the heading, 'Blessed are the Poor in Spirit', he defined 'poverty of spirit' as the state of a man 'face to face with God' and therefore opposed to the 'emphasis the world places on its belief in self-reliance, self-confidence and self-expression'. It was a reference to 'what is regarded by the Bible as the greatest virtue of all, namely humility', and an indication as to why Lloyd-Jones objected to 'a certain aggressiveness' in modern advertising which tended to project a preacher 'into the foreground'. To step onto a platform 'with confidence and assurance and ease, and give the impression of a great personality' was to turn on its head the teaching of the Apostle Paul who has said, 'We preach not ourselves, but Christ Jesus our Lord'. When Paul 'went to Corinth, he tells us, he went "in weakness, and in fear, and in much trembling" and people said of him, "His appearance is weak and his speech contemptible!"'[4] When Lloyd-Jones entered his pulpit in Westminster Chapel in his Geneva gown it was unobtrusively. Climbing the stairs of the rostrum and walking to the preaching desk his head was always down, never looking at the congregation or greeting them with a smile or word of welcome. He simply bowed his head in silent prayer and this was followed, in the mornings, with the doxology and then a short public prayer which ended with the Lord's Prayer and the first hymn. But this was, it may be said, also the expression of personality.

Lloyd-Jones explained that poverty of spirit 'does not mean that we should be diffident or nervous...retiring, weak or lacking in courage', nor does it indicate that a man should be urged to 'repress his true personality' or contrive to produce an impression of self-effacement by assuming 'another character and personality', or retire from public life 'after the manner of the monks'.[5] On the contrary, although people were changed at conversion their temperament and native abilities remained the same: they were simply redirected. The Apostle Paul, who was 'a violent persecutor' became 'a violent preacher. He was zealous in

---

3   T.H. Bendor-Samuel letter to author, 5 November, 1991, and David Winter, letter to author, 3 October, 1991.

4   Lloyd-Jones, *Sermon on the Mount*, pp.45, 44, 46.

5   *Ibid*, pp.47-48.

everything he did. That was his type. It did not change.What was changed was his direction.'[6] Poverty of spirit, on the other hand, is not a natural quality but a feeling of unworthiness: 'complete absence of pride...of self-assurance and of self-reliance...utter nothingness as we come face to face with God'. The nearest secular comparison was 'the humilty of great scholars', but even that was an insufficient comparison since scholarly humility was produced 'by an awareness of the vastness of knowledge', not by the presence of God.[7]

  Two sermons later he defined meekness as being 'ready to learn and listen' and the absence of retaliation when falsely accused: 'The Lord will revenge; he will repay.' Again, Lloyd-Jones was anxious to make the point that meekness 'does not mean indolence' or 'flabbiness': it is not 'a spirit of compromise or "peace at any price"', or a smoothing over of 'things that divide'. Quite the opposite: 'Meekness is compatible with great strength...great authority and power', and for this he appealed to the martyrs and 'defenders of the truth' who would die for the faith 'if necessary'. Lloyd-Jones had the same dogged spirit of sticking to his point whatever the cost. But meekness was also tied up with his view of the grace of God and the sinfulness of man since meekness is unattainable until a man 'has seen himself as a vile sinner'. It was the reverse of 'the popular psychology of the day which says "assert yourself", "express your personality". The man who is meek does not want to do so; he is ashamed of it.'[8]

Finally, in 'Blessed are the Merciful', he defined Christian mercy as 'a sense of pity plus a desire to relieve the suffering' brought about by the consequences of sin. He dismisses the notion of an 'easy-going' response towards transgression and the breaking of the law, and has no sympathy with the kind of person 'to whom it does not matter whether laws are broken or not' and who has little sense of justice and righteousness.[9]

So there was a tension between the acceptable and unacceptable elements of a Christian's personality, between egotism, 'that terrible thing that has ruined the whole of life. Given the opposition between the sinful nature of man and the glory of God it was not surprising that he should find pulpiteerism obnoxious because, in effect, it moved the focus of attention away from the message to the preacher and this was the reason for so few autobiographical comments in Lloyd-Jones's preaching: 'When I preach, I do not tell stories about myself or anybody else'.[10] It

---

6   Lloyd-Jones, 'Nationalism, Tradition and Language', p.6.
7   Lloyd-Jones, *Sermon on the Mount,* pp.47, 50, 49.
8   *Ibid*, pp.70, 67-69.
9   *Ibid*, pp.99, 98.
10   *Ibid*, p.107, and D.M. Lloyd-Jones, *I am Not Ashamed* (London, 1986), p.42. This was true of his Westminster Chapel sermons and his ministry in general, but in his

was an important point in his *Expository Sermons on 2 Peter* where exhibitionism was defined as 'too much interest in self, too ready to talk about self, too ready to call attention to self'. Egotism, he believed, is 'one of the last temptations to leave us', and this was something he had experienced. Inserted in parenthesis midway through the paragraph on exhibitionism, is one of his rare autobiographical allusions: 'God knows we have all suffered from this, and maybe are still suffering—God have mercy upon us if we are'.[11] It was oblique but sympathetic.

An Oracle of the Faith

What, then, of Lloyd-Jones the leader? Few in the Britain of the 1940s and 1950s provided the kind of leadership that he brought to evangelicalism. When people heard his authoritative preaching they responded and he became their leader and mentor. He may not have wanted it but neither did Sangster and Weatherhead who were treated in the same way. In this respect it was not war or social circumstances that produced great leaders in the church so much as eloquent conviction. Disciples and followers make great leaders and the success of Lloyd-Jones grew in proportion to what was thrust upon him. Being the corrector of error and signpost of the truth became habitual and the danger was that, in the end, for all practical purposes Lloyd-Jones came to assume his own infallibility. This was precisely the point picked up by a fellow evangelical in 1983: 'In a quite unique way he functioned as the Cardinal Archbishop of evangelicalism, participating in the Westminster Fellowship, the British Evangelical Council and the Evangelical Movement of Wales not as an ordinary minister but as a different order of being.'[12]

This is not how Lloyd-Jones would have seen it, and it could not be said that he aspired to papal tendencies, but what we are saying is that these things grew as people increasingly looked up to him as an oracle of the faith. It was cause and effect: the cause was the uncompromising personality and intellectual brilliance of one man who stood against the Lord's enemies; the effect was the number of people who esteemed him

---

lectures to the students of Westminster Theological Seminary in 1969 there was a glut of personal references. He justified this by saying, 'I have aimed at being practical'. *Preaching and Preachers*, p.4. It was the only time he used so many personal illustrations in public.

11 Lloyd-Jones, *Expository Sermons on 2 Peter*, p.248.

12 D. Macleod, 'The Lloyd-Jones Legacy', *The Monthly Record*, the Free Church of Scotland, October, 1983, p.209. Macleod was no enemy of Lloyd-Jones and his comments in favour were generous—'arguably the greatest British preacher since the Reformation', p.207. What Macleod wrote in his short article was the best critique of Lloyd-Jones to come from an evangelical scholar to date, and opened up the possibility of further discussion and comment, but it never came.

as a prophet for their day. The effect was equal to the cause. Lloyd-Jones knew that people would come to hear him and he believed that this was a sign of the presence of God. He was probably right. If there was a touch of arrogance here, he was at least prepared to suffer for his convictions where necessary. For example, to have been the 'only notable minister in the south of England' to stand outside and disagree with the Billy Graham Greater London Crusade in 1954 took courage, and the final break with James Packer in 1969 caused pain. There were other occasions when he stood alone and walked a solitary path, but that said, the grief he suffered was usually the result of assuming an inflexible position—that he was right and they were wrong—and the observation needs to be made that in some cases he was a poor leader.

His overemphasis on preaching is a case in point. The importance of preaching in the church is not questioned, but was it right to elevate one gift at the expense of others? It is true that he did not deny the variety of spiritual gifts for Christian people, but there is some ambivalence in what he said. In his British Evangelical Council address of 1968 he described the New Testament church as 'vibrating with life and power', its members all taking part in worship; it was 'not a case of one man doing all the talking, and all the praying, and all of everything else, and others just sitting and listening. They were all taking part. There were differing gifts but they all had some gift, and together they exercised this variety of gifts.'[13] The allusion to congregational participation is unmistakable. Speaking about worship in the early church, his comment was that he saw 'very little in common between what the Apostle describes and what we are so familiar with...the whole thing is different'.[14]

In practice, however, there was no room for any gift other than his own in the public ministry of Westminster Chapel. He allowed no soloist, no Scripture reader other than himself, and no giving of testimony. There was no other participant on the rostrum except the Church Secretary who gave brief notices. Impressive as the Willis organ was, no other instruments ever accompanied Sunday worship. The presence of a younger man to lead a service occasionally would for many ministers have been an encouragement in the ministry, but this was not welcome at Westminster. George Hemming saw this as 'a safeguard and a kindness'—a safeguard of the pulpit against any word or act which might conflict, and a kindness by avoiding a 'Doctor approved' label which would attach

---

13   Lloyd-Jones, *What is the Church?*, p.23. See also Lloyd-Jones, *The Gospel of God*, pp.238-239.

14   *Westminster Record*, September, 1968, Vol.43, No.9, p.140. That he did not minimize the gifts of God given to Christian people is also seen in *God's Way of Reconciliation* (Edinburgh, 1972), p.358; *Christian Unity*, pp.168-169, and MLJRT audio cassettes 3308-3319, sermons on Romans 12:3-8, as well as throughout *Preaching and Preachers*.

itself to a young man and make him 'immediately noted throughout the evangelical world'.[15] That might have been so but a more realistic appraisal would have seen it as an unnecessarily inflated view of one man's ministry.[16] The only time he allowed men to take part was in the Prayer Meeting before the Sunday evening service where, on occasions, they would read from the Bible and open the meeting in prayer.[17] Apart from holiday Sundays, it was one man ministering to the exclusion of all others which, in Hemming's view, was 'because of the nature of his gifts' but, seen from another angle, it came perilously close to clericalism.

Again, Lloyd-Jones's teaching on the validity of a call to preach meant that men not matching his definition of preaching could not in his view expect to see the blessing of God on their ministries. Despite his emphasis on the anointing of the Spirit he did nothing to train young men to be local preachers.[18] His views on evangelism, ideal as they may have been, left the locality of Westminster Chapel largely unvisited and unevangelized. Commuters who came from far and wide on Sundays had little commitment to the area, and when some tried to reach the flats around the Chapel during H.M. Carson's time as assistant, 'Lloyd-Jones only allowed tracts but no speaking on the door-step'. This was confirmed by George Hemming, another of his assistants.[19] Edwin King recalled Lloyd-Jones's response to a number of young men who wanted to knock on doors near the Chapel. Lloyd-Jones told them to bring family and friends first, 'then will be the time to start knocking on the doors around Westminster Chapel'.[20] In some respects this was a valid point since it is

---

15   George Hemming, interview with author, 6 February, 1995.

16   The same issue arises in Macleod's article when he refers to Lloyd-Jones's prominence among evangelical ministers: 'He should have given others an opportunity to develop their gifts of leadership (for example, by chairing the Westminster Fellowship).' *Monthly Record*, October, 1983, p.209.

17   The present writer was invited to do this on 7 March 1955, when he needed the recommendation of the church for his application to the Congregational Lay Preachers' Association and entry to Mansfield College, Oxford. In a later talk in the vestry, Lloyd-Jones fully endorsed and encouraged both endeavours.

18   Lloyd-Jones, *Preaching and Preachers*, p.305. Campbell Morgan had a Lay Preachers' Guild and a Preachers' Class in which men who felt 'called to the work of preaching' were trained and went to Mission Halls and 'neglected stations' in the greater London area and beyond. S. Harlowes, *Notable Churches and Their Work* (Bristol, 1911), p.16.

19   H.M. Carson, letter to author, 20 January, 1995. Herbert Carson was assistant to the minister, 1965-67. 'If someone approached Lloyd-Jones with visitation in mind, he said, 'If you feel like it, do it'. G. Hemming, 6 February, 1995. Hemming was assistant from 1959-65.

20   Edwin King, tape recorded conversation, 31 March, 1995. The comment is from Lloyd-Jones, and followed the question, 'have you brought any of your relatives to the services, your friends?'

often easier to knock on the door of a stranger than to evangelize family and friends, but Christ's words were that 'a man's foes shall be they of his own household'[21] and earnest people frequently found it hard to get their families to respond at all. It is difficult to understand why young people showing such zeal should not be encouraged, and the impression is that Lloyd-Jones seemed to think that only the minister of a church was the channel of grace.

Evangelism

But if Lloyd-Jones did not initiate any visitation as a planned church activity, he did nothing to deter those who were already involved in evangelism and there were some notable efforts during his pastorate. Paul Cowan, one of the deacons, had a Sunday School class of teenagers drawn from the locality and 'he visited their homes, took them out to places of interest in the week and brought some of them to the Sunday services'.[22] Joan Hall, another Sunday School teacher and member, felt there was nothing for the local children so she ran a meeting at the Chapel in the week for the neighbourhood children.[23] Mrs Lloyd-Jones had a Sunday afternoon Bible Class for women of all ages from within the Chapel congregation and a weekday meeting for women of the locality, a meeting which 'may have been a hangover from Campbell Morgan's day when there were twelve deaconesses working in the area'. There was a Sunday School run largely for children of Chapel parents although it did include a few local children, and Frederick Catherwood, who had married Elizabeth Lloyd-Jones in 1954, had a Sunday afternoon Young People's Bible Class which he ran with Elizabeth for young people within the congregation who were 'largely student types'. The Sunday School itself was run by two deacons and consisted of thirty to forty children. There were the usual anniversaries and at Christmas there was an open service at which 'Mrs Lloyd-Jones and her ladies class attended'. The Sunday School ran independently of Lloyd-Jones although he was pleased to have it remembered in Prayer Meetings. Otherwise, 'Lloyd-Jones had complete confidence' in his deacons and was happy to leave it to them.[24]

---

21   Matthew 10:36.
22   George Hemming, 6 February, 1995.
23   Edwin King, 31 March, 1995. King's comment was that Lloyd-Jones 'could not be expected to do this': the only answer was an assistant 'who was resident on the premises in the week'.
24   George Hemming, 6 February, 1995. In time the Catherwoods had two separate classes. Frederick Catherwood finally resigned after 'twenty-five years of uninterrupted leadership of the Young People's Bible Class' in July 1980, and Elizabeth resigned after

Just as important were two other examples of evangelism, highly individualistic in their leadership but successful, and loosely associated with Westminster Chapel. In the first, Elizabeth Braund, a Christian journalist, developed a pioneering work at Battersea Baptist chapel near Clapham Junction. Braund had been introduced to Westminster Chapel in the 1950s by Margery Blackie,[25] though she had been converted when alone. When 'writing minor scripts for the BBC, mostly musical biographies, and adapting musical comedies', she was asked to prepare a programme on the history of the transmission of the Bible. It was this research which ultimately led to her conversion: 'I could do nothing but submit myself to this unknown person whom I did not know but whose claims I could not go on ignoring.'[26] She became a member of Westminster Chapel and launched the bi-monthly *Evangelical Magazine* in 1958.[27]

Originally, Braund was looking for space to house the growing volume of work involved in the production of the magazine and it was in connection with this that she found the disused Baptist chapel which was offered to her rent free. But having moved in with her volunteer helpers it was not long before she became concerned about the 'mission field' on her doorstep and asked advice from Lloyd-Jones on how to go forward. He encouraged her to seek the help of the London City Mission and two local missioners eventually took on the Sunday School. Braund reopened the Women's Meeting though her major work was with the children and teenagers who began to come in off the streets. This became so popular that a junior club for children under the age of ten and a senior club for older youngsters drew sixty to seventy each week. These were children from 'the totally different subculture of Battersea in the sixties', with its old Victorian terraces and tightly-knit communities, but it also included children from the late sixties when bulldozers moved in to raze their streets in preparation for 'concrete ghettoes'.[28]

---

twelve years of leading her own Bible Class at the same time. *Westminster Chapel News*, September/October, 1980.

25   Margery Blackie, physician to Campbell Morgan and first woman physician to the Queen.

26   Elizabeth Braund, *The Young Woman Who Lived in a Shoe* (Basingstoke, 1984), pp.26, 32. These feelings were confirmed the following Sunday as she listened to Lloyd-Jones preaching.

27   It was launched at Westminster Chapel and had the full support of Lloyd-Jones. Braund ran the magazine as managing editor in conjunction with J.I. Packer and P. Tucker (minister of East London Tabernacle), until it folded in 1970.

28   Elizabeth Braund, *The Young Woman Who Lived in a Shoe*, pp.75, 35, 60, 34 and 14. The missioners who came to their assistance and who had worked in the area for a number of years were Mr and Mrs Denton, p.35.

Against such a background the clubs evolved. The format of evangelism used by Braund avoided 'evangelical jargon' or the imposition of 'a middle-class sub-culture' and adapted Christian values to the kind of society around them.[29] Integrated with simple Bible-teaching were games, sports, excursions, craftwork, drama and pageants and, in time, a football team and fishing club.[30] Because few of the children ever had holidays or knew what the countryside looked like, Braund and her helpers took 'a bunch of wild city kids' to a sheep farm in mid-Wales. This became an annual event. The owners of the farm were also friends of Lloyd-Jones. He preached at a nearby chapel on one occasion when the children were present 'sprawled along the pews': he preached, says Braund, 'without a complicated word or sentence in the whole sermon' and, for some of them, it 'made sense'.[31]

In time the chapel at Battersea was sold to Braund and her friends, and Trustees were appointed and a trust deed drawn up. It became a registered charity and was known as Providence House Trust. When the bulldozers moved into the area in the mid-1960s Wandsworth Council offered them the use of 15 Plough Road, an almost derelict house, in recognition of 'the ever-increasing number of homeless young people who turned up at the club'[32] and to ensure its continuation. Such was the success of the work that 'a lessening of juvenile crime in the area' was noted by the Local Authority. When Braund later moved to Devon, 'children were sent to her by the Authority'[33] and her influence continued.

Although not a Westminster Chapel activity as such[34] Braund's South London outreach was strongly connected through its helpers. Rosemary

---

29   *Ibid*, pp.33, 9. According to Braund, it was Dr and Mrs Lloyd-Jones who 'guided me away from an initial sinking feeling, that some how or another I would have to conform to a pattern', p.34. Lloyd-Jones's own ministry was known for its freshness and lack of evangelical clichés but this is not to say that he wholly approved of all that Braund did. Faced with such a strong personality—'I did not conform easily to many church-going habits and my old rebellious instincts and critical attitudes did not drop away', p.315—Lloyd-Jones was probably wise to encourage Braund's missionary zeal.

30   *Ibid*, p.143. The drama and pageants were based on Bible stories, *Pilgrim's Progress, The Holy War, Mary Jones and her Bible*, John Newton's life, and so on.

31   *Ibid*, pp.76, 95, 96. This is clear evidence that Lloyd-Jones could speak to the uneducated and uncultured: 'I could "hear that bloke again. It were interestin'—'E didn't talk down to us', p.96.

32   *Ibid*, pp.152, 146. Frederick Catherwood was one of the trustees.

33   George Hemming, 6 February, 1995. Braund ceased attending Westminster Chapel in 1968, when Lloyd-Jones resigned.

34   In the 'Annual Appeal' published in the *Westminster Record* in February of each year, among the recipients of gifts for 1966 and 1967 was the 'Clapham Mission'. If this refers to Braund's work at Clapham Junction it is a clear indication of Lloyd-Jones's support since he chose the causes to be helped.

Bird, a physiotherapist, became closely associated with the work: John Raynar and M.J. Micklewright, both deacons, were visiting speakers, as was Mrs Lloyd-Jones who took an interest in what was going on and spoke at the Women's Meeting. Lloyd-Jones himself recognized the value of what was happening and had advised Braund 'to take no notice of what others said, but to get on and do your own thing in the way we were led to do it'. This appears to reflect some criticism, from within Westminster Chapel perhaps, but for Elizabeth Catherwood it was the story of a 'faithful woman and her friends',[35] and this was almost certainly how Lloyd-Jones himself saw it.

The Antioch Club

The second example of personal evangelism loosely associated with Westminster Chapel during the pastorate of Lloyd-Jones was the more structured Antioch Club, a voluntary group of Christians founded by Commander Derek Elphinstone in 1953-54.[36] Elphinstone had been a wartime naval officer who afterwards founded a commercial film company with the object of getting Christians on to cinema screens as actors in suitable parts. He wrote scripts for two films and had them produced under the Meridian label and shown on the J. Arthur Rank circuit. He had also been an actor himself but 'left the theatre in order to have more time for Christian work', and became a television producer and executive consultant. Helped earlier by the Officers' Christian Union 'who took the trouble' to talk to him about Christian things and whose 'gentle follow-up work' had impressed him, Elphinstone was converted at the Kensington Temple Pentecostal Church in Kensington Park Road, Notting Hill Gate, and soon after was introduced to Westminster Chapel where he and his wife Marion became members: 'We arrived when Lloyd-Jones was preaching on the Beatitudes [1950-52] and it was heavy going to start with, but we persevered and never regretted it. We sat behind Lord Kinnaird who used to fall asleep during the sermon!'[37]

---

35   Braund, *The Young Woman Who Lived in a Shoe*, pp.22, 47, 57, 110, 11.

36   Originally it was simply called 'The Antioch', a name devised for the purposes of a bank account. Derek Elphinstone felt 'it sounded a fairly up-market name on a par with The Athenaeum'. Interview, 23 July, 1995. 'It was not a "club" any more than a missionary society would be, but there was a room at our house in Palace Gardens Terrace which was called a "club room", and that is probably where the idea came from.' Even so, Elphinstone called it the 'Antioch Club' in his follow-up folder, and we will do the same.

37   Derek Elphinstone, interview with author, 23 July, 1995. The Officers' Christian Union was founded in 1852. It 'exists to help officers of the Royal Navy, the Army and the Royal Air Force to a practical experience of the Christian faith both personally and in their duty'. *100 Days*, Officers' Christian Union, 1924. The 12th Lord Kinnaird and his wife hosted the IFES Cambridge Conference in 1939.

The work began at their home in Brook's Mews North near Lancaster Gate with informal gatherings of a few friends and with no outside help or training: 'we did it all ourselves'. They read their Bibles, made their own notes, and gradually it evolved. As time went on, 'conversions were happening at such a rate that we could not cope with them' and a larger property was needed, which they found in 13 Palace Gardens Terrace, Kensington.[38]

From its beginning the purpose of the Antioch Club was to reach the unchurched and train converts to evangelize and counsel others. It functioned every night of the week and on Sundays after the morning and evening services, with teas and suppers provided at the Terrace. In time the work became 'too big for one person to cope with at a personal level, so it was split into six groups, each with a male and female leader' who were responsible to Elphinstone, and these all met at the Terrace. In the early days there were 'up to 60 or more active members' and during the first half of its existence 'over 90 people professed conversion and were regular at Chapel and Club, not counting nearly 30 more who were in the Club for only a short time or came in later, and whose subsequent history is not known'.[39] Thus a large number of mainly young people had been contacted and brought to the Westminster Chapel services, and over a period of twenty-five years 'about 400 passed through our hands'.[40]

The 'gentle follow-up work' of the Officers' Christian Union was probably the seed from which the Antioch Club grew. Elphinstone's system of evangelism was that 'interested' contacts of members were passed on to 'a Senior Christian' who dealt with difficulties and checked professed conversions 'thoroughly'. When the new converts were established in the faith they themselves became evangelists, the older always instructing and encouraging the younger. It was self-replicating, 'each Christian doing the same thing in the same way', and in follow-up members were 'directly responsible to their Group Leader' who in turn was answerable to Elphinstone. The modus operandi was (a) Fishing, (b) Conversion, (c) *Steps One and Two*, *John's Gospel*, Personal Daily Prayer

38   Derek Elphinstone, 23 July, 1995. Ronald Eeles, later a deacon of Westminster Chapel, met with them at this time: 'I studied God's Word with them before they formed the "club"; they did much good work with quite a lot of young people'. Letter to author, 29 July, 1995.

39   Anthony Williams comments that, 'Group leaders changed as jobs took members out of town. The most...the club ever had was four at once, but most of the time, three'. Letter, 26 July, 1995. Williams himself was a leader for a time: he had been in touch with the Club since just after it was formed around 1954. He was converted in the army and was anxious for the conversion of his sister. Friends put them in touch with the group, and his sister was later converted there. When Williams left the army in 1963 he lived in London and joined Westminster Chapel.

40   Derek Elphinstone, 23 July, 1995.

and Church Attendance, and (d) Attendance on Newcomers' meetings on Thursday nights. During these stages, which might take up to a year, new converts were 'with the Antioch Club, but...not of it'. Only after they had demonstrated their conversion to be genuine, and after showing their willingness 'to work and to do it our way', were they welcomed as members.[41]

Their method of Bible study and follow-up technique was well established by the time the Elphinstones met Dawson Trotman, founder of the Navigators in 1954,[42] but they 'adapted' some of his material to their existing system.[43] The meeting with Trotman, whom they got to know well, was at the Billy Graham Greater London Crusade which the Antioch Club fully supported, providing counsellors and, in the case of Elphinstone, an Adviser alongside ministers like John Stott. As we know, Lloyd-Jones had strong reservations about the Crusade but his comment on the Club's involvement was, 'I am glad that a proper job will be done'.[44]

The Club continued to grow and lost none of its original belief that the unsaved should not only be reached but be considered their responsibility both before and after conversion. Attendance at Westminster Chapel was expected: the unconverted and 'beginners' group' went in the evening when Lloyd-Jones was more evangelistic and the others went both morning and evening. Membership of Westminster Chapel was 'treated as optional'[45] but many did join and in time, because of their youth, it was the Antioch Club which provided 'half the marriages and dedications at Westminster' and 'many of the new members welcomed into Westminster Chapel were ours'.[46] These young people, unlike Elizabeth Braund's Clapham work, were mostly students and young professionals from a mixture of backgrounds who used their memorized

---

41   'Personal Evangelism and Follow-up', The Antioch Club, n.d., pp.1, 4, 2.

42   Dawson E. Trotman formed the Navigators in 1933 which, by 1949, had spread to Europe and the Far East. It was a programme of person-to-person recruitment and training in evangelism, with systematic Bible study and memorizing of Bible verses. See *In Memory of Dawson E. Trotman* (Colorado Springs, 1957).

43   Derek Elphinstone, 23 July, 1995.

44   *Ibid.* Lloyd-Jones was making the best of what he considered to be a bad job.

45   Anthony Williams, 26 July, 1995. Apart from a few exceptions, like Williams himself, Antioch members did not attend any of the other meetings at Westminster Chapel. But if the Antioch Club was 'outside the mainstream of the life of Westminster Chapel', so too were the majority of Sunday worshippers for whom Westminster was a preaching centre and no more.

46   Derek Elphinstone, 23 July, 1995. There are no figures to prove or disprove this but allowing for an element of exaggeration, Elphinstone was probably not far from the truth.

Bible verse 'with great zeal'.[47] Tithing was also taught and this was directed towards the Antioch Club which, in turn, gave a tithe to the Chapel. Later, in the 1960s, the Elphinstones moved to Putney, but although the work continued there were not so many new members and some moved away with their work. But when Antioch members moved out of town 'they were encouraged to start an "out of town group"' and a few such groups were founded: 'one in Whitley Bay where it functioned from the local Baptist Church'.[48] The Club ceased to exist around 1974 when the Elphinstones retired to Eastbourne.

There is no question that the number of Antioch members who filled the ground-floor pews either side of the pulpit each Sunday impressed Lloyd-Jones, and he spoke 'of the encouragement this was to him'. Indeed, Lloyd-Jones visited the Antioch Club 'at least once a year and spent the evening with us. He did not preach, he sat and talked to us in general on the Christian life and various matters of interest. He always invited questions, and questions came pouring in: he loved it.'[49] In Anthony Williams's view, Lloyd-Jones saw the Club 'as part of the Chapel' and 'commended the fact that we were reaching those outside of the church'.[50]

What is interesting is Lloyd-Jones's warmth towards this group knowing, as he must have done, that it was largely based on principles which were at odds with his own preaching. There is no evidence that Elphinstone and his members were aware of Sandemanianism but they followed its ideas of 'naked faith' or 'bare assent' to Christ through the memorizing of Bible verses and the replicating of it in others. Lloyd-Jones dealt with this theme at length in 1967[51] and what concerned him was the possibility of believing without feeling, and believing without the necessity of an inward assurance of salvation by the Holy Spirit. Nor was it only a matter of historic interest since 'easy believism', that is, mere intellectual assent to the truth, was one of the criticisms brought against the Billy Graham campaigns where nightly 'altar calls', the believing and

---

47   Anthony Williams, 26 July, 1995. According to Williams, there were a few actors, an artist, a dancer and an opera singer, but it was 'not an arts group' as some have said, but a mixed group of various abilities and backgrounds.

48   Anthony Williams, 26 July, 1995.

49   Derek Elphinstone, 23 July, 1995. He recalls Lloyd-Jones saying, 'go on with what you are doing. I've got more "pillars in the church" than I know what to do with'.

50   Anthony Williams, 26 July, 1995.

51   Lloyd-Jones, *The Puritans*, pp.17-18. Sandemanianism emerged in the late seventeenth and early eighteenth century through two Scotsmen, John Glas and his son-in-law, Robert Sandeman. It was initially an attack on the idea that faith is a work which earns salvation. They taught that bare assent to what Christ had said was alone necessary for conversion. See also D.M. Lloyd-Jones, *The Righteous Judgement of God* (Edinburgh, 1989), pp.94-95.

memorizing of Bible verses, the signing of a card and registering of 'decisions for Christ' were central techniques in all the Graham meetings. Lloyd-Jones took the opposite view, that saving faith is not confined 'to the mind, or to the intellect' but includes a felt work of repentance and involved 'warm emotional preaching'.[52]

Lloyd-Jones recognized, however, the zeal of the Antioch Club and the conversions that were taking place, and was pleased with their support of the Westminster Chapel ministry. As for doctrinal differences, for Elphinstone 'The only Doctrine permissible for discussion with a pagan is "Justification by Faith"' and '"the Divinity of Christ"',[53] and until contacts were converted, it was considered a waste of time to talk about any other doctrine. In the end, the Antioch approach was more a matter of methodology than intentional Sandemanianism but, in any case, most of these issues would be straightened out as they listened to Lloyd-Jones preaching and as they sat with him at Palace Gardens Terrace.

These, then, were examples of the kind of evangelism that went on among Westminster Chapel members. They were not initiated by Lloyd-Jones but they did, in a measure, receive his blessing. His own view of evangelism was largely a reaction to campaign evangelism and perhaps for this reason it was over-cautious. But faced with people like Braund and Elphinstone there is a sense in which he could do little else than go with their momentum. Either way his own position on evangelism remained. What is clear is that he so distrusted human activity and maximized the need for unction and a divine calling in Christian service that evangelism, in effect, was completely tied in to the set-piece sermon and people were expected to attend the services and hear the Word.

The Matter of Succession

If some of this leaves us questioning his style of leadership so too does the matter of a chosen successor at Westminster Chapel raise questions. The usual response to this issue is that there was no one to take his place: 'we have lost a leader who, in our generation at least, cannot be replaced'.[54] Graham Harrison defending, as he thought, the sovereignty of God, described those who 'complained' that Lloyd-Jones had 'not designated and groomed his successor' as 'provincial oracles', men who theorized about divine sovereignty but did not believe in it or rest upon it.[55] Evidently God had broken the mould and such was the uniqueness

---

52   Lloyd-Jones, *The Puritans*, pp.180, 185.
53   'Personal Evangelism and Follow-up', p.4. It was essential to get the basics right, then move on to the next stage.
54   Murray, *The First Forty Years*, p.xv.
55   *Evangelical Magazine of Wales*, April, 1981, Vol.20, No.2, pp.46-47. Graham Harrison, minister of Emmanuel Evangelical Church, Newport, Gwent. 'To us', he said to

of Lloyd-Jones that even some members thought Westminster Chapel as they knew it was finished and had 'the temerity to say so'.[56]

But this was not in itself unusual. When W.E. Sangster died in 1960 there were similar sentiments and the *Newcastle Journal*, which saw him 'as one of the outstanding preachers of his generation', reported a Methodist spokesman saying that the death of Sangster was 'one of the greatest calamities which had come to Methodism and the wider church for many years'.[57] It was the same with Campbell Morgan, who was styled 'the greatest expositor of the Bible this century'.[58] When he died on 16 May 1945, the *Christian World*, under the heading 'Prince of Preachers', referred to Morgan as 'a towering personality, a volcanic being, with a commanding presence and an authoritative manner' who 'belonged to all the Churches' and for whom 'Christianity in two continents mourns the loss'.[59] As much could be said for other esteemed men whose ministries had touched the lives of thousands.

So far as choosing a successor went, Lloyd-Jones had gone to Westminster Chapel in 1939 as the result of the spiritual discernment of Campbell Morgan who had seen Lloyd-Jones as his successor. Jill Morgan took it as 'the directing finger of an Almighty Hand'[60] and, as it turned out, it was. But for Lloyd-Jones, although it proved to be providential, the matter was not what it seemed. 'The trouble with Campbell Morgan was that he liked preaching':'He could hear me on a Sunday and thoroughly enjoy it but on the following Wednesday, he would hear a liberal, but providing the man could preach, he would thoroughly enjoy that too.'[61] Still, events proved that Morgan had been right and there is also reason to think that Lloyd-Jones was just as concerned about his successor.

The future of the Westminster Fellowship, for example, was in mind less than a month before he died when he responded to a letter from John Caiger with a five-year plan.[62] He suggested 'an Executive committee of

---

like-minded ministers, 'he was a friend and a brother and a father all rolled into one', p.45.

56   T. Omri Jenkins, 'Annual Letter to Members of Westminster Chapel', January, 1969. Jenkins was moderator at Westminster Chapel during the vacancy until Glyn Owen commenced his ministry in October 1969.

57   *Newcastle Journal*, 25 May, 1960, p.3. The article was entitled 'Calamity for Methodism'. Sangster died on Wesley Day, 24 May, 1960.

58   T. Wilkinson Riddle, *Christian Herald*, 31 July, 1982, p.9.

59   *Christian World*, 24 May, 1945, p.5.

60   Morgan, *A Man of the Word*, p.303.

61   Edwin King, 31 March, 1995. This may explain how he was able to remain a Congregationalist while maintaining his biblical ministry.

62   Lloyd-Jones, *Letters 1919-1981*, pp.235-236. J.A. Caiger, minister of Trinity Martyrs' Memorial Baptist Church, Gunnersbury, 1942-93. Lloyd-Jones had already

six' to include Graham Harrison, Peter Lewis, and John Caiger[63] as permanent chairman, and two men from the London Theological Seminary together with a larger General Committee from which the choice of speakers would usually be made. This procedure should 'be adhered to for at least five years', so avoiding 'all elections and nominations', and giving 'time for natural leaders to appear'. These 'suggestions were made in response to the men's request', but we are not told how many of the Fellowship were behind this request nor, if they were so well instructed, why they could not formulate their own affairs. Murray's comment on the letter is that Lloyd-Jones had their continued unity in mind and Caiger, according to another letter, saw it as a matter of 'pastoral concern'.[64] Others saw it as 'the most disastrous thing he ever did'.[65] Without doubt, he was 'bishop to literally hundreds of clergy'[66] through the Westminster Fellowship, but to issue posthumous rules was more to embalm it than to preserve it.

What he needed was a natural successor like James Packer, but the events of 1966-67 when the Fellowship was closed over the ecumenical question excluded men like Packer. So apart from a last minute effort Lloyd-Jones had made no plans for the continuation of the Fellowship. The trouble was that, unlike the Eclectic Society, the Westminster Fellowship was centred on the wisdom and skill of one man. Had he adopted a less autocratic stance and developed the sort of infrastructure that Stott had done in the Eclectic Society the succession would have been a natural continuation. Because the Westminster Fellowship was essentially his fraternal and the forum where Lloyd-Jones was pastor of pastors, it could not thrive without him, nor did it do so. His five-year plan was too little too late. Caiger, for all his gifts, was not the kind of chairman Lloyd-Jones had been nor, indeed, were any of the men he recommended in the same mould, even though most of them were Welsh, and the plan did not really work. The Fellowship continued but numbers fell and at one stage a disagreement over the charismatic question reduced numbers even further.[67]

In the case of Westminster Chapel there is, nonetheless, evidence to show that Lloyd-Jones did take the matter of a successor seriously. Most

---

discussed the matter with Hywel R. Jones, Principal of the London Theological Seminary, the day before.

63   Peter Lewis, minister of Cornerstone Evangelical Church, Nottingham.

64   Lloyd-Jones, *Letters 1919-1981*, pp.235-237.

65   'Personal Information 1'.

66   Catherwood (ed.), *Chosen by God*, p.43.

67   The disagreement was over the timing of an open discussion on charismatic issues: 'Some asked for time to pray about it, others wanted immediate action without waiting. A vote was taken, the latter lost, and they left the Fellowship'. 'Personal Information 1'.

surprising is the knowledge that at one stage, Lloyd-Jones had an Anglican in mind.[68] In 1966, two years before his resignation from the Westminster pastorate, Lloyd-Jones was one of the speakers at the International Congress of Christian Physicians in Oxford and John Stott, who was also present, expounded the Upper Room Discourse in his Bible studies.[69] In Stott's own words, 'I was flabbergasted when he took me aside and said: "when I retire I would like you to follow me at Westminster Chapel." I was amazed at his confidence in me in spite of our ecclesiastical differences but what disturbed me most was his lack of understanding of me that I could be in a position even to consider that.'[70] Lloyd-Jones had misjudged Stott, but it was nevertheless a serious, if not rash, invitation which in all likelihood arose out of the strength of Stott's preaching. Perhaps he hoped that Stott would leave Anglicanism as he originally believed Packer would, but in both cases he underestimated their ecclesiological convictions. On the other hand apart from Lloyd-Jones, Stott was arguably the most outstanding expository preacher in England at the time with a strong following at All Souls, so in this respect Lloyd-Jones's judgement was right.[71]

The events of October 1966 almost certainly ended the matter and Lloyd-Jones did not refer to Stott as his successor again, although he continued to have a high regard for him. Nor did he change his mind on the strength of Stott's ministry. In a private conversation with Stott in December 1978, Lloyd-Jones spoke of his wish that they 'could be together, you and I, we belong together. Together we could make a terrific impact on the church and the country'.[72]

A second name that arose was Eric J. Alexander, Church of Scotland minister at Newmilns, Ayrshire, from 1962-77.[73] Alexander had been approached by the Pastorate Committee in 1969 and Lloyd-Jones made it clear in a letter in March 1969 that Alexander would be a good choice,

---

68   For those who believe that Lloyd-Jones left the matter of a successor in other hands, such choices were intuitive, on the-spur-of-the-moment decisions, which would vanish the next day, but this hardly does justice to the facts or to Lloyd-Jones himself.

69   John 13-17. The Congress was held on 11-15 July 1966.

70   John Stott, tape recorded conversation, 16 November, 1991. The invitation to succeed Lloyd-Jones comes from the notes and diary of Stott, the details of which were confirmed by letter.

71   On the credibility of this invitation, Stott's comment was: 'D.M. Lloyd-Jones was serious... He took me on one side to say what he did'. Letter to author, 21 March, 1995.

72   John Stott, 'Notes of a Visit to Dr. Lloyd-Jones', 19 December, 1978. Used with permission.

73   Alexander was an evangelical who had preached at Keswick and at various conferences and meetings throughout Britain. In 1977 he became minister of St. George's—Tron Parish Church, Glasgow.

and urged him 'to give the fullest possible consideration to the need of maintaining a biblical ministry at Westminster'.[74] The origin of the approach to Alexander was that six members of the Chapel had asked for him to preach, but each time H.C. Todd had taken the matter to Lloyd-Jones it was blocked.[75] Finally, after Frederick Catherwood supported the idea, an invitation was approved and Alexander preached at the Chapel on 23 February 1969.[76]

Evidently Lloyd-Jones valued the ministry of Alexander as he had done Stott, but at the second Interregnum Church Meeting when Alexander's name was put forward for the pastorate, 'objections were raised (not of a personal nature) and in view of these it was decided not to offer him the pastorate'.[77] From Alexander's point of view it is uncertain as to whether he really wanted to leave Scotland. It is clear that he was not happy with the idea of secession—how could he be as a minister in the Church of Scotland?—and felt that his position as pastor 'might lead to controversy at the Chapel'.[78] Such may also have been the reasons why Alexander declined a further invitation in 1974 when Glyn Owen resigned.[79]

Whatever Alexander's feelings, the letter of March 1969 shows how far Lloyd-Jones was prepared to go for the sake of maintaining a successful preaching ministry, overlooking 'almost' everything else,[80] even if it meant turning to non-Independent evangelicals. But nothing would have caused greater confusion among men who had taken Lloyd-Jones at his word on the issue of separation and nothing would have been more contrary to his 1966-67 position. To charge men who had remained in ecumenically sympathetic churches with 'guilt by association' and then to support such men as Stott or Alexander because of the 'overwhelming

---

74   Lloyd-Jones, *Letters 1919-1981*, p.217.

75   'Personal Information 1'. Mr Todd was in charge of pulpit supplies. According to the above reference, Lloyd-Jones told the six to 'forget about it'. A number of audio Cassettes of Alexander's sermons had been given to the Pastorate Committee to familiarize them with his preaching. Edwin King says that Lloyd-Jones was completely opposed to Alexander preaching at Westminster Chapel to start with, although in the end, he yielded to the request of his son-in-law. 6 February, 1995.

76   H.C. Todd, undermined in his efforts as pulpit supply secretary, withdrew and Omri Jenkins took over at about this time. Todd remained as Church Secretary until he resigned in 1971.

77   John Raynar, letter to author, 27 June, 1995. The date of the meeting is not given but it was probably in March.

78   Lloyd-Jones, *Letters 1919-1981*, p.217, and footnote, quoting Alexander's reply to Omri Jenkins, p.216.

79   Eric Alexander, letter to author, 18 July, 1995. He acknowledged that Westminster Chapel 'approached me again in 1974' but adds nothing more, either of this or 1969, maintaining 'complete confidentiality' in both cases.

80   Lloyd-Jones, *Letters 1919-1981*, p.217.

consideration' of the Westminster Chapel ministry was a double standard. It also clashed with his recommendations regarding the running of the Westminster Fellowship with its reservoir of acceptable speakers. Murray, anxious to credit Lloyd-Jones with the best of motives, reminds us that whatever his convictions, Lloyd-Jones continued to have fellowship with Anglican and Scottish ministers who 'did not support ecumenism' although, of course, Stott did.

There was another issue. On the face of it the 1969 letter to Eric Alexander gives the impression that Lloyd-Jones had little to do with Westminster Chapel after his resignation: 'From the beginning I have not taken any part in the direct affairs of the Chapel'.[81] But in using 'direct' he was being economical with the truth. As we have seen, Lloyd-Jones blocked the original suggestion of the six church members which Mr Todd had taken to him on several occasions and that was nine months after his resignation in May 1968. The underlying problem was that he never taught his deacons how to proceed when he retired, and this left a vacuum which Lloyd-Jones continued to fill. Perhaps, in the circumstances, his guidance was appropriate, but the impression that Lloyd-Jones had played no part in the affairs of the Chapel since his retirement was not true: 'all the pulpit supplies in the interregnum were referred to the Doctor'.[82] Edwin King recalled that Lloyd-Jones 'wanted all those who had preached over the years to have the opportunity to occupy his pulpit'[83] during the vacancy but this would have had the effect of cutting down the number of suitable candidates and encouraging men with known Arminian tendencies. In practice, however, preachers during the vacancy tended to be long-standing friends of Lloyd-Jones.[84]

In the end, as we have seen, Glyn Owen was appointed to the pastorate in 1969.[85] So far as is known, Lloyd-Jones's views on the appointment of Owen were not expressed, at least in public, although it may have surprised him since Owen was well known for his contributions as a speaker at Keswick.[86]

81   Lloyd-Jones, *Letters 1919-1981*, p.217.

82   'Personal Information 1'.

83   Edwin King, 6 February, 1995.

84   Men like S.J. Lawrence of Leicester, Leith Samuel of Southampton, G.N.M. Collins of Edinburgh, W.J. Grier of Belfast and his assistants Iain Murray, Herbert Carson and Edwin King. *Westminster Record*, April 1968, Vol.43, No.4, p.63.

85   See 'Westminster Chapel', p.92.

86   H.L. Stevenson, 'Westminster Chapel's New Minister', *Life of Faith*, 18 October, 1969, pp.3-4.

'Athanasius Contra Mundum'

A further element in the nature of Lloyd-Jones's leadership was an Athanasian or Luther-like way of thinking. It was to these two men, especially the latter, that he often turned in order to make his point. There was something about the perpetual struggle of Luther that caught his imagination. For Lloyd-Jones, Luther was a champion of the faith, a man of great energy and above all, a man 'baptized and filled with the Spirit'.[87] But it was the apparently constant and diffuse nature of Luther's struggling—with Rome, with Zwinglianism and Anabaptism, with Erasmus and the moderates, with problems in the organization of his own church, with defections of erstwhile friends and with the devil himself—that impressed Lloyd-Jones, and there is no doubt that much of this coincided with his own feelings. He was not uncritical of the Reformer,[88] but overall he saw him as an 'outstanding genius', a man of amazing courage, a 'volcano of a man' and someone who delighted in Scripture. If Luther's response to his enemies was, as Lloyd-Jones said, that he 'but read and...but expounded and...but preached'—it 'was the Word that did it; God led me on'—it was something he wholly related to in 1966-67.[89]

What Lloyd-Jones found attractive was the entrenched stubbornness and defiance of men like Athanasius and Luther. 'What are the mountain peaks in church history?' he asked when preaching on 'Submission in the Spirit'.[90] One was 'Athanasius contra mundum', God's servant standing alone against the whole world in defence of the doctrine of the Person of Christ. Another was Luther, 'a man standing absolutely alone against the great Popish church and fifteen centuries of tradition'.[91] He believed Luther's 'Here I stand. I cannot do differently. So let God assist me' to be the 'essence of Protestantism'.[92] Put another way, God had enlightened his servants so that, in effect, they stood for what was right whereas 'the church was wrong',[93] and this was largely the emphasis in *Luther and his Message for Today*. It was a case of believing the Word, that is the evangelical interpretation of it, and obeying it whatever the consequences. Thus, Luther 'was like a horse who had been blindfolded so that he could not see the enemies that were coming to attack him with their chariots and spears'.[94]

---

87   Lloyd-Jones, *Joy Unspeakable*, p.134.
88   Lloyd-Jones, *The Puritans*, pp.135, 222, 226, 7.
89   Lloyd-Jones, *Luther and his Message for Today*, pp.19, 23.
90   D.M. Lloyd-Jones, *Life in the Spirit* (Edinburgh, 1973), p.68.
91   Lloyd-Jones, *Life in the Spirit*, p.68.
92   *Barn*, April, 1963, p.171.
93   Lloyd-Jones, *Life in the Spirit*, p.68.
94   Lloyd-Jones, *Luther and his Message for Today*, p.23.

Lloyd-Jones was, in a sense, fighting the Reformation all over again and closely identified with a robust Luther-like style: 'What do numbers matter, what do sarcasm and scorn and derision matter; what does it matter though we be despised and laughed at?' Where ecumenists question the faith and practice of evangelicalism, and separatism in particular, 'Let them say it! This one man Luther was enabled to stand as it were against the whole church and against those centuries of tradition. And you and I will be enabled to do the same.'[95] He had said as much in what was surely an autobiographical comment in 1948: the evangelical 'had to stand by himself...to be misunderstood, to be defamed, to be jeered and persecuted. But he knows in the end that he will have to stand by himself before "Christ's judgement throne" to "receive the things which were done in the flesh whether they be good or bad".[96] Because he feels that he is answerable to God and to his own conscience, he is not influenced by "the right thing to do" be it in his own daily life or within the circle of the Church.'[97]

It was the doctrine of the remnant in action, demonstrating 'what one man can do when that one man is truly Christian'. It was the 'Lord taking a handful of men and making them apostles and the sole guardians and custodians of the faith—that is their message.'[98] Such was his point in a sermon entitled 'Activities and Life': 'God has repeatedly acted through a remnant, sometimes through one man... Christ left the Church in the hands of twelve men, a mere handful of nobodies. We seem to have forgotten that!'[99] It was also his theme when speaking on 'John Knox—The Founder of Puritanism' in 1972: 'No man has ever been more maligned' yet in the face of 'vitriolic attacks' it was his wisdom and energy that largely 'saved the Reformation' on several occasions,[100] and 'changed the life of the whole of Scotland'.[101] For Lloyd-Jones, Knox was of 'the same heroic character that you see in Martin Luther standing "in the Diet of Worms"'. So the nature of his style of leadership combined within it elements of this doctrine of the remnant and a heroic concept which, unconsciously, reflected the heroes of the faith. Where this brought him into conflict with other Christians, it was

95   *Ibid*, p.29.
96   2 Corinthians 5:10.
97   *Y Cylchgrawn Efengylaidd* (*The Evangelical Magazine*), November/December, 1948, Vol.1, No.1, p.5.
98   Lloyd-Jones, *Expository Sermons on 2 Peter*, p.5.
99   Lloyd-Jones, *Christian Unity*, p.272.
100 Lloyd-Jones, *The Puritans*, pp.262-263.
101 *Evangelical Magazine of Wales*, February, 1973, Vol.12, No.1, p.11.

regrettable but, as he said, this was not 'the first time...that minorities have been right'.[102]

But it was not only that Lloyd-Jones identified with such figures who stood alone against all odds: it was more than this. He saw himself as part of a chain of spiritual strength that stretched from Elijah to modern times. A minority of people 'in every country, and in every age' who were 'agreed that some things were all-important and of such importance as to render them prepared to suffer any loss or insult rather than betray or refuse to declare them'.[103] Lloyd-Jones was a twentieth-century link in the chain. For his old friend A.T. Davies this kind of certainty was 'arrogance';[104] others might say that it was the coalescence of an irresistible urge to dominate by means of a romanticized historical allusion. On the other hand, such a feeling might help to explain the complete unimportance of an 'engineered' succession, or of a 'success-ful' church or denomination in Lloyd-Jones's thinking.

In the end Lloyd-Jones was what his followers allowed him to be and this lay behind John Caiger's words on his chairmanship of the Westminster Fellowship: 'he had a secretary [Caiger] who was happy (with rare exceptions) to do what he was told, and a fellowship of pastors so hungry for the Doctor's theological learning and spiritual experience that they never questioned the propriety of it all'. It was a simple and efficient arrangement and ensured that Lloyd-Jones 'had things as he wanted them, and we were all more than delighted that he should'.[105] It was deferentialism, but the fault lay as much with the people who encouraged it as with the man himself. However, given the nature of the man, his gift for preaching and Luther-like defiance of error, some hero worship was inevitable. In the Free Church of Scotland many 'men of his early days practically idolised him'[106] and this was true in England and Wales. According to David Winter, 'he was a "guru" with a set of adoring disciples', and this was certainly so. It may not have been his wish, but such was the strength of his convictions that events overtook him. He was without doubt a genuinely disciplined Christian man but, as Winter says, there were times when even he 'could not resist papal tendencies'.[107]

One might think that if the ministry of Lloyd-Jones were so powerful, so Luther-like, then the pattern of his influence would have been extensive. As it was, in 'the eyes of non-evangelicals... Most would not

102 Lloyd-Jones, *The Puritans*, p.266, and *Evangelical Magazine of Wales*, February, 1973, p.10.

103 *Evangelical Magazine of Wales*, February, 1973, p.4.

104 *Barn*, April, 1963, p.171.

105 *Evangelical Times*, April, 1981, Vol.XV, No.4, p.14.

106 A. Sinclair Horne, letter to author, 22 November, 1994.

107 David Winter, letter to author, 3 October, 1991.

even have known his name', and those who did know, 'branded him as "fundamentalist" and fanatical'.[108]   His influence lay almost entirely within the evangelical sector of the church and, after 1967, this shrank to a minority of like-minded people. In Anglican circles Lloyd-Jones had his friends, but in general no members of the episcopate or dignitaries of the Church of England knew or cared about his views. As Packer said, 'in the little ecumenical world based on London, where the top brass of all denominations circulate, the Free Church leaders dismissed Lloyd-Jones as a freak, and the Anglican leaders took their word for it'.[109]

As for his impact on Congregationalism he was more tolerated than admired, and his way of looking at things was thought to be out of touch with the modern church. John Marsh thought that his only impact in Congregational circles was 'largely due to the fact that he was called to, and became, the Minister of a large London church'. Marsh's view of Lloyd-Jones was that 'while his own testimony received a warm reception from a sector of churches and ministers', that is to say, among those within Congregationalism who agreed with him, 'his message did not give rise to any sort of wide reception of his views',[110] and on the matter of unity Geoffrey Nuttall recalled a wry comment of John Huxtable, that Lloyd-Jones did 'more harm than good'.[111]

---

108   Alec Motyer, letter to author, 10 June, 1991.

109   J.I. Packer, letter to author, 7 June, 1991.

110   John Marsh, letter to author, 8 May, 1991. 'I have a few, but vivid recollections of him... I heard him preach and I did meet him personally. I felt that he was a sincere believer, though I did not myself follow his train of thoughts.' Marsh was Principal of Mansfield College, Oxford, 1953-70.

111   Geoffrey Nuttall, interview, 4 November, 1994.

CHAPTER 8

The Extent of his Influence:
A 'standard bearer for the faith'

We have said that in the larger, denominational sense, Lloyd-Jones had
little impact or influence, but this is not the whole picture. That he was
not widely accepted only disturbed him insofar as he felt that it was a
rejection not so much of him but of his gospel. In this final chapter we
will show that there was a real and lasting influence in spite of a self-
marginalizing tendency.

In England the oustanding aspects of his influence were his Westminster Chapel ministry, the Westminster Fellowship and Puritan Studies
Conference. There were preaching occasions in different parts of the
country and these increased after his retirement from the Chapel but, as
we have seen, from 1939 to 1968 it was the London ministry which
formed the core of his success. Set in the heart of London, Westminster
Chapel was in a strategic position 'to bear witness to the great evangelical
faith and tradition', and in 1948 he spoke about the 'many scattered
about these islands and indeed in other lands who are looking to us and
are helped and strengthened by what we are and what we do'.[1] It was no
vain boast, especially as such a ministry attracted people who one day
would become leaders themselves.

Among the agencies Lloyd-Jones encouraged from his Westminster
base the Banner of Truth Trust was particularly successful. As a new
publishing venture it had developed out of a magazine, the first issue of
which was published at Oxford in 1955. A gift from Westminster Chapel
'provided half the cost for the second issue' and the magazine grew from
there.[2] The Trust itself proved to be significant because it eventually
printed the majority of Lloyd-Jones's sermons. Such was the success of
the Trust's printing programme that by March 1996, 461,963 copies of
major titles of Lloyd-Jones had been sold, and the two-volume biography
by Iain Murray was selling at 700 copies a year.[3] Compared to other
publishing houses the Banner of Truth Trust was comparatively small, but

---

1   Lloyd-Jones, *Letters 1919-1981*, p.91.
2   Murray, *The Fight of Faith*, p.356 and footnote.
3   Murdo MacLeod, letter to author, 12 December, 1996.

such sales figures are no mean achievement and have clearly played a part in sustaining the influence of Lloyd-Jones at home and abroad.

How many people have actually read these collections of sermons—the twelve volumes on Romans for example—may be a matter of conjecture, but undoubtedly there are some. Stott, who owns some of his books, thought it a pity that Lloyd-Jones never allowed 'his spoken words to be edited for writing' and abridged:'he takes such a long time to say one or two things I cannot imagine that all these works will still be in print in 20 or 30 years time'.[4] By 1997 the sale of Lloyd-Jones titles had not diminished and other publishers such as Hodder & Stoughton, Inter-Varsity Press, Evangelical Press, Kingsway Publications in the United Kingdom, and Zondervan and Eerdmans in America, are all producing various collections of sermons under different titles. This flow of print is almost entirely from sermons transcribed from audio cassettes and has continued to fuel an interest in him and to introduce his preaching to those who never heard him when he was alive. The 400 who met at the Westminster Fellowship in the 1960s, the 200 or so who attended the Puritan Studies Conference, the weekly congregations at Westminster Chapel and the wider clientele who bought his books constitute a substantial area of influence.

A more limited area of leadership was his interest in the London Theological Seminary. Lloyd-Jones had been a member of the original Sponsoring Committee and latterly a member of the Board until the end of his life.[5] The Seminary which, according to Omri Jenkins, chairman of the Sponsoring Committee, 'owed its origin to Dr. Lloyd-Jones as a preacher' met on the premises of the Kensit Memorial College in Hendon and, during its first year, 1977-78, had five full-time students rising to twenty-one in 1981.[6] Students came from a variety of constituencies but mainly from churches of BEC background. Some came from the Evangelical Movement of Wales and a few 'from Baptist Union and Brethren backgrounds', and these have all gone on to serve as pastors at home and abroad within their own church groupings. Lloyd-Jones preached at the commencement of each new session for the first three years and also lectured on two other occasions.[7] The Seminary was

4   John Stott, tape recorded conversation, 16 November, 1991.

5   The original Sponsoring Committee also included Elwyn Davies, the Evangelical Movement of Wales, Brian Dupont, Evangelical Congregationalist, T. Omri Jenkins, European Missionary Fellowship, Clifford Pond, Strict Baptist, Roland Lamb, British Evangelical Council, and David Mingard, Fellowship of Independent Evangelical Churches. Keith Mawdsley and Gordon Murray, both evangelical Baptist pastors and not representative of any group, joined the board later.

6   London Theological Seminary, 'First Annual Report' (n.d.). Jenkin's remark was made at the Thanksgiving Service, Westminster Chapel, 6 April 1981.

7   P.H. Eveson, letter to author, 13 March, 1995.

a solid reflection of the Lloyd-Jones's philosophy of theological education, which was that it should be anti-ecumenical, non-examination centred and a training ground to 'help...future preachers', all of whom would be Protestants and men. The conservative emphasis was not his alone; it was shared by the whole of the eight strong Sponsoring Committee.[8] Whether this style of ministerial training is preferable, say, to London Bible College which had a greater number of students of both sexes studying the same kind of subjects but on a broader academic base, and whether some interaction with other theological colleges would have been beneficial, depends on one's point of view.[9] Lloyd-Jones had been in at the start of London Bible College in 1939 and in 1943 was Vice-Chairman of the Council, but the college was preparing men and women for the external examinations of the University of London and for Lloyd-Jones this involved students in the study of error. Not only so, Lloyd-Jones was unhappy over the question of student placements at the college which involved the Baptist Union and other doctrinally mixed denominations.[10] The ecumenical nature of current theological education, in his view, provoked the need for 'a Protestant Evangelical College' with a curriculum determined by conservative views of Scripture and since 'the primary need' was for preachers, such an institution was to encourage men to preach 'without fear or favour'.[11]

As we have seen earlier, the formal relationship of Westminster Chapel with the Congregational Church ended in 1966 and under Lloyd-Jones's guidance the Chapel became a member of the Fellowship of Independent Evangelical Churches and a constituent member of the British Evangelical Council in 1967. Although he was highly regarded within the FIEC and some of its men were members of the Westminster Fellowship, he featured little in it.

The new association with the FIEC followed in the wake of his call for evangelical unity in 1966. What is not clear is why the Chapel did not make a direct application to the BEC and become a member church in its own right, or why it did not join up with the Evangelical Fellowship of Congregational Churches. No mention is made of such possibilities either

---

8   D.M. Lloyd-Jones, *Inaugural Address* (1977), p.16, and David Mingard, tape recorded conversation, 28 April, 1995.

9   The number of students who went on to become ministers, missionaries, church workers and teachers in 1968 is certainly impressive. H.H. Rowdon, *London Bible College* (Worthing, 1968), p.108. On intercollegiate relations, P.H. Eveson wrote: 'We have no connection with any other theological colleges.' Letter, 13 March, 1995.

10   Lloyd-Jones, *Inaugural Address*, p.5. On the affiliation of London Bible College students from 1943 to 1968, see Rowdon, *London Bible College*, pp.109, 111, and bringing the discussion up to the present see Randall, *Educating Evangelicalism, passim.*

11   Lloyd-Jones, *Inaugural Address*, pp.2, 5, and 'Occasional Letter', London Theological Seminary, February, 1978.

in church minutes or correspondence. What is clear is that, in time, Lloyd-Jones came to see that the FIEC was not a broad enough base for his message. Initially he may have hoped that it would be: as E.S. Guest said, 'Lloyd-Jones would have us join the FIEC, but he did come round to see that we had acted rightly in retaining our view as the EFCC [Evangelical Fellowship of Congregational Churches], and then coming into the BEC'.[12]

In fact some twenty-seven ministers of the newly formed Congregational Evangelical Revival Fellowship took the Lloyd-Jones position that the new Congregational Church in England and Wales was a serious departure from historic Independency, and it was because of ecumenical tendencies and 'a departure from evangelical truth' that the CERF was set up.[13] Murray, no friend of the FIEC position, records a comment by Lloyd-Jones that membership of the FIEC was 'not the big thing. The British Evangelical Council is the bigger thing because its scope is bigger'. In reply to J.I. Packer's caustic comment 'that we should all join the FIEC', Lloyd-Jones's response was, 'that will not do, but did not say why not, nor what the alternative was'.[14] In a letter of 1980, Lloyd-Jones referred to the BEC as 'a powerful anti-ecumenical witness' in Britain and went on to say, 'we have also started the London Theological Seminary to do the same' thing, but he did not mention the FIEC.[15] So the FIEC connection fulfilled the need for non-isolation so far as Westminster Chapel was concerned, though for Lloyd-Jones it was a tenuous link.

The Charismatic Movement

His place among English evangelicals, however, took on a new complexion in the 1960s when he began to expound semi-charismatic teaching. The charismatic movement was probably the most important cross-denominational phenomenon of the mid-twentieth century but it raised problems and divided Christians as much as it united them. People who had long looked to Lloyd-Jones for guidance and leadership, and who had responded to his clear-cut views on other matters, were now not

---

12   E.S. Guest, tape recorded conversation, 11 February, 1992. The Evangelical Fellowship of Congregational Churches was founded in 1967 but it grew out of a former association of individuals known as the Congregational Evangelical Revival Fellowship that had been formed by two Congregational ministers, Gilbert Kirby and Harland Brine, the latter of which had a searching experience in the Welsh revival. Guest was appointed Secretary of the Revival Fellowship.

13   *Ibid.* Lloyd-Jones was on the original Council of Reference with G. Kirby and D. Swann.

14   Murray, *The Fight of Faith*, p.547, and Catherwood (ed.), *Chosen by God*, p.49.

15   Lloyd-Jones, *Letters 1919-1981*, p.228.

so sure of what they heard. True, his preaching was no less emphatic and, as usual, he gave no quarter to those who opposed him, but there was an underlying ambivalence. Both sides of the charismatic divide claimed his support and in a sense they were both right: he had a foot in both camps. At times he was decidedly sympathetic to the charismatic movement, hoping that this was the beginning of the long awaited revival. But he could also be strongly anti-charismatic. It was little wonder, then, that many were confused. Only his most devoted supporters could see his position to be as 'plain as a pikestaff'; for the rest, the problem was that in trying to 'avoid "quenching the Spirit"...he ended up conceding too much to Pentecostalism'.[16]

Where he differed most from other conservative evangelicals was in his belief that the gifts of the Spirit had not ceased: 'I think it is quite without Scriptural warrant to say that all these gifts ended with the apostles and apostolic era', and this view is reflected throughout his preaching.[17] What caused the sharpest reaction, however, was his belief in a two-tier experience of the Spirit, 'that you can be a believer, that you can have the Holy Spirit dwelling in you and still not be baptized with the Holy Spirit'.[18] It was a view that opened up a hornet's nest of feelings for and against.[19] In theory at least, Lloyd-Jones advocated 'a new

---

16   Catherwood, *A Family Portrait*, p.110, and *Evangelicals Now*, October, 1986, Vol.1, No.4, p.7.

17   Lloyd-Jones, *Letters 1919-1981*, p.202. Dealing with demonic depression he criticized the view of some Christians 'that spiritual gifts and similar manifestations—such as miracles and speaking in "tongues"—came to an end in the apostolic era'. D.M. Lloyd-Jones, *Healing and Medicine* (Eastbourne, 1988), p.155. In relation to the Spirit of power in preaching, he said: 'if you confine all this to the apostolic era you are leaving very little for us at the present time'. Lloyd-Jones, *Preaching and Preachers*, p.314. In this he was opposing well known cessationists like B.B. Warfield: 'some say quite dogmatically that they [the gifts] have never occurred since—that there has literally been no miracles since...New Testament times'. Lloyd-Jones, *Joy Unspeakable*, p.163.

18   Lloyd-Jones, *Joy Unspeakable*, pp. 23, 32, 36. 'The Baptism with the Holy Spirit is not regeneration', he said when commending the need for power in preaching: 'the apostles were already regenerated.' *Preaching and Preachers*, p.308. For a comparative study of Lloyd-Jones's views and John Stott's (as reflected in his *Baptism and Fullness: The Work of the Holy Spirit Today* [Leciester, 1964, 2nd edn 1975]) see M.B. O'Donnell, 'Two Opposing Views on Baptism with/by the Holy Spirit and of 1 Corinthians 12.13: Can Grammatical Investigation Bring Clarity?', in S.E. Porter and A.R. Cross (eds.), *Baptism, the New Testament and the Church: Historical and Contemporary Studies in Honour of R.E.O. White* (Sheffield, 1999), pp. 311-336.

19   See, for example, Peter Masters, 'Opening the Door to Charismatic Teaching', pp.24-31, and 'Why did Dr. Lloyd-Jones yield to quasi-Pentecostal ideas?', pp.32-35, in *Sword and Trowel*, No.2, 1988. David Mingard's comment was that 'in South Africa, the Reformed group would not read his books' because of his view on the gifts of the Spirit in *Joy Unspeakable*. Letter, 28 April, 1995.

rapprochement between Reformed and Charismatic evangelicals'.[20] This middle way could not be described as a movement in itself. People like Peter Lewis developed a freer form of worship in their churches but continued to hold Calvinistic convictions, and many of them after 1979 began to associate with Spring Harvest, an annual 'pan-evangelical' event which showed all the hallmarks of charismatic worship.[21] It was more of a trend among people who felt that it would be wrong to stand outside of what they saw as a movement of God among his people. Whether the Calvinistic position can really be aligned with Pentecostalism is an open question. For Donald Macleod it was an absurdity because they 'belong to different theological universes',[22] but seen in the light of Lloyd-Jones's Calvinistic Methodist roots it was not so bizarre, and many in the Evangelical Movement of Wales agreed with him.

There are several observations we need to make in respect of Lloyd-Jones's openness and ambivalence towards the charismatic movement. It is true, for example, that he was remarkably open to the things which were happening, especially in the early days when he and his friend Philip Hughes shared a 'hopeful expectancy' of it all. According to Hywel Jones, he was 'interested in anything which appeared to display signs of spiritual vitality', and according to David Mingard he was always concerned to 'prick the moribund bubble' of dead orthodoxy 'that can form around Reformed teaching'.[23] That he was open to what was going on is not surprising given his belief in the sovereignty of the Spirit. If God is almighty he may act as he will without restriction or question. He does not act indiscriminately or in contradiction to his written word, but he may act unexpectedly and by direct intervention as he did in the Acts

---

20   The words are those of Peter Lewis, then minister of Hyson Green Baptist Church, Nottingham, who quoted Lloyd-Jones as saying: 'I am with you one hundred percent and without reservation'. *Evangelical Times*, April, 1981, Vol.XV, No.4, p.17.

21   Ian Scott, Marketing and Development Manager, Spring Harvest, letter to author, 20 July, 1995. Spring Harvest was launched in Prestatyn in 1979, when almost 3,000 people attended. By 1986 the number had grown to 38,000 and by 1993 to over 70,000. *Spring Harvest Manual* (Uckfield, n.d.), p.27. Attenders at the event came from all denominations with about 40% Anglican and 30% Baptist. Speakers are 'drawn from the widest denominational sources', *ibid*. Peter Lewis had been one of the speakers. Among a variety of speakers were names like Robert Horn who has written enthusiastically about Lloyd-Jones in Catherwood (ed.), *Chosen by God*, p.13, and was a former editor of the *Evangelical Times*, John Stott, David Jackman, Leith Samuel's successor at Above Bar, and Roy Clements of Eden Baptist Church, Cambridge, but for all those who could be described even loosely as 'Reformed', there were many others with Arminian convictions, and many who were well disposed towards the ecumenical movement.

22   D. Macleod, 'The Lloyd-Jones Legacy', p.209.

23   Catherwood (ed.), *Chosen by God*, pp.172, 221, and David Mingard, 28 April, 1995.

of the Apostles: 'the Spirit in his sovereignty, may decide to give these gifts again' as he did in the early church.[24] Speaking of 'the lordship of the Spirit' and the 'inscrutable wisdom and severeignty' of God in the ebb and flow of revivals, it was his conviction that all preachers of the Word should 'expect' a demonstration of the Spirit and power in some measure: 'a kind of "divine afflatus"' on their ministries.[25] This sovereign intervention was to be looked for every Sunday and services should be a 'climactic experience' or 'turning point in someone's life', and this was Michael Harper's understanding of Lloyd-Jones on the work of the Spirit.[26] At the same time he was severely critical of the charismatic movement in certain areas and believed, even from Aberavon days, that 'Signs and wonders must be examined...and sifted'. The gifts, especially the spectacular ones, were for him a sign of immaturity much as they were in the church of Corinth: 'the one who is grown up is interested more in the graces of the Christian life'. He had personally never spoken in tongues but for those who had he warned against any feelings of superiority towards those who had not.[27]

Of greater importance 'was the baptism of the Spirit', but even this was not to be the touchstone of true Christianity, nor was it to minimize the importance of doctrine. He had been particularly concerned about the claims of David Du Plessis, a leading Pentecostalist in the 1950s and 60s, that the baptism of the Spirit was to be received within the cultural milieu of the recipient so that, in Lloyd-Jones's words, it brought a deeper 'appreciation of the mass and all the other various Roman Catholic doctrines and dogmas'.[28]

Although he regarded the charismata as very important he was also ready to attack the 'bankruptcy' of the Du Plessis position because it was 'not reformed' in its doctrine. So while he did not deny spiritual gifts for the twentieth century neither did he 'venture to put them into the

24 Lloyd-Jones, *Joy Unspeakable*, p.248. See also pp.56, 175 and 263.

25 *Ibid*, p.131, and *Preaching and Preachers*, p.234.

26 Lloyd-Jones, *Preaching and Preachers*, p.235. 'We must be ready for the unexpected, and not demand of God that he works in certain ways. God has sometimes surprised us!' M. Harper in *Renewal*, December, 1991, No.187, p.19.

27 Lloyd-Jones, *Why Does God Allow War?*, p.20; *Expository Sermons on 2 Peter*, p.250; and *Unity in Truth*, p.109. 'I have never spoken in tongues either in private or in public'. *Letters 1919-1981*, p.205. On the gift of unknown tongues, see also *Joy Unspeakable*, pp.254-285.

28 Lloyd-Jones, *Knowing the Times*, p.313. David Du Plessis was the embodiment of the charismatic movement. His vision was to unite people who had the Pentecostal experience, and he spent much of his time moving among churches around the world under the auspices of the World Council of Churches.

category of the essential'.[29] In the end his argument was not so much with the charismatic movement as with extremes. If we take speaking in tongues as a criterion, Lloyd-Jones was not a neo-Pentecostal, but if baptism in the Spirit is the test, then he was. And this explains why he encouraged men like Henry Tyler in his 'ministry among charismatic churches' and why he was appreciated in classical Pentecostal circles[30] such as the Gospel Tabernacle, Slough, where A. Wesley Richards, the pastor, noted that in spite of his reservations, Lloyd-Jones 'would not be smeared with an anti-charismatic brush'.[31]

Taking into account all that he said about the work and gifts of the Holy Spirit, Lloyd-Jones was conservative. In fact for all his emphasis on Spirit-baptized preaching his position was really an eighteenth-century one. Those who claimed him as a modern charismatic were wrong. It is true that he followed events closely, but it was almost exclusively with revival in mind and it was this that lay behind his remark, 'Evangelicalism is dead. God must do a new thing.' It was the idea of a powerless, failing church that urged upon him the need for 'a mighty outpouring of the Spirit of God' and that, not the gifts, was his primary interest. Certainly worship at Westminster Chapel could not have been less charismatic, but Macleod surely missed the point when he described these services as 'the most inflexible in which we have ever participated'[32] since so many people were evidently converted and renewed.

Apart from theological arguments involved in the teaching of Lloyd-Jones on the Holy Spirit, with which we are not concerned here, the ambiguity of his position lay in the fact that he allowed the charismata and encouraged people to be involved in all aspects of the church's life, but, so far as Westminster Chapel went, it was a one-man ministry with no demonstration of the gifts beyond his. In other words, it was theoretical pentecostalism.

---

29 D.M. Lloyd-Jones, *Presidential Address*, Evangelical Library (London, 1963), p.13, and *Knowing the Times*, p.354. He refers to this subject in different places but his main treatment of the Person and work of the Spirit is found in *God's Ultimate Purpose* (Edinburgh, 1978); *The Sons of God* (Edinburgh, 1974); and *Joy Unspeakable*.

30 Catherwood (ed.), *Chosen by God*, p.247. Henry Tyler, a charismatic preacher and elder at Clarendon Church, Hove. By classical Pentecostalism we mean the movement which began at Azusa Street, Los Angeles in 1906, where baptism in the Spirit and speaking in tongues marked the beginning of modern Pentecostalism. See further K. Kendrick, *The Promise Fulfilled: A History of the Modern Pentecostal Movement* (Texas, 1959), and M.G. Moriarty, *The New Charismatics* (Grand Rapids, 1992).

31 *Evangelical Times*, April, 1981, p.16. His father, W.H.T. Richards, had also been pastor of Slough Tabernacle and a friend of Lloyd-Jones.

32 Catherwood (ed.), *Chosen by God*, p.248; Lloyd-Jones, *Revival*, p.20, and the *Monthly Record*, p.209. The latter was an interesting comment coming from a member of the Free Church of Scotland where psalms and a certain ritual are noticeable.

When neo-Pentecostalism appeared in Britain in 1961 it did so mainly through articles in the American magazine *Trinity*, which began to circulate among Anglicans in 1962. It reported the events of Passion Sunday 1960 at St. Mark's Episcopal Church in Van Nuys, California, when the Rector, Dennis Bennett, and some of his congregation had been 'filled with the Holy Spirit and had spoken in tongues, just like the Apostles on the Day of Pentecost'. After some opposition Bennett resigned and it is from this day, 3 April 1960, that the modern charismatic movement is dated. By early 1963 John Collins, incumbent of St. Mark's, Gillingham, David Watson, curate at the Round Church, Cambridge, and Michael Harper, curate to John Stott at All Souls, had experienced the same kind of baptism. There was some uncertainty as to exactly what it meant so, at the suggestion of Harper, these three Anglicans visited Lloyd-Jones on 9 April to ask his advice. They did so because of his interest in revival and because 'he had surprised many by espousing the Pentecostal position in some respects, without otherwise losing any of his trenchant Evangelical views'. Lloyd-Jones believed their experience to have been genuine and some see this meeting as 'the moment when the Charismatic Movement in Britain was born'.[33] As we have said, Lloyd-Jones had a more than average interest in the Van Nuys events, but it was not long before he became concerned about imbalances and by 1970, writing about the effect of extremes on students who had visited a 'Michael Harper movement' at Chard, Somerset, he spoke of 'gross dangers and the unscriptural character of the whole thing'.[34] As Harper rightly says, 'He remained a sympathetic spectator, nothing more.'[35]

Wales

The situation in Wales as it related to the influence of Lloyd-Jones was more consistent. From the late 1940s a new grouping of evangelicals had started through 'Elwyn Davies and others'[36] uniting people from both North and South Wales, and Lloyd-Jones had shown a great deal of interest. He became involved with the Welsh Inter-Varsity Fellowship and then with a broader spectrum of evangelicals through *Y Cylchgrawn*

---

33   T. Saunders and H. Sanson, *David Watson* (London, 1992), p.71: 'Gentlemen, I believe you have been baptized in the Holy Spirit'.

34   Lloyd-Jones, *Letters 1919-1981*, p.204. There had been an 'aggressive' emphasis at Chard on Spirit baptism and unknown tongues as its evidence, with an openness to healings, prophecy and new revelations.

35   Lloyd-Jones, *Healing and Medicine*, p.169, and *Renewal*, December, 1991, p.20.

36   Murray, *The Fight of Faith*, p.247. Davies was a theological student at Bangor University at the time. He later became a Welsh Congregational minister and then a Travelling Secretary for the Inter-Varsity Fellowship in Wales, 1955-62.

Efengylaidd (*The Evangelical Magazine*) which had its first conference at Bala, North Wales, in 1952. It was renamed 'on the Doctor's own suggestion', *Y Mudiad Efengylaidd Cymru* (*The Evangelical Movement of Wales*) at the conference in Denbigh the following year,[37] at which Lloyd-Jones preached three times. By 1958, such was the interest, that a property, Eryl Aran, was purchased as a centre for camps and conferences and this was extended in 1960 to include an adjoining property, Bryn-y-groes.

All of these meetings were in line with what Lloyd-Jones felt a conference should be, an event where 'men amongst themselves be asked to read short opening papers on various subjects, and that we then discuss them together'.[38] The two-day Bala conference each June was to become a significant factor in the lives of ministers and students of theology for years to come and, until his later years, Lloyd-Jones was always there. In such a way several generations of men were influenced and this stayed with them as they went on to serve 'churches of all denominations in Wales'. Thus, 'a body of young men' were to form a major part in the development of evangelicalism in Wales.[39]

From the beginning the Evangelical Movement of Wales was a voluntary association of ministers and individuals who upheld 'the evangelical faith' and associated 'themselves with the Movement's Aims'. It was of course a denomination in the sense that it was a group having a distinctive interpretation of religious faith although it had a minimum of organization. There were and are no membership records or formal registry of members so it is difficult to assess who was and who was not in the movement. Some ministers supported it while remaining in their denominations, especially in the Welsh sector, while others from groups such as the FIEC or Pentecostal churches met in local ministers' fellowships arranged by the movement. Still, the movement has evidently grown: the Annual English Conference is now over 1,000 strong and meets in the University Hall, Aberystwyth, and the Welsh Language Conference of about 300 meets in a local church the following week. There are seven bookshops in different parts of Wales and the Evangelical Press of Wales, the movement's publishing wing, has expanded so that by 1994 it had 'sold or distributed books to 16 countries'.[40] Much of this may be traced back to the teaching and advice of Lloyd-Jones. Overall, the movement strongly reflected Lloyd-Jones's own position: separation from the ecumenical movement, holiness of life, commitment to an inerrant Bible and its systematic exposition, the need for revival and a questioning of modern evangelistic techniques.

---

37   *Evangelical Magazine of Wales*, April, 1981, Vol.20, No.2, p.25.
38   Lloyd-Jones, *Letters 1919-1981*, p.127.
39   *Evangelical Magazine of Wales*, April, 1981, p.25.
40   Gerallt Wyn Davies, letter to author, 13 February, 1995.

Seen against the general decline of membership in Welsh churches in the 1970s when 'one church in seven had less than 10 members', this is all the more impressive. As we have said, the absence of any register of churches or members associated with the Evangelical Movement of Wales makes it difficult to plot the development of evangelicalism in Wales in relation to Lloyd-Jones, but a number of churches, mainly Presbyterian, did secede after 1966 although, as J.E. Davies says, this was more 'a consequence of the deliberations of the Evangelical Movement of Wales's Ministers Conferences and fellowships in the years prior to 1966'.[41]

The Associating Evangelical Churches of Wales, a group established in 1988 to 'provide means for co-ordinating the witness and fellowship of evangelical churches, fellowships and individuals' in Wales including the Evangelical Movement of Wales, records a steady growth of independent evangelical churches since the turn of the century. Before 1900 there were eighteen older causes. From 1900 to 1959 seven churches were added, from 1960 to 1969 five, 1970 to 1979 thirteen, and 1980 to 1989 seven, making a total of fifty. The older churches were Baptist and Presbyterian fellowships which had established themselves as independent evangelical churches in the 1960s and 1970s. These figures show that about twenty-five evangelical churches associated during Lloyd-Jones's lifetime and in the crucial years, 1960 to 1969, there were five that joined. But only one of these churches was Welsh-speaking and there is no account of all the churches, ministers and members from Welsh-language areas who came to associate with these movements, and who had often heard Lloyd-Jones preach in Welsh as well as English. So this 'fifty' is only a core number: as G. Wyn Davies says, 'Associating Evangelical Churches of Wales numbers are considerably less than those who regularly associate with us',[42] nor does it account for churches and ministers outside of Wales who also supported the movement.

The situation in Wales was that the growth of ecumenical interest, as in England, had caused churches to move away from the old confessional

---

41   P. Brierley and B. Evans, *Prospects for Wales* (1982), p.5, and J. Elwyn Davies, letter to author, 3 February, 1995. Even this was only a handful of churches, 'perhaps a dozen in all but others followed' as the Evangelical Movement of Wales developed.

42   Gerallt Wyn Davies, 13 February, 1995. The AECW is incorporated with the EMW structure by means of a specific clause in its constitution, part of which reads: 'The Evangelical Movement of Wales's Management Committee recognized the Associating Evangelical Churches of Wales as a concrete expression of the Movement's church principles and cherishes its links and affiliation' with AECW. This was felt to be 'a way of securing a close supportive unity without compromising either the independence of the churches...or the independency of the EMW in relation to a wider constituency', for example the BEC. *Ibid.*

positions and Calvinism was largely a thing of the past.[43] This was Lloyd-Jones's point in 1963: 'the majority of the Calvinistic Methodists in Wales today do not believe it [the Calvinistic Methodist Confession of Faith] any more, and they do not even see the need for a confession of faith at all'.[44] As a leader in Wales Lloyd-Jones was an anachronism, his views unacceptably narrow and unyielding and if, as it seems, he rebuilt Calvinistic evangelicalism in the Principality, it was only among a minority. Many heard him preach but 'most of the church leaders would shudder when they heard his name'.[45] This is not to say that he was wrong or that the convictions of the minority were mistaken, simply that the ecclesiastical climate had changed. Even so, Lloyd-Jones regularly visited Wales and continued his pastoral concern not only for ministers but for their churches too. Where Wales differed from England in the influence of Lloyd-Jones was that English evangelicals generally refused to go along with his separatist stance, as 1966 shows, whereas the majority of Welsh evangelicals did. Where England and Wales agreed was in the way most churches rejected his uncompromising identification with conservative evangelicalism. The 'majority of ministers...largely ignored' him.[46]

Overall, Lloyd-Jones had as many enemies as friends in Wales. They could not ignore his preaching or the crowds who listened to him, but that apart, the impression of J.E. Davies that most of the church leaders in Wales would 'have been immensely relieved to hear of his call to Westminster Chapel' in 1939 is almost certainly true.[47] By then the Presbyterian Church of Wales was becoming less conservative so it was almost inevitable that, as in England, Lloyd-Jones would become increasingly an outsider so far as its mainstream congregations went: his future lay in smaller circles. Some were specific and spoke of Lloyd-Jones leaving 'a bad legacy of men who would not tolerate other views and were anti-ecumenical'.[48] Whether this was true or not, among non-evangelical leaders in Wales he had no influence at all. Thus, when Geoffrey Thomas described Lloyd-Jones as 'a colossus overshadowing Wales',[49] in the long run it was more a remark of affection than fact. The

---

43   'As time went on, the Presbyterian Church of Wales became less evangelical and more liberal so that several of the ministers left.' D. Ben Rees, tape recorded conversation, 20 May, 1992. Rees did not leave. He later became Secretary of the Liverpool Presbytery.

44   *Barn*, April, 1963, p.171.

45   D. Ben Rees, 20 May, 1992.

46   J. Elwyn Davies, 3 February, 1995.

47   *Ibid.*

48   D. Ben Rees, 20 May, 1992.

49   *Monthly Record*, Free Church of Scotland, November, 1979, p.217.

preaching over, what remains is a growing but minority group, faithful to its convictions, but unconnected with the church at large.

Scotland

There had also been a lengthy relationship with Scottish evangelicals extending from his first visit in November 1938 to his last one in May 1980.[50] Large Bible rallies were concentrated in centres such as Edinburgh's Usher Hall and Glasgow's old St. Andrew's Hall or the Kelvin Hall, and there were other venues such as Dundee, Inverness and Aberdeen.

The Bible rallies and preaching tours were arranged by the Scottish Evangelistic Council, an interdenominational society founded in 1930 which had its own caravan mission and literature outreach. These rallies were a major feature of the Council's activities and it was normal to hold them in the main centres where larger crowds gathered since they 'had the secondary aspect of being fund raising occasions' also.[51] In 1948, after preaching 'with compelling power' at a Wednesday lunch-hour service in Renfield Street Church, the Glasgow *Evening Citizen* reported that 'the Scottish Evangelistic Council gave a luncheon in honour of Dr. Lloyd-Jones which was attended by a large and representative company of ministers and laymen of all denominations'. The next morning he was at Tolcross YMCA addressing 'a meeting of men and lads' and in the evening he preached at a service in the Church of the Orphan Homes of Scotland, Bridge of Weir.[52]

There were invitations to St George's—Tron Parish Church in Glasgow, and to Kenneth Street Free Church, Stornoway, where 'people came from all parts of the island to hear this outstanding preacher and before doors were opened long queues had formed'. This meeting was linked by 'a loudspeaker unit' to Martin's Memorial Church and the Free Church Seminary, and the numerical estimate was, '5000 Hear

---

50   The first visit was to North Woodside Church, Glasgow, where he took a series of week-night meetings, 15-18 November 1938. Murray, *The First Forty Years*, p.364. His last visit was to speak at the Scottish Evangelistic Council Jubilee on 9 May 1980, in the pulpit of St. Vincent Street Free Church, Glasgow. *Ibid,* p.733.

51   A. Sinclair Horne, letter to author, 22 November, 1994. As Secretary of the Scottish Evangelical Fellowship and of the Scottish Reformation Society, Horne had known Lloyd-Jones from 1960, and it was he who arranged the Edinburgh meetings.

52   *Evening Citizen*, 11 September, 1948, p.2. The article was headed 'Business Men Packed Church to hear Him'. The meeting was all the more impressive given the time of day and week. The 'whole accommodation downstairs' and galleries upstairs were full by one o'clock. 'It was an extraordinary congregation to be drawn at a busy hour in the middle of a weekday.'

Outstanding Preacher'.[53] Professor G.N.M. Collins noted that Lloyd-Jones was known in the Highlands and Gaelic-speaking areas as well as the Lowlands, and 'the *Westminster Record* found its way into many Scottish manses' bringing 'blessing and direction to its subscribers and the congregations whom they served'.[54] Such a minister was Kenneth J. MacLeay of Lochinver who had been a friend of Lloyd-Jones: he asked to receive the *Westminster Record* regularly and Lloyd-Jones had promised to 'forward also the back numbers for this year'.[55]

But Collins's opinion that Lloyd-Jones was 'greatly loved throughout the length and breadth of Scotland' needs some qualification. Edwin King, for example, said that Lloyd-Jones's 'reception in Scotland was very mixed', and Professor R.A. Finlayson of the Free Church College, Edinburgh, said that Lloyd-Jones's 'Calvinism bends over backwards':[56] that is, accomodated more than the Westminster Confession allowed. There were, as in England and Wales, outsiders, non-evangelicals and the curious at his meetings, but the greater part of his appeal was to the Reformed constituency, those from 'true evangelical circles', which explains why he was so well received in the Free Church of Scotland.[57] It is true that Church of Scotland men like Eric Alexander and William Fitch chaired some of the meetings but they too were sympathetic to the speaker and his message. In effect, the great Bible rallies in Edinburgh and Glasgow were a kind of 'mecca for those who appreciated his testimony in defence of the Reformed faith', but generally speaking, 'many liked his oratory but deplored his theology'.[58]

---

53   *Stornoway Gazette*, 19 September, 1964, p.1, and 5 September, 1964, p.1. The reporter described Lloyd-Jones as 'a welcome visitor to Scotland' and 'One of the most outstanding preachers in Great Britain today'. The meeting, like others, had been arranged by the Scottish Evangelistic Council. K.H. Nicolson presided over the main meeting in the Free Church. K.H. Nicolson, letter to author, 22 November, 1994.

54   G.N.M. Collins in Catherwood (ed.), *Chosen by God*, pp.263, 261.

55   Lloyd-Jones, *Letters 1919-1981*, p.63.

56   Tape recording of Thanksgiving Service, 6 April, 1981, and Edwin King, tape recorded conversation, 31 March, 1995. While Lloyd-Jones and the Free Church of Scotland were Calvinists their emphases was different. Finlayson's remark reflects the strict adherence of the Free Church to the doctrine and practice of the Westminster Confession. Lloyd-Jones was more an evangelical than a Calvinist—his Calvinism more experimental than theoretical. His openness to new movements of the Spirit, his commitment to Independency and separatism, and his use of hymns and music in church, for example, contradicted the Confession of Faith. But because of Lloyd-Jones's acceptability as a preacher, and because the Free Church itself placed a strong emphasis on evangelical preaching, Free Churchmen were glad to hear him.

57   K.H. Nicolson, 22 November, 1994.

58   D. Gibson, letter to author, 20 January, 1995, and A. Sinclair Home, letter to author, 22 November, 1994. W. Fitch was minister of Springburn Hill, Glasgow, 1944-58, after which he emigrated to Canada and became minister of Knox Presbyterian

He did visit other churches in response to specific invitations as, for example, when he preached on the first evening of the Assembly of Scottish Congregationalists in Edinburgh on 30 April 1945. He visited Charlotte Baptist Chapel for the Church Anniversary on 7-8 October 1973, and the Church of Scotland in Rothiemurchus in the Highlands where he preached when on holiday in 1972.[59] Even so, he was probably more at home among ministers of the Free Church of Scotland than any other.

But if, as Donald Gibson says, the Free Church of Scotland accepted Lloyd-Jones as a 'new star in the ecclesiastical firmament',[60] there were misgivings even here. When visiting their churches Lloyd-Jones had conformed to the Free Church pattern of worship and this was his practice wherever he went, but some who went to his meetings or to Westminster Chapel when in London were disappointed at his use of hymns rather than psalms. For the majority of people who listened to him it was not a problem but there were 'certain Free Church ministers who wrote to the Doctor and took issue with him' on the subject of 'Psalms, Hymns and musical instruments'. They 'did not like his constant resorting to quoting verses of certain hymns over and over again' and there was a decided sense of disapproval that in the singing, 'all the praise consisted of hymns and no Psalms' at Westminster Chapel.[61] Lloyd-Jones-made his views on this matter clear in one of three sermons on Ephesians 5:19, which did not appear in *Life in the Spirit*. He distinguished between psalms, hymns

---

Church, Toronto. Alexander's comment was: 'In later years I myself chaired a number of meetings.' Letter to author, 18 July, 1995. Lord Mackay reminds us of others who deplored his theology also. 'In the Free Presbyterian Church of Scotland, of which I once was a member, his coming to Scotland occasioned a good deal of division with some respected members of the church thinking that it was wrong to go to hear him because of course he differed from us on, for example, infant baptism, whereas others enthusiastically went to hear him, of whom I was one.' Lord Mackay of Clashfern, letter to author, 9 September, 1997.

59   *Evening Citizen,* 5 May, 1945, p.2. 'One of the highlights of the Assembly was the evening service, with Dr. Martyn Lloyd-Jones of Westminster Chapel, London, as preacher. There was a great attendance and the preacher was at his best—which is to say a great deal!'

60   D. Gibson, 20 January, 1995.

61   A. Johnstone, letter to author, 17 January, 1995. A. Sinclair Home, 22 November, 1994, and K.H. Nicolson, 22 November, 1994. Free Church of Scotland congregations only use psalms in public worship, not hymns from 'fallible' authors. This practice, aimed at preserving the purity of worship, also accounts for the absence of musical instruments in their services. In fact Lloyd-Jones did have a metrical psalm each Sunday morning at the Chapel. It was chosen from a selection of sixteen psalms at the end of *Congregational Praise*. There was also a Psalter of four Canticles and seventy-six psalms with a system of verbal accentuation in this hymn book, as well as chants, responses, doxologies, prayers and blessings.

and spiritual songs by defining a psalm as 'a sacred poem' such as we
have in the book of Psalms, a hymn as 'a song of praise to God', and
spiritual songs as 'Odes and Lyrics'. All three were included in the New
Testament and early church. He acknowledged those who used only
psalms in public worship, those 'who would even go so far as to suggest
that it is sinful to sing anything else', but for Lloyd-Jones this exclusivity
of psalms was 'erroneous' and he went on to give his reasons. He was not
unaware of the 'doggerel' and 'sloppy sentimentality' which appeared
in some hymns, but the opposite to bad hymns is not no hymns but good
ones, and these were invariably the older ones.[62]

Again, some tended to criticise Lloyd-Jones because he did not have a
theological degree and had not trained in a theological college. This is
not so surprising since Scotland has a strong tradition of theological
education and all students in the Free Church of Scotland were expected
to complete a three- or four-year course in the Free Church College
before their ordination. Lloyd-Jones had his own views on theological
education, but so far as the Free Church of Scotland was concerned, 'On
the face of it, the Doctor was not trained', and this was a sensitive issue.[63]

There were other differences of opinion particularly over certain points
of theological emphasis: his 'concept of Christian unity',[64] for example,
and his teaching on the baptism of the Spirit as an additional experience
to conversion. In Sinclair Horne's view, as older men retired or died—the
men who had been closest to Lloyd-Jones in Scotland—'many of the
next generation became very critical of him'. These younger men were
those who had been influenced by teachers like Donald Macleod at the
Free Church College who had firmly stood against Lloyd-Jones's teaching on the Holy Spirit.[65] What is surprising is that Lloyd-Jones was so
well received even among the older men given the traditions of the Free
Church of Scotland. Perhaps it was as much Celtic similarity as historical

62   *Westminster Record*, September, 1968, Vol.43, No.9, pp.133-143. The three
sermons on Ephesians 5:19 were preached on Sunday mornings, 22, 29 November and 6
December in 1959, and appeared in September, October and November issues of the
Westminster Record in 1968. In the Banner of Truth edition of *Life in the Spirit* (1974),
there is a break between Ephesians 5:18 and 5:21. Lloyd-Jones was undoubtedly being
economical with the truth here. Clearly he did not want to antagonize his Free Church
friends or strain the fellowship they had in other matters. By 'good' hymns he meant
those by Martin Luther, 'Charles Wesley, John Cennick, Philip Doddridge, William
Williams in Wales, not to mention Joseph Hart, William Cowper, John Newton, Ann
Steele and many others', all solidly evangelical who produced hymns in times of revival.

63   *Monthly Record*, October, 1983, p.208.

64   *Ibid.*

65   A. Sinclair Horne, 22 November, 1994. See D. Macleod, *The Spirit of Promise*
(Fearn, 1986). The chapters in this book formerly appeared as editorials in the *Monthly
Record* and are largely a critique of Lloyd-Jones's position in *Joy Unspeakable*.

interest. This certainly aroused his regard for Scotland:'I always say, when I have the pleasure of coming to Scotland, that I am interested to come, not only because of my concern about the gospel, but because of the deep feeling of admiration which I have always had for you as a nation and people'. This admiration was more for the rise and development of the Protestant Church in Scotland than it was for the contemporary scene. It was 'Heroic, big men, men of granite' like 'Patrick Hamilton, George Wishart, John Knox, Andrew Melville, John Welsh', the seventeenth-century Covenanters and the eighteenth-century revivals at Cambuslang and Kilsyth, that attracted his attention.[66] Clearly, crowds went to hear Lloyd-Jones, but, according to a colleague, 'He did not feel as though he was well accepted in Scotland in spite of the numbers'. As for the man who was almost certainly his closest friend in Scotland, G.N.M. Collins, he was an Englishman.[67]

On balance, the picture of Lloyd-Jones in Scotland was of a 'standard bearer'[68] for the faith, and apart from gala occasions it was evangelical ministers who were more influenced than congregations. As these men began to die off so did much of the influence. He had his admirers, but aside from the actual preaching and personal friendships nothing actually happened in Scotland so far as unity was concerned that could be traced to him. Scottish traditions remained inflexible and church groupings stayed as they always had been. Yet there were at least two positive areas of influence. It could be said that Lloyd-Jones's identification with the British Evangelical Council encouraged the Free Church of Scotland to continue its involvement with them, and it was also true that for a generation of ministers in the 1950s and 1960s the preaching of Lloyd-Jones brought a fresh impetus for evangelical Calvinism in Scotland. For some his prestige may have gone no further than the meeting where he preached, though there was an 'awakened interest in the steady sale of his books in Scotland'[69] and, as elsewhere, this became part of his legacy.

Northern Ireland

The influence of Lloyd-Jones in Northern Ireland was on a smaller scale. In September 1967, he preached at the induction of H.M. Carson at

66   Lloyd, *Knowing the Times*, p.90.
67   'Personal Information 2'. Collins was Professor of Church History at the Free Church College, Edinburgh, 1963-82. He was born in London in 1901, but his mother was a Highlander from Sutherland, which is why he spent so much of his youth in Scotland.
68   Thanksgiving Service, 6 April, 1981.
69   A. Johnstone, 17 January, 1995. The Banner of Truth Trust moved from 78 Chiltern Street, London W1, to 3 Murrayfield Road, Edinburgh, in 1972.

Bangor Baptist Church[70] and after that he spoke at Ravenhill Presbyterian Church. According to Malcolm Coles, he was well known in Congregational Union of Ireland circles through the impact of his books,[71] but his contacts were wider than this. He was friendly with W.J. Grier of the Evangelical Presbyterian Church, with Professor Adam Loughridge of the Reformed Presbyterian Church, had fellowship with some of the brethren in the Presbyterian Church of Ireland and made a number of visits under the auspices of the Evangelical Fellowship of Ireland which, in two cases at least, 'were attended by very-big numbers'.[72] All of these provided sympathetic listeners, not only because Lloyd-Jones's evangelical Calvinism was acceptable but also because of his secessionist stance, 'which strengthened the hands of those in the smaller denominations and helped those trying to reform the Presbyterian Church of Ireland'. That he was appreciated in Congregational Churches is because, generally speaking, Irish Congregationalists had retained more of their original evangelicalism than their English counterparts. The Irish Congregational Union was never in membership with the World Council of Churches, there was no link in 1972 with the United Reformed Church and a number of churches were associated with the Evangelical Fellowship of Congregational Churches. The majority of Lloyd-Jones's meetings were held in Belfast though there was one in Londonderry and one in Armagh.[73]

Frederick Catherwood's father owned a hotel in Rosapenna, County Donegal, and the Lloyd-Joneses took their holidays there for a number of years, Lloyd-Jones speaking 'at the Rosapenna Sunday service', but these were more private occasions.[74] So far as is known, Lloyd-Jones had no contact with Ian Paisley, MP, and his Free Presbyterian Church. In some ways there were similarities between the two men: both were distinctly Protestant, both were powerful preachers, both were key figures in their group of churches and both were influential leaders, but in other

---

70   'We arranged an overflow in the Presbyterian Church across the road, thinking many would want to hear him, but very few turned up.' H.M. Carson, tape recorded conversation, 15 April, 1995.

71   M. Coles, letter to author, 19 September, 1995.

72   *Ibid*. These were day conferences organized for ministers, with an evening public rally. In R. Beckett's experience, Lloyd-Jones spoke 'two or three times' at these conferences. Letter to author, 5 December, 1995.

73   For example, 'he spoke at the YMCA, in Wellington Hall and several of the largest Presbyterian Churches which had an evangelical minister who was willing to accommodate him'. R. Beckett, 5 December, 1995.

74   F. Catherwood, *At the Cutting Edge* (London, 1995), p.44. The hotel caught fire and burned down in the summer of 1962. Later the same year Sir Frederick and Lady Catherwood moved to Sutton Hall, Balsham near Cambridge, where they remained for the next thirty years: 'the Doctor edited most of his books there'. *Ibid*, p.72.

respects they were very different. Their style of leadership was such that it is doubtful if they could ever have worked together. Paisley, an Ulsterman, was a polemicist and was as much at home in the House of Commons or on a soapbox as he was in the pulpit. He had widespread political support in Northern Ireland and was vigorously anti-Catholic. But such a mix of politics, religion and denunciation did not meet with Lloyd-Jones's approval as is seen in the case of T.T. Shields of Canada, who was fiercely opposed to all forms of apostasy but who, Lloyd-Jones noted, 'lost most of his supporters. These men are tragedies to be pitied.'[75]

Inter-Varsity Fellowship

Of greater consequence was the involvement of Lloyd-Jones in the Inter-Varsity Fellowship.[76] Until 1910 the growing number of Christian Unions in British universities and colleges had been associated with the Student Christian Movement, a group which had emerged from the Student Volunteer Missionary Union which, in 1894, had widened into the British College Christian Union. In 1914, SCM had become influential, with a branch in 'virtually every university and college in the country'.[77] By the early 1900s, however, a group of men who saw liberal criticism as 'a great movement of the Spirit' had moved into the SCM leadership, and by 1906 the movement had decided 'to adopt frankly the modern position about the Bible' and to 'shake itself free' from the old conservative approach.[78] In 1910 the Cambridge Inter-Collegiate Christian Union, which with the London Inter-Hospital Christian Union had remained evangelical, disaffiliated from SCM, and it was from this source that post-war evangelical missions in British colleges developed, emerging finally in the linking of these Unions 'under the name of the

---

75   Lloyd-Jones, *Letters 1919-1981*, p.228. I.T. Shields was minister of Jarvis Street Baptist Church, Toronto, for over forty years.

76   For another account of Lloyd-Jones's involvement with the IVF, see O. Barclay, *Evangelicalism in Britain 1935-1995: A Personal Sketch* (Leicester, 1997), pp.47-53 and *passim*.

77   Johnson, *Contending for the Faith*, pp.47, 68.

78   T. Tatlow, *The Story of the Student Christian Movement* (London, 1933), pp.260, 213, 272. Tissington Tatlow was General-Secretary of SCM 1898-1900 and 1903-29. SCM had become the British wing of the World Student Christian Federation founded by John R. Mott in 1895, and its four-yearly missionary conventions had produced a more comprehensive approach. By 1910, SCM was drawing into its membership 'Christian men of all types and points of view', p.381. It was these early SCM leaders who became part of the World Confederation in Edinburgh in 1910, a conference which was one of the factors which led to the ecumenical movement.

Inter-Varsity Fellowship in 1928'.[79] Lloyd-Jones was right to call the IVF
'a separatist movement': as he said, it was the liberalism, modernism and
Higher Criticism of 'other student movements' that 'gave birth to the
IVF'.[80]

In the early days Lloyd-Jones had resisted movements such as the IVF.
In time, however, he came to support it.[81] His first major appearance on
the IVF scene was in April 1935 when he preached at the same
conference as Bishop J. Taylor Smith at Swanwick,[82] and the next was at
an international conference of evangelical students in Cambridge in
1939, the year in which he first became IVF President. At the Easter
conference of 1941 and 1942, held at Trinity College, Cambridge, 'the
Master, Sir George Trevelyan honoured the Fellowship by attending the
Presidental addresses given by Dr. Martyn Lloyd-Jones' and Iain Murray
adds that Trevelyan was accompanied by the Cambridge philosopher
C.D. Broad.[83]

If he was hesitant initially, it was not long before he went on to shape
the outlook of a rising generation of evangelical students, so much so that
Sir Norman Anderson, a regular speaker and writer for the IVF,
considered him to be 'virtually unrivalled' in the early years of the
fellowship.[84] Lloyd-Jones was President five times,[85] but he contributed in
other ways too. As we have seen, Lloyd-Jones took part in the Biblical
Research Committee conference on 7-10 July 1941 at Kingham Hall
School, Oxford, by giving a paper on 'The Causes of Present Weakness',
but although the conference closed with unanimous objectives, what he

---

79   Johnson, *Contending for the Faith*, pp.83, 69-78, 138.

80   Lloyd-Jones, *Knowing the Times*, pp.280, 288. 'They did not decide to stay in
the Student Christian Movement and try to win it from the inside... They believed that
the only way in which they could safeguard the gospel and the truth of God was to
separate from SCM', p.280.

81   Of the IVF in Wales he said, 'I felt it was not needed. I felt that our life was based
on the Church, that we were not in sympathy with movements.' 'I opposed the setting up
of an IVF Conference in Wales, I opposed it for years.' *Evangelical Magazine of Wales*,
August/September, 1969, p.9. See also Murray, *The First Forty Years*, p.367.

82   Murray, *The First Forty Years*, p.297. The Hayes estate in Swanwick was
purchased on behalf of the SCM in 1911. It was developed and extended and, largely
through the influence of Tissington Tatlow, the Swanwick site became a popular
conference centre for different organizations, and still is. See M. Byard, *The Story of the
Hayes Conference Centre* (1944).

83   Johnson, *Contending for the Faith*, p.201, and Murray, *The Fight of Faith*,
p.68.

84   Sir Norman Anderson, letter to author, 6 May, 1991.

85   Lloyd-Jones, *Letters 1919-1981*, p.44. 'They had decided that I should remain
President of the IVF for the duration of the war!' He was President 1939-40, 1940-41,
1941-42, 1951-52, 1963-64, and Chairman of the Universities Executive Committee,
1951-52.

had to say was hardly conducive to evangelical unity. Among his eight general causes was an attack on English evangelicalism and in his three particular causes he spoke of an undue emphasis on 'the imminence of the Second Advent' which had 'left a legacy which militated against scholarship'. He criticized the 'new direction' of evangelism that divorced the gospel message from evangelical theology, and went on to attack the Keswick 'higher-life' movement.[86] How the other members of the conference responded to this we do not know, but from Douglas Johnson's remark that there had been 'a whole day of lively discussion'[87] we may infer that Lloyd-Jones did not have it all his own way. Still, the issues raised in 1941 were important not only because they shaped Lloyd-Jones's ministry among students but because they remained with him throughout his life.

His Kingham Hall paper, while it may appear negative, should be seen as part of his wider concern that IVF should be grounded in biblical doctrine. He wanted people to resist easy believism and to think for themselves. It was this more intellectual element that accounted for his encouragement of scholarship, although it was scholarship in partnership with the Holy Spirit: 'if we begin to rely upon scholarship we are finished. We must rely upon nothing other than the Spirit of the living God'.[88] Lloyd-Jones was in at the launch of Tyndale House in 1941[89] and of the Graduate Fellowship in 1955, and became a frequent speaker at theo-logical students' conferences as well as Christian Medical Fellowship meetings. But although he preached Protestant orthodoxy with an evangelistic emphasis, including appeals to trust in Christ, and

---

86 Murray, *The Fight of Faith*, pp.71-74. 'If you teach that sanctification consists of "letting go" and letting the Holy Spirit do all the work, then don't blame me if you have no scholars!' *Ibid.*

87 Johnson, *Contending for the Faith*, p.210. Douglas Johnson read English at University College, London, graduating in 1924. In October he moved to King's College where he studied medicine. Also in 1924, while still a student, he became IVF Conference Secretary and with this began a lifelong commitment to IVF as 'the midwife behind successive and significant evangelical ventures of the 20th century.' The Times, 14 December, 1991, p.16. The other members of the conference were G.T. Manley of St. Luke's, Hampstead, F.F. Bruce, Lecturer in Classics at Leeds University, Donald MacLean, Principal of the Free Church College, Edinburgh, W.J. Martin, Rankin Lecturer in Semitic Languages at Liverpool University, Alan Stibbs, Vice-Principal of Oak Hill Theological College, London, and J. Stafford Wright, Principal of the Bible Churchman's Missionary Society College, Bristol.

88 *Christian Graduate*, March, 1962, Vol.15, No.1, p.5.

89 Tyndale House was secured in Cambridge in September 1944, and dedicated in January 1945. The House is in Selwyn Gardens and houses a residential research library. In time the library attained international status, and possessed 'some rare publications which are absent from the holdings of its gigantic neighbour—Cambridge University Library.' F.F. Bruce, *In Retrospect* (London, 1980), p.127.

students were converted, he was most effective as an adviser and counsellor. The IVF Constitution of 1924 provided for 'an Advisory Committee of four' to help students in theological and other matters, but by 1928 this had expanded to six, and three more were added later, one of whom was Lloyd-Jones.[90]

Thus, contrary to what Oliver Barclay later decribed as 'an intellectual inferiority complex' among post-war evangelical students, Lloyd-Jones gave 'godly counsel' to 'leaders of student movements' on an 'enormous range of problems'.[91] One occasion was his sermon to the Advisory Committee—'In my capacity as Chairman'—on science and religion in 1959, another was his comparison between the Christian and scientific approach to truth in 1963, and a further example was his address to the Quarter-Centenary Dinner of the CMF at the Royal College of Physicians in 1973, 'On treating the whole man'.[92] His counsel in the dual capacity of doctor and pastor was obviously welcome to members of the CMF, and his name appears regularly in 'The Medical Section' of the *Christian Graduate*. He chaired the 'Medical Studies Group' (appointed to look at medical, scientific and ethical problems), and from 1959 'devoted a Monday evening bimonthly to lead the group, something he continued to do for 15 years'. His last address to the CMF was at a Study Group Dinner on 23 November 1978.[93]

There were international ramifications as well. As President of the British IVF he was present at the fourth International Fellowship of Evangelical Students conference at Cambridge in 1939, and preached on 'The One Essential', holding 'the close attention' of over 800 students from thirty-three countries.[94] There had been pre-war international conferences—Oslo in 1934 and Budapest in 1937—but it was not until 1939 that the intention to establish a more permanent relationship emerged. With the onset of the Second World War no further action was

---

90   The six were Clarence Foster, J. Stuart Holden, J. Russell Howden, W. Graham Scroggie, A. Rendle Short and H. Earnshaw Smith. Those added were Duncan Blair, Professor of Anatomy at Glasgow, Archdeacon T.C. Hammond of Dublin and Lloyd-Jones.

91   *Christian Graduate*, June, 1981, Vol.34, No.2, p.18. Catherwood (ed.), *Chosen by God*, p.124, and *Evangelical Times*, April, 1981, Vol.XV, No.4, p.16.

92   Lloyd-Jones, *Letters 1919-1981*, p.190: D.M. Lloyd-Jones, *The Approach to Truth: Scientific and Religious* (London, 1963), and D.M. Lloyd-Jones, *On Treating the Whole Man* (London, 1972).

93   D. Johnson, *The CMF—Its Background and History* (Leicester, 1987), p.36, and Murray, *The Fight of Faith*, p.675. This last address was not recorded.

94   D. Johnson, *A Brief History of the International Fellowship of Evangelical Students* (Lausanne, 1964), p.67. 'The One Essential' was faith in Christ as Lord and Saviour. IFES differs from IVF in that it is indigenously and federally controlled, not by a central office but by leaders within their own countries. It is a union of affiliated interdenominational evangelical groups, of which the British IVF is one member.

taken until, in April 1946, a committee of delegates from Europe, North America and Australia met for fellowship and discussion, particularly to debate a basis of faith and action which Lloyd-Jones had been asked to draw up earlier, probably in 1939. At the 1946 IFES general committee meeting in Regent's Park College, Oxford, he 'presented proposals, clause by clause, and ably argued for various amendments to be included in the new constitution'.[95] At the same time he was elected Vice-Chairman of the emergent fellowship. At the Boston conference in August 1947, the draft constitution was further debated, amended and finally adopted, and the chairman being unable to be present, 'Dr. Lloyd-Jones presided over the assembly'.[96] He remained Chairman of the Executive Committee until the Paris conference in 1959 when he became President until 1967, and was thereafter Vice-President until the end of his life.

Lloyd-Jones was not, of course, the only figure of note in international evangelical student circles—he was only one of the founding fathers—but there can be no doubt that his influence was formative and, set against the growth of IFES, it was extensive. His idea of an open Fellowship where each indigenous group was encouraged to develop its own style of leadership within its own cultural ethos, so avoiding Western—that is to say Anglo-American dominance—was especially relevant and a matter close to his own feelings as a Welshman. It was this autonomy of each national member that made IFES possible and was the key to its success. Just how successful may be seen by the number of affiliations from member movements: in 1946 there were nine, in 1959 twenty-one, and in 1971 there were forty. In 1983 there were fifty-nine affiliated countries 'and if we include pioneering areas IFES is active in around 100 countries' with an estimated 270,000 students involved. By 1985 there were an estimated 300,000 students linked with a movement affiliated to the IFES and by 1995, the work had 'spread to approximately 135 countries'.[97]

Such rapid growth both in the IVF and the IFES owed much to Lloyd-Jones in the early years. Indeed, according to Chua Wee-hian, it 'stirred Archbishop Howard Mowll of Sydney to propose that Dr. Lloyd-Jones

---

95   Catherwood (ed.), *Chosen by God*, p.112. The IFES Doctrinal Basis is almost identical to IVF, but it is slightly stronger in that it includes a reference to the ascension of Christ and a clause on justification by faith. The latter clause was added to the IVF (UCCF) Doctrinal Basis c.1990.

96   *Ibid*, p.113. The conference met at Phillips Brooks House, Harvard University. The missing chairman was Nils Dahlberg of Stockholm who had resigned from the International Executive the previous year.

97   P. Lowman, *The Day of His Power* (Leicester, 1983), pp.327, 368-370, and Catherwood, *A Family Portrait*, p.90.

should visit university centres worldwide',[98] though this was unlikely given the importance he attached to his Westminster Chapel ministry.

There is little question that Lloyd-Jones felt that the IVF and IFES were useful tools for infiltrating colleges and universities with the gospel and he had a high regard for them. But when he prayed 'Let us thank God for the IVF', what he had in mind was the gospel as he understood it. Accordingly, the 'genius of the IVF as a movement' was unity in a 'hard core' of biblical doctrines with liberty on secondary issues, and this exactly reflected his view of an irreducible minimum of truth. His exhortation on the fiftieth anniversary of the founding of the IVF was, 'In the name of God I appeal to you: stand in the truth that you have received; stand- fast, stand firm!' Such was his emphasis at the Schloss Mittersill conference in 1971: 'We must always keep the church under the Word, and we must keep a movement like this IFES under the Word.'[99] In 1949 about 3,000 students were involved in British IVF groups. By 1977-78 there were 14,000 members in over fifty universities and colleges, with over a thousand students in Cambridge alone who 'met in Bible Study groups'.[100] As Oliver Barclay said, 'he taught a whole generation of Christian Union members and evangelical theological students to love doctrine, and to be bold in declaring it'.[101]

Even so, there are indications that his interest in the IVF cooled off during the 1960s, although not his concern for the CMF or IFES. When speaking at the dedication of the new IVF office building in 1961 he identified liberalism, Moral Re-Armament, compromise among men who were 'once very prominent within the Fellowship', and Barthianism as part of the 'fierce battle' of early days, and under the heading 'Present Danger' he warned of complacency and intellectual pride.[102] Writing to Philip Hughes in 1960, Lloyd-Jones referred to 'anti-reformed activity' in the Advisory Committee.[103] Whether this was true or not it was clearly

98   Catherwood (ed.), *Chosen by God*, p.113.

99   Lloyd-Jones, *Knowing the Times*, pp.60, 55, 298, 315. Schloss Mittersill is an international conference centre in the Austrian mountains.

100   Lowman, *The Day of His Power*, pp.96, 99.

101   *Christian Graduate*, June, 1981, p.18.

102   *Christian Graduate*, March, 1962, Vol.15, No.1, pp.2, 4. Since 1932 the IVF had been housed in a one-room flat at 43 Russell Square, but in 1961 they moved to larger premises at 39 Bedford Square, and it was on this occasion, 29 September, that Lloyd-Jones preached. In 1976 the IVF, which had become the Universities and Colleges Christian Fellowship in 1970, moved to its present address of 38 De Montfort Street, Leicester. Johnson, *Contending for the Faith*, pp.338-339.

103   Lloyd-Jones, *Letters 1919-1981*, p193, and footnote. Lowman, *The Day of His Power*, p.98, comments that 'Many students were divided over issues of "Calvinist" theology in the late 1950s and early 1960s, and over the charismatic movement; from the mid-1960s onward student leaders and staff had to work hard at "keeping the fundamentals fundamental"', in Oliver Barclay's phrase, 'emphasizing that the groups

a reference to what he saw as a weakening of principle and doctrine, especially among the Anglicans. He was more specific in 1971: men 'have undergone a great change in recent years, some of whom admit it openly' (a reference to the IVF), and these 'would try to claim that they are truly evangelical'. At the same conference, there were men, he said, 'adhering to the old position and those who are tending to depart from it at the present time'.[104] The letter to Hughes was a comment on what he saw as a move away from the truth, but what he had in mind in 1971 was the Keele Congress and the way in which men like Packer and Stott, among others, had declared their willingness for dialogue with ecumenism. The last occasion Lloyd-Jones addressed a British IVF conference was at Swanwick in 1969, and there he cautioned, 'Be careful with whom you associate', 'be careful that in our desire to be considered intellectually respectable, we do not expose ourselves to infection'. There was to be no 'pandering to modern ideas' or 'using modern methods' in the presentation of the gospel.[105] It could be said that this cooling off towards the IVF arose out of an increasingly busy life, but that had not prevented his full support in the past. Far more likely was his growing antipathy to Anglicanism and the presence of many Anglicans within the IVF.[106]

Nevertheless, his influence in the formative years of the IVF is not to be doubted. In the 1930s and 1940s when 'Reformed doctrine was very novel'[107] and when Christian Unions were not notably strong doctrinally or numerically, Lloyd-Jones more than any other took a leading part in changing the situation. He did so by bringing an intellectual element into evangelicalism and by convincing people of its truth. Above all, it was the 'either or' effect which dominated, persuading some to accept him gladly and others to reject him outright. In the IFES his encouragement of indigenous student responsibility helped to provide the next generation of leaders and this should also be seen as part of his legacy. So too should his work on the doctrinal basis which became 'something of a rallying-point for evangelicals' and united 'all Christians who based their witness

---

were neither pro- nor anti-"Calvinist" [and] charismatic'. Among the early compromisers were F.D. Coggan, later Archbishop of Canterbury, H. Gough, later Archbishop of Sydney, Thomas F. Thomas, later Professor of Christian Dogmatics, Edinburgh, and James Barr, later Regius Professor of Hebrew at Oxford. F.F. Bruce was also suspect.

104 Lloyd-Jones, *Knowing the Times*, pp.305, 319.

105 *Ibid*, pp.296-297.

106 A view confirmed by Herbert Carson, himself an Anglican and vicar of St. Paul's, Cambridge, until 1965, and an IVF Travelling Secretary in Ireland, 1948-51: 'IVF was strongly influenced by Anglicans, John Stott in particular.' Tape recorded coversation, 15 April, 1995.

107 Catherwood (ed.), *Chosen by God*, p.16.

and life on the authority of the Bible'.[108] Lindsay Brown calls Lloyd-Jones 'the architect of our Doctrinal Basis' which 'has not changed since it was first written 48 years ago', and if, as Brown said, 'Most movements around the world base their Doctrinal Basis on the IFES version',[109] this means that Lloyd-Jones played a major part in the foundation and unity of IFES groups in over 100 countries. With the IFES basis of doctrine— 'the standard statement of biblical faith'[110]—and the IVF statement, Lloyd-Jones helped to provide a lasting summary of crucial doctrines which have anchored these movements to evangelicalism ever since.

Contradictions

By attempting, in these last two chapters, to show something of the nature and extent of Lloyd-Jones's leadership we have come across a number of contradictions. On the one hand he dismissed 'foolish talk about personality', but on the other he allowed himself to function as a 'benevolent dictator'. He appeared to have no personal ambition for leadership yet he operated at times in an almost papal capacity. While 'not concerned to defend any party line' his preoccupation with such matters as secession and the British Evangelical Council made him a party man. He eschewed movements yet he led one.

Part of the reason for this was the way people revered him. There was often a servile attitude towards him and some 'almost worshipped the ground he walked on and quoted him as if they were quoting Scripture'.[111] People at the Wednesday discussion at Westminster Chapel, for example, spoke of him 'in semi-hushed tones, almost with a feeling of papal infallibility',[112] and this was a sentiment reflected to various degrees in ministers' meetings and conferences. Congregations followed his every word and ministers of the same mind saw him as 'the prophetic voice of authority' and the 'single most formative influence on the generation of men who were called to minister in the decades following the Second World War'.[113] For others, the Westminster Fellowship under the chairmanship of Lloyd-Jones was '"a finishing school" for ministers' where members were privileged to hear him and be made 'ready for life'.[114]

---

108 Lowman, *The Day of His Power*, p.336.

109 Lindsay Brown, letter to author, 5 June, 1995: 'he told me while I was a student that others had called him "the theologian of the IFES"'.

110 Lowman, *The Day of His Power*, p.336. Lowman is quoting Derel Williams and John Capon in 'Advance and Divide', *Today*, July, 1982, p.40.

111 Gilbert Kirby, tape recorded conversation, 6 August, 1991.

112 'Personal Information 2'.

113 *Evangelical Magazine of Wales*, April, 1981, p.46.

114 Catherwood (ed.), *Chosen by God*, pp.210-211.

Another reason lay in the dogmatic, repetitive nature of his preaching. Of the former he said, 'Some may object to my dogmatic assertions; but I do not apologize for them', and of the latter, 'it is part of the very nature and essence of teaching and preaching that there should be repetition; it helps to drive the point home and to make it clear'.[115] In his Preface to *Atonement and Justification* he wrote of 'much repetition' and refers to the 'Apostle himself' who 'repeated himself frequently ...[and]...delighted in doing so'.[116] He was probably on the defensive, but the conclusion is that if repetition of this nature has the imprimatur of the Apostle Paul, none should query the need for Lloyd-Jones's recapitulations. But however that may be, sixteen relatively short chapters in Romans hardly compares with 331 sermons in twelve volumes over eleven years, and one might be forgiven for seeing this more as a weakness than a strength.[117] His dogmatism allowed no room for doubt since each sermon was 'the result of an acceptance of certain truths, and the working out of a reasoned, logical argument'.[118] Inviolable truth could not be nebulous: the 'more vague and indefinite your religion, the more comfortable it is. There is nothing so uncomfortable as clear-cut Biblical truths that demand decisions.'[119] In other words, the most notable feature of Lloyd-Jones's public ministry was a black-and-white approach to almost every issue which, inevitably, had a polarizing effect. People either liked what they heard or they did not. There was no middle ground, and this gave the impression that whatever he said was unassailable and definitive. It was not, but it seemed so to those who listened.

There were times when in pursuing the truth the nature of the man impinged on the nature of Christian leadership. Granted that Lloyd-Jones had a softer side and privately 'was a gentle-man'[120] to those who knew

---

115 Lloyd-Jones, *Preaching and Preachers*, p.4. See also pp.124, 71.

116 D.M. Lloyd-Jones, *Atonement and Justification* (Edinburgh, 1970), pp.xii-xiii.

117 The series extended to Romans 14:17 and lasted thirteen years, from 1955-68. Only twelve volumes were available at this time. At least ten minutes of every sermon was taken up with recapitulation and at that rate, it was easy to extend a sermon to sixty minutes. There is some truth in Gilbert Kirby's remark that 'he preached for an hour but he only said the same amount as you and I might say in twenty minutes'. Tape recorded conversation, 6 August, 1991.

118 Lloyd-Jones, *Why Does God Allow War?*, p.10.

119 Lloyd-Jones, *Spiritual Depression*, p.44.

120 G.A. Hemming, letter to author, 14 January, 1995. Lloyd-Jones had much of what Kenneth Slack called the '"Bossiness" of Presbyterianism'. K. Slack, *The United Reformed Church* (Exeter, 1978), p.25. There was much of the despot in his temperament and he gave the impression of 'divine right' when it came to the interpretation of Scripture, but in private 'he would admit grey areas and in personal matters to do with ministers he was remarkably soft when the occasion arose'. R.W. Davey, tape recorded conversation, 12 February, 1992.

him, but he could also be harsh in the way he put people down in public meetings. As a chairman he 'could be a ferocious beast if he took it in his head to pursue you on some point' and 'many fled in terror, not recognizing the loving heart of the man and his determination to hold the truth'.[121] The same ferocity appears in Frederick Catherwood's experience of discussion classes in the early 1970s. Confronting 'the few who could stand it', Lloyd-Jones relentlessly pursued the falseness of their arguments until, finally, their folly was exposed. Evidently one of the men who was led down the 'false trail' of his own thinking was Catherwood himself ,who afterwards received an apology from Lloyd-Jones: 'I know that a lot of people hold the view that you put, and I cannot be as brutal with them in public, as I have been with you, but I know you are big enough to take it.'[122] Whether hidden intention—'the loving heart'—is an excuse for public discourtesy, others may judge. Some may feel that the combative, forceful style of Lloyd-Jones was useful in the pursuit of truth, others might see it as bullying.

All the same, there is no doubt that he was a leader and that British evangelicalism owes much to him. Whether he desired a more obvious form of leadership is uncertain. He showed little interest in the early years when, according to Iain Murray, J.D. Jones expressed the wish that he might succeed him as a leader of the Free Church in Britain: 'I could have been President of the Free Church Council or the Congregational Union years ago. I could have had it all'. But he had declined.[123] Even so, George Hemming remembers Lloyd-Jones thinking about putting 'himself at the head of a movement in Wales because he thought there was a glimmer of hope for revival in Wales',[124] and when R.T. Kendall asked Lloyd-Jones what was 'his greatest disappointment in life?', he replied, 'I have never been asked to lead anything'. This appears to be a reference to 1966 or 1967, the point at which he came nearest to heading up a new church grouping. Nothing came of it, as we have seen, but Kendall was in no doubt that 'he was disappointed. He could have done it.'[125] This was true, yet for some reason he held back, but if there were a lack of nerve or resolution, he was quite clear about leaders who 'no

121 A. Motyer, letter to author, 10 June, 1991.

122 *Evangelical Times*, J uly, 1967, Vol.1, No.1, p.9.

123 Murray, *The Fight of Faith*, pp.62, 505. On J.D. Jones see Alan Argent, 'The Pilot on the Bridge: John Daniel Jones (1865-1942)', in *JURCHS*, Vol.5, No.10, June 1997, pp.592-622.

124 G.A. Hemming, 14 January, 1995. This was in the early 1960s. The Evangelical Movement of Wales had expanded considerably since 1952, as we have seen, and Lloyd-Jones became a key figure in it.

125 R.T. Kendall, tape recorded conversation, 8 October, 1991. In contrast to what others have said, Kendall was also of the opinion that 'he wanted to start a new denomination in 1966' but was disappointed with the lack of response.

longer lead but allow their views to be determined by the majority'. Lloyd-Jones was made of sterner stuff and there was something autobiographical in his call for 'all needed aid' for those 'who are ready to make great sacrifices and to suffer for God's cause and truth'.[126]

A Party Man?

But could it be said that he was a party man? Lloyd-Jones did not think he was. Speaking about the splintering of the Puritan Party at the time of the Commonwealth and the ascendancy of the Laudian Party in the seventeenth century, he decried the notion of thinking 'in terms of party advantage': 'There is nothing, it seems to me, that is more offensive, or more removed from the spirit of the New Testament than a party spirit that puts the interests of its own particular point of view upon matters that are not of primary and central importance.'[127] Again, '"party spirit" is always wrong... There are people who are controlled and animated by a party-spirit and by labels; and if you do not subscribe to their particular shibboleth you are condemned'.[128] In *Maintaining the Evangelical Faith Today* he said, 'Nor must we be animated by a mere party spirit' or give the impression of fighting for a 'particular theological party' rather than for the truth itself. Yet, in spite of all that he said, this is exactly what he was doing—fighting for a particular theological party. It was a party because Lloyd-Jones and those who stood with him maintained a specific cause and held certain opinions in opposition to others. For them, the 'charge of intolerance' was a compliment and the stream of evangelical witness from the New Testament down the centuries of church history[129] proved the case for evangelicalism. Others could have said the same about Catholicism. If by party we mean loyalty to a group, and if by party spirit we mean the meeting of kindred minds with a common aim, and if by a party line we mean a dogma to which all were expected to subscribe, then Lloyd-Jones was a party man. In these senses of the word the great British Evangelical Council meetings, where Lloyd-Jones preached his keynote sermons between 1967 and 1979, were party rallies.

In the early years it was more of a trend than a party line. For example, expository and doctrinal preaching before 1939 had become rare in England and it was one of Lloyd-Jones's greatest achievements to have altered this in one generation. The impact of this kind of preaching was felt in ministers' conferences, churches and student meetings. But by the

---

126 D.M. Lloyd-Jones, 'Annual Letter to Members', January, 1965.

127 Lloyd-Jones, *The Puritans*, p.70.

128 Lloyd-Jones, *Christian Unity*, p.251. By way of illustration he recalls a friend was 'once told me that he was somewhat disappointed, because in my exposition of the second chapter of Ephesians I had not once mentioned Calvinism', *ibid.*

129 Lloyd-Jones, *Maintaining the Evangelical Faith Today*, pp.6, 10.

mid-1960s, the call to separate 'from everything that is represented by the World Council of Churches and the ecumenical movement' had become a major part of his message, and this divided those whom God had united on the basis of Scripture and who had a common purpose and trust. When he said, 'I do not separate from my own brother', and when he declared of men who believed the same gospel, 'I am not going to divide from him',[130] it was not evangelicals like Stott or Packer he had in mind, but his BEC congregation. Men like Stott and Packer (and there were many more) were neither ritualists nor liberals and had equally strong views on the gospel and the church and a clear conscience about their convictions and motives. To exclude such men was sectarian. Stott believed that 'the purity and truth of the church should be our goal' and Packer's view was that he could see 'that certain things needed to be changed in the Church of England for the better and I believed I could see how those changes could be brought about'.[131]

What Lloyd-Jones may have feared above all was the strength of leadership of these men, especially that of Stott, who steered people away from separatism towards 'a third alternative of staying in under protest, and witnessing to the truth'. This was undoubtedly the issue at the Westminster Central Hall in 1966: Stott's intervention before the final hymn was a move against secession, and it worked. In fact 1966 was the point at which Lloyd-Jones's wider leadership became more limited. After this, as Alec Motyer says, 'it was never possible to look at him as a leader and a wise man in quite the same way', and by 1977 Lloyd-Jones was looking back at the Luther address as the time when 'things became clearer' as to 'the ridiculous position' of Anglican evangelicals and the Evangelical Alliance.[132]

Although Lloyd-Jones had been influential among British evangelicals up to the mid-1960s, that influence steadily declined thereafter. He had marginalized himself to such an extent that the majority of Christians outside his own circles had little knowledge of him and the religious press, which had once followed him closely, was either unaware of him or ignored him. His claim—'We are separatists. We are nonconformists. We

---

130 Lloyd-Jones, *Unity in Truth*, pp.100, 121, 120.

131 John Stott, letter to author, 21 March, 1995, and James Packer, letter to author, 7 June, 1991.

132 Alec Motyer, 10 June, 1991. Lloyd-Jones, *Unity in Truth*, p.167: 'The Evangelical Alliance...decided to adopt a position to the World Council of Churches which it described as "benevolent neutrality". I felt that I could no longer belong to that body nor function in connection with it.' Frederick Catherwood later became President of the Alliance, and in an address to the EA on 30 April 1995, complimented them on having 'stuck through thick and thin to the faith once delivered to the saints' and, he continued, 'viewed from the outside, it's on you that the future in our country depends'. *Church of England Newspaper*, 12 May, 1995, pp.7, 12.

are dissenters'[133]—was sincere enough, but it was sectarian and out of keeping with the ecclesiastical climate of the times.

The impact of Stott, Packer and to some extent F.F. Bruce,[134] may have been precipitating factors in his call for separation, as was the ecumenical trend and a growing rejection of biblical inerrancy. But ultimately it was more a matter of personality than anything else.[135] He was an individualist and not the kind of man to retreat on a matter of principle.[136] That he was alone among all the religious figures of his day would only have reflected his Luther-like resolve to defend the faith. But the fact remains, no one else came forward to lead the separatists and Independent evangelicals.

---

133 Lloyd-Jones, *Unity in Truth*, p.178.

134 Bruce's reputation as an international biblical scholar and his association with the IVF and other evangelical groups made him an influential figure among large numbers of students and churchmen in many countries. This influence extended over forty years from when he was an Assistant in Greek at the University of Edinburgh in 1935 to his retirement as John Rylands Professor of Biblical Criticism and Exegesis at the University of Manchester in 1978. See Bruce, *In Retrospect*.

135 Bruce agreed with this. Writing on the matter of criticizing other people, he says, 'I think...that may be very much a matter of temperament', *In Retrospect*, p.300. Some people are 'not the denouncing kind', *ibid*. Bruce, who had himself felt the sting of sarcasm, commented: 'sometimes the sharpest criticism has come from Christians who accept' the IVF/UCCF basis of faith. *Ibid*, p.302.

136 Lloyd-Jones's explanation was, 'I am by nature a pacific person, who does not like controversy... I envy those who have placid temperaments and easy-going, good-natured personalities... But time and again I have seemed to be thrust back into, and driven constantly to engage in, this difficult, searching and strenuous task—the maintenance of the evangelical witness.' Lloyd-Jones, *The Basis of Christian Unity*, p.3. Such words also suggest a sense of divine mission in what he was doing.

CHAPTER 9

Conclusion

The subject of this study was an outstanding figure in twentieth-century evangelicalism. In many respects he was a self-made man, although in retrospect it is clear how much Martyn Lloyd-Jones was influenced by his upbringing as a member of a rising middle-class family with strong Nonconformist roots and concern for the Welsh working man. As a Welsh-speaking Welshman his own country and people were never far from his thoughts and pervaded much of what he said and wrote. Yet he was never entirely at home among his compatriots and the overall impression is of a man embattled. Staunchly Welsh, he nevertheless remained on the fringe of Welsh church affairs and was ignored by the majority of ministers in his own denomination and, although unhappy with the English, he lived in England for forty-two years and was at Westminster Chapel for thirty of them. In his manner he was more a child of Edwardian England than the Cardiganshire hills and while he could be passionate in the pulpit his language was always precise and his sentences well formed. There was, then, a tension between what he was by nature and background and what he became as a member of the English professional classes.

His success as a preacher is beyond question. The didactic and at times prophetic nature of his sermons, shot through with man's fallibility and God's sovereignty, was in the old Calvinistic tradition which, by and large, had disappeared with the death of C.H. Spurgeon in 1892. There were a number of smaller congregations whose ministers had continued along the same lines, but Lloyd-Jones was the only person in Britain in the twentieth century to have preached such a gospel to consistently big congregations. Despite preachers' colleges, burgeoning evangelism and the ubiquitous nature of the charismatic movement no one remotely comparable has yet appeared on the horizon. Whether we care for the content of his preaching or not it has to be conceded that, from the beginning, he was consistent in his treatment of the Bible and never lost that sense of intensity which riveted the attention of people over a lifetime. There were slight changes of emphasis between his early and later preaching of the gospel but they were minimal and unimportant.

Thus, on 6 February 1977, the fiftieth anniversary of the commencement of his ministry at Sandfields, Port Talbot, he returned to preach on the same text that he had expounded on Sunday evening, 28 November 1926.[1] His convictions had not changed in half a century.

There were criticisms, of course, some from fellow evangelicals like Peter De Jong who, while thankful for Lloyd-Jones's 'incalculable influence', was not loathe to question his 'prolonged and heavy concentration' on one subject or doctrine,[2] but even his critics could not deny his unabating popularity as a communicator. He had the ability to fire the imagination and make people think at the same time and this coalescence of urgency and logic was a crucial factor in his appeal. He made Christian doctrine relevant and among those who followed him he was a prophet for his time. There is no doubt, however, that while people flocked to hear him wherever he went the peak of his reputation was as minister of Westminster Chapel. His Sunday evening evangelistic sermons in the 1940s and 1950s were full of a sense of the dramatic and this in itself imparted vision and commitment. The rhetoric and style, which had obviously been carefully planned, were very effective, although on Sunday mornings when he preached to the saints—getting them down to the depths of the faith—he could be equally moving. But having heard him regularly both before his retirement and afterwards our observation is that he was not as sharp at expounding Scripture or diagnosing events after he retired as he was during his week-by-week ministry as the pastor of a church. As the successor of G. Campbell Morgan and the minister of one of London's largest Nonconformist churches he had dominated the evangelical scene at a particularly changeable time in English history, but after 1968 the element of consecutiveness had gone and, perhaps because he travelled more, there was a stronger element of repetition and generalization in his preaching. He was also nearly sixty-nine years of age. Nonetheless he was still worth hearing and continued to draw crowds in Britain and overseas.

We have also looked at Lloyd-Jones in the wider context of Protestant evangelicalism in an ecumenical age and the efforts he made to expound an alternative form of unity. That there was no general response to his call for evangelical unity does not invalidate what he believed. His gift was preaching, not management strategy, and we cannot expect a man to do what he is not gifted to achieve. Whether it would have been possible, given the nature of Lloyd-Jones's character, for anyone else to have fulfilled this role is doubtful: his views appealed to too small a constituency. Nor can we blame organizations such as the FIEC or BEC, as Iain Murray

---

1   G. Thomas, 'Dr. Lloyd-Jones in South Wales', *The Banner of Truth*, April, 1977, No.163, p.12. The text was 1 Corinthians 2:2.

2   *The Outlook*, Journal of the Reformed Fellowship, August, 1980, Vol.XXX, No.8, p.10.

seems to,[3] for not producing the kind of men to take up the challenge: they simply were not there. Had an executive leader emerged at that time evangelical history might have looked very different. As it was, there was already a concern among evangelicals over the doctrine of the church and later the FIEC redefined its position on the church by adopting a new clause. The same interest was shown by the Evangelical Movement of Wales, the Evangelical Alliance and the British Evangelical Council. The catalyst for all this, however, was not the preaching of Martyn Lloyd-Jones so much as the ecumenical movement which had compelled churches to look again at what they believed. When ecumenism was seen as a threat evangelicals began asking what they believed about the church and how matters might be resolved. Naturally, among his friends the 1966 meeting was not an event to be forgotten and it was remembered in various articles from time to time. In Autumn 1990, for example, Kenneth Paterson wrote: 'Despite many changes during the last 24 years the challenge of the Doctor's address still remains', and Basil Howlett as recently as Autumn 1996, recalled the occasion with some vigour and still hoped for a 'close knit association of churches'.[4]

It was only a minority who warmed to the memory of 1966. Seen against the whole spread of evangelicalism the call to realign was a cause of fracture and disunity and while, as John Marsh said, it was 'a very bold and interesting idea', by its very nature it strongly 'accentuated the polarization of Lloyd-Jones's position'.[5] Historically, what he did was not unique. Separation and the dissenting tradition go back at least to the seventeenth century and ideological differences between churchmen have been so acute that new churches and new denominations have been formed, and this has continued to the present time. So arguments about whether people should remain in their churches or secede have a long history. What was unfortunate in this case was that Lloyd-Jones's insistence on separatism as a fundamentally biblical position alienated a body of opinion which was just as evangelical and loyal to Scripture. To separate from genuine evangelicals was, in our view, schismatic. In the broader sense, to cut oneself off from other Christians in order to create a separated, holy society was a form of Christianity that was no longer acceptable. Times had changed. Right or wrong, Lloyd-Jones's call to separate was out of date, and it is not surprising that as his views sharpened some came to look on him 'as a stormy petrel and enfant terrible'.[6]

Yet Lloyd-Jones was not a vain man, neither was he bigoted: his views were sincerely held and sprang from what he believed to be the truth, not from any dislike of other people. That he found it difficult to understand

---

3   Murray, *The Fight of Faith*, p.559.
4   *In Step*, BEC Newsheet No.45, Autumn, 1990, and No.57, Autumn, 1996.
5   John Marsh, letter to author, 8 March, 1991.
6   John Caiger, tape recorded conversation, 11 February, 1992.

the modern church and differed from it on a number of issues was inevitable given the nature of his faith. When he found it necessary to fight his corner it may not always have been as easy as it appeared: as he said, 'It is not pleasant to be negative; it is not enjoyable to have to denounce and to expose error'.[7] On the other hand he could not be impartial and when he did argue his case it was in the belief that he was right: it was never a matter for discussion.

There were anomalies that made it difficult to take everything he said at face value, but where contradictions did appear it was more a matter of emphasis than substance. In a way he was one man in the pulpit and another over a cup of tea. While his public utterances could be narrow, arrogant and scornful, in private he was more generous. This is not to say that he changed his mind, but he had a vestry way of speaking and a public way of speaking, and issues could become blurred. There was also a confusing openness towards modern revivalist movements and when preaching on spiritual gifts and the work of the Spirit, it sounded as if he was saying different things at different times. This was one of the reasons why so many divergent groups claimed him as their man: charismatics sought his advice, Baptists and Reformed men claimed him for other reasons, and so did Independent evangelicals. He was invited to speak in different kinds of churches, including Baptist and Pentecostal, and for some this gave the impression of someone who was prepared to 'run with the hare and hunt with the hounds'. He also tended to preach to the congregation in front of him so that where he thought there was an imbalance he would speak from the opposite point of view. If, for example, he felt too much attention was given to a subjective work of the Spirit he would emphasize doctrinal and theological commitment, and vice versa. So there were some confusing elements in his preaching, but because he had access to a cross-section of evangelical churches it should not be assumed that he endorsed everything they believed. He did not.

All the same, he had no patience with the nuances of compromise and was solidly consistent, as his sermons and lectures show. His core beliefs never varied and, in his day, his contribution to evangelicalism was outstanding: he became a touchstone of orthodoxy. Unhappily he manoeuvred himself into a corner over the issue of separation and caused a breaking of fellowship when it was within his grasp to bring evangelicals together. He knew there was substantial agreement between separatist and non-separatist on gospel essentials yet he allowed a secondary issue— church affiliation—to override what was fundamental. Not only was this an opportunity lost: it established a legacy of intolerance and perpetuated divisions among British evangelicals for years to come. For those who were sympathetic, his call to withdraw and realign was a justifiable stand

---

7   Lloyd-Jones, *Christian Unity*, p.240.

against error. On the other hand, it might just as well be seen as an example of Lloyd-Jones's idiosyncratic and independent nature.

From an ecclesiastical point of view Lloyd-Jones cannot be judged a faithful member of the Welsh Presbyterian Church, nor, as minister of a historic Congregational Church, was he a loyal Congregationalist. Indeed, it could be said that he took advantage of the large-mindedness of the denominations to which Sandfields and Westminster Chapel belonged and, in a sense, betrayed them. He used their premises as a platform for his beliefs but scarcely acknowledged them except to be critical.

Nonetheless, judged by the times in which he lived, Lloyd-Jones was a dominant force in English and Welsh evangelicalism. He restored expository and textual preaching and, in conjunction with E.F. Kevan and J.I. Packer, created a turning point in the fortunes of Calvinistic Christianity in Great Britain and further afield.[8] These men came together at the same time and there was a coincidence of interest in the 1940s and 1950s between students, churches, the Puritan Conference, the Evangelical Library and the London Bible College which consolidated the movement. It was the influential preaching of Martyn Lloyd-Jones that presented a relevant Calvinism as an answer to easy believism which largely inspired a swing in the evangelical climate. He did not do it alone but he was a major force. While he asserted that evangelicals should not separate over the question of Calvinism and Arminianism,[9] in practice he strongly supported agencies, such as the Banner of Truth Trust, which promoted Reformed literature. Indeed, from the very beginning his preaching had been overtly Calvinistic and had polarized opinion among ministers and churches. However, it was his irrepressible enthusiasm for the art of preaching that was his greatest contribution. At a time when church attendances were falling and people saw how helpless the church was in the face of social and economic pressures, Lloyd-Jones was not afraid to declare the full historic faith as he understood it. Against a background of scepticism and theological change his eloquence attracted people from all strands of society and this put heart into many young ministers. Few, if any, could imitate his microscopic analysis of the Pauline Epistles or thought it wise to try, and none had his charisma and logic, but all were inspired by him. He taught generations of Christians how to use their minds and this was probably his greatest legacy. He shaped the faith of young men and women, many of whom moved on from IVF and IFES circles to become ministers or missionaries, or to take up college or university careers.

---

8   There had been a renewal of interest in Calvin's thought among Congregationalists with J.S. Whale in the 1940s and 1950s, not least through his *Christian Doctrine* (1941) and *The Protestant Tradition* (1955).

9   *The British Weekly*, 26 March, 1953, Vol.CXXXIII, p.9.

Yet after 1966, he had relatively little influence outside of a small segment of the evangelical world. True, he continued to have friends in various quarters, Welshmen like George Thomas and Lord Cledwyn— 'his influence remains with me'[10]—or Anglicans like Sir Norman Anderson and John Stott. Among his admirers were men like Lord Mackay of Clashfern who found 'his preaching impressive, direct [and] authoritative',[11] and R.W. Davey, who was 'physician to the Queen because of Dr. Lloyd-Jones: he recommended me and it was he who was influential in that I was recommended to Her Majesty'.[12] There were others, but Lloyd-Jones had marooned himself ecclesiastically and the only way his influence could have been numerically greater was if there had been the kind of revival he wished for.

Still, we should not underestimate his importance. If the mark of a leader is that he still has a following twenty years after his death, Lloyd-Jones qualifies. Every new publication of his sermons and speeches is still warmly awaited, as are his cassette recordings. Leslie Weatherhead sold more books in his lifetime,[13] but posthumously, there has been greater interest in Lloyd-Jones than in any other of his preaching contemporaries.

About fifty Lloyd-Jones titles are currently in print in Britain from around seven different publishers. Over 1,600 cassette recordings are currently available through the Recordings Trust and an estimated fifty to seventy-five other sermons are in private circulation or are distributed through Christian bookshops. Much of this ongoing tide of interest owes its momentum to the fact that there can hardly be an evangelical in Britain over the age of fifty who has not been affected by Lloyd-Jones at one time or another, and it is largely these people who are maintaining the flow of material. But whoever sustains the publishing programme, either here or abroad, his books—especially the twelve-volume exposition of Romans—will stand and be on record for the future.

Martyn Lloyd-Jones is not a man to be dismissed. He had a thirst for godly reformation and remains worth hearing or reading if only because of his unrivalled vision of God and conception of what Christianity should be. As a bishop to his people he helped many understand them-selves and the world in which they lived. That world had changed

---

10   Lord Cledwyn of Penrhos, letter to author, 8 November, 1989.

11   Lord Mackay of Clashfern, Lord Chancellor 1987-96, letter to author, 9 September, 1997

12   R.W. Davey, tape recorded conversation, 12 February, 1992. Lloyd-Jones had put him in touch with Margery Blackie, then physician to the Queen, who had received him as her successor. Lloyd-Jones had an interest in homoeopathy.

13   30,000 copies of *Prescription for Anxiety* in 1956, 300,000 copies of *The Will of God* in the 1970s, and *Psychology, Religion and Healing* (1951) has remained a major work on the subject. J.C. Travell, letter to author, 21 February, 1990.

radically and people had seen a number of the old values and certainties fall away—which is why the historic evangelicalism of Lloyd-Jones was so reassuring—but he cared about contemporary issues and struggled to make sense of them in the light of Scripture. He was, without question, one of the greatest preachers of the twentieth century.

Appendix

Table 1
The Lloyd-Jones Family

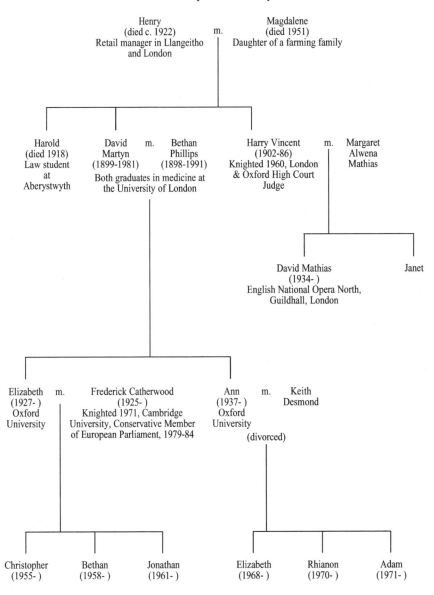

Table 2
The Phillips Family

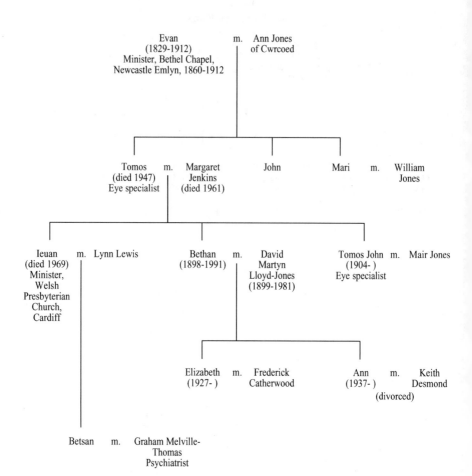

Evan m. Ann Jones
(1829-1912) of Cwrcoed
Minister, Bethel Chapel,
Newcastle Emlyn, 1860-1912

Tomos m. Margaret   John   Mari   m.   William
(died 1947) Jenkins   Jones
Eye specialist (died 1961)

Ieuan   m. Lynn Lewis   Bethan   m.   David   Tomos John m. Mair Jones
(died 1969)   (1898-1991)   Martyn   (1904-)
Minister,   Lloyd-Jones Eye specialist
Welsh   (1899-1981)
Presbyterian
Church,
Cardiff

Elizabeth   m.   Frederick   Ann   m.   Keith
(1927-)   Catherwood   (1937-)   Desmond
                                            (divorced)

Betsan   m.   Graham Melville-
                Thomas
                Psychiatrist

Table 3
Some Comparative Membership Figures for the London Area

Congregational Churches	1939	1945	1955	1965	1967
Kings Weigh Duke Street	156 E. A. Rush	N.A.	20 C. M. Coltman	26 F. R. Tomes	N.A.
Whitefield Memorial Church	New building opened October 3, 1959		110 W. Salmon	108 H. A. Jacquet	90 H. A. Jacquet
Christ Church Westminster Bridge Road[1]	N.A.	N.A.	239 M. T. Shepherd	175 L. Monteith	164 L. Monteith
Paddington Chapel	332 J. Grant	229 F. E. Quick	174 R. E. Taylor	125 L. C. K. French	113 L. C. K. French
Westminster Chapel	611 G. C. Morgan	516 D. M. Lloyd-Jones	570 D. M. Lloyd-Jones	700 D. M. Lloyd-Jones	700 D. M. Lloyd-Jones
City Temple Holborn	710 L. Weatherhead	773 L. Weatherhead	596 L. Weatherhead	505 A. L. Griffith	488 K. Slack
New Court Tollington Park	672 J. A. Kaye	462 T. J. Evans	230 W. A. Grant	148 F. J. Mortimer	143
Other Churches					
Methodist Central Hall Westminster[2]	564 W. E. Sangster	746 W. E. Sangster	1075 W. E. Sangster	994 M. Barnett	718 M. Barnett
Kingsway Hall Holborn[2]	1348 D. Soper	N. A. D. Soper	N. A. D. Soper	N. A. D. Soper	N. A. D. Soper
Bloomsbury Baptist Church[3]	568 F. T. Lord	549 F. T. Lord	585 F. T. Lord	273 H. H. Williams	332 H. H. Williams
Ferme Park Baptist Church[3]	1045 H. Cook	906 D. H. Hicks	616 D. H. Hicks	374 D. D. Black	319 D. D. Black
All Souls Langham Place[4]	260 H. H. E. Smith	N.A. H. H. E. Smith	691 J. R. W. Stott	541 J. R. W. Stott	590 J. R. W. Stott
Charing Cross Rd, Presbyterian Church of Wales[5]	1133 E. G. Evans	740 E. G. Evans	543 E. G. Evans	400 R. Jones	373 R. Jones
Marylebone Presbyterian Church[6]	647	176	103 H. T. Lewis	Closed after 1957	

[1]Combined with Upton Baptist Chapel, 1963. [2]Methodist Church Year Books. [3]Baptist Union Handbooks. [4]London Diocese Books. [5]London Presbytery Year Books. [6]Metropolitan Area Year Books.

These figures show little about the spiritual vitality of congregations nor do they say why some churches declined and others prospered. The actual sizes of congregations which in some cases exceeded membership figures and in others were much smaller, are not reflected here either. But they do indicate a general trend.

Table 4
Westminster Chapel Statistics

Ministers (with dates of ministry):

- S. Martin { 1842 – 1878
- H. Simon { 1878 – 1887
- No Settled Ministry { 1887 – 1894
- W. E. Hurndall { 1894 – 1895 / 1896
- R. Westrope { 1896 – 1902
- No Settled Ministry { 1902 – 1904
- G. C. Morgan { 1904 – 1917
- J. H. Jowett { 1918 – 1922
- J. A. Hutton { 1923 – 1925
- No Settled Ministry { 1925 – 1928
- H. L. Simpson { 1928 – 1933
- G. C. Morgan { 1933 – 1939 / 1943
- D. M. Lloyd-Jones { 1943 – 1968 / 1969
- G. Owen { 1969 – 1974

| | | Sunday School || |
Year	Members	Children	Teachers	
1841	22	N.A.	N.A.	
1863	N.A.	219	36	[1]
1877	892	N.A.	N.A.	
1879	924	323	33	[2]
1898	300	121	17	
1902	245	300	35	
1904	253	70	10	
1905	407	70	10	
1909	904	647	45	
1917	912	575	80	
1918	901	575	80	
1922	744	610	90	
1923	767	601	88	
1925	744	675	81	
1928	672	540	76	
1934	721	410	70	
1939	611	256	56	
1943	540	45	5	[3]
1945	516	N.A.	N.A.	
1950	495	150	16	
1955	570	142	24	
1960	698	100	20	
1966	700	100	20	[4]
1970	673	N.A.	N.A.	[5]

[1]S/S Teacher's Meeting Minutes, 1863. [2]Church Meeting Minutes, 1879. [3]S/S Teacher's Meeting Minutes, January 3, 1943. [4]Withdrew from CUEW in 1966. [5]Bill Reynolds, letter, June 24, 1996.

(All figures are from *Congregational Year Books* unless otherwise stated)

BIBLIOGRAPHY

Place of publication London unless otherwise stated.

Reference Works

— Holy Bible, Authorized Version (1611).
Boase, F. *Modern English Biography* (1965).
Congregational Year Book (1871, 1879, 1897, 1905, 1915, 1920, 1939, 1942, 1945, 1946).
— *Dictionary of National Biography* (1937, 1959, 1971, 1986)
— *New Encyclopaedia Britannica* (1985).
Stenton, M. *Who's Who of British Members of Parliament* (Hassocks, 1976).
Stephens, M. *Oxford Companion to the Literature of Wales* (1986).
Surman, C. *Directory of Congregational Biography, c.1640-1956* (unpublished card index)
— *Who Was Who* (2001).

Primary Sources

I. The works of D.M. Lloyd-Jones in order of publication

Why Does God Allow War? (Hodder & Stoughton, 1940).
The Plight of Man and the Power of God (Pickering & Inglis, 1945).
Truth Unchanged, Unchanging (James Clark, 1951).
From Fear to Faith (IVF, 1953).
Authority (IVP, 1958).
Studies in the Sermon on the Mount (2 vols; IVF, 1959-1960).
Faith on Trial (IVF, 1965).
Spiritual Depression (Pickering & Inglis, 1965).
Atonement and Justification (Edinburgh, Banner of Truth Trust, 1970).
Preaching and Preachers (Hodder & Stoughton, 1971).
God's Way of Reconciliation (Edinburgh, Banner of Truth Trust, 1972).
Life in the Spirit (Edinburgh, Banner of Truth Trust, 1973).
The Law: Its Functions and Limits (Edinburgh, Banner of Truth Trust, 1973).
The Sons of God (Edinburgh, Banner of Truth Trust, 1975).

The Final Perseverance of the Saints (Edinburgh, Banner of Truth Trust, 1975).

The Christian Soldier (Edinburgh, Banner of Truth Trust, 1977).

Christian Unity (Edinburgh, Banner of Truth Trust, 1980).

Darkness and Light (Edinburgh, Banner of Truth Trust, 1982).

Expository Sermons on 2 Peter (Edinburgh, Banner of Truth Trust, 1983).

Evangelistic Sermons (Edinburgh, Banner of Truth Trust, 1983).

The Gospel of God (Edinburgh, Banner of Truth Trust, 1985).

The Cross (Eastbourne, Kingsway Publications, 1986).

Revival (Basingstoke, Marshall Pickering, 1986).

I am not Ashamed (Hodder & Stoughton, 1986).

Out of the Depths (Bridgend, Evangelical Press of Wales, 1987).

The Puritans: Their Origins and Successors (Edinburgh, Banner of Truth Trust, 1987).

Assurance (Edinburgh, Banner of Truth Trust, 1988).

Healing and Medicine (Eastbourne, Kingsway Publications, 1988).

Knowing the Times (Edinburgh, Banner of Truth Trust, 1989).

The Righteous Judgement of God (Edinburgh, Banner of Truth Trust, 1989).

God's Sovereign Purpose (Edinburgh, Banner of Truth Trust, 1991).

Unity in Truth (Darlington, Evangelical Press, 1991).

The New Man (Edinburgh, Banner of Truth Trust, 1992).

The Life of Joy (Hodder & Stoughton, 1993).

The Life of Peace (Hodder & Stoughton, 1993).

D. Martyn Lloyd-Jones Letters 1919-1981 (Edinburgh, Banner of Truth Trust, 1994).

Joy Unspeakable (Eastbourne, Kingsway Publications, 1995).

God the Father, God the Son (Hodder & Stoughton, 1996).

God the Holy Spirit (Hodder & Stoughton, 1997).

Great Doctrine Series (3 vols; Hodder & Stoughton, 1996-1998).

II. Booklets and Pamphlets in order of publication

There is But One! (Glasgow, Marshall, Morgan & Scott, 1942).

Presentation of the Gospel (IVF, 1949).

Maintaining the Evangelical Faith Today (IVF, 1952).

Honour to whom Honour (Westminster Chapel, 1952).

Centenary Message (Westminster Chapel, The Lawyer's Christian Fellowship, 1952).

Christ our Sanctification (IVF, 1953).

Sound an Alarm (Westminster Chapel, 1957).

Conversions Psychological and Spiritual (IVF, 1959).

The Basis of Christian Unity (IVF, 1962) .
1662-1962 (Evangelical Library, 1962).
The Approach to Truth: Scientific and Religious (Tyndale Press, 1963.).
The Weapons of our Warfare (Westminster Chapel, 1964).
Centenary Address (Westminster Chapel, 1965).
Luther and his Message for Today (BEC, 1967).
Roman Catholicism (Evangelical Press, 1967).
An Urgent Appeal (Evangelical Library, 1968).
What is the Church? (BEC, 1969).
Will Hospital Replace the Church? (Christian Medical Fellowship, 1969).
The State of the Nation (BEC, 1971).
The Supernatural in Medicine (Christian Medical Fellowship, 1971).
On Treating the Whole Man (Christian Medical Fellowship, 1972).
Inaugural Address (London Theological Seminary, 1977).
President's Address (Evangelical Library, 1955, 1956, 1959-1969).

III. Letters and Correspondence

D.M. Lloyd-Jones, Annual Letter to Members of Westminster Chapel (1955, 1959-1968) in author's possession.
D.M. Lloyd-Jones to G.Williams (1939), Evangelical Library, used with permission.
D.M. Lloyd-Jones, Letter of Resignation (30 May 1968), copy in author's possession.

LETTERS TO AUTHOR

E.J. Alexander (1995).
Sir Norman Anderson (1991).
R. Beckett (1995).
T.H. Bendor-Samuel (1991).
F. Bowers (1994).
L. Brown (1995).
H.M. Carson (1995).
Lord Cledwyn of Penrhos (1989).
A.C. Clifford (1992).
M. Coles (1995).
J. Elwyn Davies (1995).
G. Wyn Davies (1995).
Lord Denning (1992).
A.M. Derham (1991).
R. Eeles (1995).
P.H. Eveson (1995).

R.T. France (1991).
D. Gibson (1995).
E. Guest (1992).
G.A. Hemming (1995).
C.F.H. Henry (1991).
A.S. Horne (1994).
C.D.T. James (1995, 1996).
A. Johnstone (1995).
Lord Mackay of Clashfern (1997).
M. MacLeod (1996).
J. Marsh (1991).
B. Micklewright (1991).
A. Motyer (1991, 1994).
K.H. Nicolson (1994).
J.I. Packer (1991).
I.D.G. Pickering (1995).
D. Prime (1991).
J. Raynar (1995).
W.V. Reynolds (1992, 1996).
H.H. Rowdon (1991).
T. Ruston (1995).
L. Samuel (1992).
R.Shuttler (1996).
J.R.W. Stott (1991, 1995, 1997).
Viscount Tonypandy (1989).
J.C. Travell (1990, 1994, 1997).
F. Whitehead (1991).
A.D. Williams (1995).
D. Winter (1991).

OTHER LETTERS

A.M. Derham to K.I. Patterson (1966), used with permission.
T.O. Jenkins, Annual Letter to Members of Westminster Chapel (1969).
Occasional Newsletter, London Theological Seminary (1978).
J.R.W. Stott to E. Fife (1981), used with permission.
A.F. Gibson to the editor of *Third Way* (1990).

I have also received four sources of further information referred to in the text as 'Personal Information' 1, 2, 3, 4, whose authors do not wish to be further identified.

IV. Tape Recorded Interviews

J. Caiger (1992).
H.M. Carson (1995).
R.W. Davey (1992).
A. Gibson (1991).
E.S. Guest (1992).
R.T. Kendall (1991).
E.E. King (1995).
G. Kirby (1991).
D. Mingard (1995).
J.I.Packer (1992).
D.B. Rees (1992).
M. Rowlandson (1991).
J.R.W. Stott (1991).
Martyn Lloyd-Jones Recordings Trust sermons, catalogue numbers—
4041, 5719, 5720, 5721, 5725, 5727, 5728, 5731.
Memorial Service sermon, Slough Tabernacle (1974), in private
collection of author.
Thanksgiving Service (6 April 1981), Westminster Chapel. Copy in
author's collection.

V. Notes of other interviews with author

D. Elphinstone (1995).
G. Hemming (1995).
G.F. Nuttall (1994).
D. Mathias Lloyd-Jones (1996).
I .D.G. Pickering (1995).

VI. Unpublished sources and News Sheets

Declaration of the Church of Christ, Meeting in Westminster Chapel,
October, 1841. WChA.
Westminster Chapel Trust Deed, December, 1842. WChA.
Minutes of Deacons' Meetings, October 1947, July 1956, and early
1967. WChA.
Minutes of Church Meetings, May and October 1947, January 1966,
March and April 1967. WChA.
A.E. Marsh, Retirement Address, March, 1961. WChA.
The Church, July 1965. Typescript. Author not known. WChA.

S. Curtis, 'The Church Organ: A brief account of its history', *Westminster Chapel News*, October 1965. WChA.

Minutes of Executive Council of the Evangelical Alliance, October and December 1966.

News Release, British Evangelical Council, March 1966.

Minutes of British Evangelical Council, January 1967.

Statement of Principles. Drawn up and agreed at Westminster—23 January and 13 March 1967. WChA.

Affidavit from the Reverend Edward Stanley Guest, presented to the High Court of Chancery, c.1974-75.

A. Davies, First Annual Report of the London Theological Seminary, c.1977-78.

J.R.W. Stott, 'A Visit to Dr.Lloyd-Jones', December 1978. Personal notes used with permission.

P. Collins, 'Thomas Wilson 1764-1843', September 1979. Typescript. WChA.

Westminster Chapel News, July-August 1979, May-June 1982, July-August-September 1984. WChA.

E.S. Fife, 'The Doctor Under Attack', July 1981. Typescript. In the possession of John Stott and used with permission.

In Step. News Sheet of the British Evangelical Council, Autumn 1990, 1996.

D.M. Thompson, 'Gleanings from the Archives' (n.d.). WChA.

D.M. Lloyd-Jones, 'Consider Your Ways', notes taken by E.S. Guest at the Westminster Fellowship summer meeting, June 1963.

THESES

Jung, Keun-Doo, 'An Evaluation of the Principles and Methods of the Preaching of David Martyn Lloyd-Jones', ThD thesis, Potchefstroom University, Pretoria, South Africa, 1986.

Keith, J.M., 'The Concept of Expository Preaching as Represented by Alexander Maclaren, George Campbell Morgan, and David Martin (sic) Lloyd-Jones', ThD dissertation, South Western Baptist Theological Seminary, 1975.

Penny, R.L. 'An Examination of the Principles of Expository Preaching of David Martyn Lloyd-Jones, DMin thesis, Harding Graduate School of Religion, Memphis, 1980.

Travell, J.C. 'Psychology and Ministry, with special reference to the life, work and influence of Leslie Dixon Weatherhead', PhD thesis, University of Sheffield, 1996.

VII. Other Pamphlets and Booklets

Bendor-Samuel,T.H. *One Body in the Lord* (FIEC, 1965).

Edmunds, V. and C.G. Scorer, *Some Thoughts on Faith Healing* (Christian Medical Fellowship, 1979).

Elphinstone, D. *Antioch Verse Book* (n.d.).

Elphinstone, D. *Personal Evangelism and Follow-Up* (n.d.).

Evangelical Belief (IVF, 1973).

Huxtable, J. *Traditons of our Fathers* (Independent Press, 1962).

The Moderators, *The Deacon: his ministry in our churches* (Independent Press, 1957).

Report of the Commission on Church Unity (Evangelical Alliance, 1966).

Slack, K. *The United Reformed Church* (Exeter, The Religious Education Press, 1979).

Stott, J.R.W. *The Eclectic Society* (1967).

Stott, J.R.W. *Your Mind Matters* (IVF, 1972).

This I Believe (Pickering & Inglis, n.d.).

Unity in the Faith (FIEC, n.d.).

Who Are We? (St.Albans, IVF, n.d.).

Y Ganrif Gyntaf (The First Century) (1949).

VIII. Magazines and Journals

Banner of Truth, January 1970, December 1970, June 1975, April 1977, July 1980, May 1981.

Barn (Opinion), April 1963, June 1963.

British Journal of Sociology 3, 1952.

Calvin Theological Journal, April 1966, April 1976.

Christian Graduate, September 1949, March 1962, June 1981.

Christianity Today, December 1963, December 1969, October 1971, February 1980.

Congregational Monthly, August 1966.

Congregational Quarterly, 1943 (Part 4), 1945 (Part 3), 1947 (Part 4).

Crusade, October 1966, November 1966, December, 1966.

Evangelical Magazine of Wales, August/September 1969, February 1973, April 1975, April 1981.

Evangelical Quarterly, January 1942, January 1945.

Fellowship, April 1962, May 1967.

Free Grace Record, Summer 1962.

The Friend, March 1941.

Inter-Varsity Magazine, Summer 1942.

Journal of the Evangelical Theological Society, 1982, Vol.25.

Journal of Psychology and Theology, 1973, Vol.1.

Journal of Pastoral Practice, 1981-82.
Journal of the United Reformed Church History Society, October 1987, October 1988, May 1990, October 1990, June 1997.
Life of Faith, October 1969.
Monthly Record, The Free Church of Scotland, April 1941, November 1979, December 1979, April 1981, April 1984.
Outlook, August 1980.
Princeton Seminary Bulletin, 1972.
Reformed Quarterly, United Reformed Church, Spring 1991.
Vox Evangelica XV, 1985.
Westminster Record, January 1905, June 1905, February 1906, October 1908, February 1934, August 1938, December 1939, March 1945, July 1945, August 1945, February 1947, March 1947, May 1947, May 1948, July 1951, August 1951, July 1963, February 1966, February 1967, March 1968, September 1968, November 1968, August 1976, June 1981.
Westminster Theological Journal, 1973 Vol.35, 1976 Vol.38, 1976 Vol.39.
Y Gorlan (The Fold), October 1922.
Y Cylchgrawn Efengylaidd (The Evangelical Magazine), November-December 1948, October-November 1952.
Y Efengylydd (The Evangelist), January 1929.
'Religion and Features of Nationality', a series of three talks given on Welsh Radio in 1943. Typescript translation by Dafydd Ifans. These talks, 'Crefydd a Nodweddion Cenedlaethol', were published the same year in *Y Drysorfa (The Treasury)*, and reprinted in 1947 in *Crefydd Heddiw ac Yfory (Religion Today and Tomorrow)*. As far as we know, this was not published in English.

IX. Newspapers

Baptist Times 6 May 1965, 27 October 1966.
British Weekly, 2 January 1896, 30 December 1887, 3 November 1904, 10 November 1904, 7 October 1915, 8 October 1925, 8 September 1932, 4 January 1934, 27 January 1938, 27 April 1939, 7 September 1939, 20 March 1941, 27 March 1941, 15 May 1941, 29 May, 1941, 19 December 1946, 22 May 1947, 9 March 1953, 19 March 1953, 26 March 1953, 9 April 1953.
John Bull, 25 December, 1926.
Christian, 28 November 1935, 12 December 1935, 21 October 1966, 10 November 1967.
Christian Herald, 31 July 1982.
Christian World, 1 September 1932, 29 December 1938, 24 May 1945.

Christian Age, 26 October 1904.
Church Times, 30 May 1986.
Church of England Newspaper, 3 December 1971, 12 May 1995.
Cymric Times, 4 April 1932.
Y Cymro (The Welshman), 21 August 1958.
Daily Mail, 2 October 1961.
Daily Telegraph, 11 June 1968, 13 March 1981.
Evangelicals Now, October 1986.
Evangelical Times, July 1967, November 1967, October 1970, November
    1970, April 1981.
English Churchman, 28 October 1966.
Guardian, 5 March 1991.
Glasgow Evening Citizen, 15 April 1939, 5 May 1945, 11 September
    1948.
Independent, 2 March 1991.
Liverpool Daily Post, 28 May 1954, 8 June 1954.
Methodist Recorder, 25 July 1968, 25 November 1971.
Newcastle Journal, 25 May 1960.
Observer, 19 March 1967.
People, 30 April 1939.
Sunday Dispatch, 1 March 1938.
South Wales News,7 February 1925, 9 February 1925, 11 February 1925,
    14 February 1925.
Stornoway Gazette, 5 September 1964, 19 September 1964.
Times, 7 November 1960, 25 September 1983, 14 December 1991.
Welsh Gazette, 29 December 1927.
Western Mail, 3 February 1927, 5 November 1938, 3 June 1968.
Yorkshire Evening Post, 16 November 1953.
Y Goleuad (Weekly News of the Presbyterian Church of Wales),
    November 1927, February 1933.

Secondary Sources

Ammerman, N. *Bible Believers* (New Brunswick, Rutgers University Press,
    1987).
Anderson, N. *An Adopted Son* (Leicester, IVP, 1985).
Baker, C. *Aspects of Bilingualism in Wales* (Clevedon, Multilingual
    Matters, 1985).
Ball, S. *Baldwin and the Conservative Party* (Yale University Press,
    1988).
Barr, J. *Fundamentalism* (SCM Press, 1977).
Barclay, O. *Evangelicalism in Britain 1935-1995: A Personal Sketch*
    (Leicester: IVP, 1997).

Bebbington, D.W. *Evangelicalism in Modern Britain: A History from the 1730s to the 1980s* (Unwin Hyman, 1989).

Bebbington, C. *London Street Names* (B.T. Batsford, 1972).

Bowers, F. *A Bold Experiment: The Story of Bloomsbury Chapel and Bloomsbury Central Baptist Church 1848-1999* (Bloomsbury Baptist Church, 1999)

Bowers, F. *Called to the City* (Bloomsbury Baptist Church, 1989).

Braund, E. *The Young Woman Who Lived in a Shoe* (Basingstoke, Pickering & Inglis, 1984).

Brencher, J.F. "'A Welshman Through and Through": David Martyn Lloyd-Jones (1899-1981)', *JURCHS* , December, 1998, Vol.6, No.3, pp.204-225.

Brierley, P. and Evans, B. *Prospects for Wales* (Bible Society and MARC Europe, 1982).

Brierley, P. (ed.) *UK Christian Handbook* 1985/86 and 1994/95 (Christian Research Association, 1985, 1993).

Bruce, F.F. *In Retrospect* (Pickering & Inglis, 1980).

Catherwood, F. and E. *The Man and His Books* (Evangelical Library, 1982).

Catherwood, F. *At the Cutting Edge* (Hodder & Stoughton, 1995).

Catherwood, C. *Five Evangelical Leaders* (Hodder & Stoughton, 1984).

Catherwood, C. *Martyn Lloyd-Jones: A Family Portrait* (Eastbourne, Kingsway Publications, 1995).

Catherwood, C. (ed.) *Martyn Lloyd-Jones Chosen by God* (Crowborough, Highland Books, 1986).

Carpenter, E. *Cantuar* (Mowbray, 1988).

— *Church Relations in England* (London: SPCK, 1950).

Coles, M. *I Will Build My Church* (Belfast, Congregational Union of Ireland, 1979).

— *Confessions of Faith* (Edinburgh, William Blackwood & Sons, 1957).

Cripps, S. *Towards Christian Democracy* (George, Allen & Unwin, 1945).

Crowe, P. (ed.), *Keele '67 Report* (Falcon Books, 1967).

Dale, R.W. *A Manual of Congregational Principles* (Hodder & Stoughton, 1884).

Davies, D.R. *In Search of Myself* (Geoffrey Bles, 1961).

Davies, H. *Worship and Theology in England 1900-1965* (Princeton, Princeton University Press, 1965).

Davies, H. *Varieties of English Preaching 1900-1960* (SCM Press, 1963).

Davies, R. *My Wales* (Jarrolds Publishers, 1937).

Davies, R.E. *Methodism* (Penguin Books, 1963).

Derham, A.M. 'A Momentous Ministry', *Third Way* (December, 1990), p.35.

Dudley-Smith, T. *John Stott: A Global Ministry* (Leicester, IVP, 2001).

— *John Stott: The Making of a Leader* (Leicester, IVP, 1999).

Eaton, M.A. *Baptism with the Spirit* (Leicester, IVP, 1989).

Evans, E. (ed.) *Daniel Rowland* (Edinburgh, Banner of Truth Trust, 1985).

Evans, E. *The Welsh Revival of 1904* (Evangelical Press, 1969).

Evans, G. and I. Rhys 'Wales', in Edwards, O.D. (ed.), *Celtic Nationalism* (Routledge and Kegan Paul, 1968), pp.211-298.

Fant, C.E. and Pinson, W.M. (eds.), *Twenty Centuries of Great Preaching* (Waco, Texas, Word Books, 1971).

Fielder, G.D. *'Excuse Me, Mr Davies—Hallelujah!'* (Bridgend, Evangelical Press, 1983).

Fielder, G.D. *Lord of the Years* (Leicester, IVF, 1988).

France, R.T. 'James Barr and Evangelical Scholarship', *Anvil* Vol.8, No.1 (1991), pp.51-64.

Gilbert, A.D. *The Making of Post-Christian Britain* (Longman, 1980).

Grant, J.W. *Free Churchmanship in England 1870-1940* (Independent Press, n.d.).

— *Growing Into Union* (SPCK, 1970).

Harlowes, S. *Notable Churches and Their Work* (Bristol, Rankin Brothers, 1911).

Harper, M. 'Divided Opinions', *Renewal* (November/December, 1991), pp.18-19.

Harries, J. *G. Campbell Morgan* (Fleming H. Revell, 1930).

Hastings, A. *A History of English Christianity 1920-1985* (Collins, 1986).

Huxtable, J. *As it seemed to me* (United Reformed Church, 1990).

Huxtable, J. *Christian Unity: Some of the Issues* (Independent Press, 1966).

Hylson-Smith, K. *Evangelicals in the Church of England 1734-1984* (Edinburgh, T. & T. Clark, 1989).

Iremonger, F.A. *William Temple: His Life and Letters* (Oxford University Press, 1948).

James, T.T. *The Work and Administration of a Congregational Church* (CUEW, 1925).

Jones, B.P. *The King's Champions* (Cwmbran, Gwent, Christian Literature Press, 1986).

Jones, R.T. *Congregationalism in England 1662-1962* (Independent Press, 1962).

Jones, T. *The Native Never Returns* (W. Griffiths, 1946).

Johnson, D. *Contending for the Faith* (Leicester, IVP, 1979).

Johnson, D. *A Brief History of the International Fellowship of Evangelical Students* (Lausanne, IFES, 1964).

Johnson, D. *The Christian Medical Fellowship—Its Background and History* (Leicester, IVP, 1987).

Jones, P. d'A. *The Christian Socialist Revival 1877-1914* (New Jersey, Princeton University Press, 1968).

Kirby, G. *Ernest Kevan* (Victory Press, 1968).

Lloyd-Jones, B. *Memories of Sandfields 1927-1938* (Edinburgh, Banner of Truth Trust, 1983).

Lloyd, R. *The Church of England 1900-1965* (SCM Press, 1966).

Lowman, P. *The Day of His Power* (Leicester, IVP, 1983).

Machin, G.I.T. *Politics and the Churches in Great Britain 1869-1921* (Oxford, Clarendon Press, 1987).

MacDonald, J.R. *Wanderings and Excursions* (Jonathan Cape, 1929).

MacLeod, D. 'The Lloyd-Jones Legacy', *Monthly Record* (October, 1983), pp.207-209.

Marsden, G.M. *Reforming Fundamentalism* (Grand Rapids, Eerdmans, 1987).

Martin, W. *The Billy Graham Story* (Hutchinson, 1991).

Masters, P. 'Opening the Door to Charismatic Teaching', *Sword and Trowel* 1, No.2 (September, 1988), pp.24-35.

McGrath, A.E. *To Know and Serve God: A Biography of James I. Packer* (Hodder & Stoughton, 1997).

Mayo, P.E. *The Roots of Identity* (Allen Lane, 1974).

Morgan, G.C. *Preaching* (Marshall, Morgan & Scott, 1937).

Morgan, G.C. *Notes on the Psalms* (Henry E. Walter, 1946).

Morgan, J. *A Man of the Word* (Pickering & Inglis, 1952).

Morgan, J. *This Was His Faith* (Pickering & Inglis, n.d.).

Moriarty, M.G. *The New Charismatics* (Grand Rapids, Zondervan, 1992).

Murray, H. *Campbell Morgan* (Marshall, Morgan & Scott, 1938).

Murray, I.H. *D. Martyn Lloyd-Jones: The First Forty Years 1899-1939* (Edinburgh, Banner of Truth Trust, 1982).

Murray, I.H. *D. Martyn Lloyd-Jones: The Fight of Faith 1939-1981* (Edinburgh, Banner of Truth Trust, 1990).

Murray, I.H. *Not a Museum But a Living Force* (Evangelical Library, 1995).

Norman, E.R. *Church and Society in England 1770-1970* (Oxford, Clarendon Press, 1976).

Nuttall, G.F. and Chadwick, O. (eds.) *From Uniformity to Unity 1662-1962* (SPCK, 1962).

O'Donnell, M.B. 'Two Opposing Views on Baptism with/by the Holy Spirit and of 1 Corinthians 12.13: Can Grammatical Investigation Bring Clarity?', in Porter, S.E. and Cross, A.R. (eds.), *Baptism, the New Testament and the Church: Historical and Contemporary Studies in Honour of R.E.O. White* (Sheffield, Sheffield University Press, 1999), pp. 311-336.

— *On The Other Side* (Scripture Union, 1968).

Packer, J.I. *All in Each Place* (Marsham Manor Press, 1965).

Pawley, M. *Donald Coggan: Servant of Christ* (SPCK, 1987).

Peake, A.S. *Recollections and Appreciations* (Epworth Press, 1938).

Peel, A. *These Hundred Years* (S. Tinsley, 1931).
Peel, A. *The Congregational Two Hundred* (Independent Press, 1948).
Peters, J. *Martyn Lloyd-Jones Preacher* (Exeter, Paternoster Press, 1986).
Philip, A.B. *The Welsh Question* (Cardiff, University of Wales Press, 1975).
Plutarch's Lives (Oxford, Basil Blackwell, 1928).
Porritt, A. *John Henry Jowett* (Hodder & Stoughton, 1924).
Powicke, F.J. 'The Congregational Churches', in W.B. Selbie (ed.), *Evangelical Christianity* (Hodder & Stoughton, 1911), Vol.4.
Purcell, W. *Fisher of Lambeth* (Hodder & Stoughton, 1969).
Randall, I.M. *Educating Evangelicalism: The Origins, Development and Impact of London Bible College* (Carlisle, Paternoster, 2000).
Randall, I.M. *Evangelical Experiences: A Study in the Spirituality of English Evangelicalism 1918-1939* (Carlisle, Paternoster, 1999).
Robbins, K. (ed.) *Protestant Evangelicalism: Britain, Ireland, Germany and America, c.1750-c.1950* (Oxford, Blackwell, 1990).
Robinson, J.A.T. *Honest to God* (SCM Press, 1963).
Robinson, J.A.T. *The New Reformation?* (SCM Press, 1965).
Rowdon, H.H. *London Bible College* (Worthing, Henry E. Walter, 1968).
Rowntree, B.S. and Lavers, G.R. *English Life and Leisure* (Longmans, Green & Company, 1951).
— *Sangster of Westminster* (Epworth Press, 1960).
Sangster, P. *Doctor Sangster* (Epworth Press, 1962).
Sangster, P. *A History of the Free Churches* (Heinemann, 1983).
Sargent, T. *The Sacred Anointing* (Hodder & Stoughton, 1994).
Saunders, T. and Sansom, H. *David Watson* (Hodder & Stoughton, 1992).
Saward, M. *Evangelicals on the Move* (Mowbray, 1987).
Sell, A.P.F. *Saints: Visible, Orderly and Catholic* (Geneva, World Alliance of Reformed Churches, 1986).
Slack, K. *The British Churches Today* (SCM Press, 1970).
Smeaton, W.J. *The Five Points of Calvinism* (London: Banner of Truth, 1970).
Smith, C.B. *Champion of Homoeopathy* (Murray, 1986).
Soper, D. *Calling For Action* (Robson Books, 1984).
Spangler, A. and Turner, C. (eds.) *Heroes* (Leicester, IVP, 1991).
Tatlow, T. *The Story of the Student Christian Movement* (SCM Press, 1933).
Thompson, D. *Donald Soper* (Nutfield, Denholm House Press, 1971).
J.C. Travell , 'Leslie Weatherhead', *JURCHS*, October, 1990, Vol.4, No.7, p.452.
— *Unity Begins at Home* (SCM Press, 1964).
— *Unity in Diversity* (Evangelical Alliance, 1967).

Walker, D. *A History of the Church in Wales* (Penarth, Church of Wales, 1976).

Walker, W. *Creeds and Platforms of Congregationalism* (Philadelphia, Pilgrim Press, 1960).

Warfield, B.B. *Biblical Foundations* (Tyndale Press, 1958).

Weatherhead, K. *Leslie Weatherhead: A Personal Portrait* (Hodder & Stoughton, 1975).

Weatherhead, L. *The Christian Agnostic* (Hodder & Stoughton, 1965).

Weatherhead, L. *That Immortal Sea* (Epworth Press, 1953).

Weatherhead, L. *Thinking Aloud in War Time* (Hodder & Stoughton, 1943).

Welsby, P.A. *A History of the Church of England 1945-1980* (Oxford, Oxford University Press, 1984).

Whale, J.S. *The Protestant Tradition* (Cambridge, Cambridge University Press, 1960).

Wilkinson, J.I. (ed.) *Arthur Samuel Peake* (Epworth Press, 1958).

Williams, C.R. 'The Welsh Religious Revival, 1904-5', *The British Journal of Sociology*, 3 (1952), pp.242-259.

Young, G.M. *Stanley Baldwin* (Rupert Hart-Davies, 1952).

General Index